PENGUIN B

A HISTORY OF ANCIENT EGYPT AUG 0 5 2014

John Romer has been working in Egypt since 1966 on archaeological digs in many key sites, including the Valley of the Kings and Karnak. He led the Brooklyn Museum expedition to excavate the tomb of Ramesses XI. He wrote and presented a number of television series, including *The Seven Wonders of the World*, *Romer's Egypt*, *Ancient Lives* and *Testament*. His major books include *The Great Pyramid: Ancient Egypt Revisited* and *Valley of the Kings*. He lives in Italy.

JOHN ROMER

A History of Ancient Egypt

*From the First Farmers to the
Great Pyramid*

PENGUIN BOOKS

PENGUIN BOOKS

Published by the Penguin Group
Penguin Books Ltd, 80 Strand, London WC2R ORL, England
Penguin Group (USA) Inc., 375 Hudson Street, New York, New York 10014, USA
Penguin Group (Canada), 90 Eglinton Avenue East, Suite 700, Toronto, Ontario, Canada M4P 2Y3
(a division of Pearson Penguin Canada Inc.)
Penguin Ireland, 25 St Stephen's Green, Dublin 2, Ireland (a division of Penguin Books Ltd)
Penguin Group (Australia), 707 Collins Street, Melbourne, Victoria 3008, Australia
(a division of Pearson Australia Group Pty Ltd)
Penguin Books India Pvt Ltd, 11 Community Centre, Panchsheel Park, New Delhi – 110 017, India
Penguin Group (NZ), 67 Apollo Drive, Rosedale, Auckland 0632, New Zealand
(a division of Pearson New Zealand Ltd)
Penguin Books (South Africa) (Pty) Ltd, Block D, Rosebank Office Park,
181 Jan Smuts Avenue, Parktown North, Gauteng 2193, South Africa

Penguin Books Ltd, Registered Offices: 80 Strand, London WC2R ORL, England

www.penguin.com

First published by Allen Lane 2012
Published by Penguin Books 2013
001

Typeset by Jouve (UK), Milton Keynes
Printed in England by Clays Ltd, St Ives plc

ISBN: 978-0-141-39971-3

www.greenpenguin.co.uk

ALWAYS LEARNING   **PEARSON**

For my Egyptian friends

Contents

vii

PART TWO
Making Pharaoh *(3200–3000 BC)*

PART FOUR

Step Pyramid (2675–2650 BC)

PART FIVE

Building Ancient Egypt (2650–2550 BC)

CONTENTS

Preface

*... You ask me whether the Orient is up to what I imagined it
to be. Yes, it is; and more than that, it extends far beyond the
narrow idea I had of it ... Facts have taken the place of sup-
positions so excellently so that it is often as though I were
suddenly coming upon old forgotten dreams.*

Flaubert to his mother, Cairo, 5 January 1850

Given its continuing and unrivalled popularity, you might imagine
that there are many good contemporary histories of ancient Egypt: in
fact, they are extremely rare. Certainly, you would never guess that
since the 1960s some brilliant academic research has revolutionized
our understanding of the ancient past, or that a series of ongoing
archaeological excavations is presently reshaping an entire millennium of ancient Egypt's early history. Instead of making modern
histories, most writers unthinkingly insert the products of a century
and more of the most meticulous scientific research into narratives
founded in nineteenth-century theories about human nature and the
rise and fall of nation-states. So 'ancient Egypt' yet labours in a European bondage of a grand scholarly tradition, and it is subject to both
the vices and virtues of that most powerful heritage.

The first great modern history of ancient Egypt was published in
Paris in the 1730s and had a huge and immediate effect. Written by an
elderly rector of the city university, it was swiftly translated into all
the major European languages and continuously reprinted in dozens
of different editions and for so long, that the last English edition of
Mr Rollin's Ancient History of the Egyptians, Carthaginians, Assyrians,

Babylonians, Medes and Persians, Macedonians and Grecians appeared in 1924!

Starting with the Book of Genesis, when 'the world was without form and void', Rollin introduces the first pharaoh as Noah's grandson, who had ascended to the throne, according to his calculations, in the 1,816th year of the world which, by seventeenth-century lights, had been created in 4004 BC. As a shrewd contemporary had observed, it was not the rector's 'erudition or the benevolence of his intentions' that had led to his book's success 'but above all, the piety of his sentiments, which clash with no sect or party among Christians'.

Whatever its historical merits, Rollin's history laid down the principles by which egyptology is conducted to this day, the titles of its three main sections eerily foreshadowing some of the greatest egyptological publications of the following centuries: '1. A Description of Egypt, 2. The Manners and Customs of the Egyptians, 3. The History of the Kings of Egypt' – and all of that in 30,000 words which, in Rollin's time, was sufficient to contain the bulk of Western knowledge about the ancient culture.

The last of the great histories of ancient Egypt to be written by a single scholar was completed by Sir Alan Gardiner in 1961 when he was over eighty, and is five times as long as that of Rector Rollin. Between them, the two histories mark the beginning and the ending of a scholarly tradition. Both Gardiner and Rollin were products of the classical humanist European schools, and both their histories had been based on ancient texts, their authors sharing the conviction that ancient writings held the essential truths about the cultures that had made them.

The difference between them is that Rollin had but the Bible and Greek and Roman authors as his guides, whereas Gardiner had considerable numbers of ancient Egyptian texts at his disposal, a resource that, following Champollion's decipherment of hieroglyphs in the 1820s, had already extended the span of Rollin's pharaonic kingdom by more than a millennium and its cast of characters by several thousands. So though Gardiner had retained Rollin's three fundamental divisions of ancient Egyptian culture, his emphasis, in common with all other egyptologists of his time, was firmly on the history of the court whose inscriptions he had spent his lifetime studying. Just as its title says, Gardiner's great history is truly that of an 'Egypt of the Pharaohs'.

One snag in this, and indeed one common in the flood of history books that had followed Champollion's decipherment, was that, while the translation of the ancient texts had given ancient Egypt an authentic voice, the limited nature of their subject matter had tended to screen from view almost every aspect of ancient Egypt other than religion and court affairs. In consequence, this newly emerged literary ancient Egypt seemed to live in ivory-towered isolation from the rest of the ancient world and its central narratives, as Roland Barthes described in a more general context, were 'histories in which a systematic concatenation of actions is distributed amongst a small number of characters, whose functions are largely identical from one story to the next'.

It is hardly surprising, therefore, that many traditional historians remark on the ancient Egyptians' 'innate conservatism' and describe them as ruling a venerable and static society, a vision bolstered by the translators' use of 'parallels' – the transposition of the meaning of a hieroglyphic term from later periods into earlier ones – that further tended to obscure all sense of change within the ancient state. In reality, however, the reverse was true. For early ancient Egypt had been one of those very rare places on this planet where the concept of a state, and of a regal court and of a court religion, had been developed and refined.

Another major snag in these classical histories is that the near-exclusive use of literary sources had served to cut the ancient culture into two entirely separate halves, namely, the pharaonic period, when hieroglyphs were used, and the earlier periods, so-called 'prehistoric' Egypt, when they were not. And the gap between these periods seemed so unbridgeable to these traditional historians that Gardiner, for example, sets his account of ancient Egypt's beginnings at the ending of his history because, he says, there is no real history for those times, only speculation. In reality, however, his world of 'Egypt of the Pharaohs' was not the product of a literary world with classical modes of thought, but had been created in a pre-literary age out of the humble world of neolithic farmers.

Despite such limitations, these literary histories had provided half of ancient Egypt's history with a fundamental road map. And it was nice, of course, to know that the Great Pyramid at Giza had been built for a king named Khufu, and that Ramesses the Great had ruled for more than sixty years and had a hundred children. Yet such information had not begun to answer the questions that arose in me when I first went to Egypt as a draughtsman on an American expedition, and wondered at the broken beauty that lay all through the ancient sites. In those days, in the 1960s, in Nasser's final years, Egypt was about as popular a tourist destination as Saddam's Iraq. So the pyramids and the Cairo Museum, the Saqqara cemeteries and the Karnak temples were all but empty, and the great tombs of western Thebes much as their excavators had left them, with broken funerary furnishings stacked inside their chapels and mummy fragments scattered all around.

I vividly remember a moment, standing in the open courtyard of a Middle Kingdom tomb on the ridge of rock to the north of Hatshepsut's grand terraced temple, when I held the calm and perfect face of a fine-featured mummy on my open hand, before burying it in the warm dry sand. And all around me lay fragments of the most exquisite paintings, the debris of a splendidly decorated burial chamber that lay nearby, in the darkness of the open tomb. Clearly, these people had expended huge amounts of time and energy, intelligence and skill to make such things – but to what purposes? What on earth was it that they had imagined they were doing?

As a recent product of higher education, I naturally expected to find the answer to my questions in reference books. So I looked into the splendid library of Chicago University's Luxor headquarters, which was close at hand. Yet even as I was drawn into those wonderful old volumes, with their morocco bindings, their elegant typography and their cosmopolitan scholarship, I had felt uncomfortable. Just as I had not believed the Victorians' rationale for empire building, so neither did I believe those scholars' explanations of the vanished kingdoms whose ruins I was encountering, day on day, in the Egyptian sunlight.

At the same time as I was starting to puzzle over pharaonic culture in an academic library, a radical alternative to the classical tradition of Rollin and Gardiner was being brought to bear on ancient Egypt: first of all, as part of a huge UNESCO programme to excavate large numbers of ancient sites that were threatened by the slow-filling waters of the High Dam at Aswan in southern Upper Egypt. These freshly imported archaeologists were bringing different skills to the study of ancient Egypt. Suddenly, the potential of the vast amounts of untouched archaeological material that still lay all along the lower Nile was recognized.

This new archaeology was not an updated version of the antiquarian activity of shovelling sand in the hope of finding more pyramids and more texts. These archaeologists were well-trained products of a practical, well-proven scientific discipline whose vision, at its roots, reflected the aspirations of a newly arrived and educated nineteenth-century European middle class who had wanted a bright new history for their practical commercial world. They were not bound by traditional literary sources to make their histories, and they promised some different answers to my questions. Founded amidst excavations that had been systematically uncovering the various phases of the European Stone Age, the first histories of these new archaeologists had been given a kind of ratification and a powerful contemporary model of physical change through time with the publication, in 1859, of Darwin's theory of evolution.

For many Victorians, Darwin's observations on the rise of man chimed nicely with the daily colonial experience of so-called 'primitive' and 'savage' peoples, who were often described as standing on the bottom rungs of Darwin's evolutionary ladder. Not only, then, did Darwin's theory appear to hold a model of a savage prehistoric protohistory based on modern scientific principles, but it also offered the illusion, through the colonial experience, of a living window onto the realities of prehistoric life. So the emerging discipline of tribal anthropology, the 'study of man as animal', as one Victorian described it, was brought to bear upon the archaeologists' new histories.

By the turn of the twentieth century, Freud's concept of the unconscious mind had given a powerful new dimension to the nineteenth century's notion of the prehistoric 'primitive'. Part-based, ironically enough, on the archaeological metaphor of digging down to man's beginnings, Freud theorized that the savage's rise to civilization was played out in the dreams and emotions of every generation, past and present, as part of a commonality of human nature. Best of all, as far as the archaeologists were concerned, Dr Freud continually underlined that his observations appeared to ratify the anthropologists' contention that man's rise to civilization could indeed be quantified with scientific rules. Now, it seemed, the archaeologists could evaluate the products of an excavation as if the prehistoric world had been a Petri dish and the people whose relics and remains had been uncovered were the inevitable consequences of particular sets of circumstances.

By the time of UNESCO's Nubian campaign in the 1960s, and the arrival of the new archaeology in Egypt, the prehistoric past was already globalized. So even as a novel range of scientific disciplines were being brought to bear upon the findings of the new archaeologists and often with groundbreaking results, most prehistorians naturally assumed that a single set of universal pseudo-evolutionary principles had governed all of world prehistory, and they were interpreting this new data accordingly. And so a powerful and somewhat brutal image of prehistory was constructed, a vision fortified with the omnipotence of 'science' and a tricky jargon of its own; a vision in which a diversity of communities living at different times, on separate continents, had all competed for food and land and luxury goods with the competitive and savage spirit with which humankind was assumed to have been naturally endowed.

Now, one of the great advantages of classical Egyptian histories such as those of Rector Rollin and Sir Alan Gardiner – and this is true of most of the works that were written in the centuries between – is that they are transparent in their attitudes. As with an old museum, they may be visited with pleasure, the reader relaxing as pharaoh follows pharaoh and thousands of years and lives are glimpsed through classical colonnades, and all of them are calmly and judiciously assessed. Rollin, for example, had considered the disappearance of ancient Egypt to have been the ethical failure of a pagan culture, a view powerfully revisited at the turn of the twentieth century in the histories of the Chicago historian James Henry Breasted, who considered ancient Egypt to have been an early example of mankind's potential but, as it had not been Christian, was bound to fail. Gardiner, on the other hand, a humanist, considered ancient Egypt's travails and eventual disappearance to have been brought about by bad government and invasion, a list to which more recent researches have added plagues, earthquakes and ecological mismanagement.

The longer temporal narrative of the archaeological historians, on the other hand, was a universal pseudo-evolutionary progress that ran straight from savagery through barbarism to the Ritz Hotel. But here, of course, pharaonic Egypt and its thirty dynasties of kings simply did not fit the bill. Clearly, the pharaohs that the traditional historians had so elegantly enlivened had not emerged like monsters from the swamps of evolution; nor indeed had their pyramids or governments. Neither had there been an economic or material progress in the course of pharaonic Egypt's history which, like most of the ancient world, had been technologically mature from its beginnings. Beyond the later invention and elaboration of systems of slavery and the use of iron, ancient cultures made very few material advances.

As far as pharaonic Egypt was concerned, therefore, the nineteenth-century notion of the progress of the ancient 'savage' could only find a niche at the very beginning of ancient Egypt's pre-pharaonic history, where he could be set up to represent an 'early phase' of the evolution of ancient Egypt as it rose to become a grand imperial power. And then, of course, by the savage rules of nineteenth-century archaeology, the ending of that ancient court could be explained as part of the inevitable destiny of alien kingdoms to fall to more 'progressive' civilizations.

So, though the scale and subject matter of the two histories are different, their narratives are curiously similar. Rollin's view of pagan history as a description of the workings of Divine Providence has been transformed into a view of the past as a universal capitalistic progress from primitive society to Western civilization; or, as one archaeologically based theorist recently put it, 'evolutionary traject-ories towards states occurred all over the world after the Pleistocene and were based on varying means of gaining power and access to goods and labour. Ideologies that there should be a central ruling sys-tem were created . . .'

The net result of this, however, is that modern histories of ancient Egypt now have to absorb the two quite different disciplines of trad-itional history and the new archaeology, while trying to bridge the yawning chasm between them with a rickety bricolage of myth about the 'evolution' of archaic states. Amusingly, however, that fundamental disjunction is invariably underlined by the very pages of the history books themselves, which start in the neolithic at around 250 years per page and then slow down to around four, as the courtly gossip really hits the fan.

It is hardly a convincing model for a balanced history of ancient Egypt. Nor do such histories, be they traditional or economic or evolutionary in their bias, encompass the essential and continuous central activity of the pharaonic state; those vast energies that built enormous pyramids brought great stones and precious metals out of distant deserts, and all the while created a continuous stream of beautiful and well-made things. New archaeology, on the one hand, can only set such relics into the preoccupations of more modern times, and describe them as the products of the propagandas of various social or racial competitions, or as the products of irrational impulses or as 'primitive' modes of thought. Traditional historians, on the other hand, tend to explain the impulses to make such things as if they were works for exhibition at a French Salon. Yet ancient Egypt was entirely different from all that; something new under the sun. And neither the grammarians' traditional histories nor the archaeologists' 'vulgar materialism' seem able to encompass it.

Now imagine for a minute one of those corny television documentaries in which an archaeologist drives dustily across an ancient desert in search of the bones of neolithic farmers. At first glance it might seem that there is not much to choose between the physical reality of early humankind and the T-shirted individual seated sweatily behind the steering wheel. Yet the difference holds the clue to understanding ancient Egypt and its extraordinary history.

Consider the reasons why Land Rover Man is in that car at all, why he is driving upon the right-hand side of the road rather than the left, why the buildings of his university back home look the way they do, or where the documentary's soundtrack comes from. Unlike the early farmers for whom he searches, this vulnerable individual crossing a bone-dry desert at fifty miles an hour is a complex product of 15,000 years of human culture.

A modern history of ancient Egypt should contain a great part of that story. It should describe how the first farmers slowly transformed themselves into the citizens of a sophisticated and successful state.

And then it should tell how and why the ancient Egyptians laboured so patiently and with such colossal energy and intelligence to maintain their beautiful estate. Then I would have some answers to those simple questions that I had asked myself some forty years ago, in the cemeteries of Thebes.

My ambition was to start this history from nothing, like Captain Cook mapping the antipodes. Unlike the early European explorers, however, I have tried not to label parts of this unknown land in the old familiar languages, as Wellington or Perth, nor indeed as Hunger Bay or Cannibal Creek. Best to allow a new ancient Egypt, a new world of possibilities, to emerge, that could be different from our own; no journeys from tribe to nation or archaism to decadence, no urban evolutions, and certainly, no pukka pharaohs with the attitudes of early modern European kings.

From the beginning, it was especially important to recognize the traps that lurk within the very words we use. When Cook first came across the islands that now make up New Zealand, their indigenous populations had no single name for them: Cook's Anglicized version of Nova Zeelandia, a name invented by Dutch cartographers, had made a new reality. In similar fashion, the phrase 'ancient Egypt' is but a recent addition to our language. So if at the outset you describe the language of the first hieroglyphs as 'ancient Egyptian', you have unwittingly provided the ancient people with a country without pausing for a moment to consider how such a novel notion came into being. And you have also started from the unwarranted assumption that this 'ancient Egypt' was rather like the world we live in.

I proceed, alternatively, from the evidence, which shows that ancient Egypt was both a product and reflection of the so-called Neolithic Revolution. Those early farmers could hardly have started to transform the way they lived without changing, at the same time, their conception of the world: traces of that change, indeed, are to be found in their settlements and graves, in their means of subsistence and in the things they made. I begin, therefore, with the hard surviving evidence: from the wide desert and the narrow stretch of soft diluvial silt with its ribbons of green water-meadows that ran down each side of the lower Nile.

Add a few of the farmyard items that the archaeologists have found: a small shelter, some neolithic pots and grains of wheat and, after a further fifteen centuries, the Great Pyramid of Giza, the largest and most accurate stone-block building the world has ever seen. Even by nineteenth-century standards, this was one of the most astonishing developments in all of human history. Here, then, is the promise of a lively narrative.

Clearly, there was a very powerful dynamic working inside the communities of the early farmers of the lower Nile, some kind of vision of the world and of their place within it, that eventually resulted in the creation of the Great Pyramid of Giza and of the astonishing machine that built it: the pharaonic state. Ultimately the pharaonic government, the state religion of pharaonic Egypt and all of its considerable panoply were products of the human imagination.

Look hard at the surviving bits and pieces, follow the hands and minds of generations of craftsmen, scribes and masons, and you will find evidence of an internal logic and lively human intelligence at work. And, with humility and delight, you may watch part of the story in which, over the course of five millennia, the people of the lower Nile built and maintained that astonishing creation we now call 'ancient Egypt'.

This is in no way to say that the relics of old Egypt may be read as if they held a code of symbols; such procedures have already helped produce a common mono-dimensional academic vision of pharaonic Egypt and, ultimately, those Technicolor 'mysteries of pharaoh' that are, essentially, parodies of those same mock-metaphysics. Nor am I suggesting that the ancient things are the inadvertent Hegelian manifestations of an early Zeitgeist. The ancient Egyptians did not work according to nineteenth-century notions of the purposes of art; in that specific sense, they had no 'art'. The history held within these ancient things is much fresher and far clearer, and more direct than that.

It is, however, inevitably incomplete. Just as the diverse variety of experience that once made up the living ancient past can never be recovered, so no single history, no academic school, no individual, can promise a definitive vision of pharaonic Egypt. The best that can be done, I think, is to recover various bits of the kaleidoscope through which the ancient Egyptians viewed the world, and, through that fragmented mix of endlessly repeating patterns, try to discover something of what it was those people imagined they were doing.

This history therefore, aims to serve two separate purposes: first, to provide a guide through the intellectual quagmire that modern 'ancient Egypt' has become, and also, by careful observation, to set some of the things the ancient people made back into their original realities.

This volume is the first of two, their division being set between the pre-literate and the literary cultures of the ancient lower Nile, which also marks the transformation of the pharaonic court from a progressive and inventive community into a culturally conservative society.

The second volume will describe the more familiar 'ancient Egypt' and the two millennia and more during which it was in contact with other cultures, some of whom, eventually, sacked and destroyed it. For the most part this was a time of cultural stress and interaction, and a time when 'ancient Egypt' was more concerned in rendering traditional forms than creating new ones.

The first volume, on the other hand, is the story of ancient Egypt from its beginnings to the establishment of the full panoply of the pharaonic state. Greatly benefiting from the discoveries of the last few decades and based on a mass of archaeological data gathered all across in the Middle East, it is an extraordinarily exciting tale that only twenty years ago could hardly have been told at all. And at its ending this millennially developing culture had made a king, a country and a government based on tithing, offering and stone architecture; a state founded on a system of supply embracing both the living and the dead. That is the root of the story.

A NOTE ON THE TEXT

Further details of the works cited below in abbreviated form may be found in the Bibliography.

Ancient names have been rendered in their simplest modern forms, hyphenating them only when it was necessary to show something of their current pronunciation – as in 'Hetep-heres', rather than 'Hetepheres'.

Generally, I have taken my cue from the spellings used in the recent catalogues of exhibitions held at the Metropolitan Museum, New York; see *EAAP*; for modern place names, however, I have employed the Anglicized forms given in John Baines and Jaromir Málek, *Atlas of Ancient Egypt*.

I have followed a general trend in transforming the place name 'Naqada' into the common noun 'Naqadan', which I have used to identify the considerable culture, originally from the valley of the lower Nile, that preceded pharaonic society. Following the work of Werner Kaiser – see for example Kaiser, 'Zur Innern Chronologie' – most modern textbooks have preferred to subdivide this culture into three phases: I, II and III. (Previously these phases had been awarded separate names – 'Amratian', 'Gerzean', 'Semainean' – after the cemeteries in which their wares were found.)

Note, however, that my use of 'early', middle' and 'late' to designate three successive phases of Naqadan culture does not exactly mirror Kaiser's model but has been adapted to follow the observations of Stan Hendrickx, 'The Relative Chronology'. Further technical descriptions of the periods of prehistory that I have identified by name can be found in the section called 'Names and Nomenclatures' in the Chronology.

Note, too, that absolute dates given in my text for some of the Naqadan objects and constructions I describe may differ from some of those of the original publication. Given the present uncertainties in prehistoric chronology (see further, in the notes to the Chronology), any absolute date can only be approximate. A more reliable marker of an object's relative place in history is its position in the Naqadan three-phase system; in this, I have generally followed the most recent attributions of individual objects.

In my descriptions of the early phases of ancient Egypt's history, in order to emphasize its extraordinary originality, I have used modern language sparingly, rescuing a few sound English nouns and jettisoning such loaded terms as 'civilization' and 'urbanization'. Though they may well be, as somebody once said, such things as dreams are made of, their origins are not to be found by digging in the sands of Egypt, but in the *Oxford English Dictionary*.

For those same reasons, I have also avoided the use of the terms 'towns' and 'cities'. Modern cities are products of money-based economies; beyond 'a lot of houses', hardly anyone agrees on what the word might mean within an ancient context. Generally speaking, therefore, I have employed the term 'settlement' to describe any conglomerations of buildings that are not cemeteries. I have, however, on occasion, called a pharaonic residence a palace.

I use the term 'culture' to describe a collection of objects sharing common manufacturing techniques and aesthetic properties and, by association, the people who made and used them. My use of the word 'pharaonic' describes the ages of the Egyptian royal dynasties. I have used the words king and pharaoh indiscriminately.

The word 'Egypt', on the other hand, has been employed retrospectively, either as a modern geographic designation or, as in the case of 'ancient Egypt', as a modern term that identifies pharaonic culture. It is not intended to describe any part of ancient reality. I have, accordingly, avoided using the term Upper and Lower Egypt as pharaonic designations – thus used, they produce a 'unified nation-state' by sleight of word.

To designate the area that became the kingdom of the pharaohs, the area of the Nile Valley, that is, which runs from modern-day Aswan to Alexandria, I have used the term 'the lower Nile'.

The term 'court' has been used to describe the community around the king who made and maintained the pharaonic culture. It seems to have been a non-agricultural community, supported by a network drawing its supplies from the agrarian settlements of the lower Nile. As well as people who are often pictured as being close to the person of the king – whom I identify as 'courtiers' – this court, therefore, would have included families of administrators, storekeepers, scribes, craftsmen and boatmen. Broadly speaking, I assume that at its beginnings, it had between five and ten thousand members. In this context, the 'ancient Egyptian state' would have consisted of the royal court and the population of the lower Nile from whom tithes could be exacted.

For my geographic identifications of territories outside the valley of the lower Nile, I have used the terms 'Gezira' and 'Levant' rather than Israel, Turkey, Lebanon, Iraq and Iran. The Gezira is the pseudo-island

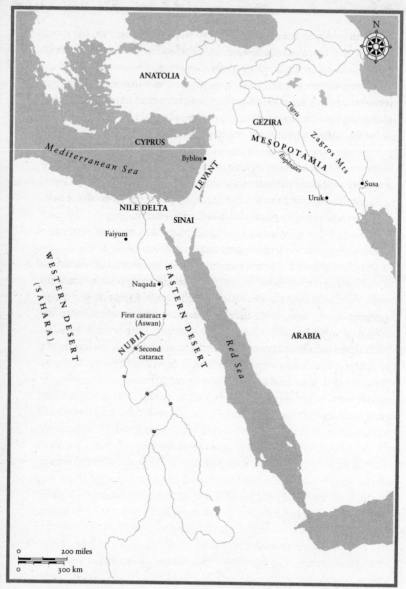

Most ancient Egypt and the adjacent regions of the neolithic Middle East

of ancient Mesopotamia that lay between the two great rivers, the Tigris and Euphrates; the Levant, the lands of the southern Mediterranean whose eastern border was the Euphrates. The southern Levant, which is often mentioned in the first part of this history, is presently set between Israel, Palestine and Jordan: all other terms are fraught with propaganda.

I have generally employed the word 'traffic' as opposed to 'trade'. For though the one may well imply the other, it is far from proven that there was a trading economy employing monetary equivalents in late Naqadan and early dynastic times.

I have also reclaimed the term 'archaic' from the academic word-police who outlawed a good and useful English term of great antiquity because, some fifty years ago, it was employed in the title of a once influential but now unfashionable handbook.

That comparatively few modern archaeologists are named in my text is solely due to the fact that archaeological expeditions are no longer undertaken by one or two heroic pioneers digging for a few months, but by a mass of archaeologists and other specialists who may well work intermittently at the same site over several decades. The interpretation of these grand projects, therefore, is seldom in the hands of a few idiosyncratic individuals as in the days of Mariette Pasha and Flinders Petrie, whose names and opinions are inextricably linked to some of the sites at which they worked, and where they made such notable discoveries.

PART ONE

Making Culture
(5000–3000 BC)

I

Beside the Pale Lake

Living in the Faiyum, c. 5000–4000 BC

It was wetter then than it is now. Though the monsoons were slowly failing, the plains were grass-green and scented with flowering shrubs whilst the valleys held exotic trees, such as still grow in central Africa. To the east of the Saharan plateau, small groups of hunters camped occasionally inside the sheltered wadis that ran down into the Nile Valley and they took fish from the river, hare, gazelle and wild cattle from the fringes of the plain above, and gathered seeds and tubers from the rushy swamps that lay along the river's edge. In the slow flow of prehistory, the changes that were transforming the Saharan plains into a hot sand sea would have been imperceptible, even to hunters living off the land. Then suddenly, some seven thousand years ago, a new way of living was introduced into this gentle Eden.

For modern archaeologists, the revolution takes the shape of storage bins. Three hundred of them, set in the crusted surface of a desert and tokening the arrival in the land of Egypt of the single greatest transformation the human race has ever undertaken: the change from hunting and gathering to husbandry and farming.

Before there was farming, the inhabitants of Egypt had lived peripatetic lives, collecting the natural resources of the land according to the seasons of the year. These storage bins, however, groups of circular pits set beside the hearthstones of small settlements, were made by people who planted grain and later on had harvested the crop and who therefore had lived in the same place for a great part of the year.

The consequences of this change were literally monumental: within 1,500 years, the descendants of those first Egyptian farmers were building pyramids for pharaoh. It is not surprising, then, that to modern minds the story of those fifteen prehistoric centuries promises a unique history.

3

When they were newly made, each one of those first-known grain bins could have held eight hundredweight of cereals, mixes mostly, of wild seed, emmer wheat and two- and six-rowed barley, crops that with a low yield would have required two to three acres of land to fill a single bin. Planted in October and November and ripened during the following months of growth and maturation, the contents of one such grain bin would have taken the farmers several days to harvest and would have needed further labour afterwards, to process the seed for eating.

In the 1920s, when the grain bins were first excavated, one of them still held a farmer's sickle, a little tree branch nicely shaped into a wooden stick, with a row of notched flint blades set end to end along one side of it to form a single cutting edge. There were, as well, some seven pounds of harvested seed. Golden dry and so perfectly preserved that a museum curator once tried, unsuccessfully, to germinate some of them. They are the oldest known examples of Egyptian grain, that bounty which, millennia later, the Book of Genesis would describe as being 'without number ... as the sand of the sea'. Here, then, the inhabitants of the lower Nile had settled down, seeded the silty soil and begun to count out their years in harvests which in later centuries became so generous as to enable the building of the pyramids and finally, at ancient Egypt's ending, to supply the bread to feed Caesar's Rome.

Four feet across and half as deep, Egypt's first-known grain bins were mud-plastered pits lined with rush-woven baskets that, after they had been filled with seed, were sealed with a strong flat lid made from a mix of salt and sand. Woven from their centre in a coil, some of these hefty grain baskets are of the same construction as Egyptian village baskets of today and, indeed, as those used by pharaoh's workmen. Similar storage facilities were also used until quite recently by the Malike people of West Africa, who stored and traded their annual harvests according to their need. If the grain was well treated, they told a visiting anthropologist in the 1970s, if it were kept dry and stirred occasionally, the seeds would live within their bins for a full three years. Elaborated and enlarged, pharaoh's seed stores, ancient Egypt's real gold, would feed priests, courtiers and craftsmen, buffer bad harvests and fuel the ambitions of the master builders.

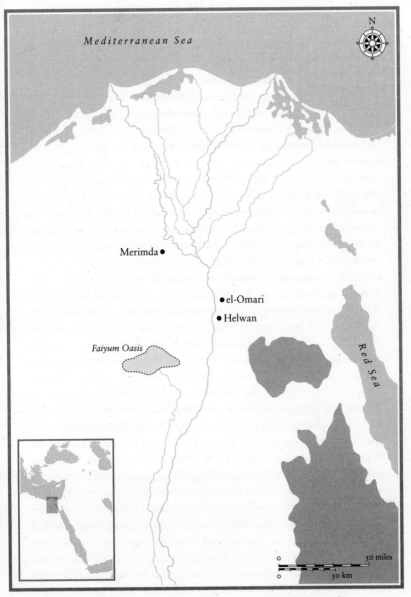

The major neolithic sites of the northern lower Nile: the principle
settlements by Lake Faiyum were along its ancient northern shoreline

Egypt's first known grain stores, however, are not in the valley of the Nile, but in a mysterious depression in the Sahara that then, as now, held a lake fed by a meandering branch of the River Nile. Lying on the west side of the river some forty miles south of modern Cairo and known today as Lake Faiyum, the ancient lake was annually revived by fierce floodwaters from the nearby river that pushed their way through a narrow breach in the valley's western cliffs and flowed into the low-lying plain of the Faiyum Depression.

That same vast flood gave life to the entirety of Egypt. Swelling once a year to twelve to fourteen times higher than its usual flow, its waters flooded the best part of the Nile Valley. Through all of ancient history and, indeed, until the last two centuries and the building of a series of retaining dams, there was no other water source in all of Egypt; no rain in the last five thousand years sufficient to sustain a single plant; nothing, other than this single river. All life flowed from the Nile and the rich organic silt it carried in its annual flooding, the product of seasonal and heavy rains in the highlands of Ethiopia. In the days of the Faiyum farmers, as in the slightly dryer times of pharaoh's Egypt, more than 100 million tons of sediment came down the river in an average flood. This then re-fertilized the narrow silty plains within the Nile Valley, the marshlands and the water-meadows of the river's delta, and the lake and fens of the Faiyum.

At the time that the lake dwellers were laying down their grain-storage bins, the annual floods were generous, the shallow lake some fifty miles wide. Today, the lake is but a ghostly mirage a quarter of that size, so that the sandy banks on which the ancient farmers set their grain bins stand high and dry, a thin light line on the horizon of a pale desert. So when you stand upon that ancient lakeshore with your back turned on the salt-encrusted mirage of the modern lake, you may still see the outlines of some of these momentous grain bins or, at least, the slight indentations of their excavation, running across a ten-foot bank above the ancient shoreline, spotted now with dusty shrubs. Once, though, thick grass and rushes had grown along this bleached-out beach; traces of their desiccated roots still snake through the ancient bone-dry silt. And nearby, there had been a pair of marshy ponds, where fishing was convenient and plentiful.

The community that gathered Egypt's first known harvests seems to have lived next to their grain stores, up on the same bankside. The absence of ruined walls, however, or even of postholes that could have supported roofing beams or tents, suggests that they moved as lightly on the earth as had their hunter-gatherer predecessors. Nor has a single grave of these first farmers been uncovered. Yet traces of their hearths remain. At some of the smaller settlements, summer storms have washed their ashes down into the now half-vanished lake, leaving dark streaks on the surface of the ancient desert. Close to the grain bins, too, the farmers' hearths were found intact, some with cooking pots still standing at their centres with fish- and animal bones within them and charcoal banked up all around. Ashes from these hearths provide a date for some of these fires at around 4300 BC, whilst other excavations at the ancient lake show that, by that time, similar communities had inhabited the area for the best part of a thousand years. All of these sometime farmers had built similarly simple shelters from animal hides and the lakeside reeds and rushes, which they had also used to weave the linings of their storage bins.

The largest known of all the lakeside settlements, some fifty yards in length and width, are those beside the grain bins. Archaeologists have distinguished at least three different periods of occupation within these settlements, each of which had flourished for considerable periods of time, one following another. So, despite the 300 grain bins, we may imagine that, at any one time, such communities were no larger than a few family groups.

All these lakeside farmers appear to have processed their crops in the same way, threshing their grain with sticks and pounding some of the harder seeds with hammer stones to split them open, then scooping up the kernels with shells and little finely woven baskets before grinding the corn to flour between two heavy stones. The hardness of some of the different grain stocks appears to have been an especial problem. Quantities of burnt corn mixed with charcoal found in one of the grain bins may have been a discarded by-product of parching, which aimed to burst the seed like popcorn, a process that may have taken place at harvest time by simply setting fire to the dry plants in the fields. A more agreeable explanation, however, is that this spoilt grain was not the by-product of careless parching, but of malting and of making beer. Although there is no direct evidence of brewing in these earliest of settlements, beer would become a staple commodity in the diet of various prehistoric Nile-side farming communities.

As well as cultivating grain, the Faiyum farmers reared animals. Large quantities of cattle, goat and, above all, sheep bones lay strewn throughout the settlements, whilst others were found in stewing pots still resting on the hearths. Nothing is known about the conditions in which these flocks were kept. What is clear, however, is that some of the hard wild seeds the farmers had stored in certain of their grain bins may have been especially gathered to support their flocks during the Egyptian summers, when there was little for such domesticated animals to forage. In wintertime, however, they could well have grazed alongside the wild gazelle and hartebeest that came down to the lake-side; and these too, so the bones within the settlements still tell, the farmers also caught and cooked. For these farmers were still hunters, and although the pig bones found within the settlements could have been those of either domesticated animals or wild boar, the remains of turtle shells, crocodile scales and the butchered bones of hippopotami, as well as those of bittern and geese which fed in the warm shallows of the Faiyum lakeside, show that they still had the catholic palate of hunter-gatherers. And the farmers still fished and hunted in the age-old ways as well, with nets and flint-tipped arrows, harpoons and spears.

Lake fish were a year-round staple. Above all others, the farmers ate the Nile catfish, a small-eyed, flat-headed, bewhiskered monster who grew to an enormous size and to whom later Nile fishermen attributed legendary powers of survival in the drying summer mud. To catch such fearsome beasts, the farmers made harpoons barbed and tipped with animal bone and ivory; these were the elegant ancestors of a millennial tradition in which the harpoon would become a chosen weapon in the internecine battles between the pharaonic Egyptian gods.

Enormous fish-bones from the settlements show that the farmers also caught some of the big old fish which lived in the deepest sections of the lake. And this in turn tells that they were also expert boatmen, constructing their craft in all probability from bunches of the same reeds and rushes which they used for their grain bins and their shelters. Such expertise was part of a millennial inheritance. Similarly sized fish-bones, gathered from the hearths of some of the hunter-gatherers who had camped beside the Nile for millennia before the farmers had come to live beside the lake, show that they were also taking huge fish from the centre of the river and that their boats must therefore have been capable of handling fish some six to eight feet long. Marks on some of the fish-bones left by these ancient hunter-gatherers, however, appear to show that, unlike the Faiyum farmers, they had filleted and smoked their catch.

Yet fish stewed upon the farmers' hearths would also have obtained a distinctive smoky taste. For the farmers made their cooking pots from clay made from river silt. And even though they part-covered the interior of some of them with red slip, and brusquely burnished them as well – which would have rendered them less porous – the modest, low-fired wares would not have stopped the distinctive taste of wood ash and smoke from the fire beneath permeating everything that was cooked within them.

The faintest traces of the activities of hunting and of modest hearths set right on the ancient lakeside beaches show that, as well as cooking on the well-established hearths within their settlements, the farmers also built small seasonal encampments and held summer barbecues in them, just as the hunter-gatherers had done before them. Now though, and for the first time in Egypt, daily life was driven by the various activities of farming.

THE NILE YEAR

Pollen caught in the fibres of the Faiyum grain bins shows that they had been woven in the weeks before the annual grain harvest, and that their makers had twisted and tied the coils of rush and grasses that had been gathered from the drying swamps beside the lake, in late March or in early April.

This was the start of summer, a time of darkening skies and violent storms, of sweeping winds and gusts of hot dry air. It was also the last month in which wild honey could be taken from the hive, a time when the meadows began to desiccate, when fish swam ever closer in the wetlands' shrinking pools until they turned into a single thrashing mass which could be harvested by hand. And that the farmers stewed this glittering annual bounty is witnessed by the considerable quantities of small and spiky fish-bones which the archaeologists found lying in their cooking pots.

Egypt is traditionally reckoned to have but three seasons; a lengthy summer followed by two months of an autumn inundation, and then a fruitful winter, when cereals were grown. Summer was the worst of times, and though it rained a little more in the times of the Faiyum farmers than it would throughout the following millennia, the difference would have been slight. Many of the native birds flew northwards out of Egypt at that time to avoid the growing heat. Plants and fruits all but disappeared, and the wild melons which grew in the lakeside gullies became so dry that the winds rattled the seeds within the gourds. Even the wild roots that were a perennial food source of the Faiyum farmers would become so hard within the grey-cracked earth they would have had to be ground to flour and soaked in water before they could be eaten.

Then, in June, in the sun's full heat, the Nile became turbid and turned slightly sour, an augur of the coming flood. And slowly it began to rise. In July, with the river's stream flowing ever swifter, ever higher, sunset winds blew cool and fresh above the stream. And then in August, when the flood was imminent and temperatures stood well above 40 °C, the universe appeared to pause.

Hardships of biblical dimensions threatened if the flood was over-generous and drowned the marshes and the meadows for too long a time. For then the flood would be late in receding, the standing waters would delay the farmers' sowing and damp and fungus would menace the seed stores, and frogs and rodents would come to plague the settlements. When they were first excavated in the 1920s some of the Faiyum grain bins held the frail corpses of whole families of mice, snuggled between the baskets and the lining clay. In lean years, on the other hand, when the flood was low, its waters may not have even breached the narrow gap within the valley cliffs that fed the Faiyum lake.

All ancient life within the orbit of the River Nile, the most placid, regular and majestic of the world's great rivers, depended on the volume of this annual watering. Even a modest difference in the height of the inundation, a slight change in the snow melt in the Ethiopian mountains or in the quantity of monsoon rains in Central Africa, could impoverish or enrich all life within the river's orbit.

For the early farmers by the Faiyum lake, a five-foot flood over the water-meadows would have been prodigal and destructive, while a three-foot flood would have been insufficient to cover the arable land and threatened not only the size of the next harvest but the formation of salt in white crusts across the surface of the drying silt, rendering it infertile. In lean times too, the five-hundred-odd square miles of the surface of the shallow lake would continue to evaporate and shrink around the year, along with the stored resources of the farmers whose livelihood depended on it.

The perfect flood, on the other hand, burst the river's banks in late August, carrying fresh, clear, fertile silt and washing away the salt that had crystallized upon the drying mud throughout the baking months of summer: all that, and the sudden bounty, when there was little else to eat, of spawning catfish in the muddy water, which were then so lazy that the normally aggressive beasts could be lifted by a pair of skilful hands.

In September, when the flood lay still and shiny right across the valley of the Nile and the Faiyum lake was twice the size of that of Galilee, there would be dew again, and dappled clouds in the bright blue sky. Then in October, when the floodwaters were starting to recede and the mornings were becoming cool and misty, sowing could have started. In later ages, Nile farmers tended to sow their muddy meadows in December and January, when the scorpions and snakes were hibernating and the evenings were occasionally cool enough to spin a gossamer of frost. By that time, though, the first Faiyum farmers appear to have left their fields behind them, for analyses of the pollen from their settlements show that they were absent for a great part of winter. It may be, then, that these first farmers shared some of the ancient habits of the hunter-gatherers who appear to have left the Nile Valley in the months following the flood, to travel east, up through the mountain valleys to the beaches of the Red Sea, or perhaps westward across the dry savannah to the exotic oases of the Sahara, before returning to the valley of the Nile in summertime.

There is no firm evidence, however, that the Faiyum farmers went on such a trek; no evidence whatever of their existence other than that found beside the lake. Nor is this surprising, for few traces of ancient life within the Nile Valley have survived. Moving erratically within the narrow confines of its cliff-lined valley, the river's course has slowly migrated from west to east over the millennia so that the great part of the remains of its past inhabitants and visitors have been washed away or are still deeply buried in the river's silt. Only the tombs and temples built along the edges of the ancient flood plain remain, along with the graves set down in the dry sands around the valley's cliffs. That no graves or cemeteries have yet been found beside the farmers' sandy settlements around Lake Faiyum, however, may be a further indication, together with the absence of winter pollens, that the farming revolution had not entirely changed these people's lives: that when the flood subsided and they had done their sowing, the farmers went travelling again, with their children, their animals and their dogs.

Whatever their peregrinations, by February the higher rising sun was breaking the cold, the Nile was running clear and sweet again, and the crops that the farmers sowed in early winter were reaching their full height. And so, by March or early April, when their cereals were ripe for harvesting, the farmers would have walked back to their shining lake, for this was the climax of their agricultural year, the time of weaving grain bins once again, and filling them with seed.

MEASURED LIVES

These then, were newly situated people leading newly measured lives. Though the hunter-gatherers had also lived in concert with the seasons, an endless round of travel prompted by the rhythms of the year, the Faiyum farmers now lived the best part of the year within a single landscape with their animals and fields and food stores. So though their lives were still marked and measured by the seasons, they were set upon another treadmill. And it was this that brought about a fundamental change in human sensibility.

Even their pottery was different. Though the farmers still made little bowls of clay as the hunter-gatherers had done, each one pinched out of a ball of the greyish Nile mud and sized, appropriately, to fit into a hand, the farmers also made tiny little cups that were whimsically supported on four small feet, as well as a variety of rough rectangular dishes, similar to the trays employed by later cultures to bake flat bread made from ground corn upon an open hearth. Now, too, the farmers made much larger pots as well, gently rounding their bases so as to allow them to stand upright in the ashes of their cooking fires. Bell-mouthed, stout and square of profile, these domestic wares were large and strong enough to have also served as water storage vessels or indeed as little ovens in which the gathered grain could have been parched or malted. Clearly, hunter-gatherers would have had but little use for such elaborations; their pottery did not have to serve nearly as many functions, nor had it been made with care, to last.

Some typical forms of Faiyum pottery; the largest vessels are around 15 inches high

This, then, was the difference. Moving continuously through a variety of landscapes all around the year, hunter-gatherers were themselves part of the natural processes which they exploited. There was no need for them to view their small communities as separate from nature: such self-consciousness indeed, might have threatened their existence. The farmers, on the other hand, lived in the same place for the best part of the year and were set into a fixed pattern of activities: a pattern that, for part of the year at least, did not immediately provide their daily diet. This then, was a life requiring forward planning, a life requiring a certain distance from the immediate environment, a certain objectivity.

In no way does this imply that the Faiyum farmers engaged in abstract dialogues about the nature of their lives that can now be reconstructed under such headings as 'economic necessity' or 'man's natural nature'. That would require the unwarranted assumption that these farmers acted on reflection and opinion, just as, we imagine, we do today. Nor is there any need for such suspect reconstructions of 'the prehistoric mind' when there are clear contemporary expressions of the Faiyum farmers' new-found objectivity within the very things they made. Just as the routine of farming had patterned and re-framed the landscape in which they lived, so too the things the farmers used and made were part and product of those same activities.

Though coarse and workmanlike, the farmers' grain baskets, for example, are expertly woven in a variety of rhythmic patterns whose regularity is emphasized by their weavers' careful choice of equally sized stems of cane and rush. In similar fashion, the fine domestic baskets, which are woven from materials just half as thick as those used by the grain basket weavers, hold an equal delight in skill and pattern, and they have patterns, too, made from the different coloured stems of straw that the weavers chose. The qualities such things display, their forms and patterning, are illustrations of the order that the first farmers were imposing on the landscapes and routines of their lives.

Nothing better exemplifies this newly developing sense of order than the scraps of linen that have been found within the Faiyum farmers' settlements. In their order and abstraction and in the precision of their planning, the tiny fragments contain the measured pattern of life in the communities which made them. Such work takes a variety of special skills, and time and planning too. In all probability, the blue-

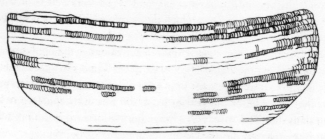

A domestic basket made and used by Faiyum farmers; about 20 inches long

flowered flax from which these cloths were woven also grew beside the lake. Such plants take three months to grow to harvest and then, in common with the farmers' grain crops, the moment of their cropping must be closely judged, for fine thread can only be made from young green plants whilst the coarser older fibres suitable for cord and rope are extracted a few weeks later in the harvest, from the flax plants' sere and yellowed stems.

Separating flax fibres from their stems is in itself a two-week process, for the plants must be rotted and then beaten before the fibres can be separated with a special small sharp tool. Disk-shaped spindle whorls found in the farmers' settlements show that the resulting fibres were then spun from the open hand, in the same way that some country people still spin wool. Compared with oily sheep's wool, however, flax fibres are hard and brittle and require a particular touch, a special skill, to maintain the constant level of humidity that keeps the spinning fibres pliable and strong. Only then could the resulting balls of yarn have been woven into the fabrics found within the Faiyum farmers' settlements.

Rough-shaped stones with various grooves and holes in them have been found in considerable numbers in the settlements and may well have been used as weights for inshore fishing nets. Some of these same stones, however, could also have been used as loom weights, for the scraps of fabric that survive have come from well-made plain-woven lengths of linen cloth, made on a loom on which the warp threads were kept under constant tension as the weaver worked. With such looms, at the very least, the weaver would have had to have fixed pegs into the ground high enough to hold the beams on which the linen warp was set and from which the loom weights could have been hung.

Such weaving necessarily entails the fastidious manipulation of rows of narrow threads. At one and the same time a physical and analytical activity, such work requires a rapt preoccupation. These, then, the first known Egyptian fabrics, are the direct ancestors of the noble household industry which provided pharaoh and his courtiers with their most splendid garments.

Immensely durable, and bleaching to an elegant whiteness under the Egyptian sun, linen improves its qualities with every wash. Yet we have no idea of how the lakeside farmers used the linens that they wove. Despite the numerous pins and needles found within the settlements, and the bone awls and flints such as are employed for working

A half-inch fragment of Faiyum linen

leather and rawhide, there is no evidence of the kind of clothing – if any – that the farmers wore.

They certainly made necklaces and bracelets, however, and probably used body paints as well. Knobs of red ochre, black carbon and green copper oxides have all been found in the settlements; raw pigments that were ground to dust on little rectangles of prettily coloured stone and then, if the evidence of later Egyptian ages may be taken as a guide, the prepared materials were used for making body paint, particularly cosmetics. By themselves alone, the little grinding palettes, which were obtained from distant rock outcrops, token the farmers' considerable interest in such processes of decoration, just as do the drilled beads cut from animal bone and desert ostrich eggs and Red Sea shells, and shining stones and beads brought from Sinai and Nubia. Such modest objects add lively decoration to the vague outlines of these vanished farmers; they also show something of how identity was shaped inside their communities. That the origins of many of these goods lay far outside the usual round of food procurement further underlines the importance of these processes; they show us something, therefore, of the farmers' predilections, of the measure of their minds.

There is as well, a further vivid indication of how these people were. For the Faiyum farmers excelled in making arrowheads as pretty as jewels, flaking the honey-coloured flint from the nearby mountains into V-shaped points, with two elegantly curved tangs with measured rows of tiny chips along their cutting edges.

These arrowheads, in fact, are an epitome of a near-three million-year-old tradition of knapping flint. As sharp as glass and twice as hard, flaked flint was the Stone Age's most durable resource. By making agricultural tools of flint – adzes, hoes and reaping blades – the first farmers had inventively extended this traditional Stone Age medium, and it was as common a material in the Faiyum settlements as it had been in the earlier hunter-gatherer settlements within the valley of the Nile.

Yet the farmers no longer worked within the hunter-gatherers traditions of flint knapping. Both in their shape and in the techniques of their manufacture, these surprising arrowheads share common pedigree with those made in the near-contemporary cultures of North Africa and the Levant. They differ from the work of their international cousins, however, in that their handiwork is finer. Nor does this token a desire to improve the arrowheads' efficiency and thus to catch more meat. Hunter-gatherers, whose lives had long depended on such tools, made sharper, stronger and less pretty arrowheads more quickly and efficiently. And though bone counts from the Faiyum settlements show that the farmers consumed similar quantities of meat as hunter-gatherers, they also show that a diet of domesticated animal meat had in part replaced the large amounts of wild game caught and eaten by their predecessors.

What the considerable amount of effort the Faiyum farmers invested in making arrowheads appears to show, therefore, is that the act of hunting and killing wild animals of itself, an act that had been an integral part of the hunter-gatherers' natural world, had taken on a new significance. At the same time, the farmers' exquisite arrowheads display, as does the weavers' rapt attention to their craft, an especial cultivation of skill within these small communities which, as the prehistorian Jacques Cauvin remarked about earlier occurrences of this same phenomenon, appear as 'an otherwise inexplicable aesthetic quest'. As far as these lakeside farmers were concerned, however, this quest became unique: one that, along with their linens, beads and body paints, would culminate in the making of the courtly culture of the valley of the Nile.

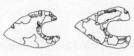

Two Faiyum arrowheads

2

Sickle Sheen

Most Ancient Egypt and the Neolithic

> *... the 'neolithic revolution' – the discovery of those civilized*
> *skills which still form the basis of our lives: agriculture, the*
> *domestication of animals, pottery-making, weaving ...*
> *Claude Lévi-Strauss 1969*

It is moving now, to see that tell-tale line of light along the cutting edge of a neolithic Middle Eastern sickle blade, that unique polish made by contact of the flint with countless stems of ripening grain as a prehistoric farmer bent to bring in the harvest.

That shine is where the modern West began. Just as the forms of the Faiyum farmers' sickles were the same as some of those used in the time of pharaoh, so the life of those first farmers is that of Adam and Eve in the Book of Genesis.

Yet the Neolithic Revolution did not originate within the orbit of the River Nile. At the time that the Faiyum farmers were sowing their first crops, other farmers to the north and east, had been employing the same techniques of cultivation for at least five thousand years. Nor were the Faiyum farmers' crops nor their domesticated animals indigenous to Egypt, or indeed to any part of Africa: not their cattle, not their sheep or goats; not their emmer, wheat or barley seed. Even the design of their flinted sickles had been imported. Their grain bins, too, with their muddy linings and their domestic baskets, were of a type that had long been made in the Levant. And though the reeds and rushes used to make their grain baskets are native to the marshes of the Nile, some of the abrasive fibres which were used to bind them together had been cut from palm trees; and these too appear to have been imported into Egypt from southern Mesopotamia.

In similar fashion, the techniques of linen weaving employed by the Faiyum farmers were equally alien, as were the flax plants whose fibres they employed. Far finer thread had been spun in the Levant in earlier millennia. With its obvious potential for use in bird traps and fishing nets, it may well have been that the plants from which such fine thread was spun were originally cultivated to serve the purposes of hunting rather than for making lengths of cloth.

There is evidence of the route by which such things first came into the Nile Valley. Bone fragments and other scant remains from the Egyptian deserts suggest that travelling herders may have grazed domesticated sheep and goats on the Saharan plains and in the Red Sea Hills millennia before farming had been established by the Faiyum lake, whilst clusters of modest campsites from Syria down to Sinai hold the faintest traces of small groups of people who, like modern Bedouin, appear to have abandoned a settled life of farming to travel in annual migration from the mountains to the sea, sowing and harvesting at intervals on their journey. Such travellers, too, may well have come into the orbit of the Nile. And as we have already seen, the Faiyum farmers appear to have undertaken similar journeys of their own, returning to their lakeside meadows at harvest time.

It is hardly surprising, then, that the Faiyum farmers' pottery also has alien origins; that the processes of tempering the clay with chopped reed, and of burnishing and slipping the finished wares also appear to have come from the Levant and ultimately, also, from the region known as the Gezira – the 'Island' – the area, that is, between the upper Tigris and Euphrates river systems which is now divided between Turkey, Syria and Iraq.

These same two areas, the Gezira and the Levant, were also the natural homelands of the stock and seed which the Faiyum farmers cultivated. Recent excavations show that, from around 11,500 BC and over a period of some fifteen hundred years, some settlements in northern Syria had exchanged hunter-gathering for the cultivation of the wild cereals and the domestication of the goats and sheep that were native to the region. And it was these, the same technologies and stock, that through the following millennia had filtered into Asia, Africa and Europe; north and west from the Levant to Anatolia, the Mediterranean and southern and eastern Europe; eastwards to the Persian Gulf, the Indies and south Asia; south along the northern coast of Africa to Spain and up the Nile to the Faiyum and beyond. In the broad scheme of things, therefore, the culture of the Faiyum farmers appears as but a tiny and somewhat isolated splinter: a few small communities in a remote oasis practising a rudimentary version of a revolutionary way of life.

Rudimentary, because the relics of the Faiyum farmers show them to have been unaffected by the cultural florescence that had developed and was still developing in some of the other farming communities. In Eastern Europe, for example, even as the lakeside farmers had gathered their first known harvests, far larger agricultural communities had been smelting copper implements for a considerable time, and some of these same settlements were also producing splendidly decorated pots and elegant ceramic sculptures of both animals and people. At this same time, too, farmers by the Black Sea were burying their dead with elaborate ornaments of beaten gold bearing lively images of their domesticated cattle – the first known use of the yellow metal on such a scale. In Anatolia, some shrine-like buildings at the centre of extensive farming settlements had long since been vividly decorated with sculptures and paintings. One of these buildings, at least, also held a hall of enormous, square-cut monolithic pillars, weighing several tons and decorated with images of animals. Each one of these enormous stones would have required large numbers of people for its transportation, shaping and emplacement, an activity which implies considerable social organization.

Nor are these the oldest known examples of such complex enterprises. Stocked with the standard Levantine range of domesticated plants, animals and farming implements, farming settlements had been established on Crete and Cyprus and some of the Greek islands as early as the eighth millennium BC. In similar fashion, such emigrations must have been considerable undertakings, entailing voyages on the open sea with substantial cargoes of animals and seed, in boats much larger than those the Faiyum farmers had built to take even the biggest catches from their little lake. The Faiyum farmers, then, were but modest outposts of this brand-new way of living, outposts established at a time when the local conditions had allowed them to flourish.

Such had not always been the case. Around 10,000 BC, when the people of the Syrian settlements were engaged in the lengthy processes of adapting from hunter-gathering to farming, there had been a disastrous and lengthy desiccation throughout northern Africa, and most living things had migrated from the scorched savannah of the Sahara to the watered highlands of the Maghrib and Cyrenaica and down into the valley of the Nile. The rains had come, however, around 6500 BC, and so fiercely that they have been called monsoons. Sweeping upward from the south they had greened the Sahara once again and re-forested parts of the mountainous deserts to the east of the River Nile.

These monsoons created large numbers of oases, which had supported bands of hunters, groups that fished and gathered local plants and fruit, ground wild grains and made distinctive types of pottery that are found today in desert graves from the Sudan to Libya. Some of these communities may also have domesticated the wild Saharan cattle, millennia before the settlers beside Lake Faiyum introduced their stock from the Levant and the Gezira. Another indigenous domestication is also suggested by the genetic components of the Saharan grain. Yet the scarcity of butchered bone within these settlements suggests that, like the modern-day herders of the Sudan, these communities kept their animals for supplies of blood and milk rather than for meat. And certainly, none of the Saharan peoples adopted the Levantine farming technologies or stock. So, presently they appear peripheral to the revolution that would spread outwards from the Gezira and Levant. Early Saharan history, however, is as yet little known and only comes into slightly sharper focus centuries after the farming settlements by the Faiyum lake had been established, when the desert dwellers were making engravings of herding and hunting on the rocks of their oases.

Direct contact between these desert peoples and the Faiyum farmers might be suggested by the beads of ostrich shell excavated in the lakeside settlements, whilst fragments of amazonite, a hard green gemstone which has also been found within the Faiyum settlements, appear to have been collected from some rocky outcrops that today are in north-western Chad on the southern side of the Sahara. Some of the spare elements of decoration – modest rows of bumps, which occasionally occur on the Faiyum pottery – are also reminiscent of forms that sometimes decorate the finer and more elaborate wares made by the Saharan herders.

'EGYPTIANNESS'

This is in no way to suggest that pharaonic Egypt was either originated by or inspired by foreign cultures, whether those of the Sahara, or the Gezira or the Levant. The influence of the Saharan peoples is highly tenuous, whilst the farming revolution which started in the Gezira and the Levant did not maintain a single cultural identity during its lengthy journeyings into Europe, Africa and Asia beyond that which was inherent in its core technologies. And even those most fundamental elements underwent considerable adaptation.

This was especially true of the Faiyum farmers who, for their very survival, were forced to radically recast the Middle Eastern neolithic farming calendar. Unlike the grasslands of Europe, Africa and Asia, which were greened and sustained by rainfall, no life-sustaining rains fell within the orbit of the River Nile in the time of its first farmers. Then, as now, most living things depended upon their direct contact with the waters of the river.

From their beginnings, then, the farming communities of Egypt were distinctively Egyptian. Just as all of life within the orbit of the Nile, one of the world's most stable river systems, was governed by the river's rhythms and its dramatic annual flood, so all external influences on those who dwelt beside the river were inevitably and inexorably transformed.

Pari passu, the particularities of the Faiyum farmers' calendar were those of pharaoh's subjects also. The fundamental technologies of their farming, indeed, would hardly change until the coming of the Persians and the Greeks. And even then, the farmers' lives stayed much the same till modern times, a fact that underlines the explosive success of the introduction of alien seed and stock into the hot-house of the narrow valley of the lower Nile. It also offers touching testimony to the unspoken presence of a peasant population that is so easily portrayed as a timeless mass of silent workers underpinning a succession of exotic and invasive governments. Until quite recently, indeed until the revolution and reforms of the last century, it was only the scribes and artists of the pharaohs who had given the Nile-side farmers a voice within their writings, and a lively presence, also, in the scenes which decorate their tombs.

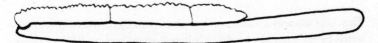

A sickle of wood and flint, as made and used by the Faiyum farmers; it is some 14 inches long

3

Merimda and el-Omari

Lower Egypt, 4800–4300 BC

> *We can only describe, and say human life is like that.*
> Ludwig Wittgenstein, 1930–31

A few centuries after the farmers had settled by the Faiyum lake, at a time apparently around 4800 BC, another community, and one far larger than any of the lakeside settlements, was established just sixty miles to their north, at a site known now as Merimda – 'a place of ashes'. Once it held the ruin of the oldest farming community that is known to have lived beside the River Nile.

Situated on a gentle mile-long slope that runs down from the Western Desert into the Nile Delta, Merimda sat on a bank of gravel, a product of the heavy rains which had deluged the deserts of North Africa in previous millennia and, in flooding down into the valley of the Nile, had deposited huge quantities of sand and flint all along the river's edge.

The settlement had survived, indeed, precisely because this gravel fan once stood a few feet above the river's annual flood; any contemporary settlements which were set upon the fields below are now deeply buried. So only the Place of Ashes yet remained of all that may have been; a fifty-acre sprawl of sand, cinders and rubbish, grain bins and threshing floors, house walls and a few isolated burials; the deposit of a millennium and more of ancient life, buried now, beneath some desert orchards.

Built directly on the gravel of the flood fan and sometimes part cut into it, Merimda's typical remains were of small round buildings with a central hearth, a house type that had long been built in the Levant.

Here, though, on the edge of the Nile's marshy delta, there had been a local touch, for some of the doorsills were made from the shinbones of native hippopotami. The frightening beasts were put to other architectural purposes, too; along with other animal bones, their vertebrae and long bones were sometimes used to form a sort of pillar to support a roof.

Now, a single hippopotamus, it has been estimated, would supply the meat of five cows or fifty sheep. Given the animal's huge size, the hunt must have been a communal enterprise, the prey brought down with harpoons with tips and barbs of ivory and bled with a stone knife or axe. A similarly communal spirit may also be detected in the disposition of some of Merimda's later houses, which were set out like streets, in rows. Here too were the ubiquitous neolithic grain bins of mud-lined pits and woven baskets. At Merimda, though, unlike the settlements beside the Faiyum lake, the bins were separated into small groups so that each dwelling appears to have had its own individual grain stores.

In one of these little houses, and most remarkably, for at Merimda almost everything had been shattered and scattered, a cooking pot survived intact, buried underneath a floor. Covered by a mat and closed with a ceramic lid, the stout round vessel held a collection of small objects which had been carefully composed in a single symmetric pattern on the curving bottom of the pot: five nicely rounded, highly polished axe heads made from a number of variegated stones, part of what appears to be a splendid ivory bracelet, two small circular boxes also made of ivory and probably cut from hippopotamus teeth, and an eroded ivory figurine of a portly hippo sporting what appears to be the head of a gazelle or goat.

Here, then, laid out in a domestic stew pot, were some fine axes and various precious little objects cut from the ivory of the most fearsome beast the Merimdan hunters ever stalked. You may, of course, put a variety of meanings on this collocation: that it is an offering to a deity or the remnants of a ritual designed to help a coming hunt or, more simply, treasure buried at the time of an enemy attack. Such narratives, however, tell more of the imaginations of their modern storytellers than they do about the ancient inhabitants of Merimda, for we know nothing of those people beyond that which has been

recovered from the ruin of their settlements; all else is merely speculation. The fact of the pattern of these objects in the pot, however,
cannot be disputed. Unlike the Faiyum farmers, where the patterns of
cultivation, object making and decoration may have been unconscious reflections of a way of life, the arrangement in this Merimdan
pot is a conscious manipulation of a group of man-made objects. Here
then, the fine-made axe heads are no longer work tools, but part of a
pattern of images and objects whose properties and identities have
been combined within a single silent dialogue; tools, that is, to para-
phrase Claude Lévi-Strauss, which have been used 'for thinking with',
and one of the first such gatherings of images to have survived from a
region that, later, would excel in just such things.

Such finds were rare, however, in the excavations at Merimda,
where the great part of what the archaeologists have recovered over
some eighty years of sporadic excavation since the site was opened in
the 1920s obtains a certain monotony: thousands of ceramic fragments, hundreds of small undistinguished objects made of bone and
stone, some spare burials dotted through the dwellings. This was not
a culture that made fine things. At the same time though, these modest
relics tell exotic tales of contact with the peoples of the Sahara and the
Levant, and this in turn shows that, unlike the Faiyum settlements, the
Merimdans were part of a lively intercontinental exchange that was
taking place during the Middle Eastern Neolithic Revolution.

Like their neighbours beside the Faiyum lake, however, the first
Merimdans appear to have led semi-mobile lives, inhabiting modest
accommodations and cultivating the neolithic staples of emmer wheat,
and vetch and barley. They also consumed large quantities of domestic
sheep, goats and pigs – especially pigs – as well as taking hippopotami
and fish, crocodiles, turtles and fresh-water molluscs from the river.
Fragments of ceramic ladles such as are required to scoop hot liquids
from a cooking pot suggest that they also cooked in the manner of
their Faiyum neighbours, on large pots on an open hearth.

Though no similar ceramic ladles have been found within the
Faiyum settlements, they are commonly found in the excavation of
contemporary farming settlements of the Levant. Some of the other
Merimdan wares from this same early phase share a distinctive her-

ringbone patterning with some of the ceramics of the settlements in the Levant and the Gezira. A solitary vase with this same pattern was left, perhaps by a wandering Merimdan, in a cave close to the Red Sea coast which had long been used as a shelter by travelling herdsmen. Along with the design of their houses and the placement of solitary human burials within the living settlement, such finds show an immediate and continuing Levantine connection.

The following centuries, however – those of the middle of the fifth millennium BC – saw a change in Merimdan material culture, which appears to have had considerable contact with the Saharan desert dwellers, some of whose distinctive maces, adzes and harpoon points, and even fragments of their fine ceramics, have been found within the settlement, along with some bones of the distinctive long-horned Saharan cattle. At the same time, though, this secondary phase within the settlement also saw the manufacture of two-barbed arrow-heads similar to those produced by the Faiyum farmers. These were so finely worked that they have usually only survived as broken fragments. One whole example however, slender, thin and more than three inches long, was enthusiastically described by its excavator as the finest of all known neolithic flints. At all events, such objects are clearly the products of a lively and adaptable society, and one, as well, with time to spare.

As with the Faiyum settlements, no cemeteries have been found at Merimda, the odd graves that were sprinkled through the houses of the settlement being the individual burials of women and children interred during the later phases of the community's existence. Crouched in death, and usually set facing north, they had been laid to rest with the scantiest of grave goods and this, along with their isolation from other graves if not the living household up above, does not speak of a strong community of custom and belief within the community. Nonetheless, several of these lonely burials had grains of wheat cast over them, a gesture that would garnish a millennial tradition of Egyptian burial and a multitude of pharaohs' tombs as well. Tutankhamun's burial crypt, for one, contained a wooden trough holding dried and sprouted grain; such were the continuing resonances of these most ancient Nilotic funerary rites.

THE CEMETERIES OF EL-OMARI

During the later phases of Merimda, in the second half of the fourth millennium BC, other settlements were established near the ending of the narrow Nile Valley and some forty miles to the south, where the bordering cliffs start to widen like a trumpet's bell in announcement of the beginning of the river's delta. Though the Saharan plains above the Nile Valley were already desiccating at this time, there was yet sufficient rainfall to sustain communities of farmer-fishermen in the wadis which drained down through the valley's bordering cliffs into the river's water-meadows. And it was these communities, at sites like those at el-Omari by the Wadi Hof, and at Helwan close to modern Cairo, that made the oldest known Egyptian cemeteries, burying their dead with their faces turned towards the north and crouched in the same poses as the house-burials at Merimda.

Here, then, for the first time, we are in the physical presence of some of Egypt's early farmers: men, it would appear, were usually around five feet six inches, women, on average, some four inches shorter. There is little, though, amongst these burials to distinguish any racial type. Just as their culture appears to have been part-African and part-Levantine, so the communities in these cemeteries are the same as those of later times in Egypt; a combination of different peoples bound into a single splendid society. More interesting, perhaps, are some of the incidental things that were buried with these people. One grave, for example, contained the oldest known Egyptian date pit; another, the body of an old lady who had been buried in midsummer with a sprig of flowering fleabane set upon her head, the yellow blooms intended, it appears, just as their properties would later be described in European herbals, to keep away the flies.

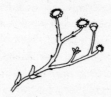

Flowering fleabane: Pulicaria undulata Kostel

THE MERIMDA HEAD

It was at Merimda, though, within the strata of the later phases of the settlement, deposited during a two-hundred-year period following the middle of the fourth millennium BC, that archaeologists recovered the fragments of the oldest known sculpture of a human being ever to have been found in Egypt. A clay head as round as a potato, it is a well-made and surprising work. It is also the earliest known evidence of how people living in the valley of the lower Nile saw themselves.

Yet it is not in any way Egyptian. Just as a prehistorian observed that 'Merimda is not significantly different from contemporary villages in Palestine, Cyprus, and Mesopotamia', so the little sculpture belongs to a world of imagery that had grown up over previous millennia throughout the heartlands of the neolithic Levant. More than a hundred such heads are known. Some of them were directly modelled over human skulls, others fitted like masks to sculptured bodies of varying sizes and proportions and were made of a wide variety of materials. All together, they appear as single series of multiplying images underlining the common circumstance, the order and identity, of the communities that made them.

Many of these heads are decorated. Some were splashed with dripping lines of bitumen. Others, like the example from Merimda, were painted with a wash of white, others with ochre, viridian or black, the same pigments that the Faiyum farmers had used for cosmetics. Several of the heads were drilled with holes and suspended in nets of macramé and knotted cord; others seem to have been placed on plinths or buried under buildings that have been variously identified as temples or storerooms, shrines or houses. The purposes of these images, however, are utterly mysterious. For there is no direct evidence from any of these communities of either gods or governments and no evidence, indeed, of any separation or inclusion of religion, cult and ritual from the daily round.

Smaller than a fist, Merimda's little head has holes impressed around its face that may have once held feathers or fibres to represent a beard and hair. It also has a hollow neck and could therefore have been mounted on a stick as part of some kind of display or joint activity. At all events, like all the other neolithic statues, it offers direct evidence of how some of the members of these communities conceived and represented human beings.

Expertly designed and crafted, as smooth and symmetrical as Merimda's barbed harpoon heads, the little face is made up of six beautifully modelled elements set in exact relationship to each other; the eyes, the nostrils and the nose and mouth being disposed in the same manner in which large flints were often worked; that is to say, in measured segments from a single centre point, like the elements of a clock face. And, like a flint, the head is small enough to fit into a human hand while the gentle work of modelling was undertaken. A miniature Brâncusi, it is one of the finest of all the neolithic images of heads to have survived.

Yet the image of itself is scary. The slanted oval holes which mark its eyes are closely set and deeply cut; the nostrils and the smaller holes beneath form an uneasy symmetry whilst the mouth is modelled like a wound, the upper lip set straighter than the lower, so that the void between them shapes a silent sound that echoes through the shadows of the eyes and nostrils.

Many of the other neolithic images are equally disquieting; the near-life-sized sculptured figures from Syria and Palestine, especially, are alien and otherworldly, plastered skulls with inlaid eyes that do not see and flattened, mask-like heads far scarier than Halloween.

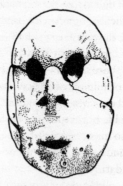

The Merimda head

In similar vein, some of the Anatolian wall paintings from the eighth millennium BC hold images of birds pecking at figures of the dead, dark images coupled with assemblages of enormous and distorted figurative sculptures, with animal skulls and savage bare-teethed felines. This, then, is the ethos of the Merimda head; life on the farm, so it appears, was not a bed of roses.

THE BIG MISTAKE

Physical evidence from neolithic cemeteries from Syria to el-Omari shows that the first farmers paid a heavy price for their way of life. Though they still hunted and gathered wild foods, their crops and livestock had circumscribed their movements and they were eating an increasingly narrow spectrum of foods and suffering a range of previously uncommon afflictions. Stress fractures due to heavy labour are common in their burials, as are the signs of osteoporosis, bad teeth and abscesses, the latter the direct result of chewing gritty stone-ground flour.

Women, especially, were physically changed by the daily labour, hour on hour, of kneeling to grind grain on a hand mill. An essential element of the early grain economies, this punishing repetitious labour had changed the shape of women's shoulders and caused their toes and heels to become arthritic and enlarged; these, the first physical signs of a separation of daily work between men and women. So, even in the hot-house of the Nile Valley, the early neolithic era was no Eden: recently, indeed, the farming revolution of itself, has been famously characterized as humankind's First Big Mistake.

Nonetheless, in the space of just a few millennia – an infinitesimal fragment in the span of human existence – large numbers of people across three connected continents had exchanged the age-old ways of hunter-gathering for a life of subsistence farming. What, then, was the attraction? Why had so many people adopted the grinding monotony of the agricultural round rather than a life of hunter-gathering?

Given that the foundations of the pharaonic state were set so firmly and precisely on this neolithic past, some understanding of its appeal – of its charisma, even, given its immediate effects – is fundamental to an understanding of the ancient Egyptian state, which in both its rituals and its imagery always looked back to these beginnings.

A NEOLITHIC REVOLUTION?

For the Victorians, such dramatic transformations, as that in which bands of hunter-gatherers became farmers and the subjects of a king in a few thousand years, were explained by tales of colonization, by acts of individual genius or by divine intervention. Such explanations are no longer popular and are now seen as a limited set of hypothetical scenarios unable to resist an ever-growing mass of contradictory data. Nevertheless, the general terms of this enquiry into what happened in this key period of human history have hardly changed at all; this, because a great deal of contemporary 'scientific' jargon, the very language of the enquiry, contains its own inbuilt and somewhat similar scenarios.

The 'Neolithic Revolution', for example, that most useful phrase, was concocted by the Australian archaeologist Vere Gordon Childe in the 1920s from two nineteenth-century terms: the word 'neolithic', Sir John Lubbock's term for the 'later or polished' phases of the Stone Age, and the medieval word 'revolution', a term originally used to describe the movement of the wheel or the passage of the stars and first provided with its present economic dimensions by John Stuart Mill. Childe later wrote that he had specifically concocted his phrase to combat the then current climate of ethnic stereotyping in European archaeology, in which the objects of prehistory were being ordered and described in terms designed to demonstrate that the motor of human history had always been the Aryan race. Childe, alternatively, had used his phrase to describe a genuine sea change he had detected amongst the relics of prehistory, one that ran right through an enormous mass of archaeological data he had gathered on three continents and which was the product of a variety of different peoples. This was a fault line in their material possessions which, he had perceptively observed, separated the tools of hunter-gatherers from those of farmers. Not surprisingly, perhaps, given the contemporary climate, Childe's newly invented Neolithic Revolution, a two-word adventure story in itself, soon became a part of Western history.

Childe's explanation for the rapid and widespread diffusion of his Neolithic Revolution was primarily economic. Farming, he argued, had enormous material advantages over hunter-gathering. In times of ecological stress, food storage and animal husbandry were first-rate survival strategies, whilst in the good times they offered prospects of a more prosperous and, literally, a more settled life. As far as Egypt was concerned, the establishment of the first farming settlements, Childe concluded, had been a direct response to the period of desiccation across North Africa which had driven populations out of the Saharan savannahs and down to the highlands and rivers at its edges. Pharaoh's pyramids, he proposed, were the triumphant signs of the Revolution's material prosperity, which had brought social and artistic progress in its wake.

The die was cast. It hardly matters that later research has shown that there had been more than enough natural resources to support the hunter-gathering communities along the River Nile, nor that many of the large 'near-urban' communities of early neolithic farmers seem to have failed, nor even that further research has proved that climate change had not forced groups of Saharan hunter-gatherers to take up farming. At around 4000 BC, indeed, when the last traces of the Faiyum farming communities disappear, the levels of the annual Nile floods were generous and rising. The seductive notion that the calorie counts of different ways of living could be turned into quasi-historical narratives offered the novel possibility of building 'scientific' histories from the relics of the distant past. Tricked out with fashionable neo-evolutionary economics, such narratives came to dominate accounts of what happened in prehistory to such an extent that, by the 1960s, the eminent archaeologist Lewis Binford would claim that 'man's culture is but the sum of his extra-somatic means of adaptation to his environment'.

Yet economics offers no explanation whatever for those rare things on which the people of the Egyptian neolithic lavished such enormous care: the clay head from Merimda, the patterns woven by the Faiyum basket weavers, their body paints, the perfect arrow-heads and all those other shapes and forms that in the course of the next millennium would be carefully and consciously expanded and extended so that they came to embody the indelible identity of pharaonic Egypt. All that economic historians can offer by way of explanation of these things are vague speculations upon primitivism, art and aesthetic urges. And that, essentially, is why most modern visions of ancient Egypt are still filled with 'ancient mysteries' and why its gorgeous tombs and temples and all those lively objects in museum cases still lie in an intellectual never-never-land.

THE CHARACTER OF CHANGE

How then to proceed? First, perhaps, by acknowledging that the early farmers were possessed of more than rumbling stomachs and a knack for knapping flint: by acknowledging that, as the human genome has not changed in the last 100,000 years, let alone the last 12,000, the early farmers were as intelligent as we are, that no 'natural' pseudo-evolutionary principles were at work, and that 'an axe', as Lévi-Strauss observed, 'does not generate another axe'. In short, there is little that was mechanically inevitable in what occurred at the ending of prehistory within the valley of the lower Nile.

We will never, of course, recreate the past's true temper: we don't even know what the man on the Clapham omnibus is thinking. The Faiyum farmers are long gone and, as with all the dead, their life and times are represented now in odd fragmented ways. Some things, though, are sure. The essence of that millennial journey in which settlements of subsistence farmers living on the lower Nile were formed into a national community and erected perfect pyramids whose corridors were filled with sacred literature, is a history of people thinking.

Hindsight is the historian's special aid to understanding something of this millennial process. Looking back, we can see changes taking place within those first communities of farmers; see choices being made; see something, then, of how they thought. Just as the things made in those communities were part of the patterns and rhythms of their lives, so the tensions that arose within them manifest themselves in images such as Merimda's fierce little head.

Hindsight, as well, points up a unique fact about the progress of the neolithic in the Nile Valley. Unlike the vast majority of their contemporaries, the communities that farmed the lands beside the River Nile undertook a series of extraordinary changes during the first fifteen centuries of their existence in every aspect of their lives other than that of the single sustaining activity of farming. There was, therefore, a powerful underlying energy at work within these small communities; an energy that, hindsight tells us, led to the creation of the pharaonic state; an energy which, as hindsight shows, held inklings of a unique conception of the order of the world.

This is in no way to suggest that these extraordinary changes were the product of an intellectual revolution. Though a common enough conceit in academia, where words are king, such a progression, from thought to deed, is utterly unproven in this silent pre-literary age where all the evidence that we will ever have is held within the things that yet remain.

These things, however, show that the beginning of this extraordinary adventure on the lower Nile lay in the change between the life ways of the farmers in their fields and those of the hunter-gatherers who travelled continuously around the seasons of the year. Survival in that hand-to-mouth existence had depended on the strong internal order of the group of travellers. The farmers on the other hand, for their survival, had to impose a strong order upon a relatively small area of the natural world through the processes of cultivation and domestication.

This, perhaps, tells something of the impulses which kept them bending at their harvests, despite their aches and pains. From the hunter-gatherers the Nile-side farmers had inherited a profound understanding of the interlinking processes of the natural world – the stars, the sun, winter, summer and the flood – an understanding that yet remained an essential component of all human life. Now, though, as they worked, the farmers were manipulating some of those same natural processes. By their very labour, they were redefining the universe in which they lived and their place within it.

We should allow the possibility, therefore, that although the lives of neolithic farmers were doubtless shorter than our own, they need not have been more brutish or more nasty. For they had changed their relationship to the world around them and sensed a new potential in it. And it was this that carried them through the hardships of the early neolithic – the inklings of a great adventure.

Within the orbit of the lower Nile, farming had unique effect. Following millennia of development in the Levant, it had immediately blossomed in the sheltered valley that held the world's most fertile soil, a burning sun and a superfluity of sweet fresh water. Little wonder, then, that after adapting the Levantine farming year to the rhythm of their river, Egypt's first farmers continued to adapt and change. The order that the processes of farming had imposed on life beside the Nile, and the order which the Nile, in turn, imposed upon its farmers, became the dynamos of a millennium and more of development and change.

Right from the beginning, change was swift. Egyptian grain put surplus food into the hunter-gatherers' hand-to-mouth economy; to that extent, and in the case of Egypt, Childe's economic thesis is correct. The later Merimdans, for example, appear to have been the first farming community in Egypt to live within their settlement right around the year. And at this same time, the change of the location of the settlements' grain bins from the communal sites of the Faiyum farmers to separate groups of bins beside individual dwellings at Merimda suggests that the community was no longer directing its efforts to maintaining the integrity of the group, in the manner of hunter-gatherers and that divisions based upon separate dwellings were arising inside their community. It was at this same time, too, that specific areas inside the Merimdan dwellings were assigned for the purposes of food preparation and for flint knapping, underlining, in all probability, a demarcation of male and female roles inside the community that may also have been reflected in a growing separation between the activities of child-rearing and hunting, which, in modern hunter-gatherer communities at least, is less pronounced. Here, then, is the beginning of the ancient Egyptian household.

Few distinctive images survive from the age of Egypt's first farmers: just the clay head from Merimda and a handful of more modest pieces, similarly cast in international neolithic style. Nor, perhaps, should we expect that such things were ever made in quantity. Hindsight shows that, of themselves, the fundamental elements of the creative processes by which such things were made were the primary ingredients of their daily lives: sowing and the harvest, the sun and moon, the silt plain, the ivory-coloured cliffs and the animals and plants and people that lived within the orbit of the river; those same elements which, in symbol and reality, came to play exactly the same role in pharaoh's courtly culture, where they held ageless and unfathomable resonance.

4

The Badarians

Middle Egypt, 4400–4000 BC

The remains of the first community that is known to have farmed within the closed confines of the cliff-lined Nile Valley were discovered in 1923 in what today is Middle Egypt, in a little village, the Ezbet Awlad el Hag Ahmed, some 220 miles south of modern Cairo, on the east bank of the Nile.

A handful of sherds had attracted the English archaeologist Guy Brunton to the site. In a decade of surveying and excavation in the Nile Valley he had handled thousands of ancient pots but had never seen anything like this high-shining nut-brown ware before, with what he later described as a 'ripple' running over its surface. And, most intriguingly, although Brunton had immediately seen that the sherds were very ancient, he had also seen that they 'could not be assigned to any known period'; that they were, therefore, the relics of a previously unknown culture.

As was common in the valley of the Egyptian Nile, the Ezbet Awlad el Hag Ahmed – 'the Farm of the Boy of Mecca-pilgrim Ahmed' – had been built on the ruins of mud-brick buildings of early Christian and Roman times which, in turn, had been erected within the confines of pharaonic and prehistoric cemeteries. And fragments from all these different eras lay all around the little settlement, in its alleyways and yards. A prime problem, therefore, when Brunton began to excavate was to separate the jumble of this common history, the ruins and the graves. So it was not until much later in that first season, whilst digging at a depth of some eight feet, that his workmen opened a grave which held another example of the same shining pottery that he had first found lying in the dust and chaff of the street above.

Though badly damaged, the body that lay beside the pot appeared to have been placed in the normal prehistoric pose, set on its side with its arms gathered together and its legs pulled sharply up towards the chest. Three objects had been put by its feet: a small, black, bell-mouthed pot decorated with geometric patterns, a large flint knife shaped like a leaf, and a slab of silvery selenite, a crystalline sulphate of lime which appeared to have been framed in wood for use, Brunton suggested, as a mirror. A round pink pot with four stout handles and a rough-made jar had been laid down the front of the body; and there as well, close by the hands, lay a beautifully rippled bowl, a near-complete example of the same high-shining pottery that Brunton had spotted at the beginning of the work.

During the following two winter seasons Brunton's excavators uncovered hundreds of similar burials in a ten-mile stretch north-wards of the village, all set in the little deserts which lay all along and underneath the valley's fringing cliffs, beyond the river and its fields of silt.

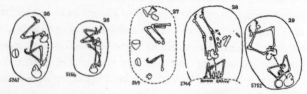

Part of Brunton's catalogue of Badarian burials. The first-found grave is labelled number 27 (569)

From the beginning, Brunton saw that the people who had been buried with these shining pots were cultivators and that some of the flints placed in their graves bore comparison with those from the Fai-yum, an observation extended by more recent studies which have shown that both the methods of flint working and the grain and ani-mal stock these people used were derived from the older neolithic cultures to the north – those excavated at Merimda and el-Omari – as indeed, were the forms of some of their pottery.

During the second season of the excavation, with Brunton working his way across a landscape filled with graves of many diverse periods, a flint specialist, Gertrude Caton-Thompson, joined the expedition with the specific aim of locating and excavating a single site that held a succession of prehistoric habitation levels, one above the other – this, to clarify the then little-known epochs of Egyptian prehistory. She had already prospected other areas of Upper Egypt to find such a location; now she found the perfect site not far from Brunton's camp, a small spur of sand beneath the valley cliffs, with flint and pottery lying just beneath the desert's surface. Her excavation was a complete success – even to the extent that, after cutting down through what we now know to have been a millennium and more of later prehistoric settlement, she found sherds of Brunton's high-shining pottery on the surface of a long-buried sand dune. So just a year after Brunton's initial discovery of some mysterious shining pots of no known period, Caton-Thompson had proved that the people who had been buried with them had been the earliest inhabitants of her site – and indeed they yet remain the first known farmers within the valley of the Nile.

Brunton dubbed the owners and, presumably, the makers of the shining pottery as 'Badarians', after the local town of el-Badari. Scientific analyses have since provided dates to show that they had flourished between 4400 and 4000 BC. The Badarians had lived, therefore, at the same time as the later phases of Merimda and the other settlements nearby, and they had also been the contemporaries of the later generations of Faiyum farmers whose settlements and grain bins were discovered by the remarkable Caton-Thompson in the same years in which she undertook her pioneering excavation at Badari.

Some typical forms of fine ripple ware as drawn in Brunton and Caton-Thompson's catalogue of Badarian ceramics. The largest example is some 3½ inches high

BADARIAN POTTERY

Since the 1920s, some further scanty settlements and yet more graves containing the Badarians' distinctive shining pottery have been discovered both in Middle Egypt and the surrounding deserts, and further south in Upper Egypt, though none of these sites have yielded anything like the wealth of artefacts and data that Brunton and Caton-Thompson first found in the area around Badari. Taken all together, however, the Badarians now comprise a population of around a thousand graves, whilst the spread of sites represents a commonality of culture amongst the first communities of farmers within the Nile Valley which is not true of the various earlier settlements to their north.

The Badarians' principal industries, so Brunton later wrote, were knapping, tanning and weaving, mat- and basket-making, and pottery. It was in the last of these crafts that they excelled. Whereas the pottery of Merimda and the Faiyum farmers has a rudimentary air, the Badarians made most splendid wares; indeed, the quality and craft of the dark-shining bowls and dishes whose sherds had first attracted Brunton to excavate at Badari was never again equalled within the Nile Valley. Not for nothing had their discoverers described those first few sherds as 'beautiful'. In the shadowed shelters of a Badarian settlement the perfect glossy bowls must have appeared as a sort of super fruit, the fragile dishes seemingly to float.

A similar striated effect to the 'ripple' which had caught Brunton's eye within the rubbish of the little village has been employed throughout the ages by many different sculptors, who, after using a variety of serrated cutting tools to establish and define the forms of their work, then left the linear marks made by those tools to emphasize the shapes they had created. Both the later bronzes of Henry Moore and the 'slaves' of Michelangelo are part-covered in just such marks; the former having been produced by clay modelling tools, the latter with toothed marble chisels. The Badarian potters appear to have used similar if somewhat simpler and more modest implements, from notched pottery sherds to fish-bones, to scrape the hard clay with a precision which produced a near-perfect uniformity and a spinning circularity similar to that which craftsmen of later ages would achieve when working on a potter's wheel. The Badarians, however, built their pots up from a fixed base and let the clay dry to a leathery hardness before shaving it down with the tools that left those distinctive rippled textures which they chose on occasion not to smooth away. Such rippled surfaces however, already had an ageless heritage in the time of the Badarians, for similarly textured patternings were regularly produced in everyday activities like scraping animal hides, weaving and flaking flints. In taking these everyday procedures and elevating them with an extraordinary finesse, the Badarian potters had done what pharaoh's craftsmen would do time and time again, in later ages.

Although monumental in their form, the Badarians' high-shining ripple ware pots are modest in their size whilst their thin and slightly wobbly edges emphasize their fragility and, to us today, who are used to a mechanical perfection, the fact that each one has been individually made. Just fifteen inches high, the grander pieces are wide-mouthed, straight-sided vessels that, as some of them show the marks of ash and evidence of mending, were presumably used as cooking pots. The smaller pieces, individual cups, and a variety of bowls with both flat and rounded bases, are very light, the work of shaving them down to their crisply sculpted profiles having trimmed the clay so finely as to leave the bowls as slim as modern porcelain and so fragile that, when they were buried with the dead, many of them were shattered at the filling of the grave by the pressure of the sand.

Though later potters did not continue to make such remarkably fine vessels, the forms of the more utilitarian Badarian wares served as a font of a ceramic tradition within the Nile Valley for a millennium and more. So seamless, indeed, was the transition to the wares of later centuries that the modern definition of the first part of this pottery tradition as a separate culture called 'Badarian' is largely geographical, for most of their pottery has been found in Middle Egypt rather than in Upper Egypt, where most of the pottery of the following phases of prehistory has been found.

That the Badarians' utilitarian wares are similar in their forms to the less-skilled productions of their northern contemporaries in Merimda and the Faiyum suggests that they may well have been adopted from the older northern settlements, along with the other technologies of the Neolithic Revolution. Yet this domestic pottery was also beautifully made, as if the extraordinary care that the Badarian potters had expended on their finest wares had trained their hands and eyes to make fine forms. Unlike their high shining pots, however, these domestic wares reflect the age-old processes in which coils and dobs of kneaded clay are squeezed and kneaded and built up into the shape of the finished pot. Given that clay shrinks slightly as its dries and shrinks again when fired in a kiln, the splendid generosity of form that enlivens so many of the Badarians' fired and finished products would have required the creation of some remarkably vigorous shapes in fresh wet clay.

As well as drawing on the traditions of the northern settlements, the Badarian potters also elaborated the shapes of some of the fruit and vegetables they harvested and which they used inside their settlements for a variety of purposes other than for eating; the shiny brown nuts of the dom palm, the dimple-textured eggs of ostriches, the swelling domes of gourds.

Some of the Badarians' domestic wares still bear the rippled marks of their final shaping; others were burnished to a high shine by rubbing the half-dried clay with a smoothly rounded sherd or stone. Sometimes these pots were left matt around the rim, so that they resemble half-peeled fruits. Many of them, however, were entirely burnished and given jet-black bands around their upper sections, a finish that was probably produced by placing a previously fired pot upside down in smouldering ash. A trademark now of a millennium of Egyptian prehistoric pottery, this distinctive lustre was first made, it has been suggested, in imitation of the way the edges of gourds that have been cut for use as containers are sometimes treated in a fire, to add strength to the rim. In the hands of the Badarian potters, the effect was most beautifully measured; the black blaze playing against the vessels' various forms in rich and subtle ways in a multiplying series of ceramic masterpieces. If ever a people was defined by its products, it is surely Brunton's Badarians, as their potters played with clay made from the silt of their slow-flowing river and the forms and textures of their daily lives.

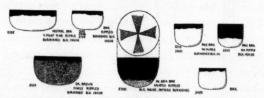

Some typical forms of Badarian domestic pottery as shown in Brunton and Caton-Thompson's catalogue of Badarian ceramics. The largest example is some 5 ½ inches high

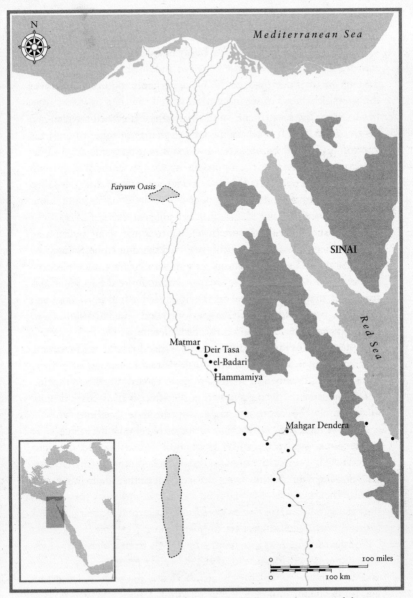

The known extent of Badarian culture along the lower Nile; some of the better known sites are named

BADARIAN LANDSCAPES

You may drive today through the Badarian heartlands, bouncing over the spurs of whitish sand and gravel, within that narrow desert that lies between the eastern cliffs and the flat-ploughed fields which run down to the Nile. It is a heraldic landscape. In one side window, the horizon is low and gentle, green and sparkling fresh with bright blue sky above. In contrast, the opposing window is entirely filled with bone-dry limestone cliffs whose surfaces are tanned with so-called 'desert varnish', a product of the deposit over long millennia of wind-borne particles of clay.

In Badarian times, the modern fields beside the river would have been water-meadows with a profusion of reeds and rushes fringed by acacia and halfa grass. In summer, these meadows were as hard and parched and hot as the out-of-season wetlands by the Faiyum lake, though in the months following the flood they could be as cool and misty as a Surrey common at a summer's dawn. The Badarians, however, appear to have favoured the little deserts at the foot of these bone-dry cliffs for their accommodation where, like Caton-Thompson, they would have been 'alternately grilled by the fierce reflected heat from the cliffs or shivering in the unbroken force of north-west winter blasts' and where, during the winter months, so the bodies in their burials imply, they must have slept wrapped up in skins and fur.

And yet there was no scarcity of food. The wetlands, which were amply spread across the valley floor and filled with game, provided abundant land for cultivation. So the Badarians stored their harvests in large clay bins within their desert settlements, where they also ground their grain as they required and sometimes, too, they turned their flour to bread, for loaves were found in several of their graves. A form of porridge also appears to have been a common food, ladled out of the cooking pots into hand-sized bowls from which it was consumed, perhaps, with the aid of the delicately made spoons of bone and horn and ivory which were also buried with the dead. Meat too, was on the menu, and in generous quantities. Alongside their domesticated herds of oxen, sheep and goats, hunting and gathering were still considerable activities; the bones of birds and fish were also plentiful inside the settlements, as were wild seeds and pulses and the roots of reeds and grasses, some of which could be as sweet as filberts whilst others would have been so fragrant yet so bitter that they could only have served as perfume.

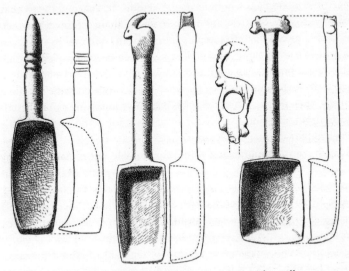

Badarian ivory spoons; the largest is 8½ inches tall

The farmers' generous and variegated diets appear to have been part contingent on a round of travel following the seasons of the year; recent excavations show that the Badarians moved up and down the valley of the Nile and into the surrounding deserts. In autumn, when the broad valley in the region of el-Badari was entirely flooded, they appear to have travelled with their herds out onto the dry plains above the valley cliffs, where the ancient rough stone walls that run across the sandy hills for mile upon mile may yet reflect some of their fences and corrals. There, too, up on the high plateau, the Badarians hunted game. Ostrich feathers, the fur of desert hare and the hides of foxes and gazelle have all been found within their settlements and cemeteries.

Some groups, on the other hand, seem to have moved further up the valley in high summer, for a small encampment 150 miles to the south of Badari in Upper Egypt, at a site known now as Mahgar Dendera, appears to have been inhabited only at that time of year, when the wider meadows of Middle Egypt were entirely desiccated and grazing had completely disappeared. At Mahgar Dendera, so the fish-bones in the hearths informed its excavators, the Badarians took catches of the large fish that lived in the middle of the river. Here, too, the steeper, narrower floodplain would have allowed the herders and their flocks to stay close to the river and later, when the flood returned, it would not have forced them to retreat to the bottom of the valley's cliffs, as it would have done in Middle Egypt. The absence of pollens within this encampment, indeed, informs us that the Badarians left it precisely at the beginning of winter when the floodwaters were receding; at the time, that is, when the wide meadows in the area of el-Badari were drying out and were ready once again for planting and, a little later on, for grazing cattle too.

Such constant journeying would explain why the remains of many Badarian settlements are so scanty and why so many of the pots that have been found within them were broken and have been mended. Such living quarters were not permanent dwellings. Sticks and matting appearing to have served as the main materials for human shelter, grain stores, generally, being more solid structures. Such transitory accommodations are similar to those of the modern Nilotic pastoralists of south Sudan who live alongside their great dusty herds of long-horned cattle, and whose predecessors and one-time contemporaries of the Badarians also appear to have spent the year in travelling and watering their animals in the oases of the Sahara.

Not that the ancient Egyptians would ever be great homemakers. Even the greatest pharaohs passed their lives in mostly modest mud-brick buildings hardly worthy of their archaeological designation as 'palaces'. And in pharaonic times, as well, the gathered grain was often better accommodated than were the harvesters themselves. Until quite recently, indeed, the villagers of the Nile Valley lived in sprawling open ways, moving during the year with their families, their bedding and their animals from house to hut, from their main dwellings in little deserts beneath the valley cliffs down to their fields below, extending and rebuilding their various accommodations all the while, as they saw fit. As they travelled, the Badarians took some of their finest and most fragile wares along with them; fragments of high-shining pottery have been found in some of their most modest settlements, in both the desert and the river's valley. In similar fashion, the requirements of the Badarian potters, their clay and fuel, access to ample water and the makings of a simple kiln to fire their pots, could also have been accommodated into this semi-mobile way of life, just as to this day some nomadic peoples carry the equipment to make fine carpets on their travels.

That the finest Badarian pottery appears to have been made in relatively small quantities yet has been found in such a wide range of locations tells a great deal about its makers; as does the fact that its limited repertoire of forms was reproduced over several centuries without suffering any loss of quality or character. That generation after generation of potters communicated their craft with such fidelity suggests an intimacy of learning; potting, so it would appear, on a modest scale such as is found in some small communities today, where it is a domestic activity in which people of different ages and status within a single household contribute to various aspects of a pot's production, from the making of its clay to the firing of the kiln. In such circumstances, the potters are usually women, which in turn suggests the possibility that the wide diffusion of Badarian pottery reflects an exchange of women – the anthropologist's 'intermarriage' – between different semi-pastoral groups. Indeed, evidence of just such an exchange is to be found, perhaps, in a flamboyant type of grey pottery known as Tasian ware, which is usually regarded as the product of a Badarian sub-culture. Similar to contemporary wares made in the Sudan and the Sahara, such small quantities of Tasian ware as are presently known to exist could well have been produced inside a single 'intermarried' group.

Tasian 'flamboyant' ware; the largest examples are around 9 inches high

Here, then, pottery has come to stand as a kind of history. Nor, in the case of the Badarians, does this equation seem unreasonable. For each one of their high-shining pots was conceived as a precious visual object, a kind of presentation. That the same few forms were carefully repeated down through generations also shows that each and every one of these precious vessels was part of a consciously maintained tradition. For both their makers and their users, the presentation which the potters offered was that of a mark of identity of a distinctive community, in the same way that today the corpse of someone buried with one of those same pots is known as a 'Badarian'.

It is this identification of a prehistoric community by pottery type and modern place name that provides the basis of a meta-history for late prehistory; a chronology of ceramic type and form which has recently been extended to take in all of Egypt's history and which has become so all-pervasive that everything excavated within the orbit of the Nile is now dated and defined by the pottery that is its inevitable accompaniment.

POTS AND HISTORY

The idea of building a history from pots came from an Englishman, one William Matthew Flinders Petrie, Guy Brunton's mentor in Egyptian archaeology and arguably the only truly original mind, other than that of Jean-François Champollion, the decipherer of hieroglyphics, ever to have worked in egyptology. Petrie had been led to his invention in the 1890s by tens of thousands of unfamiliar and rather alien pots that he had been excavating from a series of prehistoric desert cemeteries in Upper Egypt. Their sheer volume, Petrie recognized, required a simple system of classification for their accurate description in a scientific memoir, such as he produced upon a yearly basis. Possessed of the ability to order phenomenal amounts of forms and patterns in his head, Petrie sorted his plethora of pots into a small number of basic types – 'black-topped', 'red-polished' and the like, whose forms, he assumed, had slowly changed through time. He then crossed his pottery types with another data set derived from a system that he described as 'Sequence Dating', in which individual pots that he knew to have been contemporary to each other – those, that is, which had been found within a single grave – were given a single common number; say, 'Sequence Date 30' or 'SD 42'.

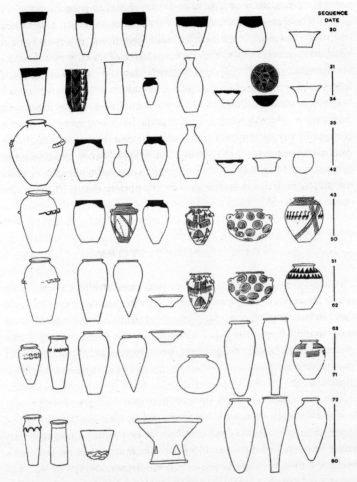

POTTERY OF SUCCESSIVE PREHISTORIC PERIODS.

Petrie's first-published Sequence Dating Chart, which begins with post-Badarian pottery, at SD 30

Using paper slips and spills of cardboard, after a deal of sorting throughout a London summer, Petrie produced a single chart that showed his basic pottery types changing within the numbered order of his sequence dates. Thus, though there were no fixed dates to which the system could be tied, the tens of thousands of pots that Petrie had excavated were accurately organized in the order of their manufacture.

So successful was Petrie's system that when other archaeologists dug other prehistoric cemeteries almost everything they found could be accommodated within the system and described by the letters and numbers of a pottery type and sequence date. All that was required, therefore, for the scientific publication of excavations such as those of Brunton and Caton-Thompson at el-Badari, was that they described their finds in Petrie's terminology, recorded any previously unknown types or sub-types with drawings and provided them with a sequence date. For more than half a century, the system was the sole measure of the order of Egyptian prehistory. Then, with the advent of scientific dating in the 1950s, the decade after Petrie's death, Carbon 14 readings provided broad confirmation of the order of the changing forms of Petrie's pottery types and awarded some of them approximate dates in time. Since then, there have been major refinements and extensions to Petrie's charts, but no fundamental changes to his system.

Its application, however, provides surprises, not the least of which is the puzzling information that, unlike the pottery forms of later ages, Badarian pottery seems to have appeared quite suddenly and fully formed beside the Nile. There is no clue as to its origin: the Badarians and their fine pottery, their bags and traps, their fires and herds, their settlements and graveyards, appear, as it were, from nowhere.

This, though, is not a cue for a modern pseudo-mystery waiting on a 'breakthrough' to reveal a hitherto unknown opening chapter of Egypt's ancient history. Unlike the continuous cultural tradition that Petrie's pottery chart so carefully lays out for later ages, all of Egypt's earliest known communities, the Faiyum farmers, the Merimdans and the rest, appear in exactly this same sudden way; like the Badarians, they all seem, as it were, to have come from nowhere.

How, then, to make a history from such unrelated fragments? First, perhaps, by observing that, although the myths of later ages variously depict the prehistoric Nile Valley as a field for invasion, repopulation and colonization, there is no evidence at all that the Badarians or any other of these prehistoric cultures came from somewhere else. There is evidence, however, though it is scanty and erratic, of people having lived within the Nile Valley for as long as there have been people – and even earlier: for the remains of a small and somewhat delicate ancestor of *Homo sapiens*, one *Aegyptopithecus Zeuxis*, have been found near the Faiyum.

One day, perhaps, traces of the Badarians' immediate predecessors may be found. It is likely, though, that their relics have been swept away, just as have the houses and settlements of most of those who have ever lived upon the flood plain of the Nile, obliterated by the changing passage of the river and its silt. All that has survived are fragments of things that were placed beyond the river's reach. Egypt's most ancient history, then, can only be constructed like a necklace, as separate beads of amber, a series of separate and sometimes vivid little moments, set upon a string of time. The trick is to construct the necklace so that more beads can be added later on, as other ancient things are brought again into the light.

THE LIVING PEOPLE

As for the Badarians, their burials show them to have been an amiable and peaceful people. Brunton found many elderly and white-haired folk within their cemeteries and few instances of broken bones or other injuries or conditions resulting from strife or deprivation. Nor were there many tools within their graves, no sickles and few adzes. Hunting equipment, on the other hand, was common in male burials, both arrows and boomerang-like throw-sticks similar to those used by the later ancient Egyptians to bring down duck and geese within the river marshes. By way of contrast, the near-contemporary graves of Sudanese herders contained considerable quantities of weapons, and sometimes, too, the skulls of long-horned bulls were intertwined amongst the corpses of the dead, a close physical identification with animals that is quite absent from the Badarian cemeteries.

As to their appearance, most Badarians were around five feet tall; a few, though, were much taller and some were very muscular. The men were generally clean-shaven and wore their hair quite long; some of the women had fringes and plaits fixed up with combs of bone or ivory. The colour of their hair varied from light brown to black; its texture from straight to curly, which is the same mixture found in earlier and later populations of the Nile Valley. As anthropological analyses serve to underline, the Badarians were of the same racial mix as the ancient Egyptians who would follow them.

The dead were usually decorated with a mass of jewellery: swags of heavy necklaces threaded on strings of animal hair or flax, with beads of shells and ivory, or hammered out from natural copper nuggets gathered from the Eastern Desert, or cut from steatite, a kind of soapstone, that was often fired like pottery so that it obtained a mysterious blue-green glaze. A wealth of other beads as well were cut from semi-precious stones brought from outside the Nile Valley, and these same stones – carnelians and jaspers, siltstones and breccias, serpentines and alabasters – along with an impressive range of local limestones – red, pink, grey and green, hard and shiny, soft and matt – were also used for making little vases.

Men sometimes wore a single string of large beads around their necks or on their arms, and ropes of glazed beads also, at their waists. Women and children might wear heavy necklaces, and most young girls had girdles and headbands made from threaded shells. Both sexes wore ivory bracelets and ear-studs, and people of all ages were buried with little pouches containing the ingredients of body paint, the makings of a maquillage that would last till ancient Egypt's ending. Nuggets of green malachite and ochres were also left beside the corpses with what appears to have been a medium of grease or fat scooped up into a shell, though one might imagine that body pigments would be better applied with a medium which would not melt or run so easily, such as the castor oil that the Badarians pressed from the seeds of the wild plant. Like the people of the Faiyum and Merimda, the Badarians ground and mixed their cosmetics on small stone palettes. Stained and polished by years of use, many of these palettes were also buried with the dead.

Both sexes, Brunton found, had been buried in clothing cut like kilts and kaftans, made from animal skins and linen. Brunton's textile specialist, Thomas Midgley, reported that the weaving was almost as refined as the high shining pottery: 'Plain weave. Ratio warp-weft 1 to 1. Picks 28 × 26. Colour dark brown. All yarns doubled, the weft slightly less twisted than the warp. The warp yarns are remarkably parallel to each other, but the weft is at a fairly acute angle. The open character of the weave is pronounced, as in other Badarian cloths.'

A half-inch square of Badarian linen cloth

Such fine linens, it appears, were worn next to the skin; the leatherwork, of antelope, goat and what seemed to Brunton to have been cat pelts, serving for the outer garments, which were skilfully worked and sometimes sewn with fringes. Needles were common in the graves of both men and women and there were many different types of them, from bone awls and bodkins such as might have been used for basketry and leatherwork, to fine-sewing points stored in special small bone cases. That hardly any instruments of common daily labour were found within the cemeteries suggests that needlework was considered an agreeable activity.

The graves from which this wealth of information was extracted were simply made and small and oval in their shape, like hearths or wheat bins, into which the dead were fitted as if into a womb. The sandy gravel in which most of them were cut was seldom stable; some graves were plastered with wet mud along their sides; others had low brick walls built in them with roofs of wood and rush. Even if such arrangements token nothing more than a desire to physically protect a corpse, they witness a belief in the vulnerability of the dead and, hence, their continuing presence in some manner, a sensibility that finds further testimony in the charcoal and ash which Brunton found within the graveyards: 'pots were set up in little hollows in the ground, and surrounded with tamarisk boughs or other brushwood. In them was cooked grain taken, perhaps, from near by storage bins, and meat which had been carved up with saw-edged knives.' These hearths, then, had cooked burial feasts, or served in some other observance of the dead.

THE BURIAL OF THE DEAD

We may not be far wrong if we suppose that the Badarians were sufficiently civilised to carry handkerchiefs.

Guy Brunton, 1928

With their fine clothes, their jewellery, their beauteous drinking cups and their carefully combed hair, one might imagine the Badarian dead had been dressed up for a party, such as would later be drawn out upon the walls of ancient Egyptian tomb chapels. Most of the goods left in these graves, as well, are those that give delight: wrapped in leathers, linens and fine furs, the bejewelled corpses were accompanied on occasion by ostrich feathers placed fan-wise in their graves.

Where though, was the party? The Badarians after all, were familiar with the realities of death in a hot climate; the sharp smell of decay coming fast and pungent in the heat, the need to dress and compose the body before rigor mortis set in, the breaking of the shining pottery with the filling of the grave and immediately afterwards, as Brunton testifies, the likelihood of robbery. Nonetheless, each grave was laid out with a fastidious and individual care. Like the pattern left in the Merimdan cooking pot, each burial was arranged as an individual presentation, a kind of dialogue.

On the broadest level, that of the language of these silent dialogues, every grave holds within it the trappings of a person whom some of the grave goods identify as a member of the culture that we call 'Badarian'. In this light, the deposition of the finest pottery within the graves, pottery whose manufacture required such concern and skill, appears like the remnants of the cemetery feasts, as a part of a dialogue of care between the living and the dead, the forging and maintaining of a joint community. At the same time, however, each and every grave also holds its own unique collection of burial goods: cosmetics, clothes and jewellery, domestic utensils and hunting gear, even a mirror in a frame, and all of them carefully disposed around the body in a different order in every separate grave. The act of burial, therefore, represented a particularization of an individual inside the common order of a close-knit and well-defined community.

Set within communal cemeteries, such burials were also part of a continuing connection between the communities of the living and the dead. Just as the living, at the time of funeral, arranged separate identities for all the dead, so the memories of the buried dead provided the people of the living settlements with a collective and individual history, a kind of afterlife. The dialogues that the Badarians conducted in their cemeteries, therefore, gave the entire community, the living and the dead together, a powerful and continuing resonance.

Such acts are not explained as 'symbolism' or 'offerings to the dead'. Saturated with human care and contact, a visual and tactile intelligence was at work within these small communities which is not easily reduced to sentences on a page. In the broader scheme of things the activities of the Badarian burial parties mark a change from people thinking about the basic activities of farming and the transformation of natural processes, to thinking *with* some of the things that they themselves had made.

Hindsight also shows that these graves stand at the beginning of a millennial process of funerary presentation and definition that would be undertaken by the people of the Nile with impressive dedication and extraordinary effect. Above all, the delectation of clear traditional design and high-shining finishes such as the Badarians established in the finest of their ceramics remained a fundamental aesthetic element within ancient Egyptian culture down to the final dynasties of pharaoh, part of the connection between community and craft, care and order, the living and the dead.

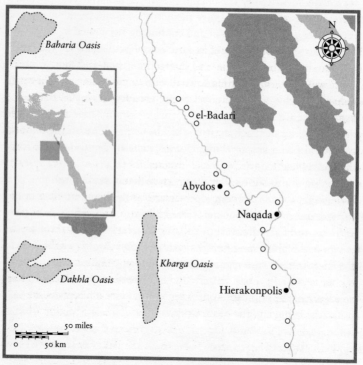

The Naqadan heartlands: the locations of some early Naqadan sites are
indicated and the three main centres are named

5

Black-topped, White-lined

Life in Upper Egypt, 4000–3500 BC

During her excavations at el-Badari, before she found a scattering of Badarian sherds lying on the surface of a buried desert, Caton-Thompson's workmen had dug down through some six feet of prehistoric debris, the residue of later settlements on the same site. Unlike the Badarians, who at that time were an archaeological novelty, the culture of the people who had inhabited the later settlements was already known, vast cemeteries of their graves having been excavated a quarter of a century earlier by Flinders Petrie, who had invented his sequence dating system to order the enormous quantities of pottery that he had found.

Although a thick deposit of limestone gravel had sealed off the Badarian strata from those immediately above, Caton-Thompson saw that it was but the debris of a flash flood which had washed down into the valley from the desert plains above, and that the strata it divided had probably been close in time. There were, as well, strong cultural continuities, for the Badarians' successors had lived in the same way as their predecessors. They had continued the same burial customs and their potters had taken up and developed many of the Badarian techniques and forms. Petrie, presciently, had started his numbering system at Sequence Date 30, so the Badarians, whose pottery had shown comparatively little change, could be allotted ten slots of their own, from 20 to 29, an estimation which the later Carbon 14 dates would prove to be appropriate.

Petrie always maintained that naming prehistoric cultures after the places where their relics were first found was 'cumbrous and inexact'. Nonetheless, just as Brunton had named the Badarians after the local county town, so the thousand years of prehistory that Petrie had excavated and then sequenced with his numbered dating system now takes its name from the modern town of Naqada in Upper Egypt, close to the first prehistoric cemetery that he excavated. The name may easily mislead, because there are now hundreds of so-called 'Naqadan' sites all up and down the Nile; at the same time, though, the label has also proved appropriate, for later excavations have shown that the heart-lands of this millennial culture lay in modern Upper Egypt, to the south of el-Badari. So nowadays this lively country town, with its clusters of minarets and church spires and a reputation for silk weaving and a fiery distillate of dates, lends its name to the better part of Egyptian prehistory; Carbon 14 analysis having determined that the various phases of the so-called 'Naqadan culture' flourished throughout the fourth millennium BC, whilst the pottery-making tradition that bears the same name only came to its ending centuries later, at the time of the building of the pyramids.

Broadly speaking, the Naqadan culture is considered to have passed through three distinct phases: 'early', 'middle' and 'late'; a progress founded on the division of the pottery sequences into three major phases labelled Naqada I, II and III, each one of which accounts for about a third of Petrie's original sequence numbers. Recent archaeology and the continuing statistical analysis of pottery, however, have enabled the subdivision and extension of these three stages into a dozen different sub-types which, in their turn, have been further subdivided to create such archaeological mnemonics for the identification of individual pots as belonging to the productions of, say, 'Naqada IC2' or 'Naqada IIIA2'.

Such typological sophistications may easily create the illusion that they represent a thousand years of history. It is not so. Despite the labelling at excavations of successive strata by such archaeological designations, the account of Naqadan culture that it provides is more like miniature geology than a modern history. Both its major phases – I, II, III – and those of some of the pottery sub-phases are counted out in centuries, and often there is little agreement as to which specific centuries they are. Change inside separate Naqadan settlements, moreover, also appears to have moved at different rates, and no two cemeteries contain the same range of grave goods. The culture, if one may call it that, is prehistoric. Reference to absolute time is always vague and hedged about with qualifying terms.

Like geology, however, a clear order and pattern may be detected in those successive phases, Naqadan I, II and III, changes that, however vaguely they can be set into a modern time-frame, tell a great deal about the ethos of the ancient society in which they were occurring. And so we may observe in general terms some of the motivations of the generations that created ancient Egypt.

THE GRAPHIC IMAGE

From the beginning, Naqadan potters drew elaborate images on some of their bowls and vases: thin, white-lined drawings that are the oldest graphic arts in Egypt and stand at the beginning of the pharaonic tradition of illustration, hieroglyphics and design. This was the beginning, therefore, of the visual cultures that the modern world now identifies as 'ancient Egypt'.

Hardly any earlier potters had drawn on their wares. Occasionally, one of the Badarian craftsmen had scratched spidery shapes or geometric patterns into the surface of the clay, and sometimes they had burnished patterns on the bottom of their cooking pots, either in the shape of a Maltese cross or, more wistfully perhaps, in hatched designs resembling vegetables or fish-bones. Now, though, the early Naqadan potters divided their finer highly polished products between those which were given a traditional blaze of carbon black and left unpainted and others, usually of different forms, that were covered with a rusty red ochre wash and decorated, on occasion, with images and patterns. Thickly painted in creamy, often rather tremulous and gritty lines straight onto the shining surfaces of simple ceramic forms, the designs impart a shimmering, gem-like quality to their pots.

These drawings share the same imagery and are delineated with the same characterful outlines as the later ancient Egyptian craftsman's fundamental repertoire: water, fish, man, boat, mountain, donkey, hippopotamus and so on, and in a manner which, like that of the pharaonic craftsmen, communicates the identity and qualities of its subject directly and unambiguously. These earliest of drawings, though, do not appear to have been a spontaneous innovation: both their sureness and their extraordinary uniformity shows that a lively graphic culture had already educated the potters' hands and eyes, and had, therefore, preceded its appearance on pots. Parallels might be drawn, perhaps, between some of these images and the rock drawings of the Saharan herders, though the latter are notoriously difficult to date and are not composed in the same careful patterns that the potters placed onto their bowls and dishes. More immediately, the Naqadan images also reflect the vigorous graphic outlines of a range of miniature sculptures that the Badarians had made in ivory and clay, and which they occasionally used to decorate their combs, spoons and jewellery. Employing the same graphic techniques to describe anything they wished to represent, the Naqadan craftsmen simply extended the Badarians' limited range of subject matter.

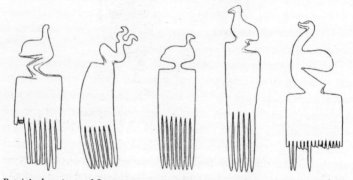

Petrie's drawings of five ivory combs from the Naqada cemeteries; the tallest is about 5½ inches high

Though the early Naqadans' images are nothing like those of Western academic art, which we pretend derives directly from 'life' and 'nature', they yet contain, as if by alchemy, the very essence of the living creatures they portray. So precise, indeed, were the Naqadan craftsmen's observations that many of the plants and creatures which they drew and carved may be identified today by their Linnaean names. The Naqadans, in fact, created a visual taxonomy of the world around them, a stocktaking of the creatures of the lower Nile that rose, eventually, to include 150 species. Many of these images had already been part of the repertoire of the early white-line pottery painters whilst others had been used in other, quite specific contexts.

The solid outlines of the turtle, crocodile and desert fox, for instance, had been employed along with various species of Nile fish as the shapes of hard stone pigment-grinding palettes, whilst the livelier silhouettes of ostrich, high-horned gazelle and ibex crown some of the ivory pins and combs that were worn as dainty decorations in the hair. On rare occasions, as if in acknowledgement of their true origins, the pottery painters drew images of combs in short, sharp lines upon their red-washed pots, beneath those of the silhouetted animals.

Two combs and a donkey drawn on a broken white-lined bowl, which is some 6⅓ inches across

It is unlikely – though ultimately, unknowable – that these archetypal images were intended for the purposes to which they are usually assigned; that is, as the signs and symbols of some unspoken primitive anthropology. Some things though, are certain. Drawn in outline on the pots, carved on occasion in glowing ivories and the most intractable of desert stones, both the subjects of the images and the materials from which they were made were the focus of intense scrutiny; a kind of meditation upon the world in which they lived, upon the rocks and clays and teeming wild life of the lower Nile. It is as if the craftsmen had sensed the contradiction between the measured, cultivated world which they were creating and the world of which they were no longer part: that natural world of animals and plants and minerals.

Sometimes, too, the pottery painters made little worlds within the pots they painted: a bowl decorated, perhaps, with zigzag watery lines across its centre and a ring of clay model hippopotami running around its rim. In such designs there is much that harks back to the Merim-dan cooking pot that was found filled with a trove of little objects, the ivory hippopotamus and the rest. This is true, not only of their subject matter but also in the patterns in which the potters set their images, and which usually divide the pots' round forms in the manner of a cross or clock or the weaving of a rush basket; that is to say, into radiating sections from the centre in divisions of four, eight and twelve.

Three Naqadan bowls with white-lined scenes of daily life

These little worlds are miniature versions of the Nile Valley. Usually, fishes, hippopotami and crocodiles are drawn in the lower sections of the vessel along with zigzag lines of water, whilst up above them and separated by triangles and horizontal lines, are images of land animals and people. One especially remarkable beaker has a lively group of model women set all around its rim; facing inwards and with every face and feature individually seen and drawn. The little group appears to be washing fabric together, at the river's bank. Part-filled with water, such vessels would have portrayed the Naqadans' Nile-side world with a striking miniature reality, the landscape of a snow globe in reverse. Other pots appear to have been designed as a single element within this re-imagined world: swaying a little out of true like living palm trees, some tall cylindrical vases are decorated with fronds around their upper sections, and the roots drawn along their bases are set in zigzag water lines. And all of these designs are based on the ingredients of life and landscape in the valley of the lower Nile, on water, and the insistent linearity of the river and the cliffs.

Unfortunately, there is no indication of what functions these fine pots may have originally performed. Certainly the images they hold were not considered as mere decorations, since the pigments that the painters used are friable and soft and quite unsuitable for daily wear. Found both in settlement sites and cemeteries, they witness the beginning of a new phase of Nilotic prehistoric culture, one following the Faiyum farmers' absorption with the manipulation of the natural environment and the Badarians' elaborate arrangement of man-made objects within their cemeteries. For the early Naqadan potters had begun to manipulate images of both natural and man-made things and to place them one beside the other to create a pictorial equivalent of the world in which they lived.

Three white-lined Naqadan pots with Nilotic scenes; they are each around a foot high

SETTLING AND HERDING

On her way down to the buried sand dune with its scattering of Badarian sherds, Caton-Thompson had excavated and removed the walls of nine Naqadan huts. Modest circles made of wattle and daub, they are rare examples of their age and show that some of the early Naqadans were building in a manner similar to those of the Badarians. Set on a gravel bank high above the flood line, the nine little circles, which are too small for homesteads, may have served as temporary shelters or as fuel and grain stores. And that in turn suggests that these early Naqadans moved as lightly on the earth as had their predecessors, travelling with their herds and returning to their crops at harvest time. With their occasional images of caravans of pack donkeys and drivers holding goads, with huts and marshlands and the ever-present river with its hippopotami and crocodiles and fish and boats, the white-lined images the Naqadans drew upon their pottery show us something of this living world, all set beneath the bordering mountains of the river's valley, and the wild animals on the plateau up above.

Though some sixty Naqadan settlements have been located, few have yet been excavated and our major source of information about the period still comes, as it did in the days of Flinders Petrie, from desert cemeteries, of which almost a hundred, large and small, have been located and from which some 16,000 burials have been recovered.

Compared with those of earlier periods, the surviving relics of the Naqadan culture are the product of a completely different order of society. The numbers of the cemeteries and settlements, for example, are larger than those of all of their predecessors put together; they also span a longer period of time – virtually a millennium – and have far greater geographic spread. Though the earliest known Naqadan objects are the products of small communities similar to those of the Badarians, those of later periods belonged to a craft culture that grew to span a near 600-mile stretch of the lower Nile, from close by the ancient Mediterranean coastline to the Nile's first cataract at modern-day Aswan, the town that is traditionally considered to be ancient Egypt's southern border. To that extent, at least, the Naqadans' relics are the first physical expression of a pan-Egyptian culture.

NAQADA, ABYDOS AND HIERAKONPOLIS

The modern town of Naqada and its prehistoric cemeteries lie 140 miles to the south of el-Badari, upon the river's western bank and at the point of sunset; other settlements of similar antiquity stood a quarter of a mile away at the point of sunrise, on the river's other shore. Though they settled north and south along the river, the roots of this culture lay deep within this symmetric landscape where the enclosing valley bestowed on those who lived within it an innate sense of place and order, flow and rhythm, life and death.

Naqadan culture appears to have had three main centres of production. Naqadan worked flints, those most fundamental tools, show three distinct traditions, whilst the pottery also seems to share a similarly tripartite division, marked by differing qualities of line and subject matter in its painted imagery, along with regional preferences for specific shapes and forms.

These three production centres roughly correspond to the sites of the three largest known concentrations of Naqadan cemeteries, which are usually assumed to have held the accumulated inhabitants of three nearby long-lived communities. The largest of these great burying grounds is close by Naqada, where Petrie excavated the graves of some three thousand souls. A second lies some seventy miles downstream and to the north of Naqada, at Abydos where the first pharaohs would be buried; whilst the third lies a similar distance upstream, and to the south of Naqada, at a lonely west bank locality known now by its Greek name as Hierakonpolis, 'the city of the hawk'.

In Naqadan times, the high deserts were still not as desiccated as they are today and people caravanned with their animals, just as the Badarians had done, along the tracks that lead out from the plateaux above Naqada, Abydos and Hierakonpolis through the Sahara to the Western Oases and eastwards also, through the Red Sea Hills down to the coast. That the later Naqadan cemeteries at these three sites became so large may well signal the ending of this semi-nomadic existence and the beginnings of settled life within the valley of the Nile.

Here, though, we are on the edge of speculation, for the settlements of the Naqadans are little known. Even those that are assumed to have had the largest populations – the prehistoric towns, perhaps – of ancient Naqada and Abydos, are largely unrecorded, and only small and mostly unrelated parts of Hierakonpolis, which appears to be the only large Naqadan site to have been preserved to any great extent, have yet been excavated. In all probability, however, there is now little left of these phantom towns; the best part of whatever there once was having been ploughed up in desert reclamation schemes, or swept away down through the ages by the lateral movement of the river in its valley. Given these ambiguities, there yet remains the real possibility that there were never any urban Naqadan centres at all, and that the three great cemeteries mark the sites of gathering grounds, like those of the modern festivals of India. Whatever the ancient reality, recent archaeology at Hierakonpolis, in a seventy-acre desert bay pocked by the moon-like craters of innumerable excavations, allows genuine glimpses of the Naqadan way of life.

When the Naqadans first lived at Hierakonpolis, rainwaters from storms on the Sahara plains still sometimes flooded down the wadis to the Nile and greened the edges of the desert. And it was, perhaps, this greening that at around 3800 BC encouraged some early Naqadan herders to build sheds and corrals within the largest of these wadis, upon fans of rubble and sand brought down by ancient torrents. Here then, in this desert bay a mile and more behind the present line of fields, are the ruins of dung-filled stockyards and such vast amounts of animal remains that its excavators have suggested that the area may also have served as a slaughterhouse. And here too is a cemetery of impressive early Naqadan graves, each one set inside its own enclosure. Nearby, and marked now by the debris of generations and enormous heaps of slag and wasted sherds, there were groups of potters workshops, whose kilns were often sited up above the level of the wadi floor, against the cliff, where they could take advantage of the evening breeze. Some of these studios, so their scattered debris shows, produced some of Naqada's finest wares: they also witness pottery making on an entirely different scale from anything that had gone before.

In the 1970s, at the bottom of the wadi's wash, close to the modern fields, amongst the scrambled relics of a long-lived Naqadan settlement, an American expedition led by Michael Hoffman excavated the ruins of a potter's kiln. Set on a circular platform some sixteen feet across and made of mud, the kiln still held some firebricks and the typical odd-shaped clay wasters that potters still make to support and protect their wares during firing. Early Naqadan pottery, so its physical analysis informs us, was fired at around 700 °C, a temperature that could have been comfortably achieved by stacking a mass of fuel and fresh-made pots on this platform, by building a low wall around its edge and then covering it all up with mud and broken potsherds to contain the heat.

Though modest in themselves, the skilful operation of such Naqadan kilns provides precise results – the Badarian potters, of course, had already mastered such techniques. And so, the potters knew that if the fire burnt too quickly and was too hot, the fabric of their pots would burst: that if, on the other hand, the fire was allowed to burn too slowly, it might not reach the temperature at which clay tempers to hardness. They also knew that if the logs of the fire were laid around the pots so as to allow a stream of clean air to rush around them during firing, they would obtain the rich colours typical of fine Naqada pottery. And that, on the other hand, if the kiln was densely packed and the fire controlled so that it stayed smoky during firing, the pots might turn completely black. Some Naqadan kilns, indeed, appear to have had a flue built into them, which could be partially closed or opened to control the updraft during firing.

The mass of ancient sherds that lay all around this kiln – which Hoffman estimated at some 300,000 pieces – represented many years of pottery production. They also showed that this particular work-shop had not made fine Naqadan ceramics but cooking pots, rough wares made from local clay tempered with chopped straw to protect them from bursting or breaking during firing.

Close by this kiln – so close, in fact, that its excavators thought it likely that an overzealous firing had set it on fire – they found the ashy ruin of one of the few early Naqadan houses ever to have been exca-vated; the cinders, ironically, preserving a date for its conflagration at around 3600 BC. Larger than the somewhat similar dwellings built at Merimda in the previous millennium, a single doorway gave access to a rectangular room some twelve feet long and ten across whose floor had been cut two feet into the surface of the desert, and whose walls were made of mud, plastered onto mats and wattle. A hearth on a mud plinth lay in a corner of the room; close by, a storage pot had been set into the floor. The roof, which like the walls was made of mud and matting, had been supported on a row of posts some five feet high; another row of posts outside the house suggests that it had also had a lean-to which, Hoffman proposed, had served as an animal pen.

A Naqadan potter's model of a similar dwelling shows that such houses sometimes had windows set opposite their entrances which could have turned the building into a little wind tunnel and allowed the cooling evening breeze to refresh its dark interior with just the opening of the door. The model also shows that this single narrow entrance may have had a wooden lintel with a rolled-up mat hanging underneath that could be unrolled to close off its interior. This is the first known appearance of those so-called roll and lintel doorways that would be sculpted in their thousands in the rock architecture of ancient Egyptian tomb chapels during the following millennia. The model also suggests that house walls may have curved gently inwards; that the palms and rushes of the mats and wattle tended to bend under the weight of the mud plaster, giving its silhouette the distinctive sloping appearance of much later pharaonic architecture.

Donkey bones found outside the house, within its lean-to, suggest that those enduring animals may have brought fuel for the kilns and carried away the potters' products in little caravans like those the white-line painters sometimes drew upon their dishes. Caravans would certainly have been required to supply this gathering of pottery workshops in the desert wadis, which would have needed substantial supplies of fuel and clay and water to keep them in production. Why, then, were those workshops sited in such an inconvenient location? That parts of that same wide wadi housed cemeteries, stockyards and slaughtering facilities suggests that some at least of these desert potters' workshops had been established to serve the needs of funerals, which, as the remnants of the cemetery's cooking hearths suggest, may well have been a time of feasting and meat-eating, just as it had been in the days of the Badarians.

It is hardly surprising that the remains of brewing vats of this same period were found close by the potters' workshops. Along with baking, the activities of potting and brewing were interdependent throughout ancient Egyptian history: bread makers required large numbers of pottery moulds in which to bake their loaves; brewers needed pots into which they could decant their brews.

A well-preserved brewery, excavated in a settlement quite close to the potter's house, had consisted of at least six ceramic vats set in pairs upon a mud platform that to promote fermentation could have been covered over and heated in the manner of a potter's kiln. As well as the remains of dates and possibly of grapes within the vats – both of which would have provided extra sugar to the brew and aided its fermentation – the dregs contained remnants of emmer wheat, that fundamental element of the Neolithic Revolution and the principal ingredient of ancient Egyptian beer.

Each of the brewery's six vats, its excavators estimated, could have held some sixteen gallons. This single establishment, therefore, may have produced around 300 gallons at a single two-day brew, though if the beer had been siphoned into jugs immediately after its initial fermentation, as its excavators propose, that quantity would have been doubled. That other similar establishments, as yet largely unexcavated, appear to have been operating at this same time shows that brewing at Hierakonpolis was undertaken on a considerable scale. Though low in alcohol by modern standards, the product would at all events have had high nutritional value.

Roughly contemporary with the potter's house, this brewery is one of the oldest known in all the world, another contender for that honour being a similar establishment excavated more than a century ago in the desert cemeteries of Abydos. Though further relics of these cottage industries have yet to be located outside Hierakonpolis, similar stockyards, breweries and potteries were undoubtedly established in the three main Naqadan centres and probably in other places too.

At Abydos and Hierakonpolis, therefore, amidst the untidy sprawl of waste and ruin that is often found along the fringes of a desert, are the remnants of a social revolution. Large, single-purpose, specialized establishments operating in the first centuries of Naqadan culture, handling and producing far larger amounts of goods than their predecessors had ever done, replacing the smaller and more complex output of the Badarian communities. It was a redefinition of an ancient way of life, a change of scale and a new attitude to food procurement and production, part-prompted perhaps by the arrival in the Nile Valley of a secondary wave of farming technologies that had been passing down through the Levant in earlier centuries and which now brought wine and figs and cheese into the settlements along the lower Nile – and perhaps had been the source of beer-making as well.

Nothing, though, is sure. Such archaeological ephemera as foodstuffs are erratically preserved and only the most modern methods of excavation and evaluation can accurately detect their presence. Nor is there anything to indicate the management systems that such enterprises as these early stockyards, potteries and breweries would have required. Nor, indeed, is there any evidence of trading systems; no budding capitalism! All that their relics show is that the hard life of the early farmers had eased, and that food surpluses were enabling some individuals within the early Naqadan communities to work at a range of specialized tasks outside those of subsistence farming. That there was, indeed, a growing communal wealth is also tokened by the increasing amounts of grave goods being placed in early Naqadan cemeteries. And it is this, perhaps, this changing way of life, that is also reflected in the white lines of the potter's decorations, as they dispassionately record the world around them, and identify their place within it.

This growing sense of ease within the early Naqadan community is further evidenced by their extension of the traditional skills of animal husbandry. For now, along with such commonplace companions as dogs and domestic livestock, a variety of exotic animals, including hippopotami, wild cats and monkeys are buried in the larger cemeteries. The remains of two young African elephants are among the more bizarre relics of this bucolic husbandry. Interred within the cemetery in the large wadi at Hierakonpolis, one of them, at least, appears to have been laid in a lavishly garlanded grave, dressed up in beads and linens in a manner similar to human burials, and accompanied by a clutch of white-line bowls, some shining, black-topped beakers and some foreign pottery imported from the north. Nodules of red ochre and green malachite and a siltstone palette were also found within the tomb – to grind the elephant's cosmetics? – and beads and bracelets too, of amethyst, malachite and ivory, along with small stone mace heads similar to those carried by southern herdsmen.

Each weighing half a ton and standing nine feet high, the two great beasts had probably been brought from a region south of the Nile's First Cataract at modern-day Aswan. Both would have required a hundredweight of fodder every day; one of them, so its stomach contents showed, had been fed on yellow water flowers and rushes like those used for making baskets. That such enormous animals had been so well provisioned and so splendidly interred is further evidence, if it were needed, that the narrow greenhouse of the lower Nile was generating considerable agricultural surpluses.

As a rule of thumb, it is generally assumed that early agricultural economies required at least ten people working directly on the land to sustain one person engaged at other tasks like keeping elephants, making pots or brewing beer. There is no direct evidence, however, of how the early Naqadans produced such surpluses. Possibly, as we have seen, the secondary wave of food technologies that had permeated the Levantine farming communities had broadened the Naqadan stock and crop base, and the introduction of ploughs and the use of farm animals for traction had increased the size of a farmer's crop. In such circumstances, of course, the growing prosperity would also increase population levels, which in turn would have provided more manpower to colonize and farm the river's semi-wild valley. Such speculative economics, though, cannot account for the individual manner in which the Naqadans deployed and organized their growing resources; nor, indeed, for the elaborate culture which they were carefully creating. All that the preserving deserts show is that, a few centuries after the Badarian culture disappeared, some of the early Naqadans were running potteries, breweries and zoos and probably, on occasion, getting drunk as well.

One wonders, therefore, what kind of society they were making.

6

A Cloud across the Moon

Death in Upper Egypt, 4000–3200 BC

... mythmaking, which scholars assume to be primarily an activity of non-Western societies, is equally prolific in European thought.

Gananath Obeyesekere, 1992

Caveat emptor! Conventional histories of Naqadan culture are by definition bogus. The information fundamental to their compilation is simply not available. Basic statistics of Naqadan society are unknown, the roughest estimates of population and settlement sizes little more than guesses. Nor did the Naqadans write: the very term 'prehistory', indeed, is popularly defined as those eras before the age of writing. There are no known events, no personalities, no cities, no wars, no clans, no cults, no evolutions and no revolutions.

Traditionally, historians of Egyptian prehistory borrowed their narratives from classical literature and those of European scholars of the last few centuries. So the material cultures of the 'Badarians,' the 'Naqadans' or the 'Merimdans' are usually portrayed as the products of separate ethnic groups, the spread and influence of their pottery and other artefacts described in political or even military terms. Crudely, those with the fewest, or most 'primitive', possessions – the 'weak' – are invaded or colonized by the 'strong', and voila! Egypt is united.

At first glance, the familiar language of such histories appears to reflect the natural order of the world. It is the same language, after all, in which the histories of the cultures of the three great Middle Eastern religions have traditionally been written, and it deals in the same passions and opinions, the same professions and offices of government, that compose our world today.

Sadly, however, such 'Old Testament' tales, as one historian describes them, obscure a strand of real history running through the relics of Naqadan society. For hindsight shows that something was taking place inside their riverside communities which in the course of the following millennium led to the creation – albeit the involuntary creation – of the first known literature, the first stone-block architecture and the first state. The real fascination of this most ancient Egypt, then, its real history, is in tracing the slow development of all that, of the invention of pharaoh's court and the idea of a state. And this, as recent evidence shows, was a process completely different from anything which traditional historians had previously described.

For, though there are few hard statistics for the fourth millennium BC and no known historical events, there is clear contemporary evidence of people making choices. The products of a century and more of excavation, for example, show that the Naqadans were engaged in developing a remarkable range of artefacts and techniques – everything from feeding bottles to stone-block architecture. They also allow, as we have already seen, glimpses of the reality of life within some of the early Naqadan communities. And it is precisely this, the unique and innovative tenor of this society, which if you attempt to encompass it within the clichés of traditional histories will run through your fingers like desert sand.

THE OVAL COURT

In 1985, and with great good fortune, American archaeologists at Hierakonpolis discovered a location that gave an entirely new dimension to our vision of Naqadan society. Within the confines of a large and long-lived settlement spread across the bottom of the largest desert wadi, they uncovered an open area where, at around 3500 BC, the people of Hierakonpolis had laid out an oval courtyard 100 feet and more in length, with a sloping, mud-plastered floor. Extended over several centuries, the courtyard had been enclosed with walls of mud and brick and stone. And all around its edges, represented by the merest ghosts of walls and postholes, the archaeologists discovered a unique group of buildings.

A row of little workshops had been set down one side of the oval courtyard, where, as scatterings of flint tools and fragmented gemstones clearly showed, craftsmen had cut and polished carnelian and agate, obsidian and rock crystal. There were fragments too, of some splendid hard-stone vessels and other well-made fragments of boxes or perhaps inlays for wooden furniture. Nearby, too, were the storerooms that had housed the craftsmen's raw materials. Here the archaeologists found slivers of lapis lazuli and ivory, malachite and turquoise and shining desert stones, some of which had been brought from the most distant reaches of the ancient world. An enormous mass of sherds lay all around the courtyard, centuries of pottery, much of it scarcely used and then discarded, and some of it imported from the Levant and the Nile Delta, from Nubia and the oases of the Sahara. And there were local wares as well, some of them domestic, some with white-lined decoration, and several in forms that were previously unknown that had been made, it would appear, for specific purposes.

Along with these accumulated intimations of energy and rare things, the excavators found fragments and chippings in the oval court from the manufacture and sharpening of flint knives such as were used in slaughtering and butchering. Developed from Badarian forms, these elegantly curved broad-bladed knives, with sections as precise and slim as aerofoils, were painstakingly produced by rubbing raw flint with abrasive dust down to the form required, which was then patterned with a final expert flaking in a virtuoso allusion to the ancient techniques of knapping stone.

Three flint knives

As sharp as cut-throat razors, the fragile blades of these fine knives are best suited to tasks requiring a deal of skill and care. Shaped so that they could be grasped in three fingers with the index finger held straight along the back of the blade as if it were a pen, some of these knives were designed to be used in an inward-curving gesture; in acts of butchery, as later images suggest, like flaying, slitting and disarticulation.

Judging from the considerable numbers of bones, shells and scales found in the long, deep trench which ran along one of the courtyard's sides, it would appear that those splendid knives had been made and used within the oval enclosure to butcher considerable numbers of animals: cattle, sheep and goats, gazelle and hares, and a wide variety of aquatica: turtles, crocodiles and catfish, as well as the gigantic perch that lurked in the depths of the Nile.

Along with the mass of pottery and the substantial quantities of bones of newborn lambs and other stock that farmers would usually have raised to adulthood, such finds suggest that some of these acts of slaughtering and butchery were preludes to lavish feasts; occasions, it would appear, accompanied by the finest utensils that the Naqadans could manufacture. At all events, it appears that, in an era when the farmers of Hierakonpolis were producing food sufficient to support the potters and brewers in a desert wadi, and were maintaining considerable menageries, this oval court had served in some capacity within a Naqadan community as a locale for the conspicuous consumption of further agricultural surpluses.

As its discoverer, Michael Hoffman, quickly recognized, there are direct links between this oval courtyard and some of the later architecture of pharaonic Egypt. Directly opposite the courtyard's entrance, across its sloping pavement, Hoffman also uncovered the scanty ruin of a large three-chambered building with four enormous postholes set along its front. Some three feet wide and almost five feet deep, these huge holes had been cut to house a row of massive pillars which, as the surviving remains of wood and bark suggest, may have been made from the trunks of conifers. Unlike the houses of the settlements, this had once been a considerable structure and of a type, apparently, that left a mark on the collective memory, for a building of the same dimensions with a similar row of masted pillars set along its high façade would be built almost a millennium later, in fine-cut blocks of stone, within the courtyard of the first Egyptian pyramid.

Nor was this the only link between this Naqadan courtyard and pharaonic Egypt. Both a mud-brick platform built on the courtyard's floor close to its entrance and what appeared to be a socket dug for a single free-standing post which had stood at the top end of the courtyard's slope were reminiscent of the throne daises and the standards that appear in a series of miniature ivory engravings and small stone reliefs made centuries later in the times of the first pharaohs. These show the early pharaohs holding court – a correspondence further underlined by recent excavation in the oval court at Hierakonpolis of a cache of fine pottery dating from the time of the first pharaohs, which had been buried underneath its plaster floor.

Some of the images on these engravings, therefore, show details of how such oval courts were used in later ages. Here then, are cattle corralled in low-walled oval enclosures, and what appear to be shrines, of a design similar to the enormous building whose scanty ruins Hoffman had found at Hierakonpolis, and whose forms would later be employed in several hieroglyphic images with connection to that same term. In many of these little scenes, the monarch sits enthroned upon a dais and people hold up standards all around him and overlook a series of presentations and slaughterings, activities that find obvious equivalence in the mass of bone and pottery excavated at the oval court at Hierakonpolis. Continuing these comparisons, and with a remarkable consistency, some of these same small drawings suggest that the posthole at the centre of the Hierakonpolis courtyard may well have held a mast bearing an image of one of the animals and birds that, later in Egyptian history, became the attributes of gods and kings. Along with the tools of slaughtering and the accoutrements that would later decorate the pharaonic court, such images may well have been made in the row of little workshops that once stood beside the oval court at Hierakonpolis.

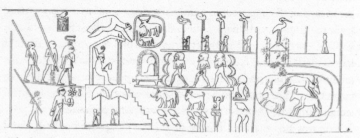

The band of engravings on the so-called Narmer mace head, as drawn for Quibell's original publication. The strip is around eight inches high

That many of the little ivory picture plaques from the time of the early kings have been found at various locations along the lower valley of the Nile suggests that such courtyard ceremonies were not reserved for Hierakonpolis alone. Nor do the events that they portray seem to have been limited to a specific era, for in the 1990s excavations in a modest Naqadan settlement close to Abydos yielded the remains of another slaughtering yard older and far smaller than that at Hierakonpolis, a yard that also held within it a wide range of ceramics and an exotic collection of butchered bone, the vague and ruined remnants, it would appear, of an earlier abattoir with direct links to the later court of Egypt.

GREAT TOMBS

A whole mythology is deposited in our language
Ludwig Wittgenstein, 1934

By itself alone, of course, the scanty ruin of a great, grand court at Hierakonpolis cannot demonstrate the presence of a prehistoric ruler in an early Naqadan settlement. At the same time, however, the organization required to establish and maintain such an elaborate establishment – and indeed, the near-contemporary potteries, breweries and menageries – shows that some kind of management was operating within the settlements of the early Naqadan farmers; that the older, simpler and probably more egalitarian society of the Badarian villages had changed.

Changes, too, had taken place within the cemeteries, where some graves were receiving far larger shares of their communities' resources than others. Although the first known Naqadan burials in the cemeteries of Hierakonpolis, Naqada and Abydos, and in the smaller burying grounds, had held a relative equality of goods like the Badarian graves before them, substantial differences were starting to appear. Differences in the sizes and locations of the graves, in the quality and quantities of their grave goods, and even in the physical attributes of the people interred are all to be found in these different burials.

Hierakonpolis once again provides the best examples of these changes. Close to the wadi potteries, and scoured by both ancient floods and nineteenth-century plunderers, faint traces have recently been uncovered by archaeologists of a dozen of the largest known graves of the early Naqadan period; the remnants of substantial brick-lined rectangles up to twenty feet in length set together in a separate cemetery accompanied by an extraordinary mix of animal burials: the two young elephants, a wild ox, an aurochs – a similar bovine that is now extinct – some dogs and cats, baboons and cows.

Each of these great graves had been enclosed in walls of matting, mud and wicker, marking generous rectangles some sixty feet and more in length upon the desert's crust. Some of these enclosures appear to have contained rows of wooden posts, and a life-sized lime-stone statue of a human figure also seems to have been set up in what, from its scant remains, appears to have been a shelter – or perhaps, the oldest known tomb chapel in all of Egypt's history. The first of a mighty line of Egyptian images of stone, the statue had been rendered into hundreds of small fragments, so that it is presently impossible to determine even whether the figure had been standing up or sitting down. Pieces of its nose and ears, however, show that it was a work of considerable craftsmanship, sculpted with the precision of the Naqadans' miniature animal sculptures and with a sense of form similar to that of better preserved examples made in the following centuries. Its reconstruction, therefore, would reconstitute a milestone in world art.

Pieces of at least four life-sized ceramic masks were also recovered from this devastated burial ground. Reminiscent of contemporary Levantine works and, like the little head from Merimda, designed around a single central point, their alien gaze jolts us into remember-

A reconstruction of a Hierakonpolis mask derived from various surviving fragments

ing that the world in which these things were made was very far from pharaoh. Though fragments of flashing Afghan lapis, of obsidian brought perhaps from Chad or Ethiopia, some prettily made flints and tiny flakes of gold and silver from the ruined tombs, hint at treasures as finely wrought as those of the later kings, the familiar style of 'ancient Egypt' had not yet been constructed when these great tombs were set down on the desert. Nor do we know anything of the objects from which the greater part of these fragments came; nor anything, indeed, of the people in whose tombs these mysterious objects appear to have been placed.

Clearly, however, the burials in this isolated cemetery were the recipients of considerable quantities of their community's resources; people whose menageries devoured part of its agricultural surpluses and whose burial suites had held the best of its craft production. Judging from the bone fragments, a minimum of sixteen people were interred in those graves and several, it appears, in a single tomb – the partial remains of two girls and a young man, for example, were found thrown into the corner of one of the great burial pits. Such practices were also common in contemporary graves of similar size in the cemeteries of Abydos and Naqada, where the early excavators found as many as five individuals curled up together. Only the bones from the great early Naqadan cemetery at Hierakonpolis, however, have been examined by modern pathologists, who found that this group of people had smaller muscle attachments than those of their contemporaries who had been buried in smaller and less well-provided tombs. The people buried in the wadi cemetery by Hierakonpolis, therefore, had not engaged in the manual labour common to agrarian societies, but lived a life apart.

Here, then, is the rub. Once archaeologists recognized that the Naqadans had begun to separate the communality of the earlier cemeteries into different types of grave that could be conveniently described as 'rich' or 'poor', 'elite' or 'working class', it was but a short step to create a sociology for the Naqadans based on the words used to describe their different tomb types and thus to bestow a kind of history on their graves. For the modern meaning of 'elite' signifies those 'considered to be the best in their society because of their power, talent, or wealth'. And so this Naqadan 'elite' is easily portrayed as a class endowed with power and wealth, and as the conduit of social and economic progress. So with passing time, the term 'elite' has allowed the occupants of those tombs upon whom it is bestowed to assume a kind of personality. Just as a common Western notion of an individual is of a man who rules himself, so the bones and fragments found within the elite tombs have come to occupy, successively, the role of 'chief' then 'local ruler' and finally transmogrify to pharaoh.

So kings are crowned, the past is colonized and history becomes a soap opera; or at least it is transported into a universe where great tombs are jargonized as examples of 'the conspicuous consumption of prestige commodities by an elite', and ostrich eggs are 'status symbols', harpoon points 'powerfacts', and those tiny fragments of Afghan lapis flashing in the sand evidence that their owners once 'dominated by the political advantage gained through exercising control over access to resources that can only be obtained through external trade'. That, though is just a history of consumer trends dressed up as old-fashioned anthropology. For there is no evidence whatever of militarism, politics or individuals at Hierakonpolis, nor even of a grand bureaucracy amongst the relics of the early Naqadans. No evidence, either, of commercial trade or of a Naqadan conception of ownership: terms such as 'rich' and 'poor', therefore, may be inappropriate.

And yet there is still a history to be made of this most distant age, a history that is not based on modern society, but on the certainty of what survives.

Skilfully excavated by an American-led expedition at the turn of the millennium a well-preserved example of Hierakonpolis' more modest cemeteries that had been part-contemporary to the great tombs in the desert wadi once lay at the edge of the large settlement in which the oval court had stood. Though heavily plundered, its 460-odd surviving graves held the remains of some 500 people; people who might have attended activities at the oval court when it was in its heyday.

A careful study of their bones shows that, in common with similar burials in other cemeteries, this section of the early Naqadan population of Hierakonpolis had been healthy and robust, enjoyed a balanced diet, suffered some of the common afflictions of humanity and lived on average for some fifty years. The same study also showed that, though these people had worked hard all their lives, they had not worked excessively, as has so often been the case in more recent times, whilst the low rates of healed fractures suggested that their labours had not been very dangerous. The fine white sand in which these modest burials were laid preserved their linen burial cloths along with the baskets and matting that were sometimes used as covering. As in all prehistoric Nile-side cemeteries, pottery too was a constant accompaniment. One of the less disturbed graves, a burial of a middle-aged woman, still held seven vessels, only one of which was of the elegant polished pottery that has become the modern emblem of Naqadan culture. Most of her burial wares, however, were cooking pots and rough domestic pottery, some of which showed signs of daily use and marks of mending. That some of these pots contained the remains of beer or ashes suggested they had been used for the last time at her funerary feast. As for her corpse, though partially robbed, in common with those of the other graves, the desiccating sand had given her, as it had the other burials, the eeriness of natural mummification.

A little bag of garlic from a grave at Hierakonpolis

There appears to have been an equitable mix of men and women within this cemetery and both sexes seem to have been buried with similar quantities of grave goods. Only the men, however, appear to have been equipped with knives. As if in further confirmation of such neolithic work divisions, a few women had been given little bags of cooking herbs and garlic. Some of these people had straight hair, others curly. Some had used henna dye and hair-pieces. Rarely, for most of the metal had been taken from these burials, a few copper needles yet remained in some of the graves, a small chisel, some simple jewellery, a comb with some missing teeth. The bodies' stomach contents showed that some of these people had eaten various forms of cereals; one had died in the heat before the annual flood, for he had just eaten the ripened seeds of desert melons. Infants, though, had been given special baby food, from which the indigestible emmer chaff had been carefully removed. But there were few children in this cemetery. Given the high infant mortality rates of ancient times, it would appear that, like other contemporary Nile-side communities, the early Naqadans of Hierakonpolis had buried their tiny corpses close to their houses, by the hearth.

As in other graveyards of the period, some of the bodies in this cemetery had been part-dismembered; heads and legs removed and replaced sometimes by pots and sticks and baskets. Such mutilations had been found in the Naqadan cemeteries of Upper Egypt since the earliest days of excavation, when European archaeologists, who considered the Naqadans to be 'primitive', had taken it as evidence of cannibalism. There is no evidence, however, that body parts were ever cooked or eaten. Some of these graves contained elaborate and individual patterns composed of pottery and flints and cosmetic palettes as well as portions of dismembered bodies. This has suggested to more modern-minded archaeologists that these arrangements were continuations of the Badarians' elaborate funerals, in which the processes of individually defining each and every corpse at time of burial had taken what must surely have been a dramatic and necessarily emotive turn.

Nor was this the only evidence of human butchery within this cemetery. There was unique evidence, as well, of other, yet more macabre, practices. Masses of small cuts on some of the skulls show that several people had been expertly scalped, while damage to others showed that their owners had been brutally bludgeoned to death.

The skulls that showed signs of scalping had belonged to men aged between eighteen and thirty. Tracing an elaborate series of cuts across the forehead and round the side of their heads, knife marks left on the bone show that the cuts would have allowed the hair and scalp to have been pulled away from the head as one might remove a bathing cap. Some of these same heads had also been most expertly butchered, to remove them from their bodies.

The people who were bludgeoned to death had been struck by objects directed with such force that some of the skulls had shattered like teacups. Others, however, had survived just such attacks; one girl, for example, had suffered a brutal crack to the head as a child and her skull had almost healed before she died in early adulthood. Five other people, though, had each been killed with one swift blow; one of these, a woman in her late thirties, had already sustained a broken arm, while a younger man, who had earlier suffered fractures of a rib and wrist and who also had a well-healed depression in his skull from an earlier blow, had finally succumbed to a hit so powerful that it had sent fragments of his skull deep into his brain, from where a palaeo-pathologist would eventually retrieve them.

These blows were to the back or sides of the skull and the wounds that they had left were consistent with those produced by rounded small stone maces such as are not uncommon in contemporary male graves. Most of the aggressors appear to have been right-handed, and the position of their strike suggests that the hair on the top of the victims' heads may have been held to steady the blow. Just as with the nearby oval court, there is later pictorial evidence of such events. Drawings and reliefs from the earliest dynasties of kings show two people locked in exactly this same deadly pose. A white-lined vase found in the Abydos cemeteries – a near-contemporary of the slaughtered bodies buried at Hierakonpolis – holds images of two bound men joined by a rope, being led by a third and larger figure who holds a mace in his right hand, whilst other fragmentary white-lined images seem to show similar scenes of violence and captivity.

Two white lined pots – left and centre from excavations at el-Mahasna and right, from Abydos – showing scenes of violence, maces and bound prisoners. Both vessels are around a foot tall

Though scalped and smitten, the victims found in the Hierakon-polis cemetery appear to have received a normal burial. One young man who had been maced to death was carefully interred as part of a double burial: a woman whose skull had been similarly smashed had been laid down so that the wound was out of sight and her thick dark hair had been arranged across her face, away from the mass of blood and bone behind. Neither abused, nor shunned nor cast away, such tender burials do not fit the traditional historian's category of 'victim'; nor indeed do such burials in themselves show evidence of prehistoric 'savagery', let alone cannibalism. Nonetheless, the ancestors of pharaoh, whose culture is popularly associated with beauty, flowers and love songs, appear to have engaged in the brutal execution of some of their own people. Such acts, indeed, became a central image of pharaonic Egypt. Precisely the same cruel practices are pictured in some of the little drawings made in the age of the first kings, images that would be writ large throughout the following millennia on temple pylons where pharaoh smites his enemies by grabbing them by their hair and hitting the side of their heads with the same kind of mace which had done such damage to those poor Naqadans buried in a cemetery at Hierakonpolis.

That killings may have been conducted in early Naqadan times on a yet larger scale than the bodies in the cemetery suggest finds confirmation in the shape of a solitary human neck vertebra excavated inside the enclosure of one of the great tombs at Hierakonpolis. It bears the marks of a beheading that took place just before or shortly after death. Such a killing presages arrangements made half a millennium later at the tombs of Egypt's first kings, where each royal vault would be surrounded by rows of modest, brick-lined graves like the cells of a honeycomb, each one specially designed, it would appear, to hold a victim dispatched at the time of the royal funeral.

Some of the same little drawings that record events in and around the early courts also hold scenes which show people being violently attacked and sometimes decapitated, and publicly displayed, and they appear to show this taking place in the presence of a king. One particularly violent tableau shows two seated figures who appear to have been partially scalped, their hair dropping down across their faces, their skulls above left round and bare. And of course, although the animals in these same small pictures are shown running free inside an oval courtyard, the physical remains at Hierakonpolis show that, in reality, the oval court had served as an abattoir, the artificially sloping floor a drain for running blood.

Like the moment at the beginning of Buñuel's famous film where a cloud slides across the moon and a razor runs through a woman's eye, the physical evidence of such events cuts us adrift from the pretty clichés of pharaonic history. And suddenly, we are in another world.

Who was it, then, who oversaw and undertook such brutal and benign activities as are witnessed by the bodies in these cemeteries? What really shaped and ordered this society? Michael Hoffman once observed that the sheer volume of pottery that yet survives at Hierakonpolis, Naqada and Abydos suggests that those settlements had been controlled by potters who had risen to pre-eminence during the exportation of their celebrated wares, black-topped, white-lined, to communities up and down the river. This would suggest a situation similar to that of the salt miners of Bronze Age Hallstatt in Austria, who became so 'rich' by pickling pork and exporting hams across the Alps that they went to work dressed up in Chinese silks and were buried with the considerable accoutrements of European Bronze Age warriors.

The early Naqadan potters, on the other hand, appear to have been subsidized by the growing surpluses of farming. The most plausible explanation of the dozens of small Naqadan cemeteries up and down the Nile which were once filled with just such wares is that they were composed of the graves of farming communities who had obtained such fine pottery through processes of exchange. This, however, tells us nothing about the situation of the people buried in the various cemeteries, grand and modest, of Naqada, Abydos and Hierakonpolis. Are they also the graves of farmers, master potters and labourers? Or are they, as traditionalists assume, the various burying grounds of nearby communities which were the size of towns and cities? Were these pottery manufactories and cattle markets operating under the aegis of an elite buried in the most opulent of their desert cemeteries and who had sanctioned acts of violence such as have been so vividly preserved at Hierakonpolis and which were undertaken as demonstrations of their civic power?

Yet there is no evidence that the cemeteries of Naqada, Hierakonpolis and Abydos served three great principalities, let alone that their burying grounds marked the resting places of urban despots and their subjects. They may just as well have contained the relics of entirely different systems of order and obligation; the residues, perhaps, of pilgrimage centres and their attendant industries, with the great, grand cemeteries holding the graves of sages, celebrants or officials, such as developed in the time of pharaoh around the prehistoric cemeteries of Abydos. Alternatively, these cemeterial conurbations could be the residues of more complex social structures, which like the relics of some near-contemporary Mesopotamian societies, may have been made up of groups of semi-interdependent household units, each one with its own head of family and its own centres of production and consumption, its own potteries and graveyards, granaries, storerooms, workshops and slaughtering yards. And each one of these, as the remains in the nearby deserts might suggest, held flocks of animals whose herders, as in many Middle Eastern communities today, were semi-mobile pastoralists living between the settlements and the plains.

As to the evidence of some kind of progress towards the unification of the land we now call Egypt and the formation of the pharaonic state, the sole surviving witnesses are the bodies in these enigmatic cemeteries and the things made within the living communities. And these show that the greatest changes and, perhaps, the greatest contemporary excitements were the Naqadans' continuing elaborations of the processes of the so-called Neolithic Revolution: the processes, that is, of the 'domestication', not only of animals or plants, but of their cultivators also.

For certainly the role that the domestic crafts and act of burial had played in earlier societies – their role in the affirmation of both the individual and the community in which they lived – was greatly changed. Farmers and herders now formed part of a wider community in which everyday goods were increasingly made by specialists; work itself, and the things that it produced, had both become commodities. At the same time too, the relics also show that some of the settlements were growing in size, prosperity and social complexity. The relative egalitarianism of the earlier farming communities, which had been small enough to allow social interaction between all their members, had been transformed. The mass of people buried at Naqada, Abydos and Hierakonpolis were undergoing such extraordinary stress as found expression in the swinging of a deadly mace and the establishment of public slaughtering yards designed to drain the running blood into a bone-filled trench.

A Naqadan mace

7

Boats and Donkeys

Copper, Trade and Influence within the Lower Nile Valley, 3500–3000 BC

My father was a merchant; not in the sense of Scotland, where
it means a retail dealer ... but in the English sense ...

Thomas De Quincey, 1845

Halfway through the fourth millennium BC, riding gently on the prehistoric river, a fleet of painted boats slides slowly into view. It is the oldest known wall painting in Egypt and one of its greatest fascinations is that it holds within it elements which, magnified and smoothed, will become some of ancient Egypt's central and most celebrated images.

The Hierakonpolis tomb painting

The sunken burial chamber that held this prehistoric painting was similar in size and construction to those of the great graves at Hierakonpolis within the wadi cemetery that lay a mile away from it, and which appear to have been abandoned before the painted tomb was made. Situated at the edge of the sprawling settlement that held the oval court and close to the cemetery of working people, with its scalped and executed bodies, it was one of a group of similar, though unpainted tomb chambers that together comprised a small select cemetery. Unlike the earlier tombs within the desert wadi, however, none of the superstructures of these tombs are known.

There are few records of the hurried excavation of the painted tomb, which took place in the winter of 1898, following its plundering by antiquities dealers. Since that time, as well, the tomb itself has entirely vanished, the fragile mud-brick wall on which the boats were drawn either covered by drifted sand or lost to a land reclamation scheme. Along with a few sad fragments, dark with varnish, that are exhibited in the Cairo Museum, only a watercolour copy of the lost original has survived. When it had first been found, however, the painting was bright and well preserved; the long wall on which the boats were painted had been prepared with a quarter-inch of yellow desert plaster that to modern eyes had given the painted images the unity of a single composition.

Set some five feet down into the desert floor, the rectangular burial chamber in which the painting had stood was about nineteen feet in length and nine feet wide, and a cross wall with some human figures drawn upon it had part-divided it into two near-squares. The six boats were painted along the full length of the chamber's western wall in two horizontal lines: two boats above and four below; five white vessels and one odd black one, which was placed at the centre of the wall and which had a shape like a stack of tied cut reeds at its stern that rose up higher than the level of the other boats and was set beside a steering oar. Though several of the boats had cabins and figures on their decks, none of them had sails or rowing oars; they simply floated on the wall as they would have done upon the river's stream: their images, indeed, were literally headed northwards, in the same direction as the River Nile that lay just a few hundred feet away from them.

Twenty groups of little figures were painted all around the boats: images of the hunters and the hunted; of humans and their weapons, animals hobbled and entrapped. Some of these images were drawn in the distinctive manner of the pottery painters; at the wall's top edge, for example, four ibex ran along a common baseline. Many of the groups, however, had been composed and drawn in different and quite novel ways: a standing man heraldically supporting two opposing lions; two elaborately costumed figures who faced each other and appeared to either dance or fight, and, in the oldest known example of an Egyptian smiting scene, a figure held a rope to which three teth-ered people were attached, and he was clubbing them.

Three details from the Hierakonpolis tomb painting. Left to right: the so-called 'master of the beasts' image, an ibex, and a group of bound and kneeling prisoners smitten by a man wielding a mace

Some of the images in the painting, therefore, were part of the trad-itional Naqadan repertoire, others were quite novel, and many survived to become core ingredients of the pharaonic arts; the tomb chamber a graphic link between prehistory and the pharaonic state. For more than sixty years after its discovery, however, there was no agreement even as to its date, for its excavators had not published a detailed account of their work and so the surviving bits and pieces from the burial could not be fitted into Petrie's sequence dating sys-tem. In different histories, therefore, the date of this extraordinary painting had fluctuated by several centuries. Was it really as old as the similar images of the early Naqadan pottery painters suggested, or was it merely a product of a provincial time lag, made at a time when such images as pharaoh smiting captives were common currency throughout the land? Was it, indeed, a tomb at all? No fragments of a corpse appear to have been found in it. Guy Brunton, who had visited the open tomb whilst excavating at Badari, had thought it to be a for-eign shrine, one made perhaps, by maritime invaders.

In the 1960s, and for the first time, a list of the excavated contents of the painted tomb was published, that had been gleaned from one of the archaeologist's rediscovered field notes, along with some damaged photographic negatives, long forgotten in an English loft. These showed that the painted chamber was indeed a tomb, and of a distinctive type that was also to be found in similar small cemeteries at Abydos and Naqada. Give or take a century or so, all of these great tombs had been made in the middle of the fourth millennium BC.

The remaining fragments of the burial goods found in the painted tomb were those of an opulent interment, whilst the piles of ash and pottery which had lain around the chamber walls suggested that a meal had been cooked at the time of the funeral, in the traditional manner. Comparisons with similar graves in other cemeteries showed that the burial had probably lain in the half of the divided tomb that the tomb's robbers had completely emptied. These comparisons also suggested that the painted tomb may well have held more than one corpse and that some of them were probably dismembered. Beside the corpses, the crypt had probably contained mats and cloth, some boxes and simple coffins and some jewellery too, perhaps of metal, lapis lazuli and other semi-precious stones. Quantities of pottery and provisions, including jars of fat and chunks of slaughtered oxen, were probably buried in the tomb as well, along with linens and cosmetic palettes and the necessary pigments, some fine stone vases, pretty pins and combs of ivory, some copper objects, harpoon heads and fish hooks, and some fine flint knives.

Of all the known tombs of this type, however, only this single tomb at Hierakonpolis had a painting preserved upon its walls, an outlandish mix of imagery which tells us that life within the Naqadan settlements was changing yet again, and that another and quite different era was already under way.

What then, exactly, did the painting represent? At first glance, both the yellow plaster of the painting's ground and the line along the bottom of the wall gave its images a unity and direction that suggests they shared a single subject; was it, perhaps, a flotilla of boats passing by various bankside activities? Was it a pleasure cruise? A trading trip? A raiding party? A royal visit, even, or a funeral?

Such questions easily arise when we view the painting as a line drawing in a book, as our eyes search for clues amidst the printed lines. Reducing the intrinsic qualities of an ancient sixteen-foot mural to an inky modern-day aesthetic, transforming the painting's brush marks to tiny symbols on a page and then puzzling over their iconography and purposes, easily translates ancient reality into a mirror of our own preoccupations. How, then, may we retrieve something of this painting's original plan and purposes?

First, perhaps, by questioning the way we involuntarily 'read' such images at all, for certainly there is no reason whatever to suppose that their makers intended them to be read by eyes trained to read lines of text, or photographs, or paintings with pictorial perspective. These ancient images, therefore, may not hold a unity in the narrative manner of a traditional European painting: they might not be a 'picture' in that sense at all. They may not have been intended to portray an event nor even to hold symbolic meaning. Alternatively, the wall might hold narratives we simply cannot see; or then again, the relationships that we can perceive between these images may be as incidental as those between different animal species corralled within a single space, one of insouciant indifference. In short, there is no way of even knowing if this wall held images of one boat shown in several different guises, or a fleet of boats together, all riding on the river's flow.

Some things, though, are certain. Every one of the painting's six great boats was drawn at a height convenient for a standing person walking up and down the wall, and the swinging shapes of their hulls echo a gesture of a human arm. Of themselves alone, such generous brushstrokes show a confidence of 'attack', a habit of such work. They show, as well, an awareness of the scale and placement of each separate vessel, which were all set in careful relationship one to the other, right along the wall.

These boats also appear to have been painted at the beginning of the work, while the little groups of animals and people were added later and mostly, it appears, in a fairly random manner. These secondary images, moreover, show a number of quite different hands at work. The line of four running ibex and some of the other beasts are fluidly drawn in the practised manner of the pottery painters, as are the six great boats, with careful emphasis on their silhouettes. In contrast, the brushwork of some of the other little groups – the man with the two opposing lions, the two facing figures, the group with the smiting man – is unskilled and untrained. At the same time though, the consistency of the tone and textures of the pigments that the various painters used – black, white and red, still visible on its surviving fragments – appear to have been used right across the wall. This would suggest that all those images had been painted in a single session, in a single period of time.

And that in turn suggests the moment of the ancient funeral, when, in the manner of the ancestors, the open grave would have served as a theatre for the deposition of the dead and for sacrifice and feasting. In all likelihood, therefore, the images were drawn by some of the participants in this ancient drama as a further individuation of the person being buried.

Perhaps the various hands that drew the smaller images were marking some kind of communal or familial affinity with the person or persons being buried in the tomb. Perhaps they had made their marks upon the wall painting before the burial was closed and when the master painters' fresh-ground pigments were still within the open tomb.

BOATS AND POTS

Whoever the draughtsmen may have been, the type of boat they drew within the painted tomb of Hierakonpolis had brought about a fundamental transformation amongst the people of the lower Nile. Older images already show that the felicitous combination of the river's south–north flow and a directly opposing wind had long since encouraged the use of oars and sails upon the great wide waterway just as is shown within the painted tomb and certainly they picture craft of similarly curved design. Such boats, however, were probably made of bundled reeds all held together by a single tensioning rope; craft that, as Thor Heyerdahl would discover, have limited life and load capacity.

The images in the painted tomb at Hierakonpolis, however, show boats that, whilst they sport the traditional up-curving prow and stern, had been dramatically enlarged and strengthened to enable them to accommodate passengers and cabins, decks and crews. And this in turn shows that by the middle of the fourth millennium BC – at the time the tomb was made and painted – the Naqadans were building boats of similar size and shape to those of later eras that have survived, and which are made of planks of wood. So, though there are many other undated and perhaps earlier rock engravings of similarly large boats, some of which have sails and banks of rowing oars, the unique tomb painting at Hierakonpolis has fixed their introduction into a specific era of Naqadan culture.

Such boats would have had an extraordinary effect. Just as the railways opened up the world to nineteenth-century Westerners and as satellites would change the horizons of following generations, so these large wooden barques with crews and cabins had revolutionized the role of traffic on the Nile and life in the Nile-side communities. At the same time, they were also a tangible exemplar of how the Nile-side settlements might be joined together as a single entity, for images of their swinging hulls and other accoutrements came to embody some of the earliest aspects of pharaonic government.

At the same time that the painted tomb was made, the Naqadans were also painting images of big boats with cabins upon a brand-new range of pottery, drawing their distinctive swinging hulls in soft-brushed lines of dark-red pigment on the surfaces of a new, light-coloured, unburnished terracotta made from a newly developed clay of marl and shales that had been quarried in desert wadis close to Naqada.

Although the earlier white-lined wares were no longer made, this new generation of pottery painters still used many of their traditional graphic devices, and they still arranged the images they painted on their pots as miniature Nile-side universes complete within themselves. Now, though, they strung rhythmic images of several boats all around the outside of a range of generously rotund vessels. And, like the boats drawn in the painted tomb, these boats painted on the newly developed pots might also be accompanied by images of animals and plants and people, set within the traditional linear devices of lines and triangles that echoed the narrow landscape of the river valley through which the boats were sailing. Now, too, the Naqadans' boats appear to have been sailing further than they had done before.

In early Naqadan times, the northernmost Naqadan communities appear to have lived close to Badari, while the southern limits of the culture lay 250 miles upstream and south of Hierakonpolis, where some of the desert cemeteries held not only Naqadan graves but those of the southern herders, whose largest cemeteries were further up the Nile, in Nubia and far beyond. By the middle of the millennium, however, the Naqadans' red-painted buff-ware pots were appearing in cemeteries and settlements all along the lower Nile. It is this that signals the ending of the first phase of Naqadan culture and the beginning of another era of prehistory. And for the first time, the geographic spread of this new Naqadan pottery marks out the full extent of the later pharaonic state.

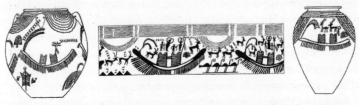

Typical red painted mid-Naqadan marl-ware pots and their decorations. The two vessels shown are a little over a foot high

Like the Naqadans' wooden boats, their new pots were a considerable technical achievement. Unlike the earlier and darker traditional wares which had been made from Nile silts, the shale-based clays from which the new buff-ware was made could be fired at higher temperatures, which made their fabric stronger and thus encouraged the potters to make thinner, lighter and larger vessels. At this same time too, the potters had developed such a precise control over their kilns that, though the fabric of the new pots was fired at higher temperatures, they were not heated to the point of vitrification, which would have rendered them impervious. So when these new thin wares were filled with water, they sweated sufficiently to allow a gentle evaporation from their surfaces and, thus, the cooling of their contents. So the potters' red-painted boats sailed on far cooler waters than before, and for the first time, too, the Naqadans made pigments that were insoluble and impervious to wear.

Not that the Naqadan potteries limited the forms of their new wares to water jars. Some of the handsome forms of hard-stone jars were now replicated in the light-buff clay and decorated with clever, dull-red designs based on the natural patterning of stone, and some of these vessels were given stout handles so that they could be hung. Other more utilitarian wares had protective strips of clay attached to their rounded forms, a device copied from Levantine studios. Prettily notched by the opposing pressure of a potter's fingertips and set like wavy handles on the swelling pots, these reinforcements served as grips and allowed the vessels to be packed side by side with less risk of breakage.

It is difficult to imagine that such practical and striking pottery was unappreciated by the Naqadans' contemporaries to the north and south: the excavated evidence, indeed, shows the extent and swiftness of their spread. And of course, these Nile-side neighbours lived in the same universe as the Naqadans and shared the same distinct experience of the great wide river as the pottery painters: the high-prowed boats, the fringing cliffs, the desert animals beyond.

As well as the swinging shapes of Nile barques and the endless horizontals of the valley landscape, the buff-ware potters also used simple patterns in polka dots or wavy lines, or, still more simply, a potter might dip three finger-tips into his pot of pigment and, with considerable panache, simply touch the surface of the pot in small curved strokes. Despite such sophistications, however, there is a novel air of haste in all of this. Even the most elaborate of these maroon decorations are but reworkings of a dozen stock graphic elements, whilst the range of the potters' forms was less varied than those of earlier times. In considerable contrast to the earlier, jewel-like, white-lined wares, these dull red-painted pots are the clear outcome of a kind of mass production.

Red painted marl-ware pottery decorated in formal imitation of stone vases and other patterns made with the stroke of three fingers. The largest pot is 7¼ inches high.

Such processes had started with the establishment of purpose-built desert potteries, such as have been found at Abydos and Hierakonpolis. At first, such potteries might possibly have been operated by part-time farmers. Yet the large numbers of pots that the early Naqadan kilns came to produce, the lengthy preparation of the clay that such work requires, the gathering of fuel to fire the kilns and the act of potting of itself, let alone the distribution of such a mass of pots, could hardly have been undertaken, or would, indeed, have been required, by a family of farmers. Here, then, the millennial life ways of the farming settlements had already broken down into different abstract zones of work, a communal redistribution of labour and resources within the Naqadan settlements that had long been under way before the decorated buff-ware was developed.

Apart from the tremendous mass of broken sherds that yet survive, some 500 complete examples of maroon-decorated buff-ware pottery have so far been found in excavations from Nubia to the Nile Delta, along with some rather wobbly local copies that underline the extent and impact of their popularity with the compliment of imitation. These pots, it would appear, were trafficked if not traded up and down the river and in considerable quantities. This, then, is the beginning of a process part-pictured on the buff-ware pots themselves, as well as in the painted tomb at Hierakonpolis: a process, one might term it, of riverization; the early stages of the creation of a Naqadan sphere of operations that would come to stretch from Aswan to the Nile Delta. It was, as well, the beginning of the transformation of settlements up and down the Nile, from small-scale subsistence economies to an Egypt-wide commodification of goods and food, labour and production, that would become the model for the supply chains which supported both the building of the great pyramids and the state-wide systems of collection and supply that were the economic backbone of pharaonic Egypt.

The changing uses of the great river may also be an underlying reason for the population movements which also took place at this time. Some of the older Naqadan settlements that had been set along the fringes of the desert appear to have been abandoned, whilst others set closer to the river underwent considerable enlargement. At Hierakonpolis, the location of the painted tomb, at the edge of the prehistoric settlement beside the oval court and a mile away from the earlier great tombs in the wadi, appears as part of this same trend, nothing less than a refocusing of communal life within the Naqadan heartlands.

Such population movements may also have been part-prompted by the gradual shifting of the river ever eastwards on its bed, just as it would continue to do throughout the course of ancient history. It may also have been a part-product of an increasing aridity of the valley's

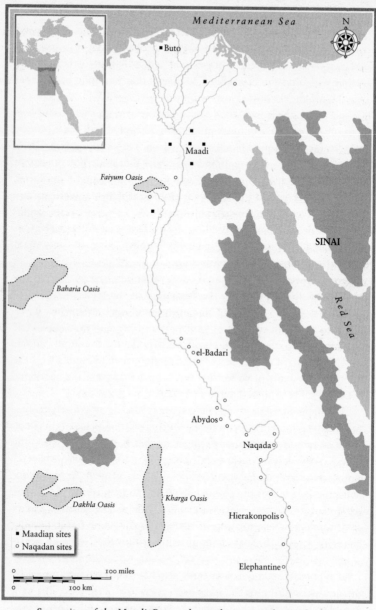

Some sites of the Maadi–Buto culture, shown together with a few mid-to-late Naqadan sites

fragile micro-deserts. The impact, perhaps, of the Naqadan cattle stations, breweries and potters' workshops on the valley's ecosystem that prompted a move away from herding and corralling at the desert's edges towards the river and its boat landings, and an increasing preoccupation with trade and water traffic testified by the wide distribution of the buff-ware pots and the appearance of images of wooden boats within the painted tomb at Hierakonpolis.

Such terms as 'trade', however, must be used with considerable care: like the 'Naqadan elite' the modern connotations of such words constrict their ancient understanding. By itself, of course, the term need not be 'trade' in either the Scottish or the English meanings that De Quincey so carefully distinguished in this chapter's epigraph; it need not, for example, signal either a desire for profit or prestige, or even individual initiative. Nonetheless, there is real evidence that some form of prehistoric trading – or, at least, a cultural symbiosis – had been in operation since the times of the white-line painters; a flow of goods between the settlements along the great wide river and, most significantly, between some of the northern Nilotic settlements, with whom the Naqadans appear to have been trading, and the peoples of the south Levant.

MAADI–BUTO: IMPORT-EXPORT

The best known of the northern Nile-side communities with proven connections with the south Levant was the prehistoric settlement known now as Maadi, after the Cairo suburb in which it is presently situated.

Like its long-defunct predecessor at Merimda forty miles to the north, the settlement at Maadi was very large and was built upon a fan of wadi silt. Extensively excavated from the 1930s by successive teams of Egyptian archaeologists, Maadi, it appears, had been founded as early as 4000 BC, around the same time, that is, as the first known Naqadan communities were established in the south. And just as their southern cousins had inherited a great deal of the earlier Badarian culture, so too the Maadians and other northern settlements of the time were the inheritors of the culture of Merimda and the Wadi Hof.

And all of them, of course, were groups of native Nile-side farmers, who had employed, as the settlement grinding stones and grain bins show, what had already become the standard set of Nile-side farming technologies and stock. One archaeological report, indeed, described the organic residues of a Maadian settlement as representing 'that typical Egyptian combination of emmer, barley, acacia and tamarisk'. Another observed that 'the only difference between the economy of prehistoric Maadi and that of mid 20th-century Egyptian peasants was that the Maadians had enjoyed pigs and soft-shelled Nile turtles, and lacked the relatively modern blessings of water buffalo and camels'.

Although the contents of their graves and houses show that the Maadians' farming methods were similar to those of the early Naqadans, a close examination of the variety of bones found in their settlements suggests that they lived quieter lives, hunting less and farming and fishing rather more. At the same time too, the goods left in Maadian graves are far fewer and much less refined than those of their Naqadan contemporaries. As if to acknowledge this lack of finesse, the Maadi potters occasionally imitated the southern wares. Their most distinctive products, however, and found in graves and settlements all up and down the Nile Valley, were pretty little vases made of basalt, a hard black volcanic stone found in impressive desert outcrops by the Faiyum and close, therefore, to the Maadian heartlands. The Maadi potters also favoured the same colour; a robust jet-black ware, indeed, has become their archaeological signature.

Though lacking the material refinement of the southerners, the Maadians were also far less isolated. In parts of the main settlement, indeed, set right next to some typically Nilotic rounded huts and grain bins, archaeologists have excavated the remains of large and obviously foreign dwellings with rounded corners and fieldstone walls. Although unique within the Nile Valley and currently the oldest known stone buildings in all of Egypt, these distinctive structures had been common in the south Levant for several millennia.

A great deal of Levantine pottery was also found at Maadi; large, globular vessels whose practical wavy handles had been taken up and adapted by the Naqadan potters, flat-bottomed wares with cylindrical necks and two distinctive handles such as the potters of the Nile Valley would never make, and jugs whose attenuated spouts were derived from some of the traditional forms of the Gezira and Mesopotamia. And just as they copied the shapes and decorations of the southern craftsmen, so Maadi's potters also copied the forms of many of these northern importations – and copied so many of them and so frequently, indeed, that their excavators came to consider the culture of the settlement at Maadi as being closer to the cultures of the Levant than that of the Naqadans in the south.

Most of these foreign pots had probably served as containers for imported goods. Just as the Maadians imported pottery and ostrich feathers, leopard skins and ivory from the upper Nile, so too in all probability they imported a range of agricultural products developed in areas to the north and east. In Anatolia and the Gezira, farmers had already extended the range of the basic neolithic economy, cultivating almonds and fruit trees and breeding sheep for wool and goats for milk and cheese. Olives and vines were also being cultivated as far south as modern Jordan, so these emollient juices, too, slopping in their rounded, wavy-handled jars, probably found their way in caravans down into the valley of the Nile.

South Levantine wares – so-called 'looped' and 'wavy-handled' pots – excavated at Maadi. The largest is about 15 inches high

Little survives of all this, however, besides the carrying pots themselves, some solid lumps of northern bitumen, a few basalt bowls whose flaring rims show them to have been products of Levantine workshops, and quantities of foreign flint, some part-worked, which would have rendered them lighter and more compact to transport. Knapped in the forms of blades and scrapers, these are typical of the workmanship of the settlements of the south Levant, where further examples have been found in considerable quantities, stacked and wrapped, apparently for shipping.

That these foreign flints are the genuine remnants of an extensive supply network is further suggested by the archaeologists' discovery at Maadi of large numbers of sharp pectoral bones of Nile catfish, which, when mounted on a reed, make excellent light arrowheads. Though not themselves great hunters, the Maadians gathered and conserved these remarkable barbed bones in special storage jars. Excavated in settlements and caravan stations in the south Levant, quantities of this characteristic Nilotic commodity confirms at least a part of the Maadians' intended markets.

Catfish bones collected by the Maadians for use as arrowheads, and the little pot in which they were all stored

Though sparse, the relics of this traffic in the south Levant are surprisingly wide-ranging. Pots made from Nile clays have been recovered in various Israeli and Jordanian excavations, along with a few cosmetic palettes of Upper Egyptian siltstone, some shells of the Nile's freshwater mussels whose mother-of-pearl was used by Levantine jewellers, two grim mace heads that may have originated as far south as the Sudan, and a fragment of a Maadian stone jar found by the shore of the Dead Sea.

Excavated both in the south Levant and at Maadi, the bones of donkeys and asses suggest the means by which such traffic flowed; the scant remains of caravan stations that skirt the biblical wastelands of the Sinai and run along the coastal margins from the Nile Delta and up the Mediterranean's eastern coastline map out their routes. Naqadan, Levantine and Maadian pottery have all been found in many of these small desert stations, along with some spiky Nile catfish bones.

It would be entirely false, however, to imagine that this is evidence of mercantile traffic between Egypt and the Levant. There is no evidence of commercial trading in this prehistoric world, nor indeed, are there any indications at this time of such geopolitical distinctions as 'Egypt' or the 'Levant'. Recent surveys in the Nile Delta, moreover, where some twenty settlements have been located with similar Levantine connections to those of Maadi, show that they too had more in common with the communities of the south Levant, to whom they were in closer geographical proximity, than with the people of the Naqadan heartlands. Here, then, such terms as 'Egypt' clearly have scant relevance.

The largest and the best known of these delta communities was set close to the Mediterranean, on an eastern branch of the divided Nile. In pharaonic times this venerable site would be celebrated as the holy city of Buto, a fabled capital of Lower Egypt whose gods were linked with those of Hierakonpolis. In archaeology, that same name now part-provides the modern name of the common culture of these prehistoric northern sites which are known as the 'Maadi–Buto culture', for Buto in common with others of these delta sites continued to flourish long after the settlement at Maadi was abandoned.

Buto's remarkable prehistory was first investigated in the 1980s by an expedition from the German Archaeological Institute, using rows of continuously operating pumps to keep their excavation from filling up with ground-water. And here again, just as at Maadi, relics were recovered of a culture that had been closer to that of the south Levant than to that of the Naqadans.

As well as the traditional northern forms, Buto's prehistoric potters had also made a range of southern Levantine wares, for which, as the surviving sherds still clearly show, they employed a spinning horizontal stand of Levantine design. This enabled them to refine the shape of their rough and part-dried wares before they were put into the kiln. Of themselves, these little spinning platforms were a significant importation. Speeded by the kick of a potter's foot on a weight set on its elongated axle, such platforms would eventually be made to spin fast enough to permit a craftsman to produce a pot by throwing a ball of wet clay down onto its centre, then shaping the spinning lump with the heels and fingers of the hands to form a finished pot. This innovation would enable ancient Egyptian potters to work at great speeds and to mass-produce a range of standard wares in considerable quantities. These nondescript fragments of early Buto ware whose markings bear witness to the use of a spinning platform within the earliest known settlement, the first known evidence of a potter's wheel in Africa, underline the significance of the continuing traffic in techniques and technologies that had long been entering the valley of the Nile from the Levant.

A yet more vital element in this secondary wave of Levantine importations was that of smelted copper. Unlike tools of flint, which were the only contemporary alternative, copper utensils permitted an extraordinary accuracy of craftsmanship; a precision that would always be a preoccupation of ancient Nile Valley craftsman. It was copper tools that shaped the stones of pharaoh's pyramids, those near-perfect monuments whose construction shaped the very order of the later state. And even in the centuries before the age of pharaoh, that same red-shining metal had provided the means of building another fundamental element of pharaonic Egypt: those wooden, high-prowed sailing boats that had been drawn within the painted tomb at Hierakonpolis.

The sources of the first copper that was used in the Nile Valley are difficult to trace. Like gold and silver, the metal was constantly retrieved, re-smelted and reused through the ages. A few unplundered graves, however, testify that the earliest Nile farmers had used small amounts of copper for pins and bodkins, fish hooks and the like and even modest bits of jewellery but, as no smelting furnace from those times has yet been found, it is likely that those little things were hammered out from naturally occurring nuggets of the metal collected by herders in the hills of the Eastern Desert, between the Red Sea and the Nile.

At the Maadi settlement this situation was transformed. Along with considerable quantities of copper ore, some sheet metal and some finished, if heavily corroded, copper tools, three cast copper ingots were found inside a single Maadian house. Maadi had been so rich in copper, indeed, that archaeologists found the earthen floors of many of its huts stained green with the verdigris of corroded and now largely vanished copper implements. Given the absence within the settlement of common axes made of flint and the rarity of the small flint blades which had long been used as the cutting edge of sickles, we may assume that, by the middle of the fourth millennium BC, within the settlement at Maadi, tools of copper had replaced most of the traditional tools of flint and bone.

The mines that were supplying the Maadians with such large amounts of copper appear to have been situated in the Sinai and the desert valleys of its eastern fringes, which run down into the Wadi Araba and the Gulf of Aqaba. These, at least, are the source of the ore from which the three Maadi ingots were cast: two as rectangular bars and the third in the form of a flat-topped bun, which appears to have been left to harden within its little casting crucible. Though of diverse shape, each of these three pieces weighed some thirty ounces, which, if more than a coincidence, would represent the oldest known example of a fundamental element of commercial trading: a basic standard unit.

Copper ores had been mined and smelted in the Gezira, in western Persia and in Anatolia, long before the technology was taken up in Sinai and the south Levant, and each of these areas had developed their own forms of copper tools, which had been trafficked far and wide. Not surprisingly, however, the shapes of the first copper implements found in Nile-side settlements are similar to those developed in the Levant – though, once again, the fact that the settlements of Maadi and early Buto shared a common culture with contemporary communities of the south Levant makes the notion of some kind of foreign trade quite inappropriate.

Just as it would be in the time of pharaoh, prehistoric copper was smelted on the scale of a cottage industry. It was hard and poisonous work. Often situated in deserts close to naturally occurring seams of copper ore, Levantine furnaces were prepared by digging simple pits some two feet deep, which were then lined with clay and filled with charcoal, wood and copper ore. After this mix was set alight, blasts from leather bellows piped air down into a rounded crucible set at the bottom of the furnace, which would then heat its contents to temperatures of over 1,000 °C, reducing them to a toxic soup of slag and copper. Being the heavier of the two, the liquid copper would trickle to the bottom of the crucible, where it was tapped by breaking down one side of the furnace pit and allowing the liquid metal to run down into little trenches, where it would harden into ingots.

Though only a few Naqadan copper tools are known to have

survived from the mid-fourth millennium BC, their effect on their communities is plain to see. Before they were available, carpenters had worked such local woods as tamarisk, acacia and Egyptian sycamore, with flint-bladed tools. Though extremely sharp, such flints, as the surviving marks still show, tended to cut the wood in gouges, which allowed but little fine control and encouraged their use in the manner of an adze or spokeshave working a trunk or branch. Around 3500 BC, however, the first known chisels and saws of copper appear in graves within the Naqadan heartlands, and at this same time, too, fragments of contemporary surviving woodwork – furniture, boxes and simple coffins – show a use of deep and well-made mortise and tenon joints, woodworking that requires levels of control and accuracy entirely unattainable with tools of flint. Such fine-made furniture also shows that a process of standardization had been adopted in which tree trunks and branches had been squared into planks and beams with saws before they were employed as elements of furniture. These carpenters, therefore, were already using a range of copper tools.

So, indeed, were the shipwrights of the day. As the paintings and drawings of the Naqadans suggest, and as the surviving elements of later ancient Nile boats still testify, these vessels appear to have been built in an idiosyncratic manner which required the large-scale production of planks and beams from the individual and often twisted wood of trees that had grown in the soft silts of the lower Nile. These were then carefully fitted one to another to make up the smoothly distinctive outline of the swinging hull. Those powerful images of boats, therefore, that appear in the middle of the fourth millennium BC testify not only to a contemporary delight in fine-made barques, the Ferraris of their day, but also to the introduction of the new tools and their associated technologies that had enabled their construction.

This new river traffic would have required copious and constant supplies of copper, both for maintenance and for its continuing construction. It is not surprising, then, that though Sinai and the south Levant would remain a major source of Egyptian copper down to Roman times, the Naqadans appear to have started mining seams of copper ore in the desert hills to the east of their great river, where their forefathers had collected naturally occurring nuggets of the shining metal and had hammered them into little beads and pins.

No one knows the routes by which smelted copper was first imported into the Naqadan heartlands – nor even the century in which it was first introduced. Nor is there any evidence of the voyages the Naqadans themselves may have undertaken for its continued procurement. Did those great wooden vessels carry captains and commanders, priests and merchants? Could they have sailed on the open sea? The delta port of Buto was open to both the Nile and the Mediterranean, and the contemporary Levantine ports of Byblos and Ugarit were only a few days' sailing with the prevailing winds, east and northwards, along the eastern seaboard.

The Naqadans may also have sailed, as the pharaonic Egyptians would later do, from ports along the Red Sea coast. The unique construction of similarly shaped wooden boats made in the times of the first Egyptian kings shows that such craft were easily disassembled. So the Naqadans might well have carried the boats' various components, piece by piece, a hundred miles and more along the desert wadis, up and away from the Nile-side settlements to the Red Sea coast, where traces of ancient anchorages and ports have recently been found, along with the planks and rigging of similar boats of later ages. The presence of such caravans walking the distant wadis of the eastern deserts, transporting planks and ropes, masts and keelsons, would certainly explain the numerous and often splendid pictures of Naqadan barques that are engraved on some of their rocks. As well as offering a short if somewhat treacherous passage eastwards to the Gulf of Aqaba, to the Sinai coast and the nearby copper mines, such ancient Red Sea anchorages could also have provided access to Aden and Ethiopia, to the Isle of Dilmun in the Persian Gulf, and to the cities of southern Mesopotamia and even to the Indies. Here, though, we have dropped off the edge of present knowledge, for we have no information whatever about Naqadan seafaring and thus we sail entirely on the seas of our imagination.

All that the surviving facts can truly demonstrate is that by the middle of the fourth millennium BC fresh waves of external influence that would be vital for the creation of the pharaonic state were already washing through the cultures of the lower Nile.

8

Rolling Along

Of Men and Monsters, 3500–3000 BC

At the same time that copper ingots were first imported into the Nile Valley, some small stone engravings of Mesopotamian origin were also entering Naqadan workshops, whose effect upon Egyptian history would be as fundamental as that of smelted copper. Tiny figures, cut on quite modest objects, that served to provide an entirely new dimension to the Naqadan crafts, enabled the workshops to create the images which would define the office of the pharaoh and lead, eventually, to the invention of a system of images that would record the sound of words. This then, is where Egypt's written history finds its true origins.

During the entire Naqadan period – and this in a region which had previously sustained a diversity of cultures – the dominant culture in Mesopotamia was one that is now named after a celebrated ancient settlement in south Iraq known as the city of Uruk. Like the contemporary though far smaller settlements along the lower Nile, the period of this so-called Uruk culture was one of communities of farmers who supported groups of people who specialized in separate and single tasks. It was a time, as well, of population movement and enlargement.

At the time that the painted tomb was built at Hierakonpolis, settlements of the Uruk culture had already been established in regions well to the north of the Mesopotamian heartlands, up along the tributaries of the Tigris and Euphrates, westwards into the highlands of Syria and Anatolia and eastwards into south-western Iran. Often built beside less-ordered and much older indigenous communities, some of these new-made settlements had high walls around them and large distinctive buildings at their centres in which archaeologists have found considerable quantities of standard-sized pottery dishes that seem to have been used as grain measures. Tokens, too, little balls and cones of clay, similar to those the Mesopotamians had long used for counting and registering goods and chattels, are also found in these settlements, along with examples of the small engraved seal stones the Mesopotamians used for stamping soft clay with an individual mark. Similar in their size to those used until quite recently in Europe for impressing sealing wax, these seals were used by the people of Uruk, in conjunction with wet clay and knotted cords, for sealing everything from house doors to the lids of storage jars.

A millennial craft tradition in the settlements of Mesopotamia and the Zagros Mountains, by the time their influence was felt in Egypt the Uruk seal engravers were employing a remarkably sophisticated range of imagery and design. By that time, too, the form of the simple stamp seal had been largely superseded by another type in the shape of a small stone cylinder which, when rolled across a bed of soft clay, produced a linear impression, a tiny patterned strip. Small, strong and often very handsome, for many of them were cut from semi-precious stones and highly polished, such seals were a perfect medium for transporting Mesopotamian imagery throughout the ancient world.

In the valley of the Nile, their impact is most obvious in the thousands of seal impressions that have been found in Naqadan cemeteries. Though they are mostly the products of seals made by local craftsmen, they show that the Naqadans took up the art of seal cutting for themselves and in the process absorbed some of the styles, designs and images developed in Uruk.

Ultimately, of course, proof of such influence rests in the eye of the beholder, for the serendipity of preservation and retrieval allows little chance of finding a seal at a Naqadan site that can be proven to have been made by an Uruk craftsman and to have had specific influence upon an object of Naqadan manufacture. The chances are so very low indeed that the employment of such criteria when dealing with the fragmented relics of this vague age serves only to deny the obvious. The impact of the Uruk designs on the crafts of the Naqadans is plain enough to see because Naqadan seals are composed and drawn in ways that are completely different to those of the traditional crafts of the lower Nile and their imagery, too, is entirely alien.

A prime example of the intrusion of Uruk into the valley of the Nile is the image of a nightmarish figure drawn full face with arms akimbo, with stars for its head and hands and two more stars projecting from its midriff. The first known appearance of this bizarre concoction comes from a grave at Abydos; a tiny image of the starry figure set amidst three lines of animals produced by the rolling impression of an Uruk-style Naqadan seal. In another grave, 250 miles north of Abydos, Petrie excavated a careful reproduction of the selfsame monster enlarged to the size of an open hand and engraved on one face of a Naqadan cosmetic palette of a slightly later date. No other palettes are known to have pictured this idiosyncratic image, which is way outside all earlier Naqadan design conventions. For its accommodation, the palette's craftsman had to adapt the foreign monster's windmill arms to frame an area where cosmetic pigments could be ground. Here, then, an Uruk image was adapted to traditional Naqadan purposes.

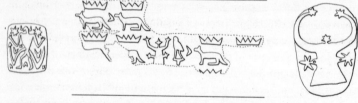

The star figure on an Uruk seal (left), a mid Naqadan seal impression, and a near-contemporary Naqadan siltstone palette. Not to scale

That starry figure was but one of a flock of hybrid monsters composed of parts of different animals that were invading the Naqadan workshops. Whereas the traditional images made by Naqadan craftsmen had been straightforwardly based upon Nilotic animals, now winged griffins and panthers with serpentine entwining necks appear alongside other beasts that, though they had haunted the Mesopotamian imagination from its beginnings and would later appear within the pages of the Bible, had no place in the paradisaical world of earlier Naqadan crafts. By the time of the pharaohs, however, court artists had become skilled in welding the forms of different animals together to create a succession of monstrous beings such as sphinxes and the images of a number of court gods.

When the painted tomb was made at Hierakonpolis, the artists had not attempted such monstrous syntheses. Nevertheless, the influence of Uruk imagery amongst the various groups of little figures in the tomb painting is very obvious. The inept composition of a standing figure holding a club and threatening three trussed and tethered figures has direct ancestry on Uruk seals, as does the roughly painted image of a man supporting two opposing lions. This so-called 'Master of the Beasts' motif is another crude copy of a much imitated Uruk motif that became general currency throughout the eastern Mediterranean in the following millennia; a monumental modification of it, indeed, is set above the Great Gate of Mycenae.

NEW SPACE

As well as herding a host of monsters into the Naqadan imagination, another innovation of the Uruk seal engravers, and one that literally opened up another space for the Naqadan craftsmen, was the linear composition produced by a continuous strip of images engraved on cylinder seals as they were rolled across a bed of clay. Its impact is already evidenced by the similarly unfolding patterns which form the basis of the composition of the boats that Naqadan potters drew on their buff-ware pots. These must themselves be revolved like cylinder seals to reveal their entire design. The six boats painted on the wall of the Hierakonpolis tomb, of course, are also set within this horizontal strip and there, as well, the line along the bottom of the wall appears to echo a standard feature of Uruk seals, most of which have just such framing lines cut round the top and bottom of their cylinders.

As well as holding compositions that roll out *ad infinitum*, like miniature wallpaper, another class of Mesopotamian cylinder seals were engraved with finite compositions with a beginning and an end; a line of people and animals, for example, all facing the façade of a decorated building of a type that stood at the centre of the Uruk settlements and which today is usually identified as a temple or a storehouse. Here, the seals' two framing lines hold a procession of images within them that together form a composition set inside a kind of time, a finite narrative.

Initially, however, it was the simple space held between the cylinder seals' two horizontal framing lines that had the greatest impact in the workshops of the lower Nile. Most earlier Naqadan images had their own unique integrity. Even when the pottery painters had set several separate images in little worlds within their pots, each one was made at its own individual scale and was usually set, unrelated, into its own space. Now, though, images of boats and men and beasts formed the components of a group or scene, as connected images that may be read as if they were a kind of visual sentence. As the Egyptian hieroglyphs for the earth and the sky, such framing lines would define the edges of the canvas of pharaonic art. The concept was also fundamental to the development of hieroglyphics, which, as with a printed line of words, depends on a common understanding between the craftsman and the viewer of the order in which the various images are to be read.

NEW FORMS

A further revelation of the Uruk seals was the manner in which their individual images were drawn. Traditional Naqadan images were made with crisp, clear outlines and near-abstract interior forms, a way of working that the best craftsmen had elevated to a Brâncusi-esque perfection. The images of the Uruk seals, on the other hand, were made in negative, every line or dot the craftsman cut into the smoothed surface of a blank seal appearing in its clay impression as a raised form. Working with the tip of a tiny drill spun on the looped string of a bow drill, Uruk seal cutters usually laid out their images by drilling indentations to indicate the body's various forms such as a head or chest, then joined these indentations into a single image with carefully abraded lines. Literally the reverse of the Naqadan method, the process gave entirely new dimensions to the Naqadan crafts, and most especially to the way human figures were represented.

Previously, the Naqadans had hardly ever treated the human figure with the same care they had afforded their other subjects. Pottery painters, for example, had usually drawn stick figures; the women distinguished on occasion, by the size of their thighs and buttocks, the men by the curled line of a penis sheath. In similarly abbreviated fashion, most of their three-dimensional images of humans had been cursory and tended to follow the natural forms of the material from which they had been made. Male figures might be outlined by a swift series of abraded grooves cut into the slender forms of tusks or bones, their gender denoted by a V-shaped beard, while females, more generously, were often drawn in fleshy rolls of clay or, alternatively, laid out on slivers of bone and ivory as stick-like diagrams of sexuality; their eyes perhaps inlaid with lapis lazuli, the nipples and pubic hair exaggeratedly indicated by rows of dots cut with the point of a tiny drill, the limbs and vulva drawn out, as with the male figures, in swift abraded grooves.

The Uruk seal cutters, conversely, used the tips of spinning drills to create the various volumes of the human figure, and, in marking out the positions of its individual forms, they had also mapped their figures' poses, a process that not only encouraged the invention of fresh and lively attitudes but imbued the finished product with an inner dynamism that the Naqadans' traditional images had entirely lacked. For the first time, the human form which the Naqadans had previously drawn in simplified abstraction took on the volume and the weight of muscle, skin and bone, and in a wide variety of poses. Now, too, the elegant, if solitary, silhouettes of the traditional Naqadan animal repertoire were no longer described by silhouette, but transformed into dynamic, wrinkling, snarling beasts, moving in their own skins and occupying a common space with other images.

Rather than imitate the gem-like miniatures of the imported seals, however, the Naqadan sculptors continued to work in their traditional materials of stone and ivory, and at the same sizes as they had always done. They chose, as well, not to imitate the concave images of the Uruk seals but to reproduce the convex impressions which the seals had left upon the clay, so that their images stood out from the surface of the material in which they had been carved.

Known today as 'raised relief', this distinctive technique, in which the gaps between the edges of each separate image are laboriously cut down to make a flat and even background, became a standard technique of ancient Egypt's craftsmen, one that would be fundamental to the decoration of pharaonic tombs and temples. It first appears, however, amidst a riot of previously unimagined images sculpted on the surfaces of such traditional Naqadan media as siltstone palettes and the ivory handles of a few flint knives.

And everything was changed. In earlier times, the Naqadans' cosmetic palettes had been small and plain, if elegant, utilitarian objects, thin slabs of siltstone polished to a dull shine and cut into simple rectangles or in the silhouetted images of animals and fish, and decorated on rare occasion only with spidery images of animals or hunters. Under the spell of the Uruk techniques, however, the Naqadan palette makers and the ivory carvers began to cover the surfaces of their work with a bustle of virtuoso craftsmanship and, finally, to create the most complex and arresting objects of the Naqadan age; objects like nothing else that has survived from the prehistoric world.

It is an enormous loss to history that most of these things cannot be fitted into a time-frame narrower than that of the second half of the fourth millennium BC, for almost all the known examples were dug up during the enormous scramble through the prehistoric cemeteries that took place around the turn of the nineteenth century – a scramble whose spoils filled European auction rooms with fine objects of no provenance or sequence dates. At the same time too, the resulting sudden increase in the market value of the objects of prehistory that had followed Petrie's pioneering excavations encouraged fakers to decorate a host of genuine if plain antiquities with clever imitations of ancient imagery. This has served to clutter and confuse the genuine evidence of what was happening in the Naqadan workshops during those missing centuries.

Despite all that, the work itself is intricate and wonderful: the Naqadan environment no longer quantified in separated images, but in complex compositions. So combs of bone and ivory which had been decorated since Badarian times with individual silhouettes of wild beasts are now engraved with lines of birds and animals, set gem-like in horizontal strips. In similar fashion, the ivory handles of slaughtering knives hold rows of docile beasts standing in carefully counted lines, as if awaiting their turn to be dispatched. Here, too, men fight, and bound prisoners are led away. Like modern Bushmen, a strip of crouching archers track their prey along the edges of a siltstone palette. And the animals they hunt are as gawkily alive as newborn calves, the line of their hunters ordered and implacable. Chased by hunting dogs, both beasts and humans sometimes flee across the surface of these stones whilst flocks of birds, with round unseeing eyes, swoop down to peck at their corpses. Here, too, are the nightmare monsters of the Uruk seals, tamed, rather, so as to appear as animals living on the desert's edge. Here, then, is a sudden multitude of images; feathers, hair, muscle, skin and bone, the sinews of feet and necks all drawn and modelled with a jeweller's care; living beings seen with a tender eye and drawn with an intensity and a vivacity that neither casts nor photographs of the originals can truly capture.

And all these masterly tableaux are carefully controlled, their images held either in narrow strips of space, in splendid interlinking patterns, or by a series of simple linear devices: a hunter's rope, an arrow's flight or, more simply yet, by the direction of a pointed bow. Here, then, the gentle arts of the Badarians and the earlier Naqadans have been transformed, the Naqadan craftsmen are beginning to tell stories and depict events, and a history of sorts begins to be recorded.

A fragment of a siltstone palette bearing part of a hunting scene

1. A freshly excavated neolithic grain bin, one of more than fifty found by Caton-Thompson and Gardner in the late 1920s at a small site on the ancient northern shore of Lake Faiyum. The stick-like object lying in the basket is a wooden sickle – three flints are still set into its wooden haft.

2. A rare unbroken cup found by Caton-Thompson and Gardner at another nearby neolithic site. A little over 3 inches high, it is made from Nile silt and was fired at a low temperature. The burnish on its interior would have made it less pervious to liquids.

3. The Nile Valley north of Aswan before the advent of mechanized irrigation in the 1980s. Such easily managed narrow flood plains were favoured by early Nile Valley agriculturalists.

4. A fine Badarian ripple ware bowl, just 3½ inches high, made from clay prepared from Nile silt, the black rim being a careful product of its expert firing in a kiln. Excavated in the early 1920s by Brunton's expedition to the region of Badari, the archaeologists' published drawing of this same bowl is shown on p. 39, where it is classified as 'DK NEUTRAL BRN'.

5 and 6. Two fine early Naqadan, so-called 'black-topped', pots. Made from Nile silt and highly burnished, they are both under 10 inches high. Excavated by antiquities dealers, their provenance is unknown.

7. Part of the Naqada cemeteries as they appeared almost a century after their excavation by Petrie in the 1890s. Many fragments of the coarser larger wares that had been buried with the dead were still *in situ*.

8 and 9. Two burials of the mid-Naqadan culture in the process of their excavation in the winter of 1909 by members of Petrie's Abydos expedition in the cemetery of Mahasna. Both burials had been placed in well-made wooden boxes. Later in the excavation, the individual in the left-hand photograph, who had been placed upon a mat, was found to be covering a number of sticks, some stone-headed maces and a copper harpoon point. Two dogs lay nearby. The burial shown in the right-hand photograph, though rich in pottery and with its wooden box relatively well preserved, lacked both head and shoulders.

10. Two examples of the so-called 'decorated buff ware', a relatively high-fired ware produced during the mid Naqadan period, that was made from clay produced from Upper Egyptian desert shale. The left pot imitates a form typical of contemporary stone vessels: the other holds a drawing of a boat with two banks of oars, two deck cabins, and a standard on a pole. Both of them are around 8 inches high and of unknown provenance.

11, 12 and 13. Until the advent of plastic containers in the 1980s, the potteries of Ballas, close to ancient Naqada, had produced the water pots used in Nile-side villages from Aswan to the Delta. And these potteries had maintained a millennial tradition, for their pots were made, like Mid-Naqadan buff ware, from clays produced from desert shale. The darker pots shown in the upper photograph have come straight from the potter's wheel and have been set to dry in the sun. The lighter-coloured pots beside them have already been fired in the kilns seen in the middle distance. The centre photograph shows stacks of finished water pots awaiting transportation to the river, whilst the lower photograph shows a Nile boatman with a shipment of Ballas water pots about to tie up for the night. All three images show something of the forms and order that are the inevitable products of manufacturing and transporting large quantities of standardized objects in non-industrial environments.

14 and 15. Frederick Green's photograph of the painted tomb of Hierakonpolis during its excavation in 1898. The rod held by Green's assistant stands by the long painted wall, on which the white shapes of three of its swing-hulled boats can be clearly seen. Green's careful drawing of the same section of that painting is shown in the plate below.

16. A detail of one of the two surviving fragments of the so-called 'Battlefield Palette' in which images of bound and slain captives being pecked by a flock of birds are used as elements of a highly sophisticated design. The lion is some 5 inches long. Most beautifully worked onto a slab of cool grey siltstone from the Wadi Hammamat, the palette's provenance is unknown.

17. A field photograph taken during the first season of their excavation at the site of the great cache at Hierakonpolis showing some mace heads and other objects found by Quibell and Green. The giant so-called 'Scorpion' mace head stands at the left; the Narmer Mace head, the smaller of the two, upon the right.

18. The tomb of King Djer at Abydos during its re-excavation by the German Archaeological Institute in the 1980s. In later dynasties, the royal tomb chamber was identified as that of the god Osiris and became a site of national pilgrimage.

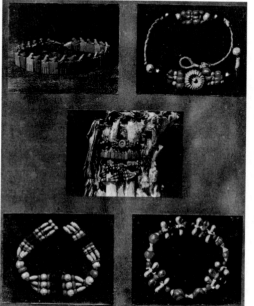

19. 'The most important discovery of this year'. The frontispiece from Petrie's annual report of his work at Abydos, published in 1901. Compiled from photographs taken in the field, it shows four bracelets of gold, amethyst and turquoise both re-strung and as Petrie had first uncovered them, resting on a linen-covered forearm that his workmen recovered from the tomb of King Djer at Abydos. This is the only photograph of this unique group *in situ* to have survived; the jewellery is now in the Cairo Museum.

PART TWO

Making Pharaoh
(3200–3000 BC)

9

Scorpion and Hawk

3200–3000 BC

For the best part of its journey, the Nile flows northwards to the sea. There is a passage, though, in Upper Egypt, where it strikes sharply to the east and curves back again in three-quarters of a circle to round a desert plateau. Known now as the Qena Bend, this 100-mile detour passes through the better part of the Naqadan heartlands, and past many of ancient Egypt's most celebrated sites, from Thebes downstream to Naqada, Coptos and Dendera, and on to Nag' Hammadi and Abydos.

Cutting this considerable voyage by half, a series of ancient tracks strike directly north and west from Thebes across the desert plateau to Naqada and Abydos, and thus complete the circle of the curving Nile. Today, these ancient highways pass over a beautiful if bleak high plain, where you may occasionally see small caravans bringing chunks of raw alabaster to the Luxor tourist workshops, or herds of camels being driven north to the Cairo markets by white-clad Nubians cracking silver-handled whips. Five millennia ago, this limestone desert still held sufficient moisture to support communities living as their ancestors had done, by herding, hunting, and gathering and grinding wild wheats and grasses. But then the plains had slowly dried and, as the ancient pottery beside the narrow tracks still shows, they were only used by parties of desert travellers.

Some of the caravanners left drawings and texts on the limestone cliffs beside these desert tracks. From their ineptness, we may assume that the best part of them were not the work of draughtsmen, but had been scratched in a moment using one of the flints that lie all around upon the surface of the desert. Amongst this multilingual babble of

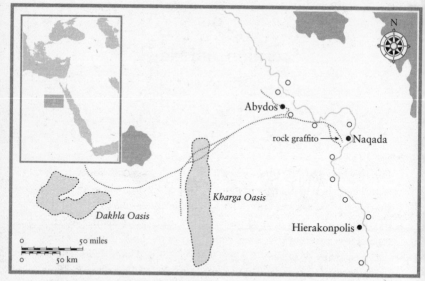

One of the ancient caravan routes from the Naqadan heartlands to the Western Desert showing the location of the Naqadan rock graffito described in the text

names and titles, dates and prayers and family trees of which such graffiti are usually composed there is an especial treasure, drawn in a little shelter that overlooks a well-trod path as it twists left and right to rise up from a wadi bed and gain the top of a limestone terrace. Set in vertical and horizontal strips, this rare graffito holds a series of some sixteen separate images: birds and snakes, a scorpion, a bull's skull set upon a post, and some human figures, one of which appears to clasp a club in one hand and a rope in the other, to which is tied – in the manner of the image in the painted tomb at Hierakonpolis – a trussed-up prisoner.

Drawings similar to several of these distinctive images have been found within the Nile Valley in archaeological contexts, so the graffito can be fixed into prehistory with a degree of confidence: these signs were drawn, it would appear, in the third quarter of the fourth millennium BC, the same period, that is, in which some of the elaborately decorated palettes appear to have been made. And here, too, though

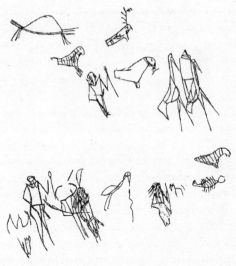

The Naqadan desert rock graffito. The man with a mace and a bound prisoner is at the bottom left. The entire ensemble is around 16 inches high

the quality of this graffito is worlds apart from those miniature masterpieces, its images are organized in lines, one following another in the manner of a cylinder seal's impression. And this in turn suggests that, like the figures drawn on the palettes and the ivories, the rows of signs in this graffito were also intended to hold some kind of linking narrative. Was it, then, like many later ancient Egyptian desert graffiti, intended to register or advertise a human presence in an empty place? Or does its setting in a rock shelter on a track between Naqada and Abydos suggest that it was made as a kind of notice?

Four hundred miles to the south, in Nubia and well beyond all trace of Naqadan settlement, a similarly drawn graffito was scratched up on a rock that overlooked the Nile's Second Cataract: an image of a scorpion dangling a trussed man between his enormous claws, with two other figures standing close by, one of which held a bow and arrow aimed straight at the scorpion's helpless prisoner.

Now, both of these graffiti appear to hold a common theme of subjugation, and both were placed outside the Naqadan homelands, in potentially strategic positions. That they contain the image of a

*A scorpion, two men and a bound prisoner; a modestly sized rock graffito
carved on a limestone outcrop above Wadi Halfa, in the Sudan*

scorpion may even suggest that they refer to groups of people, or even
an individual, who was identified by that alarming creature. That one
of the earliest known images of a person dressed as a pharaoh also
has the image of a scorpion beside it, indeed, might even suggest
that these two graffiti record the names of prehistoric kings. The two
graffiti may therefore, memorialize an event or stand as a kind of
warning; and if that were proven, it would transform these two
rough drawings into some of the oldest known documents of ancient
Egyptian history. These images, after all, were inscribed centuries
before the age of the first known pharaohs and the oldest known
hieroglyphics: those rows of images, perhaps, might represent a form
of proto-writing.

THE WINE-RICH TOMB

In 1989, German archaeologists working in the desert cemeteries of
Abydos came across an enormous tomb which had been made in the
same period as the two graffiti, a tomb that, though already plundered and half-emptied by earlier expeditions, still held part of its
original grave goods and further evidence of the beginnings of hieroglyphic writing. Somewhat prosaically, the archaeologists christened
the tomb 'U-j': tomb j, that is, in Cemetery U.

A flimsy, brick-built rectangle some thirty-three feet long and
twenty-seven wide, the tomb had been set into the side of a low, hard
sand dune and was the largest of a group of similar monuments that
were, essentially, a series of architectural elaborations of the older and

simpler two-roomed graves, like the painted tomb at Hierakonpolis. Here though, in the tomb U-j, the Naqadans' continuing urge to embellish and enlarge had transformed a modest grave chamber with a single screening wall into what appeared to have been a near-full-sized replica of the rooms and storerooms of a grand household. This impression was fortified in the course of its excavation by the surviving grave goods that still lay in the tomb's ten chambers: stores of food and drink, fragments of rare stones, ivory, obsidian and gold, splinters of exotic fine-worked woods and some bulks of flooring timber which, Carbon 14 measurement has shown, fixed the date of their deposition in the tomb within a hundred years or so, to around 3200 BC.

In extravagant continuance of the age-old Naqadan custom of burying vittles with the dead, at least two of U-j's tomb chambers had served as cellars where more than 4500 litres of wine had once been stored. Decanted into trading jars made in the manner of the south Levant and closed with lids and cords and mud bearing the impressions of Naqadan seals, the wine had been flavoured with Levantine resin and those circular strings of figs that are still sold in Mediterranean markets, whose ancestors the archaeologists found inside the jars. Many of these jars were found exactly as the burial party had left them, stacked up some six feet high, from floor to ceiling.

Considerable quantities of typical Naqadan storage jars had been piled up inside the tomb as well; robust cylindrical containers that, presumably, had once been filled with local food-stuffs, ointments, perfumes, oils and animal fats. And many of these local wares bore painted images similar to the signs in the two rock graffiti: a dozen flamboyant renderings of a bull's head set up on a post and some sixty lively drawings of scorpions.

At first glance, then, the objects in this palatial crypt appeared to put some flesh on the shade of a hypothetical prehistoric ruler, a proto-king, perhaps, named 'Scorpion' – especially when some ivory fragments from the tomb's largest room, which was probably its burial chamber, were reassembled into a stubby staff, reminiscent of a sceptre of the later pharaohs.

Had King Scorpion lived, however, he would have had to share his vague era with a host of other hazy monarchs, for many objects made at this time that have been found in excavations all up and down the valley of the lower Nile bear similarly evocative images of crocodiles, elephants and hawks. So, in a nod to the ordering of later history, Petrie dubbed the last centuries before the coming of the kings as 'Dynasty Zero'; thus, these theoretical monarchs were demoted to the role of local Naqadan princes named after animals, who squabbled amongst themselves, for to many modern eyes images of bound and threatened captives are the products of a war.

And then, with just a few small words, modern linguistics seemingly consolidated the identities of these phantom princes by translating several of their 'image names' as if they were the same as later hieroglyphs, and the doughty warriors took on such names as Ka and Djet and even, King *Nj-Hr* and King *Ḥ3.t.-Ḥr* – though not, it should be emphasized, King U-j.

Once again, however, we are sailing on the seas of our imagination, for, though several of these prehistoric images appear to resemble later hieroglyphs, it is a considerable leap to assume that these same signs are the names of individual rulers. The images, for example, that were drawn on the sides of the storage jars found in the tomb U-j at Abydos might just as well refer to the vessels' contents, or their owners or a location where the goods were made or packed or processed. Such images, indeed, may have held meanings as indeterminate as a painted flame upon the bonnet of a motor car, or as complex as a figure on a cross.

And so, of course, the prehistoric 'kings' are equally indeterminate; their totem names of 'Scorpion' and 'Hawk' derived from nineteenth-century tribal anthropology rather than the era of the ending of prehistory. Similar images, indeed, were made centuries before the era of the rock graffiti and the tomb U-j. A splendid series of scorpion sculptures, for example, minor masterpieces in translucent Egyptian alabaster that vividly encapsulate the texture and colour of the living creature, were deposited in early Naqadan tombs in the great wadi at Hierakonpolis, and images of hawks were left in those same tombs as well, all beautifully carved from lumps of lapis lazuli that flash like the plumage of the living bird.

And yet the evidence is tantalizing. Clearly, it is likely that some of the images and signs made in the last centuries before the first kings, and which resemble the later hieroglyphics, held meanings beyond those of the objects they immediately portray. What that meaning may have been, however, in this most tender age, when the offices of the pharaonic state and its arts and writing were still centuries away, is as yet impossible to know.

One thing, though, is certain. If these archaic images are 'translated', as if they were terms in standard hieroglyphic dictionaries and treated as fragments of traditional history, all they will ever provide is another chapter in a nineteenth-century history book with an added pinch of primitivism; the same old plots that animate totem kings named Hawk and Scorpion leading mythic armies on Napoleonic marches that are measured by the geographic span of their graffiti. Which, of course, is why so much ancient history writing is, of itself, something of a relic and why the phenomenal originality of prehistoric Egypt has been so obscured.

What a breath of fresh air, then, when social science promises a modern history of ancient Egypt's true beginnings! Not Dynasty Zero with its totem princes, but what Norman Yoffee has described as 'several categories of inter-societal interaction ... diffusion/migration models (which may include warfare), economic models, including colonial, imperial, and "world-systems" approaches, and symbolic/ideological models'. Read on, however, and, curiously enough, the same old ghosts still haunt this icy rhetoric, which effectively sets prehistory within the same old savage narratives, with phantom principalities 'vying for territorial, social, and ideological control'.

Archaeology, refreshingly, shows no evidence of that whatever; no layers of ash in burnt-out dwellings, no fallen fortress walls in the era of the phantom princelings. Nor do any of the bodies in the cemeteries of the period show signs of combat or evidence of military training, nor is there any trace of a warrior class or cult, or of the development of weaponry: no grave goods at all that could be classed as military, beyond the traditional accoutrements of hunting.

Nor are there any sudden changes in the material culture of the period, whose surviving relics reflect a lengthy span of slow and steady change before, during and after the appearance of the first pharaohs. Petrie's sequence dating system, for example, shows no evidence of that considerable event – arguably the greatest single happening in ancient Egyptian history – which took place some two centuries after the burial in the tomb U-j. Where then, does the evidence of this history reside?

10

The Coming of the King

The Origins of Hieroglyphs, c. 3000 BC

His Scepter shewes the force of temporall power,
The attribute to awe and Maiestie.
Shakespeare, The Merchant of Venice

The earliest known evidence of an Egyptian pharaoh was found at Hierakonpolis in 1897 by one of Petrie's key assistants, James Quibell, who had been assigned to excavate the sprawling site to rescue its antiquities from looting.

Quibell was assisted in the work by Frederick Green, another young Englishman working for the British administration of Egypt, on leave from the Government's Survey Department. And it was Green who, following Quibell's departure to take up a post in the administration's Service des Antiquités, compiled the field notes that provide the best part of our information about one of archaeology's most significant discoveries.

Quibell first chose to work in the desert wadi where more recent excavations have located traces of Naqadan houses, potteries, stockyards and cemeteries. Pocked by illegal digging and long since mined by local farmers for the fertilizing properties of desert shale and the dust of deep antiquity, the wreck of that great wide plain seems to have quickly discouraged the two Englishmen, who turned their work gangs to excavate a compact ancient mound, the so-called Hill of Nekhen, which lay in the fields below the wadi and the desert plain.

Fifty years earlier, before its sandstone blocks were carried off to serve as the foundations of a factory in a nearby town, the ruins of a little temple had stood upon that hill. And it was there, in the footings of a vanished temple, by the remnants of a prehistoric shrine, that Quibell and Green uncovered a vast agglomeration of courtly objects, a cache such as had not been seen before and has never since been equalled in all of Egypt: a pair of beautiful life-sized pharaonic statues made of sheets of beaten copper; a golden image of a hawk with glittering obsidian eyes still standing in its ancient shrine; two splendidly engraved cosmetic palettes; some prehistoric slaughtering knives; a remarkable collection of stone vases; a heap of mace heads piled like potatoes, some of which were vividly engraved in a manner similar to the cosmetic palettes. And in amongst all this, suffused by groundwater and penetrated by the roots of thorn and halfa grass, lay a mass of ivories which, Quibell remarked, 'resembled potted salmon', but on inspection proved to be hundreds of separate and delicately carved objects from the time of the first kings but which were so cemented and decayed that they are still under restoration to this day.

The excavation of these treasures continued over two long seasons, Green only briefly venturing out of the temple precincts during the second year to excavate the famous painted tomb that lay close by and which, so his workmen loyally informed him, had recently been found by dealers and was in the process of being looted.

Caught as he was between two different jobs, Quibell's publication of the finds was scanty. Green's working notebooks, however, make clear that the temple cache had been deposited in three main groups. The first included the two unparalleled copper statues that had been made some seven centuries after the first pharaohs, and the golden hawk which was probably of the same period. The second was composed of a mass of figurines and other objects made mostly during the first two centuries of the Egyptian kings, while the third, more varied in its contents and even rarer than the others, included the engraved mace heads and the two siltstone palettes, one of which, at a little over twenty-five inches, is the largest palette known to have survived, and which also spells out the name, in hieroglyphs, of a king called Narmer, the king now recognized as the first of all the pharaohs.

What gives the third group of the cache a unique significance is that it was found in a single sealed context and included objects from both the last anonymous phases of prehistoric Naqadan culture – the times of the phantom princes – and the beginning of ancient Egyptian history. In contrast, and as we have already seen, most of the other fine objects from that most crucial era were plundered from the ancient sites by dealers, and thus remain unprovenanced, undatable and so outside of history.

This third group also contained most of the surviving evidence of the invention of the office of pharaoh. Set out in fine relief on some of the decayed ivories and engraved in stone upon three mace heads and the palette with King Narmer's name, the office is defined in a group of related scenes and images that coalesce in a single figure wearing the exact accoutrements of later pharaohs – crowns, sticks, maces and the distinctive royal dresses – a figure which is larger than the others, that sits on thrones and is accompanied by body servants and standard bearers and, in the instance of King Narmer, is identified, in hieroglyphs, by name.

On all these objects, both the king and the images of other smaller figures are drawn and posed in the distinctive manner in which the later artists of pharaonic times would invariably compose the human figure. Set out on little lines an inch or so in length, some of the tiny groups of figures appear to show a royal gathering with trussed-up and mutilated captives, others, the king enthroned and holding court in the manner of the later drawings on the picture plaques of ivory and wood. Another group shows pharaoh in the guise of birds and bulls and catfish, who are identified as king by the ornaments of royal office. Many of these vivid compositions are aggressive and show

Two ivory cylinder seals, each about 4 inches high, from the great cache at Hierakonpolis

pharaoh in the act of execution, attacking trussed-up captives or breaking down the bricks of walled enclosures. There are as well some disembodied images grouped together in the manner of Egyptian hieroglyphics; a few of which, on Narmer's Palette, phonetically spell out the royal name. To Quibell and Green and their contemporaries, it must have seemed as if 'ancient Egypt' had stepped fully clothed out of the prehistoric mist.

INTERPRETATIONS

In nineteenth-century terms, such apparently inexplicable cultural revolutions were usually ascribed to the arrival of a race of intelligent foreigners in boats, to the mind of an individual genius, or to the mysterious workings of the Deity. Even these days, though they have largely dispensed with embarrassing theories of colonization, traditional historians are apt to describe the era in which pharaoh and ancient Egyptian culture make an abrupt and simultaneous appearance in phrases such as an 'age of miracles', and to portray the simultaneous arrival of the first written name as 'a dazzling intellectual leap'.

Underlying all such interpretations, even those that propose invasion as a main mover, is the common academic assumption that thought in words necessarily precedes all actions; specifically, in the case of ancient Egypt, that a clever person or some sort of prehistoric Brains Trust had thought the whole thing up, and then told a studio of humble craftsmen to delineate a set of 'symbols' that would express their ideas in some kind of a curiously abstruse visual code. Not all people, however, act, as a philosopher once put it, 'from the opinions that they hold about things', nor is there the slightest evidence that pharaonic imagery was created to symbolize abstract thoughts or even oral traditions – nor, most certainly, the comfortable saws and maxims that are so often trotted out in explanation of the pharaohs and their gods.

Given that it took close to half a millennium after Narmer's name was first inscribed to compose a hieroglyphic phrase or sentence, and yet further centuries for the first recorded hieroglyphic literature to be written out, there hardly seems to have been a rush to publication; no burning need to record imaginary intellectual deliberations. In those exact same centuries, however, before the hieroglyphs were put to literary use, they were themselves exquisitely refined, and huge amounts of care and effort were employed in their emplacement upon monumental blocks of stone. The notion, then, that hieroglyphs were created to record human thought or speech is absurd. Something different was happening: in the words of Colin Renfrew, ancient Egypt was one of those cultures in which 'the symbol in its real, actual substance, actually preceded the concept'.

At first glance, this might seem a rarefied idea. In reality, it is a universal mode of comprehension and creation. The present Queen Elizabeth, for example, attained her rank by the assumption of a crown, a cloak and a sceptre during the rites of coronation, an event whose qualities the written word lacks the capacity to encapsulate. In modern media, as well, non-literary discourse is king; most obviously in entertainment and in advertising, where complex narratives are meticulously composed and swiftly transmitted in such media as music, colour, clothes and lighting. Nor are such communication systems limited in their capacity for argument or expression; mere words, indeed, no longer compete with the universal fascination of the modern media.

An ivory Naqadan gazelle comb

ON THE ORIGINS OF HIEROGLYPHICS

That the age of Narmer was often hailed as an 'age of miracles' is because so many far-reaching changes in Naqadan society – the advent of kings, the ancient Egyptian style of drawing and, above all, hieroglyphic writing – seemed to arrive together and at once. In earlier centuries, it appeared, these things were quite unknown. Then, suddenly, around 3000 BC, identified by crowns and costumes, images of a specific king appeared whose royal name was spelled out in a group of three small signs: a house, a fish and an engraving chisel.

This, though, is largely an illusion. In reality, the metamorphosis that enabled the identification of King Narmer – the process, that is, of expanding the meaning of those three small images, of 'freeing' them from the things they pictured – had been a thousand years and more in its development. As in more recent histories, once the necessary elements were all in position, change was very rapid.

As far as pharaoh's Egypt is concerned, an early part of that long slow journey towards identifying kings was held in the gesture that had pressed an ivory comb into a knot of hair at an early Naqadan funeral. Many of those pretty combs sport images of animals on their tops – the silhouette of a gazelle, say, images that when attached to a human head change the aspect of that person in much the same way as the craftsman's cutting out the image of a gazelle on a comb had previously changed the nature of the comb itself. Here, then, a lively idiosyncratic image had twice been placed in settings where it imparted extra shades of meaning. Freed from its immediate context, the dainty desert antelope had begun to move in the Naqadan imagination. Such images, of course, hold considerable subtleties, which, as Claude Lévi-Strauss once observed, can be very good to think with!

A further stage in the journey was uncovered by the excavators of the tomb U-j at Abydos who, along with other melancholy mementoes of that once-splendid burial, found two hundred modest plaques of ivory and bone still lying in the tomb. Smaller than postage stamps, each of these tiny plaques had been vividly engraved with a few signs taken from a basic repertoire of forty images, some of which – scorpions, elephants and hawks, a bull's head on a staff – already had considerable Naqadan pedigree, and which were also drawn on other objects found within the tomb.

Ivory picture labels from tomb U-j; the largest is ¾ inch high

Each of these little plaques had been snapped from larger sheets of ivory and bone that had been scored with deep-grooved lines, their signs appearing to have been drawn out before the plaques were separated. Each plaque also had a hole drilled in a corner above the engraved signs, which would have allowed a cord to have passed through the plaque so that its images would have served as a kind of label. Like the antelope comb, the little images upon the plaque had served to modify the identities of the objects to which they were attached.

Unfortunately, the signs engraved on these little plaques are not the same as those of the later hieroglyphic repertoire, which are as specific in their identities and forms as are the letters of the Roman alphabet. They may not, therefore, be 'read' like Narmer's name nor, indeed, like many of the signs engraved upon the later, larger picture plaques. Nonetheless, the rules of the game are plain enough to see, for the standardization of the label's forty-odd signs shows that their makers were working within a well-developed system, whilst all the labels' images are well ordered and facing in the same direction, which lends them the formal qualities of later hieroglyphic texts, a visual linking narrative. These same rules, the syntax of these images, would later guide the construction of the first hieroglyphic texts and, indeed, announce the coming of a king named Narmer.

As for the specific meaning of the signs on the labels from the tomb U-j, they do not seem to have identified the contents of objects to which they were attached – not, that is, unless they were attached to the like of elephants' and bulls' heads. Nor indeed do they appear to have been elements of a previously unknown phonetic writing system that was later discarded in favour of pharaonic hieroglyphs.

Ivory labels bearing numerals. From tomb U-j; the largest is ¾ inch high

What is familiar, though, amidst all this uncertainty, is the lines and curls that accompany these tiny images, for in later hieroglyphic writing, the same forms will denote the numbers '1' and '100' and here, too, as in the later texts, these signs appear in combinations that seem to represent a single complex number which, in the manner of Roman numerals, can be calculated by counting up the duplicated signs. In later, pharaonic funerary texts, quantities of woven textiles, a significant item of grave furnishings, are listed and numbered in exactly this same way. These plaques, therefore, may be early examples of a traditional accounting system. And if that were true, their images may have identified a product, a person, a community, or work place: 'Bull's Head Wine from the Elephant Ridge Estate'?

At all events, it is a reasonable certitude that the two signs that spell out the syllables of Narmer's name upon the siltstone palette can be identified as belonging to a king by their containment within a rectangular patterning of lines known now as a serekh, a highly specific image which, for the following three thousand years, would be used to hold one of the five names of pharaoh. Later and more elaborated representations of the sign show that it represents the 'Great House'; the *per'a*, as it is spelled out in the later hieroglyphs, which is the origin of our word 'pharaoh'. Here, then, on Narmer's Palette the three little signs together would appear to signify 'the (royal) house (of Narmer)'.

Narmer's name and serekh, as drawn upon his large stone mace head

Inside the regal serekh, the sound of the two signs that compose Narmer's name have been rendered in the same way as hieroglyphic signs are in later hieroglyphic inscriptions, the bewhiskered catfish *nar,* and the chisel *mer* below it, making up the name Nar-mer. It is assumed, therefore, that those two images were carved to represent the ancient voice; this, the ultimate abstraction of Naqadan imagery which had begun when the craftsmen had created a visual taxonomy of Nilotic flora or fauna.

Sadly, however, the genuine ancient sound of Narmer's name is almost gone, those two syllables having undergone, along with those of all the other hieroglyphs, what a distinguished linguist recently described as 'a complex history of loss, assimilation and reacquisition'. At the least, the sound of their vowels is as yet unknown, so that the name represented by the catfish and a chisel has been variously rendered as 'Nar-mer', 'Nor-mer', 'Meri-neri', 'Wakh-mer', 'Nar-Ba-Thai', or on occasion, plain old 'Nar' – the last abbreviated suggestion deriving from the fact that the image usually identified as the *mer* hieroglyph is shaped like a modern stone-cutting chisel and is quite different from the image drawn on Narmer's Palette, which, with its wooden handle, is more like an engraving tool – the literal means, in fact, of making Narmer's name in stone.

Should therefore, the *mer* be abandoned, to leave us with King Nar? The adoption of another system of transcription, alternatively, one that takes into account the meanings of some of the other words in which Narmer's hieroglyphs appear, would provide our pharaoh with an entirely different set of monikers, such as 'the angry/electric/furious/excellent/mean/cleaving/catfish'. Whether any such interpretations are genuinely ancient, or are merely anthropological or linguistic concoctions, is presently beyond all knowing.

Safer, therefore – to ensure that the pure products of old Egypt don't go completely crazy – to acknowledge that there are still huge

The coming of the king: a detail of a miniature siltstone relief found in the great cache at Hierakonpolis

uncertainties about such things; and that, like the names of Khufu, Ramesses and King Tut, 'Narmer' is simply a convenient modern term for the hieroglyphs that distinguish the name of the first pharaoh.

What actually survives, of course, behind these scholarly embroideries, all that is left from Narmer's time, are the heavy solid objects, the things themselves; the mace heads, the palettes and the ivories that hold scenes upon them which can still be read like music on a page or the impression of a rolling cylinder seal; a mass of images made centuries before the first-known written phrase, that yet with hieroglyphic clarity announce the coming of the king.

11

Narmer's Palette

The Qualities of Kings, c. 3000 BC

> ... a world is as it were put together experimentally ... As
> when in the law-court in Paris a motor-car accident is repre-
> sented by means of dolls etc.
>
> *Ludwig Wittgenstein, 1914*

Of all the things Quibell and Green uncovered on the temple mound
of Hierakonpolis, one object above all has come to represent the
beginnings of 'ancient Egypt' to the modern world. Frequently described,
along with the Rosetta Stone and Tutankhamun's golden tomb as a
landmark of Egyptian art and writing, King Narmer's Palette has become
a Milestone of World History.

It was probably inescapable. Narmer's is the largest palette known
to have survived and it is perfectly preserved, so, in a period when
history is usually assembled from disparate collections of broken
scraps, its purity and completeness hold a moment of perfect clarity.
Nonetheless King Narmer's Palette's elevation to the status of World
Icon has had an unfortunate effect. Shimmering enigmatically under
its exhibition lights, the museum piece par excellence has been
removed from all reality. Set back into a living context, though, within
the ancient landscape amongst a mass of dusty broken things, this
beautiful thin stone, its size, its weight, its gathered imagery, has two
clear histories yet to tell. The first concerns its manufacture and
design; the second, its role within contemporary court society.

The material heritage is clear. Siltstone had been used for palettes
since the times of the Badarians, and, like all the other decorated palettes, the distinctive green-grey rock of which King Narmer's Palette

The Narmer Palette: the king smites a kneeling captive whilst underneath, two naked men appear to run away

The Narmer Palette's other face. The royal entourage views ten beheaded captives; and in the scene below, the necks of two monsters enclose an area for grinding pigment

is composed appears to have been extracted from a single quarry about halfway along the Wadi Hammamat, a barren valley which runs through the hills of the Eastern Desert opposite Naqada to the port of Quseir on the Red Sea coast. Mined from the times of the Faiyum farmers to the Roman emperors, the quarry holds an extraordinary range of fine, hard rock, the heavy siltstone from which Narmer's Palette was made being the raw material of some of Egypt's finest monuments. Apart from its strength and subtle colour, the stone's great virtue for the ancient craftsmen was certainly its near-perfect evenness of texture.

The techniques they used to make King Narmer's Palette were the same as those the craftsmen had developed in working on the earlier decorated palettes. First, the palette's outline was cut from a two-foot slip of quarried stone, the craftsman following a traditional design of other decorated palettes in setting the silhouettes of animals along its upper edge to make a jagged line. Here, though, and uniquely, the outline of King Narmer's Palette was given the characteristic oval shape of a large Naqadan storage jar.

This flat, blank form, less than an inch in thickness was then tapered, shaped and smoothed so that the centres of both of its faces were forward of its edges. Next, it seems, a craftsman marked out the order and design of the subjects to be carved on both the palette's sides, for the finished work is designed with some precision, the palette's width, for example, being precisely two-thirds of its height. Then the outlines of the palette's images were cut into its two convex surfaces, each one defined with a series of tiny cuts around its edges in generous and detailed silhouette using a variety of copper chisels, points and flats.

This work was then followed by a lengthy process of chiselling and abrading in which the empty areas around each of the outlined images were cut down and polished to a dull sheen so as to give the impression of a single lower surface, a ground from which the figures protrude in raised relief. This was an especially delicate procedure, in which the siltstone's innate strength allowed the sculptor to work parts of the thin slab to thicknesses of half an inch. Then, finally, after a great deal of detailed modelling and abrasion, a process in which the fine grain of the siltstone allowed the sculptor an exquisite level of control, a graphic outline was carefully drawn around each of the sculpted images with a tiny chisel point. That this final finishing, at the very least, was accomplished by a single person is suggested by some idiosyncratic details that are repeated time and time again on both the palette's surfaces; indeed, throughout all the work, the palette's very size would not have permitted more than one craftsman at a time to work upon it.

Now, Naqadan copper chisels cannot mark siltstone in any way without a hammer's blow to drive a cutting edge gently into the stone, so this final process would have been drawn out by the continual necessity to re-sharpen the chisels. All the various processes of polishing and shaping the palette's figures, in fact, would have been similarly arduous and lengthy; using much harder and more powerful tools, a modern mason took six hundred hours to make a replica. At the same time, however, the long processes of hand-working such a stone allowed the ancient craftsmen time for care and thoughtfulness, so that the forms and textures of the figures' eyes and hands, the quality of hair and feathers and papyrus fronds, are delineated with a lively sensitivity and in extraordinary detail, just as they are on many of the other, older palettes.

In that the overall composition of both the palette's faces are governed by a central vertical, its designer follows the fundamental principles of the earlier decorated palettes. Unlike them, however, with their surfaces covered in dense and clever counterpoints of void and image, the figures on King Narmer's Palette are set in relatively open spaces and held in lines between a series of horizontals, in the manner of a cylinder seal's impression. It is as if the Naqadan craftsman had sat down and unpicked a previously tangled rope and laid it out into carefully measured pieces. All the stress and dynamism of the older palettes, the graphic chaos of the hunt and battlefield, have disappeared. Isolated on an open ground, the crisp outstanding images of Narmer's Palette occupy but a third of its total area, which, to the modern eye, provides them with a novel *gravitas*. This new way of composing images was a deliberate and long-considered choice. By itself alone, the work of smoothing down the open backgrounds with abrasive powders to obtain a texture similar to that of a baby's skin, a process that, as the tiny scratches on the stone betray, was accomplished with a range of abrasive powders, from coarse to smooth, was a considerable labour. It was a labour, though, that literally produced a new-found space.

The presence of King Narmer fills these airy compositions. On earlier palettes, humans had appeared along with birds and beasts as one of many equal elements of a composition. Here, however, human figures have taken centre stage, and their relative sizes have of themselves become an essential ingredient of the palette's imagery, King Narmer's images being two and three times larger than those of other people. And for the first time, too, one of the palette's faces is dominated by a single figure bestriding its ancient centre line: the famous image of a smiting king.

It is hardly surprising, then, that this pre-eminent museum piece stands as the contemporary icon of the beginning of pharaonic art. At the same time, however, the dark oval of the palette's silhouette also encloses a range of ancient images which have been gathered together for exactly the same purposes as that for which goods were assembled and placed in Naqadan graves throughout the previous millennium; for the purposes, that is, of constructing affiliation and identity for the body at their centre. Here, however, for the first time, the body at the centre is the large and lively image of a king. And in a dozen different ways, by hieroglyphs, by the use of scale and by the very images it holds, the diminutive officials, the royal maces, kilts and crowns, the sceptres and the false tails and beards with which all pharaonic royalty will later be invested, the palette insistently and constantly identifies Narmer as a pharaoh.

So on one face of his palette, Narmer wears a headdress that later hieroglyphic texts describe as the 'Red Crown' and identify as the crown of the ruler of the regions known today as Lower Egypt – the region of the Nile, that is, that runs north from Memphis to the open sea. The first known occurrence of this crown, however, was found in Upper Egypt, where it was drawn out centuries before the time of Narmer, on the side of a burnished pot with a blaze-black rim. That the pot was recovered from the cemeteries of prehistoric Naqada, close to some native sources of copper ore, might suggest that this crown may once have been made of thin sheets of that red-shining metal.

On the palette's other face, the figure of King Narmer is once again identified by name, by size and by regalia; most obviously, on this occasion, by a tall headdress known as the 'White Crown' which is commonly identified as the crown of Upper Egypt, the section of the Nile Valley that stretches south from Memphis to the First Cataract at Aswan. Copied, so it has been suggested, from the designs of headdresses on some imported cylinder seals, the White Crown appears to have been a more recent innovation than the Red Crown of Lower Egypt. In life, it may have been made of basketwork and plaster.

PURPOSES AND MEANINGS

Why then, was this palette made? What purposes did its elaborate definitions serve? Was it an advertisement, a celebration of the making of a king, or was it made for other reasons?

Like all the other elaborately decorated palettes, its ultimate purpose derived from the simple pigment-grinding siltstone slabs of earlier ages. Indeed, a small circular pigment-grinding dish is still present on King Narmer's Palette, surrounded by two monsters, their necks and head entwined in the Mesopotamian manner, above them are the figures of the king and court inspecting ten decapitated men.

That images of hunting and fighting are the subjects of most decorated palettes has led to the plausible suggestion that they were made in preparation for these activities, because cosmetics appear to have been applied to their participants' faces before departing on such expeditions. That Narmer's Palette shares some of its subject matter with the later ivory picture plaques and other records of specific royal events, however, has led to the further suggestion that all the decorated palettes were made for similarly specific happenings. In Narmer's case, this has traditionally been interpreted not as a hunting expedition, but as the unification of Upper and Lower Egypt by force of arms, a narrative extended by nineteenth-century historians, who took the scenes upon the palette to represent episodes of martial history.

Nor, at first glance, does this seem impossible. At the bottom of one of the palette's faces, after all, there is an image of a bull trampling a man and breaking down an oval wall, whilst the same strip on the palette's other face holds two images of men who look over their shoulders as they run away; both sets of images that had been well rehearsed by figures set amidst the aggressive chaos of the older palettes. Given that pharaoh himself will later be described as a 'great bull' and is sometimes represented in the guise of powerful animals, it is most likely that the great bull on Narmer's Palette is indeed an image of the king. The question yet remains, however, whether these images record a specific event or whether, as their ancestry suggests, they are simply a reworking of traditional compositions. Similar questions may be asked of the most elaborate of the palette's compositions that contain images of Narmer, some members of his court and the trussed-up bodies of ten decapitated men. Do these also record a genuine event? Are they components of an episode of royal history?

The classic answer to such questions has been given by the palette's largest single panel, which holds a fifteen-inch-high image of King Narmer drawn in a pose derived from deep antiquity. Legs apart, with one arm raised, he is holding a kneeling man up by his hair and, in the age-old way, he is about to smite him with a mace. Above King Narmer's victim is a curious concoction of archaic signs: a complex image of a hawk with a human arm that holds a rope attached to a human head which is tethered by the nose, while the neck of the head, in turn, is attached to a particular oval shape from which rise six equal fronds of papyrus. Given that both the oval shape and a papyrus stem appear to correspond to the Egyptian hieroglyphs for 'the river delta' and '1,000', this group has often been 'read' along the lines of 'the Hawk smites the delta people', or 'Narmer takes six thousand captives', or 'the Hawk leads six thousand captives'.

Recent archaeology, however, clearly contradicts these traditional interpretations, for it has proved that the northward movement of the Naqadan population into Lower Egypt began many centuries before the time of Narmer and that it did not appear to have been accompanied by warfare. Nor is there archaeological evidence that Narmer the Hawk, or any other military force, 'conquered' the Nile Delta. And at the same time, too, further research has provided explanations of the palette's purposes beyond that of advertising an illusory invasion.

For Narmer's Palette was found along with a host of objects that, as more recent archaeological discoveries have shown, were typical of the contents of contemporary shrines. And this in turn has led to a suggestion that its grinding dish was intended to supply pigment for the decoration of the figurines that were often housed in such shrines, some of which appear to have had some kind of make-up drawn around their eyes. If, the theory then continues, these palettes had been part of the equipment of such shrines, the presence of these elaborate reliefs inside such simple mud and wattle buildings may have been the root and inspiration of the reliefs carved in later Egyptian temples.

Other objects from the cache of Hierakonpolis, however, suggest that Narmer's Palette may also have served a more active function. For along with the great palette, the cache also contained some limestone mace heads that are as large as footballs. Inflated, like King Narmer's Palette, beyond all other known examples, they too were covered in scenes of royal ceremonial. In similar fashion, the cache also contained an enormous pair of slaughtering knives, the largest worked flints ever to have been excavated. Brittle and very heavy, at over two feet long, like the giant mace heads, these knives were hardly practical. Here then, some of the traditional utensils of Naqadan society had been enlarged and transformed so that mace heads and long flint knives, the tools of ancient slaughter, had become powerful and archaic icons of some of the acts pictured on King Narmer's Palette.

Though larger than all other palettes and carved and polished so that its upper edges have the weighty quality of an engorged water skin, King Narmer's Palette is nonetheless deceptively thin and thus conveniently light, whilst its tapered shape and carefully smoothed edges have clearly invited its being grasped in both hands along its lower edges, as ancient wear along them clearly shows. This suggests that it was designed for carrying, together, perhaps, with the giant knives and maces, those images of royal power, just as enlarged and highly decorated swords and maces are still carried in procession at parliaments and universities. Held high above the head, the palette's upper edges enlivened by the jagged outline of two silhouetted bull heads, King Narmer's serekh, an archaic microchip upon a slaty circuit board, formed the very sounds of pharaoh's name.

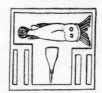

The king's name as it appears upon the recto of the Narmer Palette

Was this, then, the presentation that Narmer's craftsman was working to achieve, an exhibition piece used in parade? Certainly the palette's careful images were designed to be read and understood; their balance and composure, a careful exercise in visual logic, laying out precisely and insistently the attributes and the identity of the new office that we now call pharaoh. Nor did its every detail have to be open to immediate inspection. Like a great jewelled Bible carried in procession, the scenes on Narmer's Palette hold their own wisdom, their own internal dialogues, their own tremendous potency. Made as carefully as written words and designed to be read up close, it was enough that they were there.

Amid images of suffering and death, the defining signs of kingship, courtly rank and hierarchy are laid out in ordered and precisely balanced compositions. Some have claimed, as we have seen, that such sufferings record genuine invasions, real wars; archaeology does not support this supposition, and modern 'translations' of many of the palette's signs are as yet uncertain, imprecise.

What is certain, though, is that the images of Narmer's Palette lay out the attributes, the qualities and the identity of pharaonic order. Rather than merely documenting the earthly exploits of a single man, as in an ancient newsreel, its craftsmen employed images far older than any text or written histories to display a novel governmental system and to offer in its balanced compositions, stark recognition of, a meditation even, on the suffering required to maintain a social equilibrium within the new-made order.

12

The Hawk upon the Wall

History, Land and Naqadan Resettlement,
3500–3000 BC

In the study of Egyptian society, ideology has usually had the
advantage over reality, whether it is the ideology of the histor-
ian or the ideology of the Egyptian ruling class itself.

Christopher Eyre, 1999

Though today we easily describe this Narmer as a 'king', as wearing
'crowns' and occupying the post we now identify as that of a ruler of
all Egypt, in reality, of course, in Narmer's time there were no modern
notions of a 'king' or 'kingdom' nor, indeed, in all pharaonic history
would there ever be a denominating hieroglyph for 'Egypt'. And so
the very words we use give false voice to the people of the distant past.

Nor was the concept of a nation-state with fixed borders and an ethnic identity a part of pharaonic Egypt; it is, of course, a creation of early
modern Europe. Even those words that, a millennium later, pharaonic
scribes occasionally used to define the ancient kingdom, such popularly
quoted terms as '*Kemet*' – the 'Black Land' – or '*Sema-Towy*' – 'The
Two/Joined lands' – were essentially poetic. More typically, when ancient
Egyptian scribes referred to pharaoh's kingdom in non-literary texts,
they used terms like 'residence' – that is, the royal residence – to denote
the controlling centre of the networks of trade and traffic, tithing and
taxing, that operated in the regions of the lower Nile. The assumptions
that led traditional historians to capitalize the 'Black Land' as if it were
something other than a description of a cultivatable tract of earth beside
the Nile, would have been entirely foreign to the early court of Egypt.

So, just as there is no gene pool that may be described as 'ancient Egyptian', so there could never have been a 'unification' of the 'Land of Egypt'. Given that the span of the lower Nile is similar to that from Rome to Hamburg, it is unlikely that its various ancient inhabitants even spoke a common language. What then, had Narmer's assumption of the two crowns actually signified?

To European eyes, the tumbled ruins of old Egypt have long provided an obvious explanation. Pharaoh's shattered visage, after all, looks much like those of Roman emperors. So Narmer and his successors are enlisted as archaic representatives of a European narrative of history in which nations rise and fall and everything is explained by drum-and-trumpet Darwinism. Pharaonic Egypt, however, was not just another version of those later histories, and had an entirely different tenor.

In many ways, indeed, it was the antithesis of a modern nation-state. In no sense, for example, could ancient Egyptians be said to have been interested in the modern idea of 'progress'; the maintenance of an ancestral order was a paramount objective. At the same time, the formation of Narmer's state had provided the foundations of a truly original order for society that would last for millennia and which, as pharaoh's Egypt, became a wonder of the ancient world, a byword for wisdom, piety and wealth.

Certainly, the role of pharaoh has clear elements in common with the many later kings who ruled by tradition and divine right; this is why, at first glance, a commonly used term like 'kingdom' appears to be appropriate. Yet the pharaonic state stands at the beginning of all that. It was created from the ground up, without the benefit of an exemplar and, indeed, without the aid of writing or the presence of a national faith. Thus, it was made in an entirely different environment from those of subsequent states. Only centuries later, when the pharaonic state was well developed and cultural continuity established, did this unique creation find literary voice and only then did the scribes examine and define their silent and already ancient kingdom and reflect its order in a mirror image, in elaborate descriptions of a literary cosmos. By then, however, the moment of the state's creation, the making of the king and gods, had long since gone.

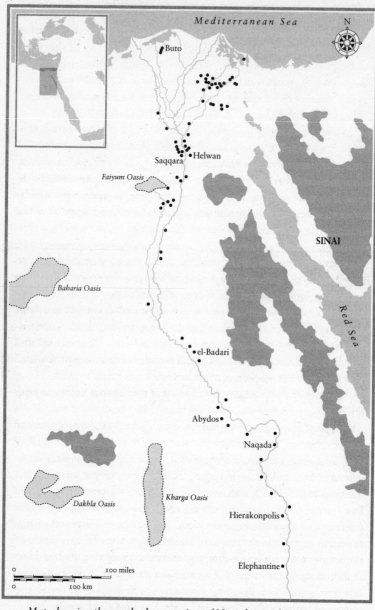

Map showing the northerly extension of Naqadan settlement into the regions of Memphis and the Nile Delta

MIGRATIONS

Memphis, in parchíd Egypts soyle:
Flankíd with old Piramides, and melting Nyle.
William Lithgow, 1632

Setting aside traditional histories, the true origins of the pharaonic state lie in the middle of the fourth millennium BC, at the time, that is, when the first known images of wooden boats appeared and the Naqadans began to move out of their homelands and settle all along the valley of the lower Nile.

At first the wooden boats appear to have sailed right through the middle of Egypt, where the broad flood plains were ill-suited to Naqadan farming, and settlements and cemeteries were founded both in the river's delta and in the narrow fifty-mile strip of land between the ending of the Nile Valley and the latitudes of Lake Faiyum. In this region, Naqadan colonies became so large that to Flinders Petrie, whose expedition had been the first to excavate them, it appeared that the core of the culture had itself shifted to the north. And so he dubbed this new and mobile phase of Naqadan prehistory 'Gerzean', after some of the settlers' cemeteries which his staff had excavated by the little village of Girza, just forty miles south of Cairo.

Like other Naqadan sites within this area, Girza's cemeteries and settlements were set upon a rising desert plain above the west bank of the river, just as they had been in the Naqadan heartlands. Here, however, the river valley was only half as wide as in Upper Egypt and in ancient times the western bank was exceptionally narrow. The ancient Nile was different from the modern river, too, its flow much stronger than it would become in later phases of its history. In consequence, the beginning of the delta, where the fast, wide river broke into half a dozen different streams and spread out like a fan, was further south than it is at present, at a point where the valley cliffs nip close together near the pyramids of modern-day Saqqara. And it was there, within this narrowing plain at the ending of the river's valley, where Naqadans had never lived before, that in the last centuries before the reign of Narmer they came to settle in their thousands.

As the northern settlements grew in both size and number, the ancient cemeteries back at Naqada fell into disuse so that, by Narmer's day, apart from a few alien mortuary monuments set at their edges and built apparently for members of the royal family, they were accommodating hardly any burials at all. Nor did the later, non-royal graves contain splendid craftworks like those of earlier times. Ancient Naqada, it appears, had descended into an obscure provincialism, which is probably why most of its magnificent prehistoric cemeteries had lain undisturbed beneath its gravelled plains until the ending of the nineteenth century.

This was not the case throughout the rest of the Naqadan heartlands. Narmer himself would be buried at Abydos, along with his successors to the throne, in a most ancient desert cemetery that had earlier accommodated the wine-rich burial in the tomb U-j. At Hierakonpolis, as well, new cemeteries were established in the time of Narmer's successors and several large impressive monuments were constructed.

Add this archaeological evidence to the warlike scenes on the mace heads and the palettes, and it is easy to imagine that Abydos and Hierakonpolis had ganged up on Naqada, impoverished that city and marched northwards to control all of Egypt, and then, just as ancient Greek and Roman historians describe, had founded a fortress-capital at the site of Memphis, a pharaonic metropolis of later eras situated close by modern-day Saqqara. To traditional historians, the familial struggles of Horus and Seth, those great pharaonic deities, appeared as a reflection of these imaginary archaic wars, especially as two pharaonic temples were later dedicated to those same two deities at Hierakonpolis and Naqada. And was not the very name of Memphis' greatest temple, Hikuptah, transformed by the ancient Greeks into *Aigyptos*, and employed by them as the name for the entire kingdom? Translated into English, the word is literally 'Egypt'. Had not ancient Egypt's history begun, therefore, within this mythic glooming?

At first glance, Egypt's own records appear to part-confirm the story. For if Narmer had also been called Menes – and that is not impossible, as later pharaohs bore as many as five separate names – he may well have been the individual that some pharaonic king lists name as the first king, the same monarch that Greek and Roman texts describe as uniting Egypt by force of arms and founding its first capital at Memphis.

'What follows rests on the accounts given me by the Egyptians, which I shall now repeat,' wrote the historian Herodotus in the fifth century BC.

> The priests said that Menes was the first king of Egypt, and that it was he who raised the dyke which protects Memphis from the inundations of the Nile ... and having thus, by turning the river, made the tract where it used to run, dry land, proceeded in the first place to build the city now called Memphis, which lies in the narrow part of Egypt ... Next, they read me from a papyrus, the names of three hundred and thirty monarchs, who they said, were his successors upon the throne ...

Unfortunately, Herodotus' story is little more than a recasting of a typical Greek tale about a heroic founder of a classical city; cities like those named after Alexander, cities that were not the products of population movements but had been established by acts of policy and deeds of engineering specifically to service the needs of trade and serve as naval bases. The story, too, is flatly contradicted by the excavation of a series of opulent and enormous late Naqadan cemeteries on both banks of the Nile in the region of ancient Memphis, which prove the Naqadans had been established in that area a century and more before the time of Menes/Narmer. And then again, despite extensive surveys, there is no trace of the archaic city that the heroic Menes is said to have founded, the dusty mounds of ancient Memphis that are visited by modern tourists being the residue of buildings of much later periods.

Nor is there any trace of Menes in the contemporary record. Narmer's name, on the other hand, though it is never mentioned in later ancient Egyptian texts nor in the tales of the Greeks and Romans, is common enough in excavations of the late Naqadan period, and lists of kings compiled in the reigns of his immediate successors insistently record his name as the first in the line of pharaohs. So the later ancient Egyptian historical records and the reports of the classical historians are simply not true; nor indeed are nineteenth-century history books.

Some of the other later ancient texts, however, now appear closer to the facts of modern archaeology. Wonderfully oblique writings inscribed on temple walls and on papyrus scrolls tell of the voyages of a god, a hawk named Horus, whose primordial progress was not that of a conquering and city-founding king, but is marked up and down the lower Nile by the establishment of shrines that in the following millennia would be transformed into some of ancient Egypt's grandest temples.

The image of a hawk, of course, itself an ancient Naqadan sign, also appears upon the Narmer Palette. Other near-contemporary images of the same bird were frequently drawn on storage jars and also appear as rock graffiti all along the lower Nile and in the surrounding deserts. In later times, indeed, the name of the caravan route that joined the Nile Valley to the regions to the north of Egypt would be called the 'Way of Horus'. The 'Temple of the First Horus', so these texts tell, was established at Hierakonpolis, the same site, that is, where Quibell and Green had found an image of a golden hawk, sitting in the same pose as earlier Naqadan images of hawks that are drawn on the red-painted jars, where they are shown perched on standards and riding on the wooden boats. It is indeed the voyages of that same distinctive image which these ancient texts seem to describe.

So the hawk sailed upstream, ten miles south of Hierakonpolis, to a site that is now the modern town of Edfu, where, so it is written on the high walls of that city's splendid temple, a special shrine was made for him. Though any archaic buildings that had once stood upon that venerable site have long been swept away or lie buried beneath the later temples, the texts tell how a perch was made from a split reed and planted in the silt at the river's edge, and that the golden hawk had settled there. And the mound where the perch had been set up was known as 'Horus' Elevation'. And an enclosure of precise dimensions with a central shrine three cubits wide was built to house the Edfu Horus; a literary description that tallies both with surviving models of archaic shrines and with images that are drawn on many of the picture plaques.

Other texts tell of Horus shrines that were established downstream from Hierakonpolis, in both the river's valley and its delta. Like the shrine of the Edfu Horus, the sites of some of the Horus shrines that were established in the Nile Delta are buried now, beneath such modern towns as Damanhur – whose name still defines the city as the 'settlement of Horus'. Ancient Buto, too, is listed as one of the hawk's foundations, whilst the locations of several similarly described Horus shrines within the delta are yet unknown and appear in ancient Egyptian funerary texts as lost and legendary cities.

The greatest of all the northern Horus shrines was at Heliopolis, which now lies under Cairo's northern suburbs. Though its surviving relics are few, Heliopolis is described in ancient literature as a grand religious centre. In Heliopolis, so it was written, the 'Horus of the Eastern Horizon' leaves its perch and takes wing every day, to rise in glorious confabulation with the sun god Re, as Re-Harakhty, Re the Horus.

In these later literary worlds, the dead of Hierakonpolis in the far south are united with those of Buto in the delta. Known as the 'Souls of Pe and Nekhen' – the souls, that is, of Buto and Hierakonpolis – the two groups of spirit voyagers appear as mysterious ecstatics in funerary texts where pharaoh himself becomes a Horus, his courtiers are known as the 'Followers of Horus', and all prehistory – the age, that is, before the coming of the kings – is glimpsed as a golden age when history had not yet begun and the pharaonic state was ruled by gods.

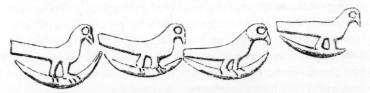

Four late Naqadan voyaging hawks

13

Taking Wing

Naqadan Emigration, 3500–3000 BC

> *We don't start from certain words, but certain occasions or
> activities*
>
> Ludwig Wittgenstein, 1938

INTO THE DELTA

Until the 1980s, the immigrations from the Naqadan heartlands that
would define the full extent of pharaoh's kingdom and indeed the
land of Egypt, were but little known or understood. A plethora of
recent excavations has changed all that, however, some fifteen flourishing Naqadan settlements having been discovered within the Nile
Delta alone.

Here then, in the region that would become the other half of ancient
Egypt, the southerners' distinctive pottery has recently been found in
typically Naqadan graves set close to simple huts of daub and wattle.
The delta's indigenous populations, on the other hand, the people of
the Maadi–Buto culture, lived in relatively well-built settlements and
made spare and simple graves that showed little of the southerners'
millennial preoccupation with the dead.

Hints of what had encouraged the Naqadans to leave their narrow
valley and voyage downstream into the wide and windy flatlands of
the river's delta may yet be held in some of the region's ancient place
names, which, as they are recorded in the language of the later hieroglyphs, are derived from such Levantine phrases as 'low lands', 'free
pastures' and 'ears of wheat'.

Such abundant visions were probably a reflection of environmental change. In distant prehistoric times, both the Nile's flow and the intrusions of the sea into its delta had been so violent as to delete all record of earlier human activity. In the seventh millennium BC, for example, the Nile had flowed so fiercely through its delta that it had channelled into a single outflow to the Mediterranean, the so-called 'Great River', which had run due north from the ending of the valley's limestone cliffs. A process that had desiccated the delta's wetlands and extended the river's length by dropping huge deposits of silt and sand into the Mediterranean, and, with the aid of the prevailing sea currents, had cast up mounds of sand and silt along the shoreline of the river's delta. That fierce flow slowed, however, during the following millennia, and some of the silts which came down in the annual flood had dropped within the river's single stream, dividing it again into half a dozen branches that fanned out into the river's ancient delta lands, reviving marshlands and meanders and watering a hundred miles of fertile silt and rush. And it was this that promised the Naqadan herders a leafy paradise rustling with fine game.

The first Naqadan settlements in these reviving pasturelands, those established in the middle of the fourth millennium BC, consisted of the usual simple huts set on the gentle alluvial sandbanks typical of the delta landscape and known today as 'turtlebacks'. Sited up above the level of the river's silt, such settlements offered relatively dry, year-round accommodation within the marshy delta plains, and many of them flourished for centuries, furnished for the most part with the distinctive Naqadan pottery and other imported goods, for there is no native stone or metal in the silty delta. Recent excavations have shown that the settlers had brought the traditional Naqadan technologies of baking and brewing along with them.

Despite the striking scenes of Narmer's Palette, there is no archaeological evidence of a brutal colonization of indigenous populations on the part of these Naqadan settlers; no communal fortifications, no warrior burials. Nor would there have been any strategic or economic reason for such aggression. With the combined populations of both the valley and the delta estimated at a third of a million people, and with a great part of the landscapes of the lower Nile still wild and empty, there was hardly a 'competition for resources' between the two groups. So of the twenty known delta settlements and cemeteries of the Maadi–Buto people, only five had Naqadan farming communities founded on the same site, and all of these appear to have been established after their original inhabitants had either left or, perhaps, had adopted the manners and culture of the southern immigrants.

Nor does violence of itself appear to have been a 'natural' human response to migrants in the ancient Middle East. Excavations at contemporary Uruk settlements built beside more ancient, well-established communities show a variety of passive cultural exchanges taking place over long periods of time. And in the Nile Delta, too, there is modest evidence of similar processes of selection and assimilation between the southerners and the indigenous inhabitants.

Such were the delta's continuing attractions that many of the later pharaohs would pass their lives within it. Harbours and pleasant palaces were erected beside its streams and water-meadows, and temples made of imported stone were decorated with fine statues from Upper Egypt and granite columns floated down the river from Aswan. That the delta's many channels chopped and changed down through the centuries according to the height and rhythms of the annual flood caused the harbours that gave the pharaohs access to the open sea, and were the ancient Mediterranean's entrepôt to Egypt, to silt, to be abandoned and then re-established once again beside another, deeper delta stream. And all the while, within this softly tractable environment, rulers hunted duck and wild bulls amongst the rushes and papyrus plants, and farms and Bronze Age factories flourished. Courtiers and craftsmen, shepherds, cowherds and sailors lived side by side with people from the south Levant, Syria and Crete. And so today the delta's silt preserves a part of ancient Egypt different from that held in the more familiar relics from the valley of the Nile. The delta's evidence, therefore, is complementary rather than additional to the usual sources of information about pharaonic Egypt. These were not the dry and literary environments of ritual and death, but fragments of the domestic, cosmopolitan, day-to-day, caught now in the roots of the spiky grasses that green the delta's dusty mounds or lie beneath sweet-smelling fields of clover, onions, beans and lentils.

A considerable bonus for delta archaeologists is that, in comparison to the Naqadans' southern homelands where only the sparest domestic remains have been excavated, the northern settlements are well preserved within its soft and silty strata. Egyptologists had theorized for centuries about the contents of the fabled delta sites, yet, apart from Flinders Petrie, and a handful of Victorians vainly searching for the 'Cities of the Exodus', there had been more plundering than excavation. Nor is the excavation easy work. The delta's earth is damp and its remains are often frail, so that their successful excavation requires the skills of modern archaeology rather than the sand-shovelling of traditional expeditions. Pioneering work at delta sites was undertaken in the early 1960s by Egyptian and Austrian archaeologists but was halted by the Arab–Israeli wars, and intensive surveys and excavations have only really been under way in more recent times. Hard-won, and sometimes dug down close to the water table, these typically wide and shallow excavations reveal dun-coloured mazes of walls built directly one on top of the other. These are the remains of ancient settlements and towns that today are known by the names of the modern villages which lie close by them: settlements such as Tell el-Farkha, Minshat Abu-Omar, Tell Ibrahim Awad, Tell Hassan Dawud and Tell el-Fara'in – which is ancient Buto – the 'Tell' in several of these names denoting the presence of a hill that is usually of ancient origin.

Such sites, their archaeologists report, show that both indigenes and Naqadans alike had hunted rhinoceros and hippopotami and taken large quantities of fish from the delta's many streams, catfish mostly, and large quantities of fresh-water molluscs. The delta's opulent pasturelands had also supported splendid game, so that the pigs caught by the Naqadan immigrants stood a good six inches higher than those they had hunted in the valley of the Nile. In similar fashion, the immigrants' stocks of cattle, sheep and goats were larger than those within the narrow valley. The southern settlers also harvested the delta's wild grasses and cultivated cereals. Most of the imported flints found in the Naqadan settlements still shine from their contact with stems of ripened wheat. The considerable quantities of husk and other residues of threshing found within the ruins of their settlements, along with the rough-made pottery that the southerners traditionally made for use as bread moulds and beer vats, show that life could have

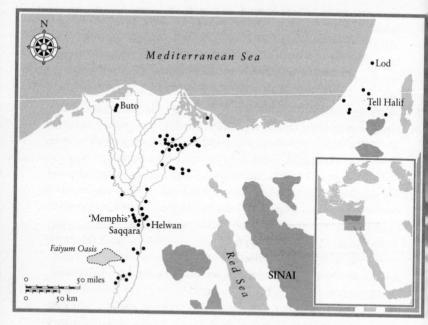

Some of the key settlements of the late Naqadan expansion into the south Levant.

been fairly comfortable. Nor did their tombs' contents differ greatly from those of the southern heartlands, for, though the pottery and stone vessels were sometimes miniaturized, much of their contents had been imported from the south and thus bear the stamp of traditional Naqadan craftsmanship.

INTO THE LEVANT

The Naqadans did not stop at the Nile Delta. Following in the footsteps of the ancient Maadian traders, they also moved into the hinterlands of the south Levant, where the scanty ruins of late Naqadan settlements have been found containing quantities of flint and ceramic storage jars, whose massive mud-silt stoppers still bear the impressions of their sealing, and even, on occasion, a few of the cylinder seals themselves were found close by.

By Narmer's time, there were least twenty of these settlements. Set now within the coastal plains and hills of southern Israel, they were connected to the Nile's eastern delta by the old Maadian trade routes that ran along the Mediterranean littoral, across the top of Sinai and into Palestine. Holding both Naqadan and Levantine wares, some two hundred and fifty caravan stations and small shelters have been identified along this ancient highway that runs up through the Gaza Strip as far north as the Yarkon River close to Tel Aviv.

Three-quarters of the ceramics found in these caravan stations were of Naqadan manufacture, which suggests that the traffic on this route was mostly from the lower Nile. At the same time, though, there was a considerable two-way traffic in ideas. Just as some of the buildings in the Naqadans' Levantine settlements were built in Nile Valley style, so too some contemporary delta settlements show Levantine influence, both in the design of the houses and also in their inhabitants' material possessions.

As with the Naqadans' delta sites, there is no evidence whatever that the Levantine settlers had fought to either take or hold the land on which they had come to live. Quite the reverse. The little site of Nahal Tillah/Tell Halif, for example, on the edges of the south Palestine desert, held both Naqadan and local Levantine wares that had been used side by side within the settlement, with a preponderance in some areas of the settlement of one pottery tradition and of the other in other quarters. Here, then, separate Naqadan and Levantine households had lived side by side within the same community, though with little interchange of pottery between the two different cultures.

Now, the forms of a household's domestic pottery are the means of its daily life, and they reflect its methods of food storage and preparation, the very food its people ate. It would appear, therefore, that different households in these small, close-knit communities were choosing either one tradition or the other, according to their cultural predilection. So, in a statistical analysis of a heap of potsherds, we discover something of the genuine ethnicity of Naqadan culture, traces of a living identity consciously maintained and based on hearth and home, amidst the alien hills of another land, 250 miles from the valley of the Nile.

INTO NUBIA

At this same time and in similar fashion, new Naqadan settlements were established to the south of the Naqadan heartlands, in the region between Edfu and Aswan at the Nile's First Cataract. Here, their fore-fathers had long coexisted with the settlements of Nubian cultures whose centres lay far further south. No borders had ever separated these two distinct communities, who, indeed, had shared common origins, both having originally been peripatetic and travelling with herds of cattle. In previous millennia, indeed, the Nubians' splendid pottery had often been indistinguishable from the products of the Badarian and early Naqadan kilns.

Set leapfrog style along the river-bank, one culture following the other, these various cemeteries and settlements ran south from Hiera-konpolis into a region where the landscape of itself is a variegated forty-mile strip of geological change, from the familiar verticals of the high, white limestone cliffs to the horizontal ridges of rusty sandstone that begin at Gebel Silsila and run southwards to the granite boulders of the First Cataract at Aswan.

Despite the aggressive images in several late Naqadan rock graffiti that were inscribed 200 miles to the south of Aswan at the river's Second Cataract, there is no evidence of Naqadan settlement south of Aswan. Nor, once again, is there any trace of violence or friction between these two different communities, despite the common mod-ern assumption that the rock graffiti hold militaristic significance. So, in a Naqadan cemetery by modern Cairo, a man who was presumably a Nubian was buried in the manner of his people, his grave provided with a traditional roofed burial chamber and marked on the surface of the desert by a distinctive stone circle, in a burial now known, in clunking archaeological parlance, as typical of Nubian 'A Group' cul-ture. And on the Isle of Elephantine at Aswan, at the furthest southern point that was navigable by the wooden long boats, some Naqadan settlers were buried with some of their traditional grave goods, in little hollows that the swirling river had sculpted from the granite rocks.

Though the Naqadan settlers appear to have preferred to use their own distinctive material possessions, the products of their workshops were greatly prized by their southern neighbours. So in the last centuries before King Narmer, some of the largest and most splendid Nubian graves were stocked with Naqadan work of a quality that has only otherwise been found in grand burials at Hierakonpolis and Abydos – goods, it is usually suggested, that were buried along with local Nubian rulers. Excavated by a succession of rescue expeditions mounted at different times throughout the twentieth century, as Lower Nubia was part-flooded by the construction of a number of great dams, these graves held many types of object that had not survived within the Naqadan homelands themselves: some splendid incense burners, for example, one unique piece being decorated with an engraved image of a man enthroned upon a large swing-hulled boat and wearing a White Crown, some pretty little jugs that had been made in the Levant and which may have been used for carrying imported oils, and a singularly beautiful gold-handled mace, whose decoration has an elegance shared only by such images as those on Narmer's Palette.

Such imported treasures have traditionally been viewed as evidence of the growing reach and power of a Naqadan proto-state, a scenario of ambition laden with its own implicit narratives: that, for example, the borders of this proto-state must have been secured by violence, as must access to the 'strategic materials' required to construct such vital elements of supply and control as the Naqadans' great wooden boats.

Yet in the periods both before and after Narmer, Egypt's borders appear to have been largely undefined, and there is no evidence from either Nubia or the Levant that the late Naqadans were caught up in that militaristic mix of avarice and insecurity that has accompanied the foundation of more recent empires. Nor is there evidence of large-scale trade in or stockpiling of strategic materials such as timber or copper. What actually remains, therefore, what can be seen on the ground in Nubia, in the Nile Delta and the south Levant, tokens neither conquest nor control nor exploitation, but a *convivencia*, an amiable exchange of technologies and goods following considerable

Naqadan resettlement. This was a straightforward extension of that age-old continuum of international exchange in exotic products that ran right through the ancient East, a traffic which, as the beads of the Faiyum farmers and the Levantine pottery in the wine cellars of tomb U-j at Abydos both suggest, was based on novelty and delight.

Rather than demonstrating the grim-faced strategic imperatives of an imaginary Naqadan proto-state, the facts on the ground from the centuries before King Narmer show broad movements within various populations with no accompanying evidence of the idea of a national ownership of land, let alone the conscious creation of the boundaries of a kingdom. They show, therefore, that the physical extent of what would later be known as pharaoh's Egypt was first defined by Naqadan settlement and the communication networks that were established at that time, all along the lower Nile.

14

Taking Stock

Ordering and Accounting within the Early State

In Narmer's day, the hub of his new kingdom was the sixty-mile stretch at the narrow ending of the Nile Valley, which, thanks to centuries of immigration, already held more Naqadan graves within it than the ancient burying grounds of Abydos, Hierakonpolis and Naqada combined; a process that would continue unabated during the reigns of the first kings. Just twenty-five miles south of Memphis, for example, the necropolis by the village of Kafr Tarkhan, one of a dozen sites on the west bank of the river, eventually came to hold two thousand graves, while the span of Naqadan cemeteries beside the Cairo suburb of Helwan, directly opposite the site of ancient Memphis, encompasses the largest known burying grounds in all of ancient Egypt, holding at least ten thousand tombs.

Given that these huge cemeteries had probably accommodated the burials of heads of households rather than those of every individual within a community, there is little chance that the fields within that slender strip of river valley could have supplied the produce to support the living communities such graveyard populations would imply. This, however, need not have been a cause of hardship, for in later times, as the cemeteries appear to show, the character of the Naqadans' continuing relocations had changed from the modest emigrations of colonizers settling virgin lands to entire households that were not subsistence farmers, and who would be buried in large tombs along with considerable quantities of manufactured and imported goods.

Coupled with the decline in the number of burials that took place in the great cemeteries of the Naqadan homelands in the final centuries before the coming of the kings, the contents of many of these later tombs suggest that their occupants were participants in various aspects of craft production and supply. This section of Naqadan society, indeed, had long been supported by the farmers and now, more than ever in this narrow strip of land at the valley's ending, had to be sustained by goods and provisions shipped on the river.

The fact that in the generations after Narmer these same cemeteries in the region of Memphis continued to accommodate considerable numbers of people who were not farmers suggests that the households of craftsmen and seal holders – those, that is, involved in tithing and court activities – were moving, lock, stock and barrel, out of the Naqadan heartlands.

Unlike their copious desert graveyards, few of the settlements of these immigrants have yet been excavated. The contemporary accommodations of the Naqadan communities within the Nile Delta, on the other hand, are yet under excavation and these show that, like the settlements within the Memphite region, they too had undergone great change. In earlier times, as we have seen, the Delta Naqadans had lived as they had always done within the river's valley, making modest shelters for their harvests and their families. In the last centuries before the kings, however, as non-farming communities were established in the Memphite region, enormous mud-brick complexes were built within the delta, long, low, four-square architectural compounds on top of the gentle mounds that stood above the water-meadows.

Of a size and quality of build unequalled by any contemporary structures yet excavated in the Naqadan heartlands, these later delta settlements were considerable *fattorie*, with warehouses, threshing yards and slaughterhouses and a complexity of rooms and corridors reminiscent of the temples of the later pharaohs. Here, then, flour was ground and bread was baked, beer was brewed and fodder stored, and animals were raised and butchered. Now, too, so some cylinder seals and other goods from the settlements' larger graves suggest, factors and managers were living alongside the farmers on these delta estates.

Apart from the growing need of the various Memphite communities for continuous supplies of food, these impressive developments within the delta may also have been encouraged by the erratic behaviour of the Nile. In the last centuries before King Narmer some of the annual floods had been so low that temporary buildings erected on the river's flood plain that would usually have been dissolved by the rising floodwaters were preserved, their remains part-buried in ancient, windblown sand. From Hierakonpolis in the south, to the Faiyum and Tell el-Farkha in the eastern Delta, excavators have recorded similar telltale strata; yellow aeolian sands sandwiched between two dark strips of silt, strips that by their very thinness show that in these years the river's flood had been mean and low.

Within the narrow valley, the early parching of the fields caused by such low floods would have stopped the crops growing to maturity. This precipitous desiccation could, however, be slowed by making extra ditches and embankments to retain the receding waters of the inundation within the river's flood plain. This is still done today in river basins in Ethiopia and Senegal, just as Herodotus recounts in his tale of early Memphis. Just such a project, indeed, also appears to have been described in the generations before King Narmer, in a scene cut in low relief upon a giant mace head. This shows a man with the ubiquitous scorpion engraved beside him and wearing what would become the White Crown of Upper Egypt, in the act of opening a water channel with the stroke of a farmer's adze. Though it is hardly proven that this so-called 'Scorpion Mace Head' records an actual event, it is improbable that this unique object, which was found by Quibell and Green in the great cache at Hierakonpolis, does not reflect something of the age in which it had been made.

Broad and flat, the delta plains would have allowed the convenient conservation of such floodwaters as had come down the river in lean years. Barley, too, which unlike wheat tolerates the dry and salty conditions of a drought, was grown in larger quantities; and, as the ancient Egyptian terms for each of the two crops show, it had a different taste from Nile Valley produce. Yet there is also evidence that even the delta harvests in those times were hard-won, for the weak inundations appear to have dropped their silt in some of the delta's slow-flowing streams, part-blocking them and turning water-meadows into swamps which, as some of the bones excavated in contemporary delta cemeteries appear to show, encouraged fevers and malaria. Certainly, the delta farmers of those times were less healthy than their compatriots within the Nile Valley. Slipped discs and other skeletal features show that many of them were working very hard, and that most were dying in their thirties. No wonder that in those last centuries before the kings a great part of the northward movement of the Naqadan population had stopped so abruptly at the valley's ending.

Yet the considerable quantities of bread moulds and brewing vats found in the ruins of the delta estates suggest that the settlers were producing food in larger qualities than subsistence settlements would have required. The presence of seals and storage jars within their cemeteries also suggests that, like the imported wine in tomb U-j at Abydos, their produce was being packaged and controlled. It would appear, therefore, that there were direct and pressing reasons for the establishment of these large, efficient farm estates and that they had continued to supply the ever-growing settlements at the ending of the river's valley in a time of decreasing harvests. That considerable quantities of animals were butchered and cooked within these delta farms further suggests that meats and fats were being shipped as well – in later centuries at least, the Egyptians were adept at storing meat and game in jars, preserved under dripping or honey. At this same time too, though life down on the farm may well have been hard, the graves of some of the seal holders on these large estates were as lavishly equipped as some of the larger contemporary tombs in the cemeteries at the ending of the Nile Valley, which once again suggests direct connection.

Given the absolute dependence of the people settled in the area of Memphis on regular supplies, it is hardly surprising that this unique community developed an obsessive concern with the supply and control of materials and food, an obsession that would dominate the nature and activity of the pharaonic state down to its very ending.

So, in the generations before King Narmer, the mythic city of archaic Memphis may not have been a settlement at all but a gathering of the houses of managers, workers and controllers set beside some shipyards, docks and storage magazines that had been built to develop and maintain Naqadan river traffic, to house and ship the raw materials such as flint and copper that the delta farms required and to store the produce gathered from both the Nile Delta and the river's valley for distribution throughout the Memphite communities. And certainly this narrow landing at the ending of the river's valley has proved a perfect place for such an entrepôt. Just a few miles to the north of ancient Memphis, modern Cairo still serves something of the self-same function.

COUNTING AND ACCOUNTING

With such continuing and pressing reasons for the development of an efficient system of supply, it is hardly surprising that in the last centuries before the coming of the kings, Naqadan culture was, of itself, carefully and deliberately standardized. As Renée Friedman, one of Hierakonpolis's modern excavators, has described, its wonderfully diverse tradition of ceramics now suffered a 'striking and complete loss of regional intervariability'; a remarkable uniformity of the products of the potters' studios all up and down the lower Nile that would remain throughout the best part of pharaonic history.

So the individual ceramic masterpieces traditionally buried with the Naqadan dead quite disappear and are replaced by a small range of utilitarian storage jars that on occasion might be accompanied by a few exquisite dishes and vases cut from desert stone. Clay had become the plastic of the day, the potters making ever larger quantities of wares in ever simpler, regularized shapes. As well as being placed in graves, some of these practical yet still handsome pots were used in Naqadan households. The larger and more robust vessels, designed for the transportation and conservation of a wide range of commodities, were marked with a range of little images such as scorpions, hawks and serekhs – the box-like sign that later came to hold the hieroglyphs of Narmer's name. Like the images engraved upon the ivory tags found in tomb U-j at Abydos, such pot marks may denote some kind of provenance, an owner, a region or the name of an estate. In truth, however, their significance is yet unknown, as is the order and administration of the traffic that they seem to represent.

Yet these powerful little serekh signs are one of the great historical seductions of this last vague age before the coming of the kings.

Serekhs drawn into the wet clay of late Naqadan storage jars excavated in the south Levant, in the eastern Nile Delta, and in the region of Memphis

Swiftly drawn into the clay of storage jars before they were put into a kiln for firing, the image of the serekh is so frequently found on pots and sherds along the valley of the lower Nile, through Nubia and the Levant, that to many modern eyes it appears as if it were a logo of late Naqadan internationalism, the mark of the offices of administrators operating a powerful widespread trading system.

Now the serekh sign, as we have already seen, is an image of a compound or a residence and came to denote, in Narmer's day, the royal name. Buried around 3200 BC, one of the earliest datable examples of a serekh was engraved upon an ivory label in the tomb U-j at Abydos where it may also have signified a kind of residence, as in the time of Narmer, as might indeed a variety of early serekhs drawn on a range of surfaces, from cylinder seals to desert cliffs. That many of these serekhs are topped by images of hawks, just as they would be in later times when they enclosed one of the five names of pharaoh, might suggest that they also denoted some kind of pre-pharaonic bureaucratic entity. The phantom kings of 'Dynasty Zero', indeed, owe their fifteen minutes of prehistoric fame to signs drawn inside some of these prehistoric serekhs. Unfortunately, however, there is little more to any of those phantom kings than these signs upon some pots. Do these early serekhs, therefore, really advertise archaic governments? Or are they simply a kind of branding, as one might mark a sheep or cow or, indeed, a potter's workshop?

With or without such fundamental information, the fact that these early serekhs have been found on late Naqadan storage jars from Nubia to the south Levant and in considerable quantity, makes it difficult to imagine that they are anything other than the debris of a consistent pattern of some kind of trafficking. In the modest settlements of the south Levant, for example, serekh pot marks are as common as they are in excavations in the area of Memphis and are often accompanied by jar sealings impressed with cylinder seals. This further hints that strings of some kind of 'trading posts' were operating within that region.

Whatever the realities of the system may have been – and it is neither necessary nor appropriate to turn these ancient pot marks into an empire run by some archaic entrepreneur – the distribution of these marked and standardized storage jars appears to represent not only a trafficking of goods but also the consistent operation of a common system of accounting. They represent, therefore, a traffic, not only in commodities, but also in ideas. And here at last, and most intriguingly, there are indications that, along with their adoption of Mesopotamian design and imagery – and even the serekh itself has Mesopotamian precedents – the Naqadans had also taken up accounting systems first used in the Gezira and in the Uruk settlements of the Levant.

Though frequently described as 'gaming pieces' or 'unfinished beads', the dozens of pretty little cubes and spheres of semi-precious, semi-polished stones that are often found in excavations at Naqadan sites are equally reminiscent of so-called Mesopotamian 'tokens'. These had been in use for several millennia in the Gezira, where they appear by their quantities and different shapes to have represented a variety of goods and chattels commonly stored in Mesopotamian communities.

Now, at about the same time as the Naqadan expansion, the Mesopotamians had also developed a system by which groups of their traditional tokens were encased in balls of clay to create a physical record of a specific group of goods or chattels which could then be marked on its exterior with the impression of a seal. A somewhat cumbrous form of book-keeping, it was swiftly augmented by another system of accounting in which frameworks of grids were drawn onto small pillows of soft clay. These compartments were then impressed with the shapes of tokens, so that many different groups of goods were recorded together – a muddy spreadsheet, so it has recently been proposed, that was the origin of writing in the Middle East.

Such Mesopotamian grids would have resembled the contemporary grids drawn on sheets of bone and ivory in which the images of the little labels from tomb U-j had been engraved before the individual pieces were snapped apart. The same grid system, with hieroglyphs set into its separate compartments, was also used in some of the first ancient Egyptian tomb reliefs to record lists of tomb offerings. Later, it would be employed to order and contain the accounts of pharaonic temples and a wide range of other records too, from land registers and lists of booty to the accounts of the Memphis shipyards and lists of successive kings.

Another residual trace of this prehistoric traffic in mercantile ideas may well be the ancient Egyptian words for numbers such as 6, 7 and 8, which are Levantine in origin. Though modern scholars consider such terms integral to the language of ancient Egyptian hieroglyphic writing, which they describe as a mix of African and Semitic language groups – a mixture that is, of the ancient languages of northern Africa, of the Levant, Arabia and the Gezira – these Levantine phonetic numerals could well have been introduced along with the Mesopotamian accounting grid centuries before writing was invented or, indeed, before the establishment of kings. Such borrowings, of course, would not have represented a traffic in mathematical abstractions, simply the need in a growing mercantile non-monetary society for a quick and ready method to record groups of objects with a degree of accuracy.

THE ORDER OF THE STATE

Could these faint surviving traces of accounting systems, along with the distribution patterns of the early serekhs, offer genuine evidence of archaic governments that, in the generations before the coming of the kings, established farms within the Nile Delta and set up trading posts within the south Levant?

Though there is no hard evidence of such organizations in the regions of the lower Nile before the appearance of King Narmer, it is scarcely credible that his great grey palette documents their invention. Courtiers and kings did not emerge one morning like monsters from the swamp. They were not natural phenomena but products of ancient Naqadan culture and imagination: like many other of the images on King Narmer's Palette, they were also products of a pre-literary age.

Exactly similar activities to those shown on Narmer's Palette and on other objects that bear his name were certainly taking place long centuries before his time within traditional Naqadan society. At Hierakonpolis, for example, people were being smitten in the manner shown on Narmer's Palette five centuries before the kings, as we have already seen. There is as well a direct link between King Narmer and that most ancient slaughtering yard, the oval court at Hierakonpolis, for objects of Narmer's time were found buried in its floor.

By then, however, Naqadan society had completely changed from that represented in the earlier graves in the Naqadan heartlands. The considerable Naqadan communities that were well established in the region of Memphis were members of societies entirely different from those of their farmer forebears and, in similar fashion, the subsistence farmers who first emigrated to the delta had lived in very different circumstances from those of the estate workers of King Narmer's time. From Aswan to the settlements of the south Levant, all these later Naqadan communities had been joined in a common material culture and in common networks of supply. And so too, they would also have obtained a sense of joint identity that extended well beyond the ancient settlements and culture of the traditional Naqadan heartlands.

This is the age that the Narmer Palette shows us. Not the imaginary creation of an early modern state by force of arms, but a conscious awareness, shared by the officers and craftsmen and the families of King Narmer's court and also, to some extent, by Naqadan communities up and down the Nile, of a brand-new order in society: an awareness that they were part of a cultural entity that was greater than any single settlement, part of a single system, also, that covered the entire valley of the lower Nile and beyond and was controlled by a bureaucracy operating in the name of a single person that today, as he is shown encrowned, we call a king.

The egyptologist John Wilson once famously remarked that ancient Egypt was 'a civilization without cities'. This, perhaps, was not so much a sociological analysis as an intuition formed from the impression of the peripatetic nature of the pharaonic court and from the air of comfortable provincialism that the modern eye so easily detects in many of ancient Egypt's relics. Though they controlled a considerable kingdom, from the little group of standard bearers pictured on Narmer's Palette to the families of nobles in fine linens, with their cats and comfy chairs drawn on the walls of innumerable tomb chapels, the pharaohs and their courtiers seem never to have lost the immediacy of human contact: the atmosphere, indeed, of a parish council that found later literary expression in a host of stories and the simple fiction that the monarchs personally controlled the state's activities.

Underpinning those benign images of government and order, though, beneath that gentle air of feudal domesticity, there was a range of

powerful courtly imperatives that were overseen with such determin-
ation, such intelligence and efficiency, that just a few centuries after
Narmer's time the court could initiate the building of a line of colossal
pyramids.

At the beginning, the dynamos that drove King Narmer's court
were products, and probably, initially, inadvertent products, of the
Naqadans' proclivity for manufactory and travelling, activities that
had first been developed by community potters and metalsmiths, by
carpenters and shipbuilders and all of those professions whose hierar-
chies were derived from the practical imperatives governing their
activities. The master potters, for example, overseeing the provisioning and distribution of their studios, the boat captains controlling
their vessels' voyaging and repair, would all have developed their
individual systems of supply and command within the Naqadan
heartlands. It is this that was extended by processes of immigration so
that, eventually, these archaic networks ran throughout the region of
the lower Nile and into the Levant.

Centuries before King Narmer's time, however – and certainly in
the time of the owner of tomb U-j at Abydos – those fundamental
structures were already being overseen by a secondary level of bureaucracy, which controlled the activities of Naqadan trading networks
and all of the communities' logistic processes beyond the needs of
boatmen, potters and subsistence farmers. This was a professional
hierarchy that was not itself composed of potters, farmers or boatbuilders, but which ensured the continuous supply of tools and
implements to the delta estates and undertook the collection and
delivery of their produce to the communities in the region of Memphis and whose members were themselves buried in the cemeteries of
the Memphite region. Such managers would also have directed the
standardization of Naqadan material culture and ensured deliveries
of wine and desert stone and other exotica as well as provisions and
materials to the shipwrights, the craftsmen and the communities of
Memphis. These managers, therefore, would have controlled the living networks of supply whose traces still survive in mud sealings and
pot marks and in the fragmented records impressed on muddy sealings and engraved on ivory and bone. They may be considered,
therefore, as the seal holders; and, in the times of the first king, as the

surviving sealings found within the tombs still testify, many of these managers were royal courtiers; and some perhaps, were of the families of the king.

Whether or not, in late Naqadan times, these networks of supply were controlled by the phantom princes of 'Dynasty Zero', the serekhs, the hawks and all the other signs that the potters of that age drew on their wares represent, in some way or other, the diversity of networks for which those Naqadan storage jars were made: the same networks into which, around 3000 BC, King Narmer's name was suddenly introduced.

In modern terms, it represents the branding of previously existing systems under a single authority. That Narmer's name appears in greater quantities and in more places than those of all of his supposed predecessors with 'image names' further suggests the integration – the 'unification', even – of many smaller, previously separated networks, a view borne out by the large numbers of monuments and inscriptions made in the time of Narmer's successors, which would further indicate that the supply systems had not previously been in the hands of a single ruler. This, then, was a brand-new order of Naqadan society, an order that the lists of kings engraved upon cylinder seals in the reigns of Narmer's immediate successors tell us began with Narmer's name and received pictorial representation and definition with the objects made in the court workshops.

So the numerous images engraved on stone and bone and ivory that

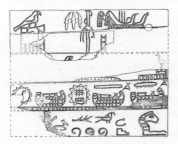 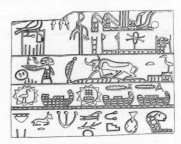

Two ebony labels around 2½ inches high, bearing the name of Aha, Narmer's successor. Each one shows a court enclosure and a shrine, some boats and lists of various goods: the essential offices of the early Egyptian state

show the archaic kings crowned and cloaked and surrounded by an entourage are more than records of events, more even than the lists of tithes that were essential to the existence of their brand-new enterprise. For their depictions of state exchange hold the very essence, the very nature of the state itself, whilst the disposal of the court around the king are realizations of the hierarchy it maintained.

Exactly this same system was literally laid out in hard, clear lines along the Memphis skyline during the reigns of the kings who followed Narmer to the throne, when an impressive row of mud-brick monuments was built to house the graves of some of the kings' closest courtier-officials. These men and women, so the copious collection of seal impressions gathered from such tombs appear to show, controlled both the estates and the flow of goods that supplied the communities living in the regions surrounding Memphis and the households and flotillas of the royal court.

As elaborate and as well built as the contemporary delta *fattorie*, these great tombs held models of the granaries and warehouses, the magazines and storage rooms that many of their owners spent their lives in organizing. Some of them, too, had dozens of life-sized modelled bulls' heads set out in rows around them, each one topped with a pair of horns taken from the herds of animals such as were kept on the great estates. In similar fashion, the tombs' internal chambers were storerooms of produce and supplies and held enormous stocks of wood and flint, of copper tools, thousands of standard sealed storage jars, and meat and bread and grain and a range of other produce. Boats were buried alongside several of these monuments: wooden boats with gently swinging hulls such as supplied the estates with farming implements and shipped their produce to the royal court and to the communities at the ending of the valley.

These great tombs, with their funeral boats and well-filled magazines, their stores of fine stone vases and their domestic treasures of ivory and exotic woods, show that the centralization of the Naqadans' supply systems in the time of Narmer was already creating surpluses of treasure-house proportions. At the same time, however, the great row of skyline tombs still stood in the same relationship to the Memphite settlements as had the modest cemeteries of the early Naqadan communities, as part of the public panoply that established the identity and permanence of the living community and offered a continuing connection between the quick and the dead. Now, though, this ancient Naqadan practice, this advertisement of death and burial, was used to give the royal court identity and afterlife; the royal enterprise, the state itself, a powerful and continuing resonance. In time, these same processes would lead to the construction of the pyramids and they, in turn, defined the very nature of the mature Egyptian state.

15

The Shadows of Birds

Rite and Sacrifice within the Early State

Standing again before the oval of King Narmer's Palette, the museum's case a dark, reflecting mirror, brings us sharply to ourselves. Narmer smites, and the evidence of that same act has been excavated in the flesh from a cemetery five centuries older than the king. Intimate and violent, the same tableau had been drawn time and again before it emerged, iconic, on Narmer's Palette; later, it became a central image of pharaonic culture. It is an image of a killing king. From the beginning of the kingdom, then, the public panoply of death was used by the royal court in the age-old ways, to reinforce the identity and presence of their community. And on Narmer's Palette the king himself literally takes the matter into his own hands.

It is not a subject that most modern visions of old Egypt care to entertain, for it is not a part of the 'ancient Egypt' that seems familiar to us. Even in the years before the First World War, when Narmer's Palette was discovered, most of Quibell and Green's contemporaries had managed to convince themselves, in an extraordinary *volte-face*, that images of death and execution made in the times of the early kings were the province of the savage, as if the qualities of this 'savage', which was of itself an invention of mid-nineteenth-century anthropologists, had governed prehistoric human mentality.

Nor, as we have already seen, is there any evidence that Egypt's so-called unification was a military event. And certainly, the brutal gesture of the king upon the palette is one of formal execution, as practised at Hierakonpolis, and not of war, which, though it was certainly a living issue to archaeologists at the time of Quibell and Green, appears to have been born as a mythology of heroic national armies, with the words of Homer and the Greeks.

After Quibell and Green, the following decades saw the wide adoption of those evolutionary principles of intellectual development so alluringly described by the likes of Freud and Frazer. These held that the 'primitive' – that is, the non-Western mind which, they imagined, was expressed in Narmer's Palette – was the opposite of the scientific mind and close to the world of 'feeling' and to mystical and childish thoughts, where savage passions lurk just beneath the surface. Once again, this was based on the assumption that the behaviour of ancient peoples was similar to that of nineteenth-century tribal communities which had been studied and evaluated by the founding fathers of anthropology – people who often shared the same attitude to their subjects as their colonial administrators and whose view of their subjects has now become a part of intellectual history.

And yet the vision still prevails. Kings like Narmer are portrayed as living in a time when humans were 'closer to nature' than we are today, and Narmer, the first pharaoh, is presented as a primal hero whose killing gesture symbolized the struggle of humanity emerging from the chaos of the primitive world. Thus everything is explained; ancient people were automatons with no facility for thoughtfulness, and all you have to do for their explanation is to find the key with which to wind up their imaginary clockwork. As for the early kings, caught in imaginary wars and forever planning for a mumbo-jumbo afterlife, Narmer's gesture is explained as a method of filling his contemporaries with shock and awe.

Archaeology, on the other hand, shows that most of Narmer's subjects were practical subsistence farmers, who lived lives similar to those led until quite recently by the majority of people on our planet. And certainly, if we today were set down in the conditions in which the Naqadans had lived and thrived, most of us would surely perish. We may usefully conclude, therefore, that, whatever the imagined savageries and superstitions of these 'simple' people, their communities had practical skills and sensitivities that we today have mostly lost.

The Naqadans were as well, inventive and discriminating. By Narmer's time, continuous processes of improvisation over considerable periods of time had already led to the invention of hieroglyphic writing, the initiation of a state-wide bureaucracy and a royal court. And all of that had been the product of an integrated process in which the Naqadans viewed the things that they were engaged in making in terms as practical as the millennial requirements of subsistence farming. And ever since the foundation of the oval court at Hierakonpolis, the organized killing and dismemberment of both animals and people had commanded a great deal of the settlements' resources, a practice that was continued, with some fanfare and in good order, in the times of the first kings.

So a body count of Narmer's Palette provides a list of ten people dead and mutilated and two who are about to die, and, though the scenes on Narmer's giant mace head appear to show but a single vulnerable figure, bound and squatting in a pose that other images suggest is one of execution, the hieroglyph engraved beneath is a tadpole, which, in later hieroglyphic, signifies '10,000'. Other signs, beneath the nearby images of a goat and cow, suggest that they, too, represent considerable numbers. In similar fashion, the scenes of royal assembly on the little picture plaques made in the time of Narmer's successors to the throne show just such slaughterings and executions taking place alongside the presentation of goods and chattels to pharaoh and his court.

More than a hundred of these plaques are known to have survived, though most are now in fragments. Translating some of their numerous signs in the manner of the later hieroglyphs, it would appear that some of their images depict specific events, numbering the years of the reign in which they took place, describing the nature and amounts of the goods received, and sometimes even quantifying the slaughter. That plaques have been found at Naqada and Abydos and several sites within the Memphis region suggests, as we have already seen, that such 'oval court' assemblies were established in many Naqadan settlements other than Hierakonpolis. Some specific details on a few of them, indeed, allow the tentative identification of one of their locations as Buto in the northern Nile Delta, where one picture plaque shows a local shrine with an enclosure standing close to the court of ceremonies. It would appear, therefore, that settlements and estates all along the lower Nile delivered part of their annual yield, alive and dead, to the enthroned figure at the centre of these gatherings, and at that same time people were sometimes stabbed and scalped and maced to death in the old Naqadan ways and that bowls, as the picture plaques occasionally show, were held up to collect their blood.

A 2-inch ebony plaque that was once attached to a jar of oil. It shows the presentation of furniture (?), a statue, a catfish, and other goods to the serekh of King Djer. And in the upper register to the right, a person is plunging a dagger into a victim's chest: it has been suggested that the two seated women in the register are portrayed as being partially scalped

Such insistently recorded butchery brings back to mind the Naqadans' magnificent flint knives. Though fragile, some of the later specimens were designed to accommodate a handle so that they could be grasped in the manner of modern knives and employed for sterner tasks than that of flaying or of slicing meat. A dozen or so of these handles have survived. That they are of polished ivory, decorated on occasion with fine designs and covered with sheets of shining gold, suggests that they were intended for display. That one of then shows rows of bound and kneeling prisoners accompanied by guards on one of its faces and a settlement shrine upon the other, further suggests that some of them, at least, were the tools of human sacrifice.

TITHE AND CEREMONIAL

What makes human sacrifice something deep and sinister anyway? Is it only the suffering of the victim that impresses us in this way? All manner of diseases bring just as much suffering and do not make this impression. No, this deep and sinister aspect is not obvious just from learning the history of the external action, but we impute it from an experience in ourselves.

Ludwig Wittgenstein, after 1938

Taking life at funerals had been common in the Nile Valley from the time of the first farmers. Animals were often killed and buried in the cemeteries, and butchered, cooked and eaten at the grave. By early Naqadan times, it would appear that people, too, were being killed and buried with the dead, for multiple burials are common in the cemeteries of the time and it is difficult otherwise to explain how several bodies could have been simultaneously interred within a single grave without such killings. At the same time, as we have seen, some of the Naqadan dead were dismembered at the time of their funeral, their body parts laid out in careful patterns with the funerary goods. At least five per cent of Naqadan burials, show evidence of *post mortem* butchery.

These deathly dramas appear to have declined from around 3500 BC, when images of wooden boats appear at Hierakonpolis. At this same time there was as well, a growing preoccupation with the protection and physical preservation of the dead throughout the Naqadan heartlands, with increasing numbers of burials placed in coffins and set inside brick-lined burial chambers. Techniques were also introduced that would later be elaborated to become the complex processes of pharaonic mummification. Resin-soaked linen cloths were placed round some of the Naqadan dead to turn flesh and bone into a solid, long-lived image. Now, too, the goods which had traditionally been buried with the dead were changing, the splendid pottery, household goods, plates of food and remnants of cemetery feasts replaced by a few stone vases and provisions, stored, for the most part, in the same types of ceramic jars that the Naqadans were trafficking along the lower Nile and into the Levant.

At Hierakonpolis, the prime locale of the Naqadans' interchange between life and death was moved from the desert cemeteries to the oval court close by the settlements and the river-bank. And it remained in sporadic use down to the time of Narmer.

In those last years, when the settlement that had once surrounded it had moved away and some of the courtyard's installations were covered with wind-blown sand, traces of new-built mud-brick walls and fragments of fine stone vases among the dereliction show that it was restored for the last time. That this work was undertaken to serve some kind of rite or presentation at the oval court is suggested by the findings of the archaeologists who in the 1990s succeeded Michael Hoffman in its excavation; they uncovered a cache of exotic objects made in Narmer's time which had been smashed up and buried in a pit dug in the courtyard floor.

The pottery in this cache was the key to its understanding. Alongside some clever antiquarian imitations of the lustrous black-topped Naqadan wares of earlier ages, and some exceptional pieces imported from the Nile Delta and the south Levant, were sherds of locally made jars whose elaborate forms were similar to those of later hieroglyphs that designate words like 'praise' and 'libation'. Thus, some of the pottery in this rich cache could be identified as an early type of the so-called *hes* vase later used in rituals performed in the great pharaonic temples. A further indication that it was indeed the residue of a rite or ceremony was the presence of a rounded pot whose form had only previously been known from a drawing of just such a vessel shown standing in the forecourt of a shrine: a detail from part of the engravings on Narmer's mace head which was also found at Hierakonpolis, and which had itself formed part of the deposit that contained King Narmer's Palette.

Nor was this the sole connection between the cache of objects from the oval court and the enormous deposit excavated by Quibell and Green. Both locales clearly held the residues of ceremonial or ritual activities, while some of the great mass of objects recovered bore clear comparison to more modest groups of objects since recovered in the excavation of archaic shrines at Abydos, at Aswan and in some of the Naqadans' delta settlements.

Composed of figurines of animals and humans, and made in a variety of materials, these caches were usually accompanied, as they were at Hierakonpolis, by flint knives and incense burners, by *hes* vases and by exotic pots and dishes. All of them, therefore, appear to have been the residues of ritual activities and some, at least, so the images from King Narmer's time quite clearly show, were part of courtly pageantry.

We may imagine, then, by combining the archaeology and the scenes on the picture plaques, a grand flotilla arriving at settlements such as Buto, Naqada or Hierakonpolis and setting up a court inside an especially designated area, where the king was enthroned upon a plinth, and various scenes of tithing, butchery and presentation unfolded underneath him; that vivid mix, in short, that – tempered, sanctified and bejewelled – was the essence of the pharaonic enterprise. Enacted throughout the networks on which King Narmer stamped his name, by their very repetition such awful tableaux must have taken on the qualities of a theatrical or liturgical event.

The first kings would also take the act of killing back into the cemeteries, so that the line of courtly tombs on the horizon of Saqqara and other grand contemporary tombs were framed by rows of smaller graves, the burials of craftsmen and other servants, killed apparently at the time of funeral and buried on occasion, along with herds of bulls, with the gathered wheat and wine from the great estates and with some of the finest products of the royal workshops – exactly that same mix, in fact, which had so enlivened presentations at the living court.

And so the networks of the early state were extended to include the generations of the living and the dead. And the centrality of death and

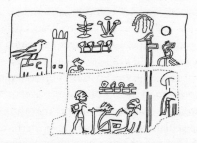

Fragments of two different plaques, one ebony, one ivory, holding drawings of similar courtly locations. The lower fragment also holds an image of an executioner stabbing a victim; typically, he holds up a bowl to catch the spurting blood, in a gesture that is later pictured at the slaughtering of animals

butchery in the Naqadan tradition had continued resonance in pharaonic culture. Death, indeed, came to define its very limits. The pyramids, the tombs of pharaohs, were set on its horizon, and every major temple possessed offering altars and a slaughterhouse. With the delineation of a single, awful gesture, Narmer's craftsmen had encompassed the essentials of pharaonic government.

SACRED AND PROFANE

At first glance, Freud's and Frazer's notions of the 'primitive mind' provide us with a simple explanation of what was really happening within those oval courts: the slaughterer's contact with death, in which his victim stood as intermediary, had transformed him into a magician-priest in direct contact with the dead. So the office of the king, in whose name the slaughterer had worked, became a sacred office, and tithing at the royal court, which ensured the welfare and continuity of the state, was transformed into a sacred ceremonial of offering that ensured a so-called 'cosmic continuity' in a savage and chaotic universe.

In reality, however, there is no evidence at all that rites conducted in the oval courts were undertaken in a religious context, or even that they held some kind of symbolism. Centuries later, when pharaoh's scribes first found a voice, they describe some of these age-old rites and tableaux, and in those writings there are the first literary intimations of the king's divinity. In the silent and archaic age of the first pharaohs, however, before the scribes composed their verses, before the artists of the courts drew kings in company with gods, there are just burials and bones, silent objects, images and architectures, and the sparest traces of a network of tithing and supply operating all along the lower Nile.

Taken all together, this evidence suggests that the early kings were commanding rites that had previously been performed within the oval courts and, earlier still, within Naqadan cemeteries. Rites that were conducted under the heavy halo of real, bloody and emotive dismemberment and death. Rites that reinforced the identity of the archaic court in the same way they had for earlier communities of farmers, at times of funeral.

Nor, in this silent world, should we bother much to differentiate between the sacred and profane. The ancient Egyptians seldom did so; such navel gazing, as a later Egyptian caustically observed, came with the Greeks. As for the subjects of the early kings, their tools and their utensils, their burials and boats, their drawings and their architectures all hold their own intelligence, their own integrity, the imperatives that were the very order of their world. So if a modern definition of religion, or indeed of art, is that it gives meaning to objects beyond the utilitarian, then it is better to leave King Narmer's Palette and the relics of the oval courts and the pyramids and temples of old Egypt outside such discussions. For if such things were made in the conscious service of the sacred, as far as pharaoh's kingdom was concerned it was a necessary sacredness.

And still today in the Egyptian countryside, just as they appear upon the serekhs of the early kings, hungry hawks sit high up on the walls of village stockyards above the butcher's block, and look down upon the living world below with round, unblinking eyes.

Narmer's name and serekh, as drawn upon the large stone mace head

PART THREE

Making a Kingdom
(*3000–2650 BC*)

16

The Serekh Tomb

The Story of the Naqada Mastaba, c. 3000 BC

Driving north from Thebes to Dendera on the west bank road through the narrow desert that lies between the cultivation and the cliffs, it is easy to pass the sprawl of celebrated cemeteries known by the collective name of 'Naqada' without noticing them at all. In a low light, though, in the early morning or at sunset, the shadows of Petrie's excavations stand out across the little desert. Stop, then, and walk through the emptied graveyards, and it is as if his excavation finished yesterday. The gravel mounds raised by Petrie's workmen as they dug the grave pits are still scattered with slivers of white bone, and lying all around are sherds of the fine pottery that first drew Petrie to the site.

In the winter of 1895, as Petrie dug those cemeteries, he knew neither the age nor the identity of the people he was excavating and knowledge of Egypt in the age before the pharaohs was virtually non-existent. Fortified by the discovery of some inscriptions on the granite doorways of a nearby pharaonic temple that had been dedicated to Seth, a god of foreignness and of confusion, Petrie at first thought that he had uncovered the unlettered relics of a previously unknown foreign tribe – a 'New Race', as he called it – that had emigrated to the land of pharaoh. The French prehistorian Jacques de Morgan, however, the director of the government's Service des Antiquités, believed the graves to be prehistoric, and two years after Petrie had finished his excavation, he visited the Naqada cemeteries as part of a general survey of prehistoric sites within the Nile Valley and proved by further excavation that their inhabitants had lived before the age of kings.

Walking just a few miles south of Petrie's cemeteries, de Morgan had first noticed a pattern of low rectangles among the sand dunes, and decided to investigate. Then, as his workmen dug into the enormous, custard-yellow drifts, he found that they were covering great smears of dun-dark, dirty mud-brick dust, the remains of some enormous and utterly enigmatic buildings. Unfortunately, though he had counted the outlines of at least three separate structures on the surface, only one of them still contained the identifiable remnants of a solid building: the lower sections of a massive mud-brick rectangle some thirty yards wide and almost twice as long, with walls some nine feet thick that had been built straight onto the surface of the desert plain.

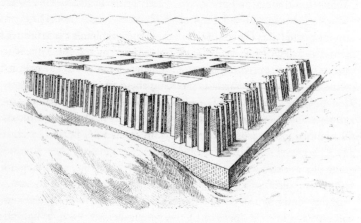

de Morgan's reconstruction of the lower sections of the great brick tomb at Naqada

A strange, slope-sided structure such as no archaeologist had ever seen, with twenty-one internal chambers and no connecting doorways, the building that owed its preservation to an enormous fire which, as de Morgan found some intrusive burials of the second millennium BC, unburnt and interred, set into the ash of its destruction, must have taken place quite early in pharaonic history. Though the great blaze had partly fired the sun-dried building bricks and thus preserved them, at the same time it had burnt so long and so intensely inside the kiln-like structure that most of its original contents had been reduced to ash and clinker. Most of the pottery was distorted and some had been reduced to slag; porphyry had cracked and vitri-fied, limestone calcined and granite granulated, while palettes of fine, hard siltstone from the Wadi Hammamat had split, melted and bubbled in the heat. Apart from a single room that de Morgan found still stacked with sealed storage jars, only tiny fragments of the original contents remained, glistening in the soft ash of the building's burnt-out chambers.

These, though, comprised a unique collection of small objects: a shoal of little fishes, like English eighteenth-century gambling tokens, made of slivers of fine ivory; some tiny flasks most beautifully cut from black obsidian, a glass-like volcanic stone imported from the Yemen or Ethiopia, and polished as highly as the little fish. There were, as well three sets of small, exquisite sculptures – some model lions and hunting dogs of ivory and several three-inch sphinxes cut from rock crystal – which bear comparison with similar pieces that have since been found in other near-contemporary tombs, where they appear to have been pieces of board games that were buried with the dead.

Quantities of ivory labels were also scattered through the building; one of them hinting of considerable amounts of jewellery, of which de Morgan would recover but a single golden bead. Decorated furniture had once been stored within its dark brick magazines, as well. Along with the remains of numerous bone inlays, there were some exquisitely modelled ivories in the shape of bulls' legs that, when tied to wooden frames, were a traditional motif for the legs of beds and chairs. Mixed in with all those tiny treasures, de Morgan found a mass of traditional Naqadan grave accoutrements such as Petrie had recovered from the nearby cemeteries: Naqadan pottery and vases, some gloriously flamboyant flint slaughtering knives, a few Red Sea shells and fish-bones, gazelle horns, faience bracelets and ivory hairpins.

From the outset of his excavation, de Morgan had seen that this great brick magazine with its ruined stores and single central chamber had housed a burial. And yet, despite a plethora of elegant if enigmatic hieroglyphs engraved on ivory and stone and impressed on dozens of clay jar sealings, he could find no indication of the name of the person for whom the tomb was built.

The following year, however, Ludwig Borchardt, the founder of the German Archaeological Institute at Cairo, returned to Naqada to re-survey de Morgan's excavation. An architectural specialist engaged in excavating pyramids, Borchardt had been intrigued by the discovery of prehistoric Egyptian architecture and exasperated by the perfunctory nature of de Morgan's report upon the excavation, which he had entitled the 'Tombeau Royal de Négadah'. So Borchardt reopened the tomb, made detailed plans of its complex brick-work and, in a subsequent analysis of its numerical subtleties, established that the tomb's designers had employed the standard pharaonic measuring unit of a cubit, which at around 1 foot 8.61 inches, is usually described as the length of the human forearm.

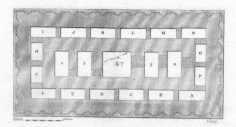

de Morgan's plan of the great tomb at Naqada compared with part of the resurveyed plan of the same monument by Borchardt

Noticing that de Morgan had found a broken picture plaque within the tomb which held a drawing of a serekh-like building containing an image similar to that of a hieroglyph with the phonetic value *men*, Burkhardt published his observations on the tomb as 'Das Grab des Menes', – the tomb, that is, of the legendary Menes. In its time this identification generated a great deal of heat in archaeological journals, but it has since been discarded with the re-examination of seal impressions from the tomb which contain the names of King Aha, Narmer's successor, and a queen, Neithhotep.

More important than these archaeological shenanigans – part of the rivalries between European archaeologists in Egypt which, in the 1890s, were very fierce – was the fact that de Morgan had realized that the contents of the great tomb were directly related to those of the tombs which Petrie had excavated in the nearby prehistoric cemeteries. And just two years later, Petrie, after inspecting the finds from de Morgan's great brick tomb in the storerooms of the Cairo Museum, had seen the same connections, observing that they were of a slightly later period than the majority of objects he had found within the nearby cemeteries. De Morgan then, had found a missing link between prehistory and the pharaohs which, along with the discovery in that same winter season of the great cache at Hierakonpolis, had convinced the usually intransigent Petrie that he had been mistaken and that the cemeteries he had been excavating for several years were in fact 'predynastic', as he now termed them. Indeed, it was during that same year, in the summer of 1899, that Petrie completed the refinement of his sequence dating system that still forms the basis of modern descriptions of the last thousand years of Egyptian prehistory, a sequence that he could now attach to the beginning of the classical histories of the Egyptian pharaohs.

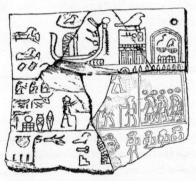

The broken picture plaque from the Naqada tomb in which Borchardt claimed to have found the name 'Menes' in the last sign of the upper register. The fragments in heavy line were excavated and drawn by de Morgan in 1897, the piece in a lighter line was recovered a few years later, during a third re-clearance of the tomb.

URUK IN EGYPT

Might we consider . . . that what we see in the construction of elite graves and royal tombs is the production of ideology in itself . . .

Adam T. Smith, 2007

Just as remarkable as the calcined contents of the great burnt tomb of Naqada was the fact that, as Borchardt realized, the building of itself, its size, its proportions and precisions, represented the beginning of ancient Egyptian monumental architecture. Standing, when it was freshly built, at an estimated height of some thirty feet, it was an entirely unexpected debut, since all four of its gently battered walls had been enlivened by a complex and distinctive design, a pattern composed of series of stepped verticals that between them created sequences of niches. When the sixty-yard-long tomb had stood to its full height, these would have produced a regular repeating pattern of sun and shadow lines, making it stand out dramatically in the desert's flattening glare.

Though the upper sections of the tomb had entirely disappeared, the plan of these elaborate brick niches showed that their original appearance had been the same as the drawing of the serekh hiero-glyph, the sign that showed a royal compound and had denominated and enclosed the names of the first pharaohs. Consequently, the full-sized architectural version of the striped walls that de Morgan found at Naqada is now known as a 'palace façade', more recent excava-tions having shown that the structure shared its distinctive patterning with many other near-contemporary brick-built monuments, most obviously, perhaps, the line of great tombs that stand on the horizon at Saqqara. Later, too, the same pattern would become a staple elem-ent of pharaonic culture and was widely used in various forms in temples and in tombs, where it enlivens everything from the shrines of gods and the sarcophagi of pharaohs to humble coffins and domestic furniture.

Like much of later Naqadan design, this highly distinctive pattern was a local adaption of an Uruk design; specifically, the 'palace façade' which had long been a characteristic architectural ingredient of temples built in the Gezira and the Levant, and which, like the great tombs of Naqada and Saqqara, had also served as storerooms for produce and for precious goods.

Though engravings on Uruk seals made centuries before the build-ing of these mud-brick tombs hold clear images of Mesopotamian temples with serekh-like patterings, it seems unlikely that such tiny images alone would have prompted the introduction of full-blown decorative mud-brick architecture into the valley of the Nile. It is more likely that the sudden appearance of this powerful and idiosyncratic design was a consequence of the so-called 'second wave' of Uruk expansion. This, so recent archaeological analyses suggest, was taking place in the centuries before King Narmer, when impressive buildings with similarly niched façades were being built in settlements in Anatolia and Syria and which, as the presence of some Naqadan pottery and other Nilotic goods that have been found within them would suggest, were in contact with the Naqadan trafficking networks.

Nor were these later Uruk settlements temporary or slight affairs. Habuba Kabira, for example, a Syrian site on the banks of the Euphrates some 600 miles upstream of the city of Uruk, had a population of six to eight thousand people; though large, it was only one of dozens of such colonies. Like the Naqadan trading networks, these settlements had made extensive use of traditional cylinder seals on the mud stoppers of jars, for sealing doors and on the ties of leather bags. And tokens too, those basic elements of Mesopotamian accounting, are not uncommon in these same settlements. From such locations, therefore, wool and other products of the later Neolithic Revolution such as cheese and oils may have been trafficked, and stone, wood and metal sent back to the mother cities on the silty Mesopotamian plains which, like the Nile Delta, were largely lacking such commodities.

Standing like many a contemporary Egyptian site, on a low desert terrace by a river, the colony at Habuba Kabira was enclosed within substantial, elaborately niched walls that ran on for a mile and more. At least one splendid temple stood within the town and that, too, sported similarly niched interior walls. Six miles to the north, at Jebel Aruda, an old indigenous settlement had a similar structure with a near-identical niched façade built at its centre that imitated similar Uruk originals and also had an elaborate series of thick-walled rooms in its interior similar to those de Morgan had excavated in the tomb at Naqada. Travelling Naqadans, therefore, would have seen impressive architectural examples of the serekh pattern at many sites like these. Engravings on an elephant's tusk found in the great cache at Hierakonpolis, indeed, show just such a prospect; carefully drawn images of a series of palace façades with rows of accompanying animals lined up as if for slaughter – though this, of course, could also have represented similar structures built within the valley of the Nile that have long since vanished.

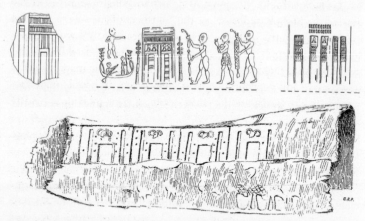

Serekh designs drawn on Uruk seals and upon an engraved elephant tusk from Hierakonpolis

Like the Victorians' appropriation of elements of medieval Venetian architecture to decorate the buildings of nineteenth-century England, the influence of Uruk on the Naqadans was limited to pattern and to style. So, though beautifully bonded brickwork was intrinsic to the form and structure of both Venetian palaces and Uruk temples, the Naqadan bricklayers, like the followers of Ruskin, simply imitated the patterns that the original bondings had produced. Thus, in comparison with the originals, the Naqadan imitations of Uruk façades were as ponderous as the Victorian's mock-Venetian architecture, their builders simply piling up enormous stacks of bricks to produce elephantine facsimiles of a foreign, traditional design that had originally made elegant and economic use of the available materials.

Historians have traditionally concluded that the Naqadans had taken up Uruk's monumental architectural imagery because of exotic connotations of 'prestige' and 'power', and, indeed, Naqadans visiting Habuba Kabira on the Euphrates could hardly have failed to notice the city's mile-long decorated walls. The Naqadans, however, were nothing if not discriminating. Everything that entered the charmed environment of the Nile Valley passed through local filters of choice, rejection and adaptation, a continual process, also, of reinvention that would continue throughout all stages of pharaonic history. Nor did the Naqadans build Mesopotamian fortifications or temples in the time of the first pharaohs, when the courts' craftsmen were engaged in creating a courtly culture, one in which foreign forms were bent to serve local purposes. Just as they had taken over the serekh sign and used it to hold the names of their kings, so they now magnified that same device and appropriated its simple, strong and easily manufactured forms to designate the architecture of their individual courtly culture.

It is unlikely, however, that the great tomb of Naqada was built to house the burial of a king, for the tombs of the first kings have all been found within a single separate cemetery, and they are entirely different. Tombs such as the one de Morgan found at Naqada, as later excavation has confirmed, were a distinct group of monuments, and most of them were built in the region of Memphis, housed officials of the court and were colourfully decorated. Known today as 'mastabas' from an Arabic word for 'bench', most of these great tombs contained the produce and equipment of rich estates, along with little treasure troves of courtly manufactured goods and an elaborate burial chamber.

To that extent, at least, the mastaba at Naqada seems to have been exceptional, for its contents appear to have been far richer in exotic objects than those built in the north. Traditional historians, indeed, speculate that this unique building was made for Queen Neithhotep, who had been born at Naqada of the ruling family and who was married to King Narmer as part of a military coalition and was the mother of King Aha, for Aha's officials, so some of the sealings would appear to show, had overseen her burial. The hard truth, however, is that we have no evidence that, at its beginning, the throne of the pharaonic state was held in dynastic succession, no evidence either of the institutions of marriage or strategic alliance, nor indeed the slightest knowledge of prehistoric politics. Nothing but our modern understanding of the world, and the charred remains of an ancient, burnt-out tomb.

17

A Line of Kings

The First Dynasty Royal Tombs, 3000–2825 BC

> *At Abydos the cliffs, about 800 feet high, come forward and*
> *form a bay about four miles across which is nowhere more*
> *than a couple of miles deep from the cultivation. Along the*
> *edge of this bay stand the temples and the cemeteries of Aby-*
> *dos; while back in the circle of the hills lies the great cemetery*
> *of the founders of Egyptian history . . .*
>
> Flinders Petrie, 1900

King Narmer and his seven immediate successors to the throne were
entombed in a dramatic series of subterranean chambers set into the
desert of Abydos. It is a magic place. An open, four-mile semicircle in
the valley's western cliff that, like those at Thebes and Hierakonpolis,
holds the dust of evening sunset in a golden cloud. Only at Abydos,
though, is there a hidden wadi that runs down from the high plateau
into the valley of the Nile. And sometimes, as you struggle through
the dunes that fill that lonely place, your lungs filled with hot dry air,
the loose sand all around you makes an eerie music, like the sound of
organ pipes.

The royal cemetery was situated on the flat stage at the centre of
this natural amphitheatre, right on the wadi's flood fan. Pitted by
plunderers and excavations, and blurred by drifts of wind-blown
sand, the site was so deeply strewn in ancient bricks and sherds that
the local villagers called it the 'Mother of Pots', the Umm el-Qa'ab.

Here, then, all histories of the pharaonic state begin. Here it was
that the better part of our present knowledge of the first Egyptian
kings was found.

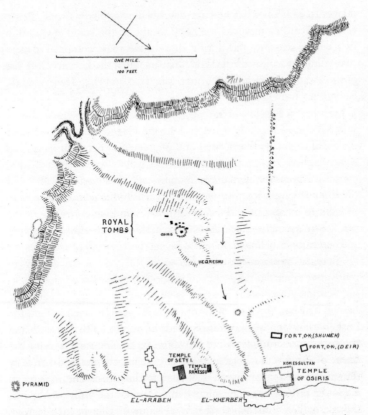

Part of Petrie's map of Abydos, surveyed and drawn in 1900, showing the relative positions of the celebrated temples and the royal tombs in the desert beyond

Petrie went to excavate on the Umm el-Qa'ab in the winter of 1899, following in the footsteps of a French coptologist, Émile Amélineau, and a hundred local workmen who had been ripping through Abydos' ancient cemeteries for the previous three winter seasons, digging up to thirty tombs a day, using some of the ancient wood from the royal burial chambers to fuel the expedition's cooking stoves and on occasion smashing the growing stock of ancient pots and vases to ensure that the perfect objects which Amélineau had selected for the European salerooms would also be unique. Bringing his extraordinary talents to bear on what he later described as a 'piteous ruin', Petrie re-cleared and re-surveyed the royal tombs on the Umm el-Qa'ab in two winter seasons, and during those same years compiled a lucid two-volume account of the work that included the first accurate list of the first eight pharaohs: Narmer, Aha, Djer and Djet; Den, Anedjib, Semerkhet and Qa'a.

Even before Amélineau had visited Abydos, the Umm el-Qa'ab had suffered considerable destruction. Like the Naqada mastaba, most of the royal tombs had been fired and plundered in deep antiquity, and some had been soaked and part-dissolved by floodwaters from the desert gully. The early Christian communities of Upper Egypt had attacked the tombs as well, for they were frightened by the demons that were thought to inhabit such empty pagan places and which, as one of the priests wrote, could be heard screaming in the desert in the winter night.

Then came Amélineau. In truth, his methods were not untypical of his time; his great misfortune was to be followed at Abydos by an innovative genius at the height of his powers who was given to making scathing comments about lesser mortals. At all events, the Frenchman had the pick of what treasures yet remained among the broken tombs, packing crates of goods off to the Cairo Museum and the Parisian salerooms, saving souvenirs for friends and reserving the finest pieces for the Louvre, including a magnificent and perfectly designed five-foot royal stela. Cut from creamy limestone, it bears an elaborate serekh topped by a hawk and contains the image of a snake, the hieroglyph from which the royal name of Djet is part derived. Once this stela had marked the tomb of Narmer's third successor.

One especial treasure that Amélineau collected was a considerable haul of pots and dishes of stone, many of them very small and shaped with the same exquisite care and sensibility that had informed the finest work of the Naqadan potters. Polished to a rare perfection – not, that is, to a mechanical high shine, but to a texture that resembles human skin – enclosed in their museum cases, they still glow with desert colour. Some, too, yet possess their fitments of fine gold; yellow lids as stiff and straight as playing cards and handles made from twisted wires wound prettily around pots cut from blocks of amethyst, serpentine and porphyry, rock crystal and fine breccias; flint, basalts and siltstone and the most beautifully variegated alabasters.

Amélineau, however, worked in haste, and so his workmen only dug up half of the tomb U-j and missed its real treasure: the oldest hieroglyphic imagery that has been found in Egypt. He also missed, as Petrie found to his delight, the lower section of a human arm still garlanded with bracelets. These bracelets are elaborately composed in ridged and rounded beads of gold and polished amethyst, of lapis lazuli and turquoise, some of them cut into the shape of little serekhs, topped by a lively image of a hawk, such as Naqadan craftsmen had made for centuries past. One of Petrie's workmen had seen the severed arm wrapped in ancient linen and jammed between the mud bricks of a burial chamber wall. Hidden, perhaps, by a one-time robber who had not returned to collect his loot, its archaeological dislocation made it impossible to know the tomb from which the arm had come: that a museum curator later threw the bones away along with their linen wrappings has since rendered it impossible to know if the four bracelets had been worn by a woman or a man. And yet the little treasures by themselves provide a glimpse of what once was buried in the Umm el-Qa'ab, especially when it is recalled that, at one time, the royal graveyard had held at least a thousand tombs.

Though earthly treasures pleased the patrons who had subsidized his work, Petrie was not after gold but history, and so the previous ravishment of the site had not discouraged him at all. Over those two long seasons, Petrie later estimated, he and his five co-workers had examined a hundred thousand fine-worked vase fragments and drawn hundreds of fragmented seal impressions, most of which had originated from the bulky, cone-shaped sealings that had closed the open mouths of storage jars. Often more than eighteen inches in diameter and weighing up to fifteen pounds, the varying textures and colours of these sealings, so Petrie noted, suggested that they had been made up and sealed in many different locations. Many, indeed, would appear to bear the names of delta estates, though, in reality, their contemporary meanings remain elusive.

Petrie recovered considerable quantities of other ancient goods as well: a variety of ancient woods, often burnt and splintered and some of it carved so as to resemble woven reeds in the manner of much early furniture. And there were furniture legs as well, in the familiar form of bulls' legs carved in bone and ivory, and copper pans and dishes and mountains of ceramics, mostly fragments of the standard-ized storage jars, some of which bore serekhs with a royal name. Some of the pots still held the remains of animal fat; more rarely, some ele-gant Levantine containers held the remnants of what appear to have been vegetable oils. Such produce was delivered to these tombs in enormous quantities. Petrie said that the sand in parts of the cemetery was still dark and perfumed.

From this colossal wreck, Petrie recovered and registered every-thing he thought of interest, from two perfectly preserved hair-pieces, still with their rows of curls, to tiny fragments of faience and gold foil. And always, and especially, he recorded anything that bore designs or hieroglyphs, and, in these great tombs, they were everywhere; signs for numbers, signifying one and ten, hundreds and thousands; dates and names, the scrambled cursive fragments of the book-keeping and accounts of the court's traffic of supply, were engraved on tiny tags of bone and ivory, impressed on mud seals and scribbled onto the wet clay of new-made storage jars.

As well as this, there were hundreds of other fragments that bore perfect and precisely drawn hieroglyphs. Some, like the stela of King Djet, were arranged in beautifully balanced sets, their individual hier-oglyphs as carefully made as ever they would be in later history. Others, though far smaller, and carved on wood and ivory, on furni-ture and stone dishes, were as precisely made.

There were some lively picture plaques as well, a few of them in fine condition, others smashed to fragments, and all of them drawn with the same clarity and style that would decorate the walls of tombs and temples for the following two thousand years. Scenes of royal smiting, of the kings at oval courts; kings seated on thrones; kings running and overseeing executions. And there were elaborate images of bound-up captives, and people whose carefully recorded appearance, in later ages, would designate them as non-Egyptians.

Yet hardly anything remained intact, and it is impossible today to reconstruct the best part of the objects of which these fragments had once formed a part, a million fragments from a broken treasury. A treasury, however, that in the variety and richness of these remaining splinters shows that in the times of the first pharaohs the quality of craftsmanship was already at the highest level. Fragments, too, that in their richness, tell us that the role of the first kings within their realm was now a world apart from other people.

Fragments of a granite and of a rock crystal bowl – two of the many thousands of such pieces – drawn and part-restored to their original forms by Petrie during his excavations on the Umm el-Qa'ab

RECONSTRUCTING ANCIENT ABYDOS

In 1977, Werner Kaiser, a Munich egyptologist, undertook the re-excavation and conservation of the Umm el-Qa'ab at Abydos, a task that might at first appear to be a thankless one. Yet the techniques of archaeology had greatly changed since Petrie's day and in the richly funded final decades of the twentieth century the necessary resources were available. And so, to date, most of the ten known royal tombs upon the Umm el-Qa'ab have been re-excavated, cleared out and restored, and many of the enormous embankments of sand and chip thrown up by previous excavations, which were still loaded with considerable quantities of ancient things, have been re-examined. And in the process, new swathes of history have been recovered from the pre-serving desert.

In many ways, Kaiser is Petrie's natural successor. In the 1950s, when egyptology was still driven by traditional language studies and there was little interest in pre-literary ages beyond the sporadic excavation of the mastabas at Saqqara, he had undertaken a fundamental reforma-tion and refinement of Petrie's sequence dating system. Later, as director of the German Archaeological Institute in Cairo, while he initiated the reinvestigation of the early royal cemeteries of Abydos, he also oversaw the scientific publication of the prehistoric sites at Maadi, Merimda and Helwan. He also established a long-term excavation on the Isle of Ele-phantine at Aswan, where three thousand years of fascinating provincial archaeology was packed cheek by jowl. And at Abydos, apart from re-investigating the early royal tombs, Petrie's original excavations have been extended into the nearby Naqadan cemeteries. As a result, German archaeologists have recovered a five-century-long sequence of graves, from the modest tombs of early Naqadan times, to the cemetery that includes the tomb U-j, which lies less than a hundred yards from the later royal tombs of the Umm el-Qa'ab.

That King Narmer's tomb, or, at least, the structure at which various loose objects that bear his name were excavated, lies between the cemetery which includes tomb U-j and the later royal tombs, had led to the suggestion that the early cemetery was the burial place of 'pre-dynastic' kings. Narmer's tomb, indeed, is in that same tradition, for it is a simple, thin-walled mud-brick construction, half-buried in the sand. Built in two separate phases, the tomb is composed of two inter-linking pits some twenty-six feet long and lined with rough-plastered, flimsily stacked mud bricks, and roofed, as the remaining impressions made in the drying mud still show, by a ceiling of mats and mud plaster supported by wooden beams laid across the chamber's walls. Close by this modest monument, the German archaeologists recovered some decorated inlays of ivory and bone, one of which bore Narmer's name. They are similar to other pieces found by Amélineau and Petrie, and one day, perhaps, all of them will be reunited and a unique object, a box of ivory and ebony from the grave of Egypt's founding Pharaoh, may be reconstructed.

Many of the thin walls of these early tombs had bowed, and some had collapsed, this in all probability following the rare rainstorms and flash floods that ran down the desert gully. The tomb of Aha, Narmer's successor to the throne, shows the ancient builders' answer to this problem, for here, inside each of the royal burial pits – three large, equal and equidistant rectangles – the royal builders stacked up five layers of stout mud bricks as regularly and massively as they had done at the mastaba at Naqada.

Slowly, then, the pharaohs' burial vaults were transformed from a set of temporary walls into a substantial work of subterranean architecture. And though, in later tombs, the original elements of this design would be elaborated and enlarged, from now on the tomb of Aha was the way they liked it. Its design formed the basis of a pro-

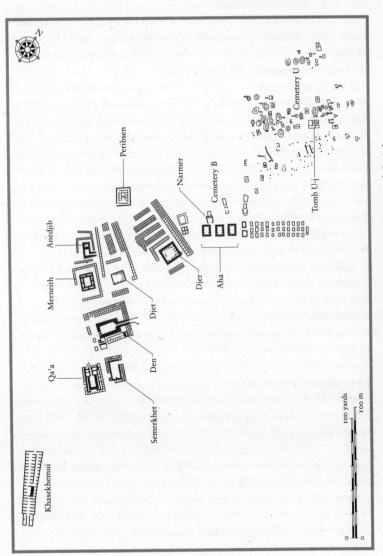

A recent plan of the royal cemeteries at the Umm el-Qa'ab

Khasekhemui

Qa'a

Semerkhet

Den

Djet

Merneith

Anedjib

Peribsen

Narmer

Djer

Aha

Djer

Cemetery B

Cemetery U

Tomb U-j

N

100 yards

100 m

gramme of intelligent and inventive change which would continue in the classical manner of pharaonic culture, throughout the construction of the tombs of his successors.

So, in the royal tombs that followed Aha's on the Umm el-Qa'ab, those three stout chambers were transformed into a series of great, grand burial chambers, some of them more than thirty feet in length, with ceilings supported by joists set up on great brick piers. Reign by reign, the royal crypts were cut ever deeper into the desert, and slowly, too, their interiors took on the appearance of a court, several of them being given floors and walls of wood. One at least had granite paving brought from the cataract at Aswan – the first known use of this material as building stone in Egyptian history. Then too, stairways were made to run down into these burial chambers and stone portcullises were set within them that could be lowered after the burial had taken place. And small side rooms were also built beside these staircases, one of which, at least, had statues set within it; an arrangement reminiscent of some of the tombs made several centuries earlier, in mid-Naqadan times, within the wadi at Hierakonpolis.

The most striking of all of these elaborations were the long lines of little mud-brick chambers built around the central royal tomb, which had held subsidiary burials. Though neither Narmer's tomb nor any of the earlier Naqadan graves appear to have had these satellite cemeteries, King Aha's tomb already had three rows of them; a solemn procession of dark-squared chambers set out in measured lines, whose staring open shapes cut into the soft sand are reminiscent of a modern sculpture. More than thirty of these pits were set into the desert beside King Aha's grave, their occupants accompanied in death by two young lions – not the little crystal sculptures such as were buried in the contemporary Naqada Mastaba, but animals of flesh and bone, killed and buried amid the rows of human graves.

The next royal burial chamber to be built, that of King Djer, had seven trenches set around it, each one with thin brick walls that were, in turn, divided into grid-like cells that made three hundred burial vaults. Though these numbers lessened in the following reigns, subsidiary graves were sometimes placed between the brick piers within the royal burial chambers, and the names of some of the individuals who were buried in them were painted in red paint onto the yellow plastered walls.

Though hardly any bodies from these graves have been examined by modern pathologists, it seems certain that many if not all of the people for whom these little graves were made were killed for burial with the king. It seems unlikely, after all, that a king's tomb would have been reopened after burial, the portcullises raised, the burial chamber penetrated, simply to entomb someone in a subsidiary vault, while the lines of tombs set around the royal graves share common roofs. This would imply that all the burials beneath took place at the same time. Another indication of communal burial is that the names of some of these unfortunates were painted and engraved on various similarly sized stones in groups of images that are so alike in quality and dimensions that these sad memorials appear to have been made at the same time.

There is no evidence, however, that this considerable slaughter was accompanied by acts of ceremony such as are portrayed upon the Narmer Palette. No evidence of smiting or dismemberment of the corpses has been found. From their accompanying inscriptions, the occupants of these little tombs appear to have been courtiers, perhaps, and craftsmen, and members of the royal household. Judging by their names, the majority of them may also have been women. The presence of dried blood in some of the surviving teeth appears to show that some of these unfortunates were strangled before they were placed into their graves; other analyses suggest that, on occasion, poison may have been used.

Unlike the massive mastabas at Saqqara, there is hardly any trace of how the graves on the Umm el-Qa'ab, royal and non-royal alike, were marked upon the surface of the desert beyond a handful of great stone stelae holding the kings' names, which appear to have been set up to mark the presence of their tombs. Small fragments of plastered brick and matting recovered by the German archaeologists suggest that the kings' burial chambers may have been covered by rectangles of sand, mud and matting, in the manner of the largest Naqadan graves at Hierakonpolis. As for the subsidiary tombs, unlike Saqqara, where the little burials that surround the great brick mastabas were usually marked in some way, none of the smaller tombs within the royal cemetery appear to have been marked by even the briefest of external architecture.

A mile from the Umm el-Qa'ab, however, set between the royal cemetery and the ancient settlement that lay beside the cultivated land, first Petrie and later an expedition from the University of Pennsylvania uncovered the foundations of a cluster of massive mud-brick enclosures that give an entirely new dimension to the royal burial arrangements on the Umm el-Qa'ab. Made in the time of the first kings, at 500 feet in length, with walls that, by comparison with better preserved examples built in the following dynasty, had once stood to a height of some 40 feet, the largest known of these enclosures could have accommodated the entire cemetery on the Umm el-Qa'ab. Though others may yet be discovered, the earliest known and, at just 110 feet long and 70 feet wide, the smallest of them appears to have been built in the time of King Aha.

Though modern plans now show these great enclosures clustered side by side, each of them appears to have stood for only a short period of time before it was dismantled, its building materials perhaps incorporated in the nearby enclosures of its successors in the manner of some of the later royal mortuary temples. The seemingly temporary nature of these enclosures suggests that they may have housed activities connected with royal funerals. To the archaeologists' chagrin, however, the excavation and re-excavation of their interiors has yielded very little.

Outside the walls of these enclosures, though, all set in rows like the subsidiary burials on the Umm el-Qa'ab, further burials have been excavated, some of them provided with exotic goods and fine jewellery, others basic and austere, while similar pits even contained the burials of some hard-worked donkeys. And in the 1980s, to everyone's surprise, a fleet of buried boats was found near these enclosures, fourteen yellow-painted craft, each one some seventy feet in length and all of them encased in brick and all of them moored with limestone anchors, in the driest of deserts.

Such evidence suggests that these temporary enclosures were used by the royal court and that the associated burials of people, boats and donkeys were part of a system of supply. For the fact that similar buildings were built two centuries later at Hierakonpolis, a site that never held a pharaoh's grave, shows that these grand enclosures were not specifically designed for royal funerals. Though enormous of themselves, such elephantine constructions made of sun-dried mud

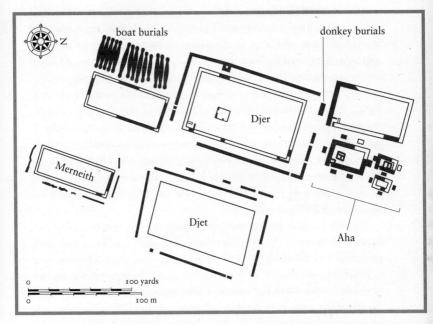

A recent plan of the First Dynasty enclosures at Abydos

brick would not have been a major drain on court resources. Similar arrangements, indeed, may well have been built at various points along the lower Nile to hold the produce of the estates of the delta and of Upper Egypt – arrangements that may well be reflected in later texts, some of which mention the docks and warehouses of Memphis 'of the white walls' while others specifically refer to 'storehouses' in the vicinity of Abydos, a term that is reflected to this day in the local Arabic name for one of these enclosures as the Shunet el-Zebib, 'the raisin storehouse'.

At Abydos, then, beside the royal tombs and far from the court's centre in the region of Memphis, such architectural arrangements may well have served as reception centres in which to stockpile and protect the mass of goods being gathered from all up and down the lower Nile for emplacement in the new-made royal tomb. Certainly, it is precisely such elaborate processes of checking and distribution that are reflected in the mass of scribblings and sealings found within the tombs themselves. Some of the sealings found in the royal tombs, indeed, show that some of these activities were under the control of the same people who were managing the royal estates within the delta and who were themselves buried in the great tombs at Saqqara, close by the dockyards and enclosures that supplied the living court.

Rather than serving the mundane functions of magazines and store-rooms, however, these grand enclosures at Abydos are usually described in traditional histories as being built as theatres to hold as yet undefined and undetected rites which, on the basis of later hiero-glyphic texts, are imagined to have accompanied the first pharaonic burials. Indeed, it is these later texts that still inspire the continued re-investigation of the grand enclosures, as archaeologists search for traces of pharaonic ritual.

Though at first glance these two differing interpretations might appear to be at odds, in reality they need not have been mutually exclusive. In this silent, pre-literary age, however, it would seem more appropriate to proceed, as Wittgenstein once observed, not from cer-tain words, but from the traces of genuine activity. So, leaving aside the primitive superstitions that are often given as the inspiration for such ancient monuments, it is clear that, whatever else it may have represented, this huge gathering of royal burial chambers and enclo-sures and subsidiary burials in the deserts at Abydos was part of the same system of supply, accommodation and provisioning that these kings had overseen in life.

These great enclosures, therefore, could also have served as accom-modation for the living court, and for the tomb makers and craftsmen while they prepared the great tombs to house the royal burial. We may well imagine, therefore, that the internal facilities of these great enclosures were similar to the buildings beside the courts set up throughout the land, that were used for acts of royal ceremonial and for tithing and slaughtering.

Nor should it seem surprising that the death of kings should occupy such a great part of their courts' attention. In life, their very role had been part-defined by death, while the elaborate reactions to the kings' demise was simply and quite logically a continuation of the order and functions of the very culture of the living court.

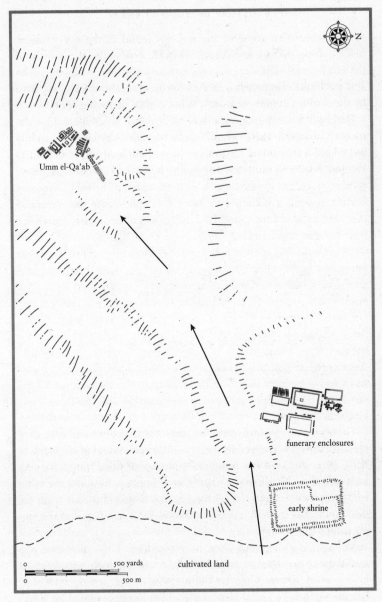

Umm el-Qa'ab

funerary enclosures

early shrine

0   500 yards
0   500 m

cultivated land

First Dynasty Abydos; the recent discoveries at the enclosures and on the Umm el-Qa'ab have been placed upon a section of Petrie's map shown on p. 197

HISTORIES AND KINGS

It was Flinders Petrie who, by comparing the positions and contents of the Abydos tombs with later ancient lists of pharaohs, had first set the eight kings who were buried on the Umm el-Qa'ab in the order of their succession. It was not until Kaiser reopened those earlier excavations after seventy years, however, that the accuracy of Petrie's reconstruction was confirmed with the recovery of two contemporary king lists.

Some of the fragmentary mud seal impressions that list the kings of the first Dynasty, in this instance, the rulers from the reign of Narmer to the time of Queen Merneith and King Den. The hieroglyphs are around a half inch long.

The first of these remarkable documents was gleaned from the partial impressions of a single cylinder seal on five fragments of dark-grey clay which had been used to seal the lids of jars found in the tomb of King Den. One of these, a nondescript chip of dried mud barely an inch high, had been found by Petrie and is now in London; the other four were recovered by the German Archaeological Institute from the tomb itself and are now stored at Abydos. When put together in a single composite drawing they named the first five kings in order of their succession; Narmer, Aha, Djer, Djet and Den, a list to which was added the name of a woman, Merneith, whose tomb had also been set in the royal cemetery of the Umm el-Qa'ab. At just thirty feet in length, Merneith's burial chamber – which Petrie describes as 'finely built and well-made' – had been relatively modest; but Merneith was buried with the panoply of kings and so is usually described, in the

European manner, as a queen regnant. For Merneith, it would appear, had flourished during the first part of the lengthy reign of Den, who, it is assumed, had been too young to reign alone.

The second, larger king list, in which Merneith's name does not appear, was gleaned from a still larger number of impressions, shiny fragments of dried silt that had been so finely sieved as to look like sealing wax. These, it seemed, had been broken from the sealings of some leather bags placed in the tomb of King Qa'a. When the partial impressions of this single seal were put together once again, they were found to list no fewer than eight successive kings, which both confirmed and extended the older, shorter list.

That both these lists start with the name of Narmer showed that, in the times of his near-contemporaries, at least, if not in those of later pharaohs when that name is never mentioned, Narmer was regarded as the first king of the pharaonic state; the man, therefore, that we would consider as its founder.

And yet, however great a warrior or unifier or ritualist this Narmer may have been, one reign by itself cannot represent the establishment of the unique office that the compilers of those two king lists celebrate in their seal engravings.

Such lists, it would appear, were elaborate versions of a contemporary preoccupation, for at this same time many shorter versions were also cut onto a range of fine stone vases, the names of just two or three kings written in different hands, one following another. At the same time, too, this same line of rulers was literally and most obviously advertised in the row of mastabas set on the horizon at Saqqara.

Set out in a wide variety of media, such insistent representations of a line of kings represent a conscious historical awareness of the continuity of the office and an order that, in life and death, was the embodiment of the pharaonic state. Whatever the physical relationship of one pharaoh to his predecessor may have been – and there is as yet, no hard evidence of what that may have been – it was this fundamental concept of a line of kings that enabled the office of the pharaoh itself to take on the aspect of an entity that has existence of itself and which, like Keats's immortal nightingale, was not born for death.

It was at once a novel and an entirely artificial creation. Before those eight named kings, there is hardly any evidence of the conscious cultivation of an historical communal identity along the valley of the lower Nile beyond that which the Naqadan burial parties had left in the cemeteries. With the coming of the kings, however, the culture and continuity of their kingdom would be continuously and most scrupulously defined by generations of court craftsmen, scribes and builders. These lists, therefore, represent nothing less than the invention of a new order and identity within human society. And a great part of that order was forged and held within the narrow valley of the lower Nile, beside the great slow river.

AIGYPTIAKA: MANETHO AND THE DYNASTIES

Not only were the Egyptians conscious of a long history but they tried very seriously to come to terms with it. No Near Eastern society was more meticulous in its record keeping . . .
John Van Seters, 1983

When Petrie had begun his excavations at Abydos in the last year of the nineteenth century, contemporary historians could only describe the entire history of ancient Egypt before the building of the pyramids in a few short pages. Little more was known about the early kingdom than a few ancient, enigmatic king lists and some classical scraps and stories, many of which quoted a Greek text called the *Aigyptiaka*, which is now lost but, as it was generally regarded by classical historians as the soundest of their sources for the ancient history of Egypt, is fragmentarily preserved in their quotations and their comments.

The *Aigyptiaka* appears to have been written in the great library of Alexandria in the third century BC by one Manetho, an Egyptian priest and one of a group of scholars in that learned institution who were compiling histories of the ancient cultures of the pre-classical world. Manetho appears to have been a man on something of a mission: some of the surviving fragments of his work are critical of the considerable errors and inaccuracies he had found in earlier Greek accounts of Egypt. Indeed, he is portrayed as having travelled to

Alexandria from his home town in the delta especially to represent the living ancient culture of his country to the City of the Greeks.

The bits of the *Aigyptiaka* that survive are but a series of tiny narratives laid over a list of kings such as ancient Egyptian scribes had compiled since earliest times. Manetho's history, however, was composed in Greek and written for a Hellenistic audience. So, at the same time that these capsule histories emphasize such traditionally pharaonic concerns as the making of sacred statues and the building of temples, they also present ancient Egypt to the Hellenistic world as a holy kingdom of unfathomable antiquity, as a kingdom of architects and astronomers where medicine and writing were invented; a kingdom gifted by gods, ruled by heroes and attacked by foreigners.

Nonetheless, modern archaeology has shown that the chronological framework of Manetho's history – its lists of rulers – is remarkably accurate. Certainly, the priest read hieroglyphs, which, in his day, had been in use for more than three millennia and would continue to be used on public monuments for six further centuries. So, one of his commentators tells us, Manetho had access to some king lists written out on leather or papyrus, and he probably also used some of the state records that had been inscribed on a variety of stone blocks centuries after the time of the first kings. So, though the *Aigyptiaka* in its present broken form contains errors and obscurities, it yet reflects the historical knowledge of his own country as it was perceived in classical times by an educated patriot and is, therefore, a genuine and touching record of old Egypt.

For egyptologists, however, the overriding contemporary significance of the *Aigyptiaka* is that, for better or worse, Manetho divided the kings of ancient Egypt into successive 'dynasties' a handy jargon that subdivides a succession of 165 major pharaohs into thirty-odd numbered groups of kings, and an innovation for which there appears to have been no precedent at all. Rather than appearing as an alien imposition upon the order of the distant past, however, Manetho's system not only pinpoints disturbed periods of rapid change in which his 'dynasties' come and go in very quick succession, but also reflects several long-lived familial lines that are known from other sources to have held the throne of Egypt for considerable periods of time. Manetho's scheme, therefore, appears to have been a genuine historical perception of the order and succession of the ancient kings. And it is certainly a very great convenience. So, though many of Manetho's dynasties may not have been dynasties in the sense that we would use that word today, they are universally employed, for as Rector Rollin, the eighteenth-century historian of ancient Egypt, observes, they help us to avoid a 'confusion of the times'.

The name of Djet engraved upon a vase fragment from the Umm el Qa'ab; the original is an inch and a half high

18

The Lost Dynasty

Fake Histories, Real Lives: Dynasty Two,
2825–2675 BC

The appearance, at around 3000 BC, of a dynasty of eight named kings one following the other might, at first, appear to signal the ending of Egyptian prehistory. After a century and a half, however, this regular royal lineage disappears.

It is as if the history of the newly founded kingdom had run into an Alpine tunnel and emerged in an entirely different landscape. At the tunnel's entrance stands the First Dynasty of kings, all named and buried in good order in their subterranean cemetery at Abydos, surrounded by the graves of murdered court officials. At the tunnel's exit, however, at the beginning of the Third Dynasty, human sacrifice at royal burials had stopped, the classical ancient Egyptian courtly arts were at a peak of excellence, and the state bureaucracy was embarking on the construction of the first Egyptian pyramid, a free-standing structure some two hundred feet high entirely made from blocks of stone whose manufacture had employed more than a thousand people. Thus, in that dark tunnel, Narmer's Naqadan principate had been transformed into the kingdom of the pharaohs.

Most ancient history is pieced together from flashes of information that light up the landscapes of the distant past like the flashes of a thunderstorm. There is but precious little left to illuminate the life and times of the early pharaohs, however, and the period known as the Second Dynasty is especially dark. Evidence of its court and kings is presently contained within a few partial and broken monuments and a mass of brief ambiguous descriptions. Most of the monarchs of the time are little more than names, there is no firm chronology of their succession and thus the landscapes of traditional history cannot be established.

In great part, this hiatus is due to the fact that most of the kings of the Second Dynasty abandoned the royal burial ground at Abydos and moved their cemetery up onto the plateau of Saqqara, the great wide desert plain which became the greatest courtly cemetery of ancient Egypt. So the royal tombs of this elusive dynasty were swept away by later builders, and all that now remains of them are some corridors excavated in the rock beneath the desert, a half-dozen mazes with slope-sided storerooms set around some central chambers that may once have held the royal burials. Empty, or still awaiting excavation, and often lying underneath later tombs and chapels, even the names of some of the kings for whom these subterranean apartments appear to have been made are as yet unknown.

No tombs, no history. For, in the supply economy of the early ancient Egyptian court, building tombs and their accompanying architecture in the preserving landscapes of the valley's deserts now represents the best part of the early courts' activities. So traditional historians are forced to compile their king lists from much later sources, some royal names engraved on bowls and dishes, a handful of seal impressions, and a list of three kings scratched one after the other on the shoulder of a little granite statue. For just two named rulers of this vague period had funerary monuments made on their behalf on the Umm el-Qa'ab at Abydos, and thus their names achieve a kind of substance.

And so, it would appear that, halfway through the Second Dynasty, the builders of one of these pharaohs, a certain King Peribsen, cut a rather modest rectangular burial chamber close to the tombs of the First Dynasty of kings and lined it in the traditional way, with sun-dried mud brick. At the ending of this hidden dynasty, the court builders of another king, one Khasekhemui, followed the same pattern, building a similarly unpretentious chamber to which was later added a long line of storerooms that appear to reproduce in mud brick the arrangements of the rock-cut magazines of the near-contemporary Saqqara tombs.

Khasekhemui's tomb, however, suffered heavy damage in the king's own lifetime. Excavated in the desert's underlying gravels, the tomb chamber and storerooms had been set into a long, wide trench which soon served as a conduit for a flash flood which had washed down from the high desert, part-dissolving and greatly weakening the tomb's sun-dried mud bricks. So the royal workforce had returned to buttress the sodden walls and also to rebuild the royal burial chamber in limestone, in the manner of the Saqqara tombs. Here, though, unlike Saqqara, there was no underlying rock within easy reach, so the builders imported blocks of quarried stone to remake the royal burial chamber – and built the first known stone-block structure in all Egypt.

As the last king to build a tomb on the Umm el-Qa'ab, Khasekhemui's accompanying brick enclosure down on the plain below was not dismantled like its predecessors, and so it still survives. Set alongside the foundations of the earlier enclosures and the largest of them all, it is a dramatic, dark, imposing structure with two buttressed, battered and part-plastered enclosing walls some sixteen feet thick and more than thirty-five feet high, two framing rectangles set one inside the other, enclosing an area the size of a football pitch.

In common with the other earlier enclosures, archaeologists have found scant evidence of contemporary structures inside Khasekhemui's enclosure. At Hierakonpolis, however, the similarly massive building which was also built during Khasekhemui's reign, the so-called 'fort' of Hierakonpolis, was found to hold the remains of formal architecture, parts of which had been made of blocks of granite. Some of these blocks were decorated with reliefs holding both the royal name and some groups of figures that are similar to, though larger and more formal than those drawn on the little picture plaques.

That there are no traces of a royal burial of this period at Hierakonpolis underlines the fact that these grand enclosures were not made exclusively for royal funerals. Along with the recent discovery of near contemporary ceremonial activity within the nearby oval court and the cache of objects found by Quibell and Green, some of which bear Khasekhemui's name, the 'fort' stands as physical evidence of a continuing royal progress of tithing and appearance through the ancient kingdom, a progress in which the great enclosure served as focus and enduring testimony of the royal presence at the settlement.

Such architectural enterprises during Khasekhemui's reign may also have included a rough stone-walled enclosure which still stands in the desert at Saqqara, for pottery found at the site was made at about the time he ruled. Almost a third of a mile long, this largely buried and highly enigmatic rectangle in the desert is further evidence of the enlarging royal building programme that was taking place. It is, as well, a powerful indicator of the growing efficiency of the court's supply system during the late Second Dynasty, part of an economic history that is underlined by Petrie's discovery of some jar sealings in Khasekhemui's tomb on the Umm el-Qa'ab, which show that a part at least of the king's burial goods were installed by the officials of King Djoser, his successor – for whom the first Egyptian pyramid was built.

LET ME CALL YOU SWEETHEART?

How, then, to recover a coherent courtly narrative for the Second Dynasty of kings? Traditionally, egyptological histories have been compiled, as the great egyptologist Sir Alan Gardiner described, from 'an avowedly philological point of view'; that is, from inscribed papyri and inscriptions. That so few texts exist from the period of the early dynasties, however, has left traditional historians to shift as best they can, 'translating' such signs and objects as have survived as if they held the meanings of the later hieroglyphs.

In similar fashion, a group of signs drawn on some fragments found by the tomb close to that of Aha on the Umm el-Qa'ab were translated as 'sweetheart', a common popular term at the time of Petrie's excavations. Working on the assumption that the signs may also have been a name, Petrie and his co-workers proposed that it had belonged to one of Aha's daughters, and they formally transcribed it as 'Berner-ib': more recently, as you might imagine, Aha's sweetheart has also been described as a concubine or queen.

Yet there is no firm indication that the signs which make up Sweetheart's name were in fact a name at all. Sweetheart, indeed, which has been recently rendered as 'one who is pleasant at heart', could just as well be an official title, a royal epithet or none of the above, and there is nothing that would indicate Sweetheart's sex.

Nonetheless, the narratives that such 'translations' imply can spin most wondrous tales. Take King Peribsen, for example. Impressions on jar sealings found at his Abydos tomb show the royal serekh topped, not by the usual hawk, but by a monstrous beast that egyptologists describe as the 'Seth Animal' and identify as a manifestation of the state god of that same name. Now, in tales of the later religion, Seth appears as the rapist and uncle of Horus and the murderer of his own brother, Osiris. Could it not be that such disturbing stories – in the course of which Seth assumes the form of a black pig, and tears out young Horus' eye, who in turn castrates him – reflect more earthly struggles in this 'primitive' age? Or, alternatively, was poor Peribsen a 'fervent worshipper' of the evil Seth, as several other historians suggest?

Such speculations are underpinned by the common assumption that sudden gaps in courtly history like those presently afflicting the Second Dynasty were the product of civic violence, a view encouraged in this instance by some other sealings from Peribsen's tomb bearing a word that may mean 'tribute' or perhaps, 'the conqueror'. Peribsen's name is rarely found in excavations as far north as Saqqara, and this has further suggested that he ruled only in the south – hence, therefore, his tomb is at Abydos rather than Saqqara with the other kings of his time. In similar vein, the fact that the Seth Animal on some of Peribsen's sealings may be named as 'Ash', a name that has connection with Libyan deities associated with Seth, even provides him with an invading international enemy to fight, for Seth, after all, was the sometime god of foreigners!

Like all good fantasies, it all ends happily enough; on this occasion at Byblos in the Lebanon, where, according to another legend, the murdered body of Osiris fetched up on the beach, and where, in the 1920s, French archaeologists excavated some fragments of a stone vase showing Horus and Seth standing peaceably together on top of a single serekh which contains the name of Khasekhemui – a sure sign that, in this delirious maze of myth and mistranslation, peace had broken out within the warring dynasty, that Upper and Lower Pharaoh Land had been united once again, and, as an extra bonus, that Khasekhemui had revived trading missions to the Levant! Huge histories built upon the thinnest evidence.

FROM ANTHROPONOMY TO HISTORY

As the oldest, richest and most successful of all ancient cultures, the pharaonic state had a remarkable reputation throughout the later ancient world. Thus, in the Old Testament, the land of Egypt is shown as the home of a uniquely splendid court with much wealth and powerful mystery, a pungent biblical description that has influenced the order and the role of Western governments down to this day. And so, with crowns and kings, with fighters, sweethearts and defenders, we conjure easy stories about boy princes and heroic queens, warring generals and wily priests. Such stories gain acceptance as a kind of truth because they provide comfy pedigrees, pseudo-scientific prefigurations even, of standard roles within our own society. Those qualities, indeed, that are frequently attributed to 'human nature'. And so the shattered relics of old Egypt become shards of a mirror in which we glimpse phantoms of ourselves playing stories from our childhoods.

Specifically, as far as the history of the Second Dynasty is concerned, dubious affirmation of such tales is built on two assumptions: first, that the seven hundred-odd known inscriptions of the period reflect an ancient court of biblical complexity, and secondly that, though the means of indicating grammar had not yet been invented, all that is required to help those stuttering scribes to tell their tales is to fill the gaps between their images with prepositions.

Yet the images and signs that have survived from the period of the Second Dynasty were not fragments of a system intended to imitate speech or written narrative. Just as the earliest identifiable hieroglyphs are those signifying numbers, so too the labels, seals and pottery on which the later hieroglyphic images are preserved show that their uses were still restricted to a narrow range of functions within the court's network of supply. They record ownership, checking, accounting and describing the quantities and qualities of things. It would take several centuries for some of these same images to be selected and then be set within the grammatical structures of hieroglyphic texts. To their contemporaries, the combined meanings of these early signs were comprehensible only in the context of the living system of which they were a part; the system that was itself the 'grammar'.

Thus, though these archaic signs and images hold a highly restricted range of meanings, they promise histories way beyond the traditional narratives of Western historians. These fragments of an archaic information system, these early signs of patterning and quantifying, are the inadvertent records of a rising order in the early state, the early history of a powerful system of supply that eventually enabled the building of the pyramids, and fuelled and financed the mature pharaonic state.

Right from the time of the tomb U-j at Abydos, where the signs and numbers seem only to identify the amount of goods and, perhaps, some elements of their origins, this is a history of elaboration and enlargement. It manifests itself in more complex records like those on Narmer's mace head and the picture plaques of the First Dynasty, documents that not only named and numbered tithes and offerings but also record the year, the place and the occasion on which the goods were taken into the royal court. Here, then, in the First Dynasty of kings, centuries-old accounting methods had been adapted to record data within a living system, so that they are capable of listing events in passing time and of transmitting unique sets of information from one generation to the next; taken together, they record patterns of trafficking and tithing down through generations and are, therefore, a genuine recorded narrative compiled without the aid of abstract or literary conceptions.

So though the surviving lists of images and words made in the first two dynasties may not tell us who Aha's sweetheart really was, nor recount soapy tales of harems, marriages or wars, they can inform us of a fundamental development in human history. For these scant inscriptions are the first known records of specific events in passing time. History itself was born within the early offices of the pharaonic state.

ASWAN 1 – 2 – 3

A Hollywood of wars or times of mellow fruitfulness? Whatever else was taking place at the court of the Second Dynasty of kings, it is clear that the fundamental institutions of pharaonic government, its systems of supply, not only survived throughout that century and a half, but flourished to the extent that, when the kings emerge into the light of history again with the pyramid builders of the Third Dynasty, the state on the lower Nile was more efficient than it had ever been: that there was, therefore, strong institutional continuity.

Hard evidence of this, indeed, which contradicts the usual gloomy rumours of the history of the period, has been found in recent years, in excavations undertaken all over Egypt, from Aswan in the south to Helwan and the delta in the north. At Aswan especially, ongoing excavations on the granite outcrop of the cataract, provide a marvellous microcosm of the times, and, indeed, of day-to-day life throughout the period of the first three dynasties.

Aswan always was 'stone city'. Though the ancient Egyptians took a variety of stone from other sources, the finest quartzite and best part of the red and black granite used by ancient Egyptian builders and sculptors of all periods came from Aswan. Plentiful and of consistent quality, Aswan stone was shipped along the river to all parts of the ancient kingdom.

As an organized state enterprise, the quarrying of Aswan granite seems to have started in the reigns that followed Narmer, when the hard, red stone had first been used as an element in royal architecture and boulders lying close to the river were shipped downstream to the royal building sites. So several speckled spears of grey Aswan granite were erected on the Umm el-Qa'ab at Abydos which identified the kings within the tombs beneath, the royal names pounded into their shining, water-rounded surfaces. Three centuries later, some of the fifty-ton granite blocks used in the interior of the Great Pyramid would still have similarly water-rounded surfaces. In yet later centuries, however, when all the stone suitable for use in building had been taken from the riverside, the quarries were moved half a mile and more back, into the hills of the granite outcrop with their broad, near-perfect horizontal seams of rock. And there it was that the great obelisks and the granite colossi of the pharaohs were extracted, from sites that are still filled with the millennial dust and chips of lives passed in the quarrying of hard stone.

With its cascading bougainvillea, grand hotels and white feluccas, modern Aswan is not as it once was. Calmed now by two great dams, the last and largest of which now forms the city's southern horizon, the river's flow is slow and low around the year. In ancient times, however, the annual flood had run so high, so full and fast and overwhelmingly, that the cataract had been impassable in certain months – the so-called 'autumn boats' of ancient texts perhaps describing craft adapted to shoot those rapids in such times. In those days, too, the granite islands that now stand high and dusty in the slow-flowing stream were but a scattering of rounded rocks and boulders, lying on the belly of a white-water cataract.

Judging by the pottery they left behind, the Naqadans had lived in small settlements set on the river-bank between Hierakonpolis and Aswan alongside the settlements of their Nubian contemporaries. At Aswan, too, though the granite islands were mostly inundated by the annual flood, a small Naqadan settlement was established on a little outcrop at the ending of the white-water, where the river had begun to widen out again to fill the centre of the valley. Here, then, on the southern part of what is now the Isle of Elephantine, they set up reed huts in some strips of river silt which had been caught between the granite boulders. And they buried their dead close by, some of them in nicely rounded sink holes carved by the fast-flowing river, so that eventually archaeologists found fragments of their bones and burial goods broken up and water-rounded, like pebbles in a stream.

Though they fished and, in the traditional way, kept herds of cows, it is unlikely that even this modest settlement could have supported itself on its granite island, where there was precious little vegetation other than that which grew upon a few narrow, silty beaches. One may imagine, then, that the plain of silt the surging river had dropped in the lee of the granite outcrop and which now accommodates the modern city of Aswan, served as their pasturelands, where animals were grazed and grain was cultivated.

By the middle of the fourth millennium BC, when the Naqadans had begun to sail the river in large, wooden boats, the islanders were using some of the decorated pottery imported from the Naqadan heartlands. At the same time, they also used the products of Nubian potters, whose wares were common in the settlement. Then, in the last centuries before the kings, a large rectangular building made of sun-dried mud brick was erected at the middle of the settlement. Some twenty-four feet long and slightly less than half as wide, the building shared the same proportions as some of those which were being erected in the Nile Delta at that time. And, just as those new buildings in the northern settlements had done, the appearance of this structure signals the beginning of a transformation of the island settlement, from a gathering of the random accommodations of subsistence fishermen and farmers to a measured colonization. And at this same time, fragments of the storage and transportation jars that had become the currency of the Naqadan supply networks start to appear.

Unlike the contemporary delta estates, this development could hardly have been concerned with agricultural production; these colonists, it would appear, had come south to Aswan, to this island in the river's stream, to harvest stone. That, too, is the message of a simple kiln of the same period that was constructed in the colony, which, though it may have been used for firing pottery, could also have been employed for smelting copper or casting copper tools and so aid in stone extraction and the maintenance of the Naqadan networks of boats and barges.

In the mid-First Dynasty, at around the same time that granite pavements were being introduced into the royal tombs at Abydos, a massive seventy-yard-square enclosure built of stacked and bonded brick with high, battered walls was built upon the island's northern end. Made in the manner of the architecture of the great contemporary tombs, it was set straight onto the granite boulders and sited so that a tiny beach sheltered by some enormous water-rounded boulders could serve as a quay. With fifteen-feet-thick walls, a grand entrance doorway and an impressive line of semicircular bastions along its sides, the building's plan is reminiscent of some of the fortress-like images carved upon the siltstone palettes: later in pharaonic history, Aswan's name would be signified by a similar hieroglyph.

An image of a storehouse engraved upon the Narmer Palette

There is no archaeological evidence, however, within this considerable ruin, of the presence of a military garrison; nor indeed of any conflict or destruction at the site. Like so many of the splendid architectures of later periods of ancient history that are identified as fortresses, the structure appears to have embodied the resources and the order of the state, at once powerful and protective, in much the same way as the enclosures and great tombs at Saqqara and Abydos.

This architecture, though, was for the living. That it was set directly and without regard over the flimsy dwellings of the earlier settlement – the fortress's western wall cut over and across the entrance of an ancient shrine – also signals the blunt intrusion of external authority into an established community; a feature that once again it shares with several other contemporary buildings in the Nile Valley and in the delta. At Aswan, however, and uniquely, it not only marks the southernmost extent of the pharaonic transport network but, as the debris of their workshops implies, the establishment of a state settlement in which families of craftsmen worked hard stone. Both the products of these workshops and the stores that kept the craftsmen and their families supplied with grain and copper, food and tools, seem to have been held inside the fortress's imponent walls.

By the mid-Second Dynasty, so its German archaeologists have shown, the size of the island fortress had been doubled, a wall and tower having been added to its entrance gate and two further walls built out from the fortress's northern end, to run some eighty yards down along the edges of the narrowing island and meet at its tip. Inside this new-made triangle of space, the walls enclosed a series of simple mud-brick dwellings all laid out within a carefully measured grid, just as many later pharaonic building projects would be throughout the following millennia. On Elephantine, the grid held just two rows of houses with at least twenty family plots in them, each one a little over sixteen and a half feet wide and twice as deep; or, as the state's contemporary surveyors would have expressed it, in the traditional units that were related to the human forearm, plots that were eleven cubits wide and some twenty-two cubits deep.

As well as houses, this grid also accommodated at least six communal spaces, the largest of which was about 150 square feet whilst others were so small that they could only have served as grain bins or cupboards. Some of these spaces were roofed, others left as open yards. Inside the individual housing units, though each of them shared common dividing walls, every one was of a different plan. Those rooms with small windows that were open to the river's evening breezes may have been used as bedrooms; others, with little baking ovens, were clearly kitchens, and there were also animal stalls and storage areas. Most were less than six feet high, though many of the housing units also had upper storeys built against the fortress's inner walls. As Aswan is close to the Tropic of Cancer, we may well imagine that the families, who, from the size of the housing grid, could have consisted of three generations at most, sometimes slept up on the open roof.

Such well-regulated communities – and in later ages many more of them would be built up and down the Nile – lived cheek by jowl, so close, indeed, that the narrow passages which gave access to the various family dwellings were set inside the individual housing units. Here, then, public and private spaces were undifferentiated and people would have brushed by one another as they moved around the settlement or indeed from room to room within an individual unit. So the settlement would probably have appeared as one large dwelling, its external appearance not unlike that of large traditional Upper Egyptian houses of the recent past. And the ancient island families used both wind and shade in individual and clever ways, just like their modern counterparts, and with a similar understanding of the excellent insulation afforded by mud architecture.

Like the earlier Naqadan settlement on the same site, this imported community of at least twenty nuclear families living within the First Dynasty fortress could hardly have been supported from the natural resources of the little island. We may imagine, therefore, that though the river gave them fish and the nearby fields continued to provide grain and cattle pasturage that, as the copious fragments of the large state storage jars suggest, the foursquare settlement was part-provisioned by the supply systems of the royal court. At all events, the settlement certainly thrived, for after a century or more, at some point in the Third Dynasty, another complex of rather larger, stout-walled dwellings was set up just 130 yards away, on another island, close to the centre of the river's stream.

Today, both these little islands form part of the southern tip of the modern Isle of Elephantine, for they have been joined together by silt

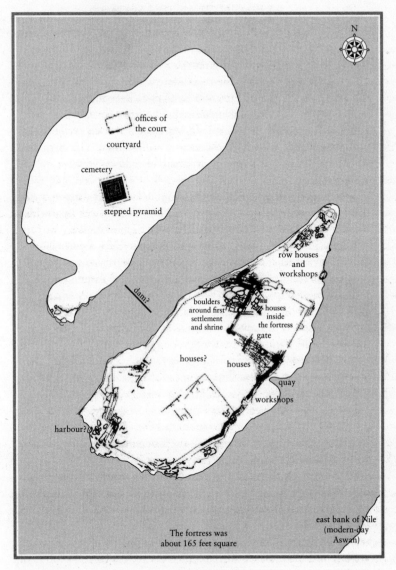

The Naqadan settlement and its subsequent enlargements upon two ancient islands in the Nile at Aswan. The section of the east bank of the Nile shown at the bottom right is now in the grounds of the Cataract Hotel

brought down in the floods of later centuries. In the Third Dynasty, however, they were still apart, and the settlement on the second island, which had been built directly on the rock, was being changed and adapted as circumstances required. Here it was, at the beginning of the next dynasty, that one of these buildings was reduced to dust and rubble and buried within a higher, wider floor, a process which, as its German excavators discovered, had protected the debris of earlier occupation and, with it, a treasury of information. For here they found a mass of seal impressions, many of them in coarse clay and broken from the ties of bags and the lids of pottery jars, and other smaller and more delicate sealings that had closed long-vanished sheets of papyrus, a common enough writing medium that has entirely disappeared from the archaeological record of those times.

Taken all together, the hieroglyphs on these rare scraps showed that, in the time before the room had been demolished, its occupants had been in contact with the officials at the court of at least one Third Dynasty monarch – part of a process of communication and supply that, as the tens of thousands of bread moulds found in the surrounding area implied, was part concerned with the provisioning of the fortress families and the supply of granite to the court.

This demolished building, then, appears to have been a Third Dynasty administrative centre, a government office set up within a colony, which, like the delta estates, had been a place where goods and supplies had been handled in large quantities. Here, state officials had controlled the delivery and dispatch of comestibles and presumably, at Aswan, the shipping of the dull-red stone that the court builders were using in increasing quantities.

Such excavations – and there are several others in Egypt, though none that have yielded such richness of detail as those at Aswan – show something of the realities of life within the tunnel of the Second Dynasty. They show, too, that, though the order of the pharaohs remains unknown, the period had been a time of continuity and growth. Indeed, it was a time in which the craftsmen and officers of the royal court were still engaged in transforming the realm of Narmer and his successors, a world of farmers, boat captains and estate managers, into the mighty state machine that would construct the pyramids of ancient Egypt.

19

The Wheeling Hawk

Refining Egypt: Dynasties One, Two and Three

At the same time that the mid-First Dynasty fortress was being built upon the Isle of Elephantine, pharaoh's northern networks of trafficking and settlement were being slowly yet drastically transformed, a process that not only served to shape the physical extent of the later kingdom but had a profound effect upon the cultural identity of the court and its attitude towards its neighbours.

There are but faint indications of what provoked such transformations, and, as we have already seen, the records of the succeeding Second Dynasty are especially sparse. Something, though, was in the very air. To the north, the Uruk settlements in modern-day Syria and Turkey, those considerable fortresses by the Euphrates, were abandoned, while in the Levant, as at Aswan, populations that had previously lived in small and open settlements were moving into larger towns set inside walled enclosures. At this same time, too, the old Naqadan settlements in the south Levant which had long enjoyed a close relationship with the region's indigenous inhabitants began to shrink, so that by the time of the Second Dynasty they had entirely disappeared.

TRADING CLICHÉS

Such drastic realignments are often ascribed to those Four Horsemen of the neo-Darwinian Apocalypse: plague, invasion, avarice and politics. So pharaoh's dissolving settlements in the Levant are described as an example of a 'loss of empire'; as something that, in a more modern idiom, had threatened the supply of a number of 'essential strategic commodities'.

Burgeoning nation-states, so this eerily contemporary narrative continues, have growing and indeed imperative requirements for access to a range of strategic raw materials: so the ancient Egyptians needed continued access to baulks of timber to construct the boats that were such a vital element in the foundation of the pharaonic imperium. Such great boats, it is affirmed, would have required wood as straight and massive as that of the great firs and cedars which grew in the forests of the mountains of the Anti-Lebanon, whose timbers were certainly imported by the officials of later pharaohs. In similar fashion, the officers of the early kings would also have required plentiful and secure supplies of copper, that essential component of the Naqadan toolbox, which had long been imported from the south Levant along with further supplies of the red metal that had been mined and smelted in regions even further to the north.

Even as the Naqadans had first moved up along the Nile to Memphis, the scenario continues, there had been moves to protect the flow of these strategic commodities. This, indeed, had been the prime purpose of establishing the settlements within the south Levant, a policy that Narmer's governing elite continued. In the Second Dynasty, however, after these settlements had been abandoned and the native Levantines had moved into larger fortified communities, these trade routes would have been inaccessible, and pharaoh's officers had therefore taken to the sea. Citing 'Byblos boats', a term used in later hieroglyphic texts to describe a class of square-rigged seagoing ship, it has been estimated that a voyage from the port of Buto, east and up along the coast to Byblos in the Lebanon, could be accomplished in just three days. This re-routing was archaeologically underpinned by the discovery of the names of some Second Dynasty kings engraved on stone vases found both in the temple compound at the ports of Byblos in the Lebanon and at the ancient harbour city of Ugarit in modern Syria.

The story, though, is based on a string of unwarranted assumptions. There is no evidence, for example, that before King Narmer a central authority of any kind was operating on the lower Nile, let alone controlling a network of settlements in the south Levant with the aim of ensuring a supply of strategic materials to the inhabitants of the Nile Valley. Nor indeed is there evidence that the boatbuilders of the time used imported wood. The oldest Nile boats that are known at present – the flotilla uncovered at Abydos and buried in the reigns of Narmer's immediate successors – are entirely made of smaller native timber.

By Narmer's day, as well, the mariners of the eastern Mediterranean already had long experience of sailing on those waters. Traces of a millennial coastal traffic, in particular, have been found off the Levantine littoral, where fishing boats occasionally bring up Levantine and Nilotic pottery even older than that of the Naqadans' northern settlements. At Byblos, too, there is an ancient lighthouse with six mid-Naqadan anchors – large rectangles of limestone perforated to hold substantial cables – built into its walls. Nor would a cargo trade from a port like Buto need to have been conducted with substantial so-called 'Byblos boats'. Recent voyages have shown that four men in a large canoe could have carried two hundredweight of copper from Byblos to Buto in less than twenty days. So centuries before pharaoh's Levantine settlements had disappeared, a variety of boats were already plying the Levantine seaboard and, of course, the strong, high-shouldered so-called 'wine jars' made by the Naqadan potters are perfectly designed for stacking in the hulls of boats.

There are, as well, more fundamental objections to such dreams of empire. Just as there is no evidence of the notion of a 'land of Egypt' in King Narmer's time – no denominating hieroglyph – so too there is no trace of a modern sense of nationhood, let alone an incipient imperialism, in the relics of the period. So at the island excavations at Aswan, modern ceramic specialists are no longer classifying the excavated wares of these early centuries as 'Egyptian' or 'Nubian' as if they were the separate products of two different cultures, but rather as the various components of a local island culture whose roots were spread between the north and south.

Here, too, in excavations from Aswan to the delta a new history is beginning to emerge; a history that, rather than recounting the rise and fall of phantom empires, is concerned in showing how the culture of the pharaohs was itself created: how its style and physical dimensions were first defined, and how at the same time the court employed an exclusive, narrow range of rare materials to identify and define its order and its offices.

Imported and exotic things, of course, had been prized by the people of the lower Nile long before the pharaohs – since the time, indeed, when the first farmers had gone to live beside the Faiyum lake – and many of these same materials appear in pharaonic regalia. Naqadan cemeteries had held magpie collections of lapis lazuli and turquoise, obsidian and faience, along with tiny quantities of gold, silver and copper; traces of an international prehistoric traffic in delight. Many of these bright materials could also be obtained locally, of course. Washed out of their lodes in antediluvian floods, nuggets of pure gold had been picked up from the dried-out beds of Egyptian wadis since prehistoric times. Carnelians and sard lie on the surface of some Egyptian deserts and they too had been used as beads since the times of the first farmers, along with chalcedony and jasper, fluorspar and garnet. Malachite, the leaf-green copper ore that, along with smoky black galena, the Naqadans had ground into dust to make the pigments of their eye paints, is to be collected in the eastern deserts, while rock crystal and other rare and gleaming stones which had been used since earliest times can be found in a barren desert some forty miles west of Abu Simbel.

Afghan lapis had long since found its way down to the lower Nile along ancient Asian trade routes, together with the technique for making faience, the bright shining glaze that that had been used in jewellery since Badarian times. Ebony, too, had long been imported into the Naqada settlements from west Africa. In the early years of the nineteenth century, the Swiss explorer Jean-Louis Burckhardt had seen small logs of that same dark wood still being traded on the Nubian Nile. And though the Nile hippopotami had always been a source of sport and meat and ivory, the Naqadans, as we have already seen, had imported live elephants, and quantities of tusks as well, from both Africa and Asia.

There is little need to impoverish the motives of this ancient international traffic with discussions of market economics or the politics of prestige. Both the Badarians and the Naqadans had possessed a hunter's eye and a sophisticated appreciation of fine craftsmanship. As their graves clearly show, they well appreciated the exact qualities of a diversity of both colours and materials from fur and fish skin, fine linens and turtle shell, to creamy alabasters, soft-shining silver, black obsidian and jasper red, and lapis lazuli of such intensity that, still today, in a world saturated with chemical colour and illuminated screens, the blue stone engenders fascination when it is glimpsed in the darkness of an ancient tomb or, indeed, in the window of a Bond Street jeweller.

It would be wrong, therefore, to assume that in the period of the first three dynasties, at the outset of pharaonic history, the procurement of such venerable delights had automatically endowed the early pharaohs with status and prestige. Rather, we should endeavour to discover how and why it was that, in the period of those first few dynasties, some of those exotic materials – gold, lapis and the rest – seem to have been employed exclusively within the royal workshops and came to stand at the very centre of pharaonic culture.

THE MATERIAL WORLD

It is difficult today to locate with any great exactitude when and where the international prehistoric traffic in bright and pretty things had begun. Apart from lordly lapis lazuli, which appears to have been mined in just a few locations in northern Afghanistan, few of the exotic materials used by the Naqadan craftsmen have been subjected to scientific tests to determine their origins, and such tests as have been made are not infrequently disputed.

There are problems, too, of terminology. Is the jade that had been collected by the people of the lower Nile since the earliest prehistoric times really jade at all, or its harder, heavier cousin, nephrite? The former would have been mined in Asia, the latter at various European sites. Had the obsidian found in the mastaba at Naqada originated in Chad, in Ethiopia or Anatolia, or indeed from all of these, or from other sources yet unknown? Were the ambers and resins that had been placed in Naqadan and early dynastic graves gathered in Syria or Libya, or from the beaches of the Baltic?

Nor are these simply problems of physical identification. There is, for example, an intrinsic difference between the odd nuggets of alluvial copper which were hammered into beads and needles by the Badarians and early Naqadans, and the copper ingots that first appear in mid-Naqadan times, when the great wooden boats had begun to ply the Nile and copper had become the primary raw material of ancient Egyptian tools. At that same time, from the middle of the fourth millennium increased amounts of lapis lazuli, obsidian, gold and silver have also been found in contemporary graves, a funereal enrichment that spread with the Naqadan cemeteries as settlements were established at Girza and Memphis, at Helwan and in the delta.

Recent surveys in the Egyptian deserts have shown that local sources of copper were hardly being exploited in mid-Naqadan times, which suggests that its increased use in that period, along with the simultaneous rise in the amounts of gold and silver, lapis lazuli and obsidian, was another consequence of the increasing traffic on the trade routes down which copper ingots were being imported into the valley of the lower Nile. These routes, as we have already seen, seem to have extended right through the settlements of the south Levant to the metal workings of the Wadi Feynan in Jordan and similar sites much further north.

These, then, are the established land routes that were broken in the mid-First Dynasty when the pharaonic settlements in the south Levant began to disappear. At exactly this same time, the considerable traces of copper tools being used in the court workshops, along with the large numbers of copper tools being buried in the cemeteries of Memphis and Abydos, show that, at the same time as these long-established trading networks were disappearing, supplies of copper, along with those of other rare materials, rather than diminishing had actually increased.

It is likely, of course, just as the presence of fine alabaster vases made in the court workshops of the Second Dynasty and excavated in the Byblos temples suggests, that a continuing trade in materials such as copper was conducted by sea-going craft docking at Lebanese ports. These same routes, indeed, facilitated the smaller traffic in lapis lazuli and other alien materials. At exactly the same time, however, large numbers of small copper mines were established in the eastern deserts of Egypt, at sites strung out across the hills midway between the Red Sea and the valley of the Nile: a fact that makes it highly likely that the great copper mines of Sinai that would be so heavily exploited from the Third Dynasty onwards were also prospected and opened up at this time.

Now too, halfway between this line of copper workings and the beaches of the Red Sea coast, a string of gold mines was established. Using two-handed stone hammers, weighing between fifteen and twenty pounds, their miners worked in trenches, some of them above ground, others, like the tomb makers of later times, following the rock faults which run down deep into the desert cliffs. Here, then, in the same territories where their ancestors had freely walked and picked up loose nuggets of metal, teams of professional miners now pounded at the lode within the rock and washed its dust to reveal the yellow-sparkling grains.

This, of course, was also the period in which the fortress at Aswan with its colony of granite workshops had been established. This same period as well – the reigns of Djer and Djet and Den – witnessed an explosion of the products of the court's stone vase workshops as the traditional Naqadan taste for fine designs and exotic materials extended and enlarged to produce those myriad masterpieces of design and ingenuity whose tantalizing fragments Amélineau and Petrie excavated by the ton at Abydos. There were marvellous imitations of rush baskets and fig leaves cut from blocks of siltstone; hard-stone vases worked so finely that they obtained the luminosity of flowers; a range of beauteous alabaster forms, jars and dishes such as were found in distant Byblos; and fine round offering tables and elegant tiny pots for oils and cosmetics.

At this same time too, marble, amethysts and feldspar, and other stones that were hardly used in Naqadan times but which naturally occur in the desert mountains to the east of the valley of the lower Nile, appear in ever growing quantity in the royal graves. The famous bracelets of gold, amethyst and turquoise that Petrie found still wrapped around their owner's arm are among the first known examples. Alabaster, too, much of it mined in the great quarries of Hatnub, 140 sailing miles to the south of Memphis, now became the commonest stone of royal stone-working workshops.

Pharaonic inscriptions of later periods record that expeditions to the Egyptian deserts organized to collect some of these same materials required hundreds of people to carry the water and supplies in such inhospitable environments. The early desert mines and quarries, therefore, represent a considerable investment on the part of the early court

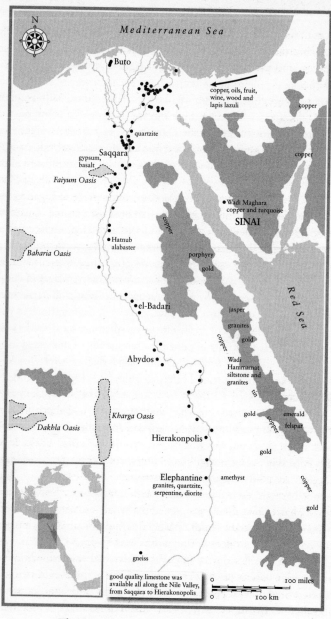

The mineral resources of early dynastic Egypt

and, as in the workshops in the island fortress at Aswan, it is unlikely that such projects could have been undertaken in the centuries before the kings, and the resources of a centralized supply system became available.

Not surprisingly, therefore, as the use of materials such as hard stone and copper seems to have been restricted to the court, so too from the times of the mid-First Dynasty, other materials – such as silver and gold, obsidian, ebony and Afghan lapis that in earlier times had been used in burials all along the lower Nile – are now only to be found in the royal tombs and, to a lesser degree, in the tombs of their courtiers and estate managers. As the court began to be engaged in the procurement of most of these materials, so their use became restricted.

The ancient Naqadan identity had been subsumed. The ageless skills that Naqadan craftsmen had employed for a millennium had been taken over by pharaoh and his court. The ethereal beauty of rare gems and precious metals, goods that reflected the primary colours and ingredients of the Nile Valley landscape, had become part of court identity.

BEFORE AND AFTER

With the retreat of the northern settlements, the cutting of Levantine traffic and the prospecting of the Egyptian deserts, changes may be detected in attitudes within the royal court towards other communities. It is as if the court had withdrawn into itself. Cultures outside its orbit, with their different modes of dress, comportment and behaviour, were increasingly shown as different; as foreign.

And at exactly this same time, the exotic mixtures of articles that had long since filled the largest and most lavish Nubian burials with masses of late Naqadan wares, with fine furniture and Levantine pottery, came to an abrupt end. This, it has been suggested, was because the kings of the First Dynasty had blocked the trade routes along which a wide variety of materials and goods from central Africa and the Levant had previously been trafficked. At this same time, however, the Nubian A Group culture, whose northern settlements had flourished alongside those of the Naqadans for centuries, entirely disappear:

not just its northernmost communities, between Hierakonpolis and Aswan, but the entire culture that had lived along the 300-mile stretch of river-bank between Hierakonpolis and the Nile's Second Cataract, south of Wadi Halfa in modern-day Sudan. Had those ancient herding communities simply died away, were they attacked, or had they travelled southwards with their herds? For whatever reason, there is scant evidence of anyone inhabiting lower Nubia for several centuries after the coming of the pharaohs.

Such emigrations, of course, were not exclusive to pharaoh's neighbours; the ancient communities of the Naqadan heartlands, after all, had been moving northwards along the lower Nile for centuries so that, by the time of the early dynasties, the region around Memphis had become the central focus of the newly created culture of the pharaonic court. And it was there, whilst the other settlements along the lower Nile had remained inside the broad material world of late Naqadan culture, that, by the beginning of the Third Dynasty of kings, the court workshops had already developed the essentials of that narrow and distinctive repertoire which they preserved throughout the following millennia. Here, then, was created that specific mix of raw materials and imagery, the style and the distinctive visual order that would be applied to everything from the design of groups of hieroglyphs and the drawing of the human body to the forms of stone-block architecture.

A great part of this process of selection and reformation must therefore have taken place after the extensive changes which occurred in the court workshops of the mid-First Dynasty. All that may be gleaned of the following phase, however, which must have taken place within the Second Dynasty and in the region of Memphis, is by a comparison of the products made in the periods before and after that dark tunnel. Clearly, the traditional methods of placing signs in ordered registers and the techniques of raised relief developed in late Naqadan times were retained and refined so that they triumphantly re-emerge in the surviving products of the court workshops of the Third Dynasty. So, too, many of the hieroglyphs, patterns and devices introduced during the First Dynasty were retained and formalized.

Yet at the same time, many long-used images were discarded. The two entwining monsters of King Narmer's Palette, for example, were

expunged from the courtly repertoire, along with other alien exotica.
Some of the survivals, though, were quite remarkable. The serekh, for
example, and those most ancient images of bulls' heads, the distinctive shapes of staffs and staves, furniture legs made in the ancient
shape of animals' limbs and a myriad other prehistoric forms would
be as widely used in the courtly arts of the Third Dynasty as they had
been in previous millennia in the neolithic farming communities of
Europe, Africa and Asia. Now, though, after the darkness of the
Second Dynasty, they appear as highly formal elements in the well-
ordered regalia of the pharaonic state, as images upon a royal belt, as
sceptres or as parts of the royal throne: the unfathomable neolithic
underpinnings of an exclusive well-ordered society.

*Petrie's drawing of an 8-inch spill of wood – a gaming piece perhaps –
bearing an image, so its hieroglyphs suggest, of a so-called 'northerner'*

20

The Realms of Pharaoh

Dynasties One and Three

> *It was the best of times, it was the worst of times, it was the age of wisdom, it was the age of foolishness, it was the epoch of belief . . .*
>
> Charles Dickens, A Tale of Two Cities

The single greatest change to have taken place during the Second Dynasty of kings was in the status of pharaoh. Evidence from the First and Third Dynasties shows an increasing consecration of the office and, at the same time, a growing discernment of the existence of a realm, a supra-geographic kingdom spanning life and death, within the region of the lower Nile.

That the royal role had been in a continuing process of development since the time of Narmer is best seen in the fast-changing burial arrangements of the kings themselves, a process that had first differentiated the tombs of members of the court from those of the rest of the population and which by the beginning of the Third Dynasty had climaxed in the isolation of the kings' tombs from those of all other people and monuments so large that their construction had taken over the great part of the state's efforts and resources. At that same time too, a different image of the king had been created: the tremendous statue of King Djoser that was found beside his pyramid, a life-sized masterpiece of stilled ferocity, with sculptural qualities unrealized by earlier generations.

A subtle early indicator of the changing status of the kings had been the shift in their relationship to time. In the days of Narmer and his successors, specific royal events of tithing had been identified by the years of a monarch's rule, a process that had effectively inserted the names of individual kings into the court's food chain. Then, in the middle of the First Dynasty, the compilation of lists of the names of successive rulers had effectively extended the earlier role of individual monarchs as court providers to the office of kingship of itself.

That such concerns had been genuine preoccupations of the court is shown, as we have already seen, by the two surviving king lists of the time and also by the careful corrections made to the shorter of the two lists at a later date. That such concerns were widespread throughout the later parts of the dynasty is attested by no fewer than ten surviving bowls and vases inscribed with the name of King Den, to which the names of his successors to the throne have been added with some care by different hands at later dates.

As the Aswan fortress testifies, these early redefinitions of the status of pharaoh were taking place at the same time as the state was beginning to guard its enterprises; the same era, too, in which pharaoh's north-eastern networks were shrinking, the court was looking to local sources for its raw materials and the royal workshops were producing masterpieces in extraordinary quantities. This period, therefore, the reigns of Djer, Djet and Den in the mid-First Dynasty, was the time in which the court had started to create and cultivate its own cultural identity; to regard itself as an institution. And at exactly this same time, killing at courtly funerals reached extraordinary proportions.

Such slaughtering, which also took place on a smaller scale at the funerals of some contemporary courtiers, appears to have begun quite suddenly. No one, for example, seems to have been killed at the funeral of the person buried in tomb U-j, human sacrifice in Naqadan cemeteries having died out centuries before, when the focus for community killing had shifted to venues in living communities like the oval court at Hierakonpolis. Nor does anyone appear to have been killed at funerals on the Umm el-Qa'ab in Narmer's time. King Aha, however, Narmer's successor, had a tidy regiment of thirty-odd young men buried beside the royal crypts and half that number again entombed by his funerary enclosures close to the Nile-side fields. Subsequently, more than eight hundred people, men and women, were immured at the funerary monuments of Djer and Djet, after which there appears to have been a slackening in the killing so that in the time of King Qa'a at the ending of the dynasty, just twenty-five small graves were made beside the royal tomb.

It is impossible, in the obscurity of the Second Dynasty, to determine precisely when this slaughter stopped. Briskly introduced and, as we shall see, mightily impactive, the fierce custom seems to have been abandoned by the king and his courtiers by the beginning of the Third Dynasty of kings, when the first pyramids were made. Such dark acts, however, threw long shadows.

An ivory plaque showing King Den smiting a so-called 'easterner'. That the label has a pair of sandals drawn upon its other side suggests that it was once tied to footwear intended for burial with the king. It is 1¾ inches high

THE POLITICS OF SACRIFICE

At the ending of the second century AD, Tertullian famously observed that 'the blood of the martyrs is the seed of the Church': that the sacrifice was fundamental to church identity. So, too, memories of the First Dynasty royal funerals upon the Umm el-Qa'ab became a fundamental part of the later state's identity, and Abydos became ancient Egypt's greatest single shrine, a place of pilgrimage throughout the following millennia.

Dozens of later pharaohs would embellish and enlarge the modest shrine that, in the time of the first kings, had stood within a settlement at Abydos and which had been rededicated to the state god Osiris, the ruler of the dead, who was also identified specifically with the dead kings. At Abydos, too, some of Egypt's most celebrated queens and pharaohs founded monuments of their own in a two-mile line that ran along the edges of the fields to the south of the Osiris temple. And from the compound of the Osiris temple, close by the enclosures of the early kings, a grand, wide, processional way ran out across the desert to the ancient royal tombs upon the Umm el-Qa'ab. Thousands upon thousands of more modest monuments, graves, altars and cenotaphs, built by people from all over pharaoh's kingdom, were set up in the surrounding deserts. Sometimes on winter nights, so it was said, the dead could be heard howling in the wind that blows along the sandy gully in the cliffs, down over the ancient royal tombs and out across the living land. No wonder, then, that a common prayer of later ages was that the spirit of a dead person might join the annual pilgrimage to Abydos, or that burial parties would leave model boats in tombs all over Egypt, their sails rigged to take the winds that would speed their spirits on that sacred voyage.

After some fifteen centuries of such devotions, the tomb of Djer on the Umm el Qa'ab, where some three hundred and fifty victims had been buried all around the royal burial chamber, was refurbished and re-established as the tomb of the great god Osiris, who by that time was regarded as a prehistoric king, as the sovereign ruler of the underworld and a god of resurrection. So when Amélineau had excavated the royal tombs, his workmen had first to dig through the debris of millennia of piety. And in Djer's great burial pit, they found a life-sized black stone statue of Osiris lying on a funerary bier which had been set inside a sarcophagus of fine white alabaster. And all around the ancient tombs were the remains of the Abydos pilgrimage, great drifts of broken pottery in the soft yellow sand; water jars, incense burners and dishes as small as penny pieces, which had once held a pinch of grain, whose sprouting was a vital part of Osiris' annual resurrection.

Those dark archaic tombs with their framing lines of tiny graves had come to occupy something of the same space in the psyche of the pharaonic state as the earlier multiple burials in Naqadan cemeteries had for those earlier communities. Yet the focus of these deathly dramas had entirely changed. Rather than the unique arrangements of each and every Naqadan burial, the regularity, the uniformity of this mass of little graves upon the Umm el-Qa'ab, set out in straight lines all around the royal tombs, suggests that they were not designed to provide each king with unique resonance in the manner of the Naqadan tombs. Now, it would appear, the offices of the state rather than their individual holders were the intended beneficiaries; an impression reinforced by the fact that many of the victims of these burials, some of whom were named, seem to have served as officers of the court, or as members of a court household.

These gatherings of secondary tombs around the great regal burials, therefore, were a literal extension of the order and offices of the living kingdom into the province of the dead. Just as the great graves had been designed to hold the goods of the living state, just as the stamps and sealings of those goods served to delineate the range and reach, the space and substance of the court, so these extraordinary assemblies were a simulacrum, a definition even, of the constitution of the 'great house'; that is, of the offices of the pharaoh.

KING DJET'S COMB

Petrie went back again to Abydos in 1921, and pitched his expedition tents inside Khasekhemui's grand funerary enclosure. In the winter season of the year before, an expedition had uncovered some previously unknown graves of the First Dynasty close by, and further excavation, Petrie expected, might shed more light on the royal tombs that he had excavated some twenty years before. In this, though, he was disappointed, for the new cemeteries proved to raise more questions than they answered.

A month or so of digging showed that the recently uncovered burials were but a small part of a series of cemeteries that had been cut in long narrow trenches in the desert, which were lined with parallel brick walls and subdivided into small partitions, each one of which had held a body. Such arrangements, Petrie saw, were reminiscent of the subsidiary graves on the Umm el-Qa'ab, and these new tombs, he suggested, might have been a kind of overflow. In reality, however, more recent excavations have proved that Petrie had uncovered most of the graves laid down around three of the First Dynasty funerary enclosures, which had been built in conjunction with the nearby royal tombs and then apparently dismantled, one after the other.

In his account of these excavations, Petrie estimated that, in the reigns of Djer, Djet and Den, some five hundred people had been immured in these linear cemeteries. Most of the surviving bodies showed that they had been carefully laid down in their four- and five-foot vaults, legs bent, arms gathered in the old Naqadan fashion, accompanied by a cache of storage pots and a few personal possessions. That a few had been found in grotesque positions led Petrie to suggest that some people, at least, had been buried whilst they were still alive.

A series of swiftly scribbled field notes hold Petrie's records of the intimate detail of these little burials; as the greater part were robbed, however, their clearance must have been depressingly repetitive. One grave, though, which he describes as having been made for a woman named Mer-nesut, still contained some copper tools, a few small bone labels and a pretty little comb cut from a sheet of ivory. In the manner of the times, only the bottom quarter of the comb had tines which were exquisitely cut and were similar in proportion to those of the wider sections of a modern comb. The remaining surface, almost two-and-a-half inches high, had been reserved for the owner's guiding hand. And on one face of this elegant handle, golden with age and still shining from its ancient use, was a remarkable engraving. For in accurate and vivid lines, a craftsman had engraved the name of King Djet on the ivory; 'Djet' the snake, within a serekh, with a hawk set on its top, to form an elegant little group that was balanced by a single so-called *ankh* sign set beside it. And high above them both the craftsman had drawn a swing-hulled boat of the type that had been painted in the tomb at Hierakonpolis, and on this boat, perched upon its cabin, there is a second, smaller image of a hawk.

At first glance, the upper section of the composition appears to be an image of the pharaoh's progress along the networks of the lower Nile on which King Narmer had first stamped his name. Here, though, the king's boat does not float on the river, but has been carried up into the sky on two huge outstretched wings, which, as many similar later images will show, would come to hold the red disk of the sun.

In the direct imagery of the early hieroglyphs, the small engraving apparently depicts the pharaoh as king of earth and sky; a message emphasized, perhaps, by the hieroglyphic images of two distinctively

Petrie's drawing of the ivory comb engraved with the serekh of King Djet.
It is almost three inches high

shaped staffs that heraldically support the outstretched wings and
frame the royal serekh and the *ankh* sign, an image of a sandal strap
that later scribes employed to signify 'life' or 'to become'. Later, those
same distinctive staffs will come to represent the notion of stability.
Here, though, they may well represent the fringing cliffs that frame
the sky within the Nile Valley, the sky through which the royal hawk
is sailing in the royal brigantine. If this is an accurate interpretation of
those little signs, they represent an entirely different aspect of the
pharaohs' kingdom; one not formed by evidence from the networks
whose goods and produce filled the great graves of the time, but a
part-representation of the networks' physical extent, along the living
valley of the Nile, and from the river to the sky.

TITHE AND SACRIFICE

Entire theologies have been erected round that pretty scene. In the
light of later evidence it is usually described as an early version of how
'ancient Egyptians' viewed the universe in which they lived; a world
under the aegis of a divine pharaoh who rules both earth and heaven
and brings stability and life to the regions of the lower Nile; a universe, in short, in which everything under the Egyptian sun was part
of a single sacred order, the order of the pharaoh.

Yet it seems a heavy burden for a little comb to bear. Made at a time when the courts of the early pharaohs were beginning to both guard and to regard themselves, when they were still arranging their millennial heritage to reflect their changing status, its immediate purpose may simply have been to designate King Djet as the ultimate overseer of the valley in which state activity was taking place. At all events, the rare scene certainly identifies a new stage in the development of that concept, that considerable journey, in which the ancient colonies and trading networks of Naqadan times became a kingdom.

First, Narmer's name had been set inside a serekh on his great stone palette so that it appeared, quite literally, as the occupier of a 'great house'. Then, in the mid-First Dynasty, the dual signs of a bee and a rush had been drawn side by side beside the royal name on some fine stone dishes, a composition designating, if later usage serves as an indication, that the king's realm spanned both the river's valley and its marshy delta – landscapes that the images on Djet's comb seem to have extended up into the sky and into the living land itself. And at precisely the same time as pharaoh's realm was in the early phases of its definition, at the same time as Djet's name was balanced on the little comb by a hieroglyph signifying life, so too a thousand souls and more were being killed at royal funerals.

Egyptology's traditional explanation of this sudden outburst of killings is that it represented the last knockings of a savage progress on the road to 'civilization'. In this reading, the early kings and some of their most powerful courtiers had come to harbour the Sardanapalian desire to take their possessions with them to the grave so that their spirits could maintain the life they had enjoyed on earth. Thus, in this consumer paradise, they required attendance from their servants. It is not, then, surprising that, as the lines of little graves house more women than men, the doleful cemeteries at Abydos and Saqqara soon came to represent to traditional historians the inhabitants of an *orientaliste* haremlik that had been launched into the 'next world' as if they were passengers on the barque on pharaoh's comb.

Though one might well doubt that, in a time of increasing royal exclusivity, hundreds of courtiers and servants would be killed to enable their participation in an ecumenical afterlife, the fundamental belief that the dead had continuing existence was certainly extremely old. Guy Brunton found evidence of offerings and funeral feasts in

Badarian cemeteries, customs that were continued in Naqadan cemeteries, where the excavated pots of food and other goods provide further evidence that the dead were thought to have some of the same needs as the living and were, therefore, present in forms other than their physical remains. In similar fashion, the German expedition on the Umm el-Qa'ab uncovered just such an *Opferplatz* by tomb U-j which, so the presence of a fragment of an alabaster vase engraved with Narmer's name suggests, had been used to tend to the spirit of the tomb's dead owner long after the burial was made. At the nearby royal tombs as well, further traces of contemporary offering places have also been found.

Such ancient acts of offering, of making direct contact with the dead within a specially appointed space, would become a primary function of the office of the pharaoh, just as the ancient act of killing had been a primary function of the royal office from its beginning, as is shown on Narmer's great stone palette. And as the picture plaques made in the times of Djer, Djet and Den all underline, such events were conducted in the royal name within the royal tithing courts, just as they were at contemporary royal funerals.

Similarly deadly acts had previously taken place within the cultures of the early Nile Valley in periods of stress, when the identity of a community was in a process of formation. So in Naqadan times, the focus of these dramas had moved from the graveyards of the small early settlements to courts set inside the larger, more complex settlements which were developing within the Naqadan heartlands. So, too, in the First Dynasty, when the identity and culture of the royal court was in the process of formation, the long lines of little graves at Abydos and Saqqara represent part of an overwhelming dialogue that, like those which had always taken place within communities along the lower Nile, were carried out in images and objects, goods and chattels, flesh and blood.

After the office of the pharaoh had gained an institutional stability and there was continuity in the royal court, so the killing had diminished. Then, later in the First Dynasty, as the practice of making little picture plaques with their records of killing, tithing and the restless royal round also disappear, so the killings at the graveside further slowed. And in the historical hiatus of the Second Dynasty, it appears to have stopped completely.

Yet in the reign of Djoser, a large figure of a smiting king in the pose of Narmer on his palette – the first known monumental work by an ancient Egyptian sculptor – was engraved upon a desert cliff at Sinai, close by the mines that would supply a great part of the considerable tonnage of copper chisels which pyramid building would require. In later reigns as well, a line of similarly regal images would be placed on nearby rocks. That their inscriptions name turquoise, a green-blue stone also quarried in the area, rather than the tons of copper that were being extracted, serves to underline the contemporary importance of those gemstones that, unlike the copper that was used for tools, were elements of the royal regalia.

These scenes of smiting on the rock of Sinai are often taken to show the physical subjugation of the local people. And yet, of course, they are the purest definition of a sacerdotal pharaoh; a post that had already been defined throughout the previous two dynasties. Here, then, is pharaoh, the provider and protector of his realm, shown as the conduit linking the landscapes of his kingdom to this world and the next, a single image marking the physical and metaphysical extent of a new-made universe.

A reworking of a badly weathered inscription of Djoser carved upon an uneven rock face at the quarries of Wadi Maghara in Sinai. The smiting King is attended by an unnamed goddess, one of the first-known appearances of a deity in human form. The figures are approximately half life size

21

Two Gentlemen of Saqqara

Merka and Hesi-re: Dynasties One and Three

> *Let us suppose ourselves, then, at some time about the end of*
> *the IIIrd Dynasty standing on the broad ridge running north*
> *and south and immediately overlooking the valley. Below us on*
> *the west is a wide depression, bare and windswept, where later*
> *the stone mastabas of the Vth Dynasty are to rise and then to*
> *disappear under the drifting sand. The pyramids of Abusir, even*
> *those of Giza, are as yet unbuilt; only one great monument*
> *rises from above the desert, but its aspect is most imposing.*
>
> *The Step Pyramid to the south of us, newly finished, towers*
> *above its mighty panelled wall of white limestone as great a*
> *work as the pyramid itself looking from here more magnifi-*
> *cent than the white walls of Memphis which glitter in the east*
> *across the marshes.*
>
> James Quibell, 1923

A great courtly drama must surely have been played out in the region
of Memphis, where Djoser's pyramid now stands. And yet, despite a
century and more of survey and excavation, the white walls of the
settlements of the early dynasties still only glitter in imagination, for
no trace of them has ever been uncovered.

There is, of course, an extraordinary continuity at Memphis. Many
of the ten-thousand-odd tombs in the vicinity of Helwan on the river's
eastern bank, those huge cemeteries founded in the times of Naqadan
emigration, had continued to be used throughout the early dynasties
for the burials of a great diversity of court officials. On the west bank
as well, on the plateau that lies between King Djoser's pyramid and

the line of First Dynasty mastabas that runs along the top of the cliffs, are extensive cemeteries of the same period, the greater part of which have yet to be excavated. And in the deserts to the north there are other cemeteries of this same period, mostly modest tombs sprawled over desert wadis, lying deep in drifting sand.

The living settlements that once stood at the centre of this vast arc of archaic graves, so it is generally agreed, must have been a considerable conurbation, with dockyards and magazines that stood near the later city on the west bank of the river. By a process of deduction and core sampling, which has determined that the river in Narmer's time flowed nearer to the western cliffs than it does at present, the most likely site of early Memphis appears to lie a mile or so to the north of Djoser's stepped pyramid and in the wash of a considerable wadi, close to the desert's edge.

Might this phantom Memphis, then, be termed a city? Not, perhaps, in the modern sense of the term, where commerce plays a fundamental role as magnet and provider for an urban population. But in the classical world, when cities were expressly founded to serve as entrepôts and mostly thrived, it may certainly have qualified. The manpower, materials and supplies required to build Djoser's pyramid alone would have required previously unseen levels of court traffic on the river.

Nowadays, however, that energy has largely gone. The fields of the village of Saqqara and the town of el-Badrashein stand by the mounds which hold the ruined palaces and temples of the later city that the ancient Greeks describe. Behind them both, a glimmering backcloth glimpsed through groves of shaded palms, Djoser's pyramid stands high above great screes of debris, the products of centuries of excavation on the plateau.

MERKA

The southernmost of the half-mile-long line of mastabas that stand on the cliff top of Saqqara, and the last and the most mature of all those monuments, was made for a man named Merka, a courtier who in life appears to have been concerned with the supply and conduct of the royal court and who died in the reign of Qa'a, the last ruler of the First Dynasty. Merka lived, therefore, in the period immediately before the early pharaohs and their courts all disappeared into the historical hiatus of the Second Dynasty.

Well over 200 feet in length and more than 90 wide, and standing, originally, to a height of some 20 feet, the enclosure that once held Merka's mastaba is the largest structure to have been excavated in this long line of tombs. Set inside several massive walls, two great buildings had entirely filled this grand enclosure. One of them, a maze of corridors and chambers reminiscent of some of the contemporary estate buildings in the delta, seems to have been an elaborate offering place equipped with storerooms and is usually referred to as a temple. The other building was a mastaba, 120 feet in length, which, though its exterior of four fine palace façades was similar to those of the two-century-old mastaba at Naqada, had no interior magazines at all, and was a solid mass of brick.

Merka's burial chamber lay underneath the mastaba. A large and elaborate affair, it consisted of two small chambers cut either side of a single staircase. This ran down into a splendid funerary crypt whose roof had been held up by two massive beams which, following a colossal fire, had collapsed so that the brick filling of the mastaba above dropped down upon the ashes of the burial. When it was excavated by British archaeologists in the 1950s, fragments of human remains were found lying on the wooden planks of what appeared to have been either an enormous coffin or some kind of wooden catafalque.

Consumed by fire and subsequently ransacked – even the huge stone portcullis that had blocked the passage to the burial chamber was smashed to pieces – the remaining fragments showed that the three subterranean chambers had held some fine stone vases and dishes, some flint tools and quantities of storage jars and a few small jugs imported from the Levant. Though it contained but a fraction of the quantities of goods stored in the similarly sized mastabas of earlier times, there was provision, in the shape of the elaborate temple which had stood beside it, for fresh offerings to be made at Merka's tomb after the burial was closed. And in a niche inside that building, the archaeologists found the feet and ankles of two standing wooden statues, presumably of Merka, set in a typical pose of pharaonic statues, with one leg placed in front of the other, of which they are the oldest known examples.

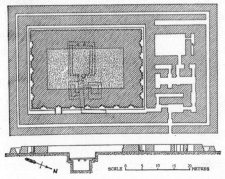

The plan of Merka's mastaba as drawn by its excavator, Walter Emery

The greatest of all the treasures from this courtier's tomb, however, was an enormous limestone stela that the archaeologists found lying across one of the mastaba's enclosing mud-brick corridors. Spear-shaped, like some of the granite stelae placed beside the royal tombs of Merka's time, the six-foot slab holds hieroglyphics and a drawing of a man seated on a chair, a somewhat inept rendering of a relatively common image of the time. Beside, above and underneath this figure, however, there are no less than seven lines of hieroglyphs which, though individually ill-formed and inexpertly cut, are collectively one of the oldest continuous inscriptions to have been found in Egypt. Though much of their detail remains obscure, their burden was to name the owner of the tomb and describe his relationship to the king and his role within the living court.

Even before the stela had been moved, the archaeologists were able to identify Merka's name by its proximity to the seated figure immediately below it, for in later times such images were used as a determining hieroglyph for the names of dead members of the court. Then, the transcription of several of the more prominent hieroglyphs set above Merka's name identified him as *iry-pet*, which, as later occurrences of the same term suggested, showed that he had probably been a member of a small group of courtiers who were close to the king, and even, perhaps, a member of the royal family.

Merka's limestone stela

Another section of the inscription further identified Merka as *sem*, a word that in later times defined a group of people who performed some of the functions of a priest and who held senior posts in the regiment of ritualists who both accompanied the living king and specialized in robing sacred statues. In further confirmation of that role, Merka's seated figure seems to have shown traces of that same dramatic cloak of leopard skin which appears on images of the so-called *sem*-priests throughout pharaonic history. Taken literally, the term *sem* appears to have been borne by a man who dressed the king in the royal regalia. That another of Merka's titularies apparently describes him as 'master of ceremonies' puts one in mind of the little figures that accompany King Narmer on his palette, one of whom, though unidentified by an inscription, also wears a leopard skin.

In Merka's day, when the kings were still buried at Abydos, the activities of the royal court, as we have seen, seem to have centred on an annual round of voyaging and court appearances. These events, so the picture plaques of the First Dynasty depict, involved acts of offering and slaughtering, tithing and presentation. Marking out the years of each king's rule in panoply, death and economics, at localities such as Abydos, Buto and Hierakonpolis, such events appear to have been somewhat similar convocations. The monarch is shown bejewelled and crowned and surrounded by an array of costumed courtiers: a royal progress of tithe and slaughter that ended at the royal graves of Abydos.

That Merka bore the title *sem*, therefore, suggests that he performed functions at such royal appearances, which would have required a caste of specialists with the skills to organize the court and its regalia and to count and circulate the goods it had accumulated. At this time, then, the roles of priest and body servant to the king may have been practical and indivisible, and the tasks of a royal inner circle, consisting, perhaps, of family members. People, at all events, who spent their lives in ensuring that the equipment of the court appearances – the crowns and costumes, the slaughtering knives and sceptres, the throne, the record keeping, the great boats and the architecture that marked and facilitated the royal progress up and down the Nile – was in good order.

By Merka's time, therefore, at the ending of the dynasty, this core group would have performed the tasks of both tithing masters and ritualists – for such appearances, their images suggest, are properly described as recording pageantry, even ceremonial. This group, therefore, of which Merka was probably a member, would have formed a close society around the king and had an intimate understanding of the order of royal appearances, and a practical knowledge of the cycles of the river's flooding and of the quantity and quality of the harvests that were the fundamental components of the court's survival. These, then, are the origins of the panoply and complex ceremonial of the pharaonic court.

It is usually assumed that such posts as are implied by the inscriptions on Merka's stela – and there are many shorter, less informative examples of them – were developed as a political means of governing an emergent state. It is an argument *ex silentio*. What in reality the archaeology shows is that the practical apparatus of this developing kingdom – the sealings, year tags and the like which ultimately served to record the amounts of food it collected – grew in sophistication with the enlarging court, whose organization was bound closely to the king and his endless round of tithe and offering.

Serving and supporting the households of the court, of course, were the people who were visited and tithed by it: the farmers, colonists and craftsmen who, as a later text observes, it was not good to harm, as they 'make everything'. The descendants of the old Naqadan settlements, the inhabitants of various communities, dockyards and colonies, were now part of the culture of the pharaonic state, whose people, both alive and dead, were dependent on the produce of the land and, thus, the good order of its farmers and its network of supply.

On occasion, those people outside the orbit of the court and the households of its courtiers and craftsmen, seem to have been called *rekhyt*, a term identified by a hieroglyphic sign of a lapwing, a bird that wintered on the Nile but which would later be regarded in the literature as ill-omened and even as alien – which may suggest that the modern notion of an 'ancient Egyptian' does not equate with all of the ancient population of the lower Nile.

The *rekhyt* do not appear on Merka's stela. There are indications, however, that, even at the beginning, the relationship between the court and the people of the lower Nile may have been somewhat fraught. The topmost frieze on the Scorpion Mace Head, for example, was decorated with a ring of dead lapwings hanging from ropes, as if a gamekeeper had set them on a fence to keep the crows away. Tied to some of the standards that would be carried in the company of the king, such images are reminiscent of the 'Peasant's Column' with its impaled farm worker, which Dürer drew for Luther's delectation, and it suggests a certain courtly fear of the *rekhyt*: sometimes the later lapwing hieroglyph would show the bird with dislocated wings.

Though only a handful of people are shown on the palettes, mace heads and picture plaques of the First Dynasty kings, it is easy to assume that, like the images of modern rulers and their ministers, these little figures token the tips of considerable governmental structures; yet such need not have been the case. In Merka's time, the entire population of the Nile Valley was well below a half a million people. Outside the delta colonies, the land may hardly have been organized at all, and the king's immediate retinue only composed of a small number of people. Nor is there evidence that in Merka's day the communities along the lower Nile were held within a rigid, highly structured society. Certainly there were nobles and a court, tithing and killing, and the making of great tombs. Yet in reality, nothing more is known of Merka's time than what modern archaeology has recovered and there is no evidence at all that what we now dub a 'royal court' was an organization similar to that of the military, hereditary or property-based elites of traditional Western societies. This, after all, was a time when kingship of itself was a very new idea.

MARIETTE AND HESI-RE

British archaeologists had not been the first to dig at Merka's tomb. Over the ages it had suffered a variety of excavators, from early Christian stone thieves rummaging for building materials for a nearby desert monastery, to medieval treasure seekers sieving the Saqqara sand for grains of funeral jewellery, and, in the mid-nineteenth century, the Frenchman Auguste Mariette, egyptology's most passionate pioneer, who had opened Merka's burial chamber and left some telltale tackle blocks behind him.

Mariette, a linguistic prodigy who had already catalogued all the hieroglyphic texts in the Egyptian collections of the Louvre, had arrived in Cairo in 1850 at the age of twenty-nine, and created a sensation when his excavations at Saqqara had uncovered a vast catacomb filled with enormous sarcophagi and a mass of bright antiquities. It was the beginning of a remarkable career. Over the next thirty years, the one-time journalist from Boulogne-sur-Mer went on to mount enormous excavations the length and breadth of Egypt, freeing many of its now familiar temples from vast mounds of debris, digging thousand upon thousand of ancient tombs, recovering great treasures, founding the first national museum of the Middle East and what would become the Service des Antiquités. Encased in a great granite sarcophagus of his own and surmounted by a fine bronze statue, the tomb of Mariette Pasha now stands in the grounds of the Cairo Museum.

Mariette's greatest single achievement was to stop the plundering of ancient Egypt that had started after the retreat of Napoleon's invasion of Egypt in 1801, when the remains of pharaoh's kingdom had first been quantified and mapped. Beyond carrying off some of its prettier objects to their museums, the European powers had not known quite what to do with the extensive ruins of this newly revealed kingdom, and consequently bands of foreign treasure seekers had done more damage to its fragile relics in the following decades than had occurred throughout the two previous millennia.

With the patronage of Ferdinand de Lesseps, who, with the encouragement of France, was engaged upon his scheme for financing and excavating the Suez Canal, Mariette gained the ear of Egypt's Ottoman governor, the Viceroy Said, who in 1858 instituted a regime to protect and conserve the national monuments and appointed Mariette as its *mamur* – its director. Now, as part of a thirty-year programme of conservation and mass excavation, Mariette returned to dig at Saqqara, where he discovered some of the most celebrated objects ever to have been found in Egypt. And there it was, just a few hundred yards from the mastaba of Merka, that one of his work gangs uncovered a similarly enormous tomb that had been built, so its inscriptions told, for another courtier, a man called Hesi-re.

In the 1860s, as Mariette was excavating at Saqqara, the early dynasties of kings were little more than a succession of strange names culled from the surviving fragments of Manetho's *Aigyptiaka*. Given that he found no inscriptions bearing a royal name within the tomb of Hesi-re, he could do little more than list the tomb as '*archaïque*' in his publication, signifying that it had been made in the time of the pharaohs who had ruled before the Great Pyramid had been built. Today, however, we know that the mastaba of Hesi-re was built in the reign of Djoser, whose pyramid stands nearby. Thus, like Djoser's pyramid, this courtier's tomb stands at the other end of the historical hiatus of the Second Dynasty; that period which had begun after the death of the courtier Merka and the reign of Qa'a, his king.

Even bigger than the mastaba of Merka, the tomb of Hesi-re had been one of the larger monuments that stood within a vast, dense and as yet only partially excavated cemetery of nobles' and servants' graves, both large and small, that had extended from the cliff-edge line of First Dynasty mastabas far back into the desert of the Saqqara plateau. Like Merka's funerary enclosure, the tomb of Hesi-re had been contained within a similar series of enclosing mud-brick walls, which, on this occasion, had encompassed but a single structure, a massive mastaba built in the old tradition, with a large and elaborate burial chamber system cut into the desert rock beneath. Here, too, the alleyways behind these enclosure walls had given access to a single narrow corridor that ran along the mastaba's east face, the only one of its four walls to have been decorated with a palace façade. Here, however, unlike earlier mastabas, the centres of the eleven niches of this lone palace façade had held great thick slabs of dark brown acacia wood, each one as finely grained and vigorously veined as a panel of decorative marble. And each one of these slabs, so the surviving panels showed, had stood some four feet high and on their lower sections had held a sculpted inset panel, each one of which, so their inscriptions told, had borne an image of Hesi-re, a tall young man with a short wig and a moustache, and often with a scribe's kit of pens, inks and palettes slung like a bandolier over his shoulder.

Unlike the sorry images on Merka's stela, the figures of Hesi-re's reliefs had been designed to stand in open space. And just as the Naqadan vase makers had used the veins in the hard stone to flatter the lines of their dishes and vases, so too the crisp lines of the figures of Hesi-re had been set against the grain of the acacia wood, the gentle curve of face and wig echoing its powerful twist and flow.

Set in an envelope of fine texture and high design, even the most damaged image on the surviving panels still has its own life, an intense tactile quality of surface; the pulse of living things. Here, then, is that precise coalition of high formalism and direct realism with which later Egyptian craftsmen would always be especially concerned – and it was never better done throughout the following millennia.

Above all else, perhaps, Hesi-re's reliefs display a joy of craftsmanship, of making things, of magically endowing heavy planks of wood with the qualities of life. The formal qualities of earlier sculpture have been largely stripped away to enable the description, with the aid of copper chisels and discrete abrasion, of a living chest, the exact quality of skin and muscle, a heart beating underneath a ribcage, an arm, a finger and an eye, even, perhaps, a sneer of cold command. Even the rows of hieroglyphs that accompany the images of Hesi-re are similarly endowed, like figures of the scribe himself, with the qualities of life.

Though such intense and exquisite work is very rare, the pose and style of Hesi-re's reliefs are not unique for the time in which he lived. What in this instance encouraged these particular craftsman to work to such extraordinarily skilful levels is unknown. In following centuries, however, some tomb owners appear to have taken considerable interest in the way the craftsmen represented them. Perhaps, then, Hesi-re himself had encouraged such extremes, examining each of the panels as they were being made in the craftsmen's workshops. Certainly their qualities could hardly have been assessed in their set positions in the mastaba, where the mud plaster of the architecture obscured part of their carefully measured frames and the relief was cast in shadow in the narrow corridor and set so deeply in the niches and so close down to the floor that their viewing, let alone their manufacture, would have been well-nigh impossible.

At all events, the formal qualities of Hesi-re's surviving reliefs may now be seen to represent that fragile yet decisive moment in the culture of the royal workshops when the mature court style was first realized. At its best, it would remain a meditative art created by a small number of specialists working in isolation as part of the circle of the court, an activity that, in great part, seems to have been a private dialogue between the craftsmen and their courtly patrons. Such comments, though, treat Hesi-re's reliefs as if they were Western works of art, when in reality their placement in an uncomfortable and lightless gallery has nothing, whatever, to do with the modern roles of viewers, patrons and practitioners. Here, then, were worlds that we no longer know or really understand.

Mariette removed the five best preserved of Hesi-re's reliefs for public exhibition in the viceroys' growing collections, where they received the celebrity that they still retain within the Cairo Museum. Mariette did not, however, map or even fully excavate the tomb itself, which in consequence was swallowed by the sand again for half a century and more, until an elderly workmen, Osman Duqmaq, told the English archaeologist James Quibell that he had seen Mariette take the wooden panels from the side of a high mound of mud brick on the Saqqara plain.

Quibell had gone to excavate at Saqqara in 1901. After his work at

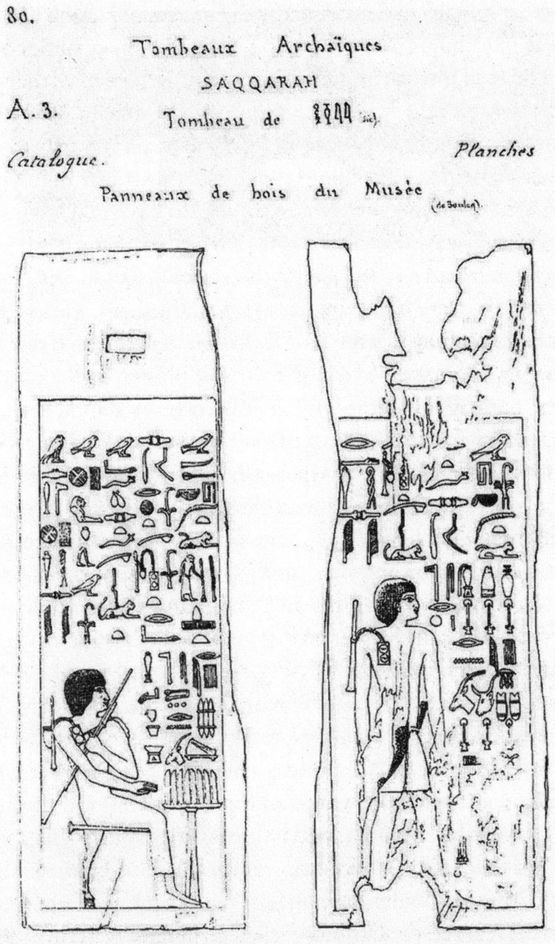

80.

Tombeaux Archaïques

SAQQARAH

A. 3.   Tombeau de 𓎛𓋴𓂋𓇾 (iii)

Catalogue.   *Planches*

Panneaux de bois du Musée (de Boulaq)

*Two of Hesi-re's acacia wood reliefs drawn by the architect Geslin for
Mariette's original publication. They are some 3 feet 9 inches tall*

Hierakonpolis and the preparation of a catalogue of archaic objects
for the newly founded Cairo Museum, he had become an acknowledged expert on the period and, as a senior inspector of Mariette's
Service des Antiquités, planned to excavate an enormous mass of
early tombs which lay behind the line of cliff-top mastabas.

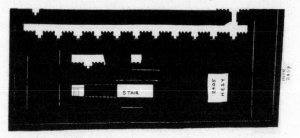

The plan of the mastaba of Hesi-re and its row of niches as drawn by its excavator, James Quibell. The superstructure is almost 140 feet long; the stairs lead down to a series of shafts and to the burial chamber

It was there, at the largest of those tombs, in the monument that Osman Duqmaq had remembered as the tomb of the wooden panels, that Quibell found, in one of the last baskets of debris that his workmen removed from Hesi-re's burial chamber, some jar sealings bearing the name of King Djoser. These showed the reign in which Hesi-re's burial had been sealed and thus the king in whose court he had served. Now, indeed, the images of the two men, king and courtier, could be seen to share the same distinctive stone-faced demeanour – and even the same-shaped moustache.

Quibell also found the sad remains of the other panels. Though part-consumed by ancient insects, they were still standing in their original positions in the palace façade. This had been decorated, Quibell records, in the traditional way – and in similar fashion to the grand façades of Merka's tomb painted two centuries before – as a series of *tromp l'œil* renderings of wooden frames and rope bindings that held brightly coloured geometric images of mats, such as might have been set up to make a screen within a garden or in the desert during a hunting trip.

On the opposite wall of this narrow corridor of niches, and apparently unnoticed by Mariette, Quibell also found faint traces of some remarkable drawings of courtly furniture, beds, stools, sticks, cabinets and canopies, cloths, mats and gaming boards, many of which would not have looked in the least out of place, in the following millennium, amongst the goods piled up in Tutankhamun's tomb. Another section of the same finely plastered wall held images of weights and measures, of oil jars, and boxes of tools, utensils and supplies, such as were trafficked in the court's systems of supply. Here, then, draughtsmen had painted images of the very goods that, in reality, had been stacked and stored within the chambers of the great mastabas of the First Dynasty.

Just a foot or so away from these careful drawings, half-hidden beneath bulging lintels and set between the gaudy patterns of the painted rugs, the tender wooden reliefs of Hesi-re would have been barely visible. Yet, in the darkness of that corridor they had been set up close to this enormous diagram, a visual stocktaking of traditional tomb furnishings. Between the two of them – between the living, breathing qualities of Hesi-re's reliefs and the painted spreadsheet on the opposing wall listing everything his spirit would have traditionally required – the installations at the tomb's east wall had taken on a quality of magic realism, a quality that would have been enhanced by the placing of fresh offerings at the bottom of the niches, rites given architectural expression by the little maze of corridors and chambers set around the mastaba that led to the niches in its eastern wall.

In the darkness of the tomb, images have been pushed hard against reality and are transforming into objects, words and sounds. In the wooden panels alone, image, word and object are transposed to the extent that, on one of them, the figure of the scribe carries the hieroglyphs that form his own name, Hesi-re, in his two hands: the distinctively shaped archaic *hes* vase in one, the rounded, sun-like disk, the *re*, in the other. Rather than demonstrating a proclivity for punning, as this quality is usually portrayed, the designers of this transformative environment were dealing in a new-found language of writing and of image, one with dimensions that are both visual and metaphysical and which in later centuries would be used to define and categorize the realms of life and death within the kingdom.

Here, then, image and the written word have taken on especial power. In comparison to the mass of goods stacked up in earlier mastabas, just a few provisions appear to have been placed in the apartments of the tomb of Hesi-re, the bulk of them having been replaced by written and painted lists and facilities for future offerings. Hesi-re's spirit is served by words and images and a few chosen objects, and the relationship of all these categories one to another has been transformed.

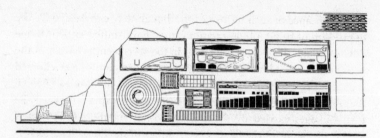

Annie Quibell's drawing of some of the wall paintings in the corridor of niches at the tomb of Hesi-re. This section holds images of offering tables and gaming boards such as were often placed in earlier tombs – and further images of chests filled with tools and sticks, weights and measures. The largest of the boxes is some 18 inches long

ORDER AND THE COURT

And every pillour decked was full deare
With crownes and Diademes, and titles vaine,
Which mortall Princes wore . . .
          Edmund Spenser, The Faerie Queene 1590

The burial of Hesi-re in such a large and splendid tomb suggests that he had been an influential member of the court. None of his inscriptions, however, describe him, as Merka was described, as *iry-pet*, as a member of the royal inner circle. That he is often shown in his reliefs carrying a scribe's set of brushes and a palette suggests that the role of scribe may have been a significant part of his position. Translated in the manner of later inscriptions, some of the elegant hieroglyphs in his reliefs tell that he was indeed 'overseer of the kings scribes' but that at the same time he was the 'greatest of doctors and dentists' and a 'captain of work gangs'. That Hesi-re's own name may be loosely rendered as 'sun offerer, or worshipper' might even seem to further gild the image of what at first appears as a master scribe and a prodigious personality.

Yet in reality there is scant understanding of the precise contemporary significance of such terms which, though they can easily give the impression of being job descriptions, may have shifted in their usage down through the dynasties, just as, in the seventeenth century of the present era, a field-marshal had been a subordinate officer charged with the organization of military encampments. In similar fashion, the origins of Hesi-re's appellation as work-gang captain may well lie in the images carried by the little bands of standard bearers that accompany some of the figures of the kings of the First Dynasty. It is a common designation amongst the courtiers of later centuries, when it apparently describes some of the posts of the supervisors of a wide range of separate units within the court, from pyramid builders to temple servants and divisions of the royal household. In the time of Hesi-re, therefore, when mature pharaonic society was still under construction, it would be misleading to take such translated terms at face value.

All that the tomb of Hesi-re really tells us about its one-time occupant is that he was not of the same social group as Merka had been, but an official of the royal court and most probably literate; that either he or some of the members of his household were interested in the finest craftsmanship of the day and that, as Quibell found in the course of his excavations, he may well have had a partner, a woman named by the excavator as Ankh-efes, whose name was found in Hesi-re's burial chamber on fragments of stone vases, along with the disconnected bones of several individuals, some of whom were also identified as female. And yet, and more importantly, perhaps, it also tells us that the times, the very air of the society that Hesi-re inhabited, had greatly changed since Merka's day.

CONSTANCY AND CHANGE

Crown him, and say: 'Long live our Emperor!'
Shakespeare, Titus Andronicus

Although they lived a century and a half apart, there is considerable constancy in the burials of Merka and Hesi-re. Both were nobles of pharaoh's court and buried close to each other on the plateau of Saqqara in tombs of traditional design. In similar fashion, the images on Merka's limestone stela and the reliefs on Hesi-re's acacia slabs are drawn in the same way and share the same essential subject matter: a figure of the tomb owner set beside lines of hieroglyphics naming the man and something of his status at the court, a traditional composition that was elaborated in the century after Merka and remained a fundamental feature of Egyptian tombs throughout the following millennia. Such images usually show the dead tomb owners with lists of offerings – a *post mortem* system of accounting that is also common in the later courtly tombs – and on several of his panels, too, Hesi-re is shown seated at an offering table loaded with bread, while some of the texts above his figure hold written lists of offerings.

Yet though the two tombs show a constancy typical of the later kingdom, an accumulation of changes that occurred in the period between the times of Merka and of Hesi-re hints at huge transformations in the order of the state. The vast numbers of seal impressions that have survived from the First Dynasty, for example, record the names of courtiers who, like Merka, were engaged in some manner in the traffic and supply of goods. By the time of the Third Dynasty, however, and certainly in the tomb of Hesi-re, the kings' names alone appear on the preponderance of jar sealings. By that time, as well, the records of the annual round of tithing and ceremonial which had been compiled throughout the period of the First Dynasty seem also to have stopped.

Such changes echo others in the structures of the court itself. In the days of Merka, the monuments suggest, it had been a relatively small affair, composed of men close to the king who were directly concerned with the provisioning of the court and who had accompanied the royal progress up and down the river. By the time of Hesi-re, the fundamental processes of tithing and supply seem to have been organized as they would be in later ages; conducted, that is, from a series of regional bases up and down the Nile in the manner of the offices beside the stone workers' workshops at Aswan. In the time of Hesi-re, indeed, those same court offices would have been engaged in the supply of thirty ponderous blocks of the dull-red stone, weighing up to twelve tons each, to make King Djoser's burial chamber.

Faint traces of similar offices have been uncovered in recent excavations in the delta, whilst some surviving sealings hint that just such a supply base may also have existed at el-Kab on the eastern river-bank by Hierakonpolis. Here, too, if the titles on some seal impressions may be said to reflect contemporary circumstance, granary inspectors might have been operating as early as the Second Dynasty. And certainly, by the time of Hesi-re, a series of five mastabas – some of the largest ever made – were being built in the cemeteries of Beit Khallaf, a site close to Abydos, to house the burials of men who appear to have fulfilled something of the role of provincial governors. Sealings from these tombs show that some of these burials enjoyed pharaonic patronage and further hint, therefore, at the extension of the royal reach beyond that of personal appearances at the ancient ceremonials of slaughtering and tithing.

Apart from the provision of materials and supplies required for the ongoing construction of King Djoser's pyramid – a work that, by itself alone, would have required the equipping and provision of more than a thousand individuals – a newly developing regional network of supply would have encouraged the refinement of the state systems of collection and accounting, and thus prompted the need for scribes to transmit data, beyond the simple listings of Merka's time. Writing, as the seals from the lost papyrus scrolls at Aswan and several other sites appear to testify, had gained importance. Beyond the increasing sophistication of the hieroglyphic system in contemporary inscriptions, further evidence of a new emphasis on writing is the growing role of scribes within court society. Scrolls of sheet papyrus, a tough writing medium made of plant fibre, were certainly in use at the court by Merka's day, but there is no mention of the scribes themselves on the contemporary monuments. Images of later nobles, though, such as those of Hesi-re, who is the very model of a modern major courtier, are sometimes shown carrying a scribal writing kit and described, apparently, as holding positions in the court scriptorium. Life and death, it would appear, had changed with the systems of state accounting.

Now, too, as the offices of court diffused throughout the land, signs of royal patronage increased in their importance. At the same time, the great cemeteries of the people of the farms and settlements seem to disappear, along with the millennial Naqadan burial culture.

When the hawk had wheeled, when pharaoh's court had turned in on itself, the use of rare materials and the products of the mining and smelting industries were increasingly restricted to the royal work-shops. Along with the copper chisels that, from vases to pyramids, were essential to the production of courtly works, such exotic raw materials as alabaster and cedar wood, granite, ebony and gold were all procured by courtly enterprise, so that, by the time of Hesi-re, their employment in the finer furnishings of noble tombs and households was probably dependent upon royal patronage.

Although the mastabas of men like Merka and Hesi-re appear similar, the circumstances of their creation were entirely different. The relationship of courtier to king had changed so much, indeed, that, by the time of Hesi-re, men like Merka would have seemed impossibly independent. By the time of Djoser's dynasty, the surviving tombs and pyramids suggest that there was a greatly increased focus and efficiency within the systems on which King Narmer's name had first been stamped.

The scale of the enterprise had changed as well. In Merka's day, the tombs of courtiers had held the wholesale wealth of great estates and had been set up like lighthouses along Memphis's western skyline. By the time of Hesi-re, however, the royal tomb in the gigantic form of Djoser's pyramid had risen up to dominate that same horizon, and the sizes of the courtiers' mud-brick tombs, though similar to that of Merka's mastaba, were but a tiny fraction of the size of that enormous stone-block building. Here, then, is a monumental differentiation between the fate of kings and that of their subjects, and one whose crisp unmoving lines still loom over the dissolving mud-brick monuments of the royal courtiers.

Now, too, unlike those of Merka's dynasty, the monuments of Djoser's nobles occupy relatively modest situations on the desert plateau, like court attendants standing round a throne. And, if the inscriptions of slightly later monuments may stand as guide, it would appear that the desert plateau of itself was part of the royal monopoly. Tombs like Hesi-re's, therefore, signal the next stage in the transition of the pharaoh from chief officer of supply to a ruler whose office is the linchpin of the living state and whose spirit after death had unique and even supernatural potential. It is the beginning of the mature pharaonic kingdom.

ARS BREVIS

The craftsman's gaze had shifted. For the first time in Egyptian history, the craftsmen of King Djoser's time – for there are other monuments of those same days though none, perhaps, as fine as those of Hesi-re's – show individuals made of skin and bone, living people whose pulsing bodies will change when their hearts have stilled and they are placed inside their tombs. It is as if pharaonic time, that new non-cyclic history based on the span of human life, had entered the sensibility of the court workshops and the craftsmen's skills were now employed to scrutinize the qualities of living people.

Such changes should not be attributed to some kind of technical, Vasarian advance within the craftsmen's workshops. The images of Hesi-re show no more evidence of improved craftsmanship or observation than, say, the Naqadan animal sculptures, and they are also built upon the same subtle balance of silhouette and interior form. In their time, however, society was changing.

Traditionally, such striking visual evidence of cultural change has been taken as a symptom of other changes which had previously taken place in politics or religion. Yet in the deep silence at the very edge of history, there is no evidence of that at all: no evidence that such assumptions were the prime movers of that age. What is known, however, is that Hesi-re lived in a society in which the internal order of the early court had been overtaken and a new culture had been installed around the overwhelming image of the pharaoh, and that, without that figure, there would be no later state, no fine materials or tools, no pyramids, no images of the living man in Hesi-re's reliefs; only the anonymity of prehistory.

Now, too, there is a single order all along the lower Nile: a silent social contract whose viability within the confines of a tough Bronze Age economy was ultimately dependent on the office of the pharaoh and the Nile's phenomenal fertility; a contract in which a well-ordered population chose to live and die as part of the pharaonic order; a contract whose first draft had been manifested in living pageants and the figure at the centre of the oval court.

Now, though, the temper of the court itself had changed. In the days of Merka, the nobles' tombs of the Memphis region were engorged with provisions and supply but had relatively little of the finest productions of the royal workshops stored in the royal tombs at Abydos. Now, however, the tombs of courtiers like Hesi-re were not filled with the contents of great households nor the produce of their estates but with far fewer, often finer things, the qualities of which had spread to include parts of the monument itself. More individual in their architecture than the monuments of their predecessors, the contents of these new tombs represent the more intimate aspects of their owners' lives and are increasingly concerned with different aspects of the living person. Hesi-re's reliefs, as we have seen, were probably made while he was still alive. It is as if, within the small society of courtiers, there had been a lessening in tension after the slaughter stopped.

Though parts of Hesi-re's tomb survived, most of the reliefs and statues placed in other contemporary monuments at Saqqara had been taken out and sold to various European collections in the decades before Mariette began his work. The majority of the surviving reliefs are cut on limestone blocks rather than the warm wooden panels of Hesi-re's reliefs, and they are generally of lesser quality. Some sculptures, though, have something of those same rare attributes. Two near-life-sized limestone statues of a man and a woman with smudges of green-painted eye make-up bear similarly ambiguous epithets to those on Hesi-re's reliefs. A group of twenty stumpy seated statues, whose courtly style, though yet emerging from a heavily archaic past, bears resemblance to the famous statues of the king. Their forms and manners would be echoed later on, in some of ancient Egypt's later masterpieces.

Here, then, is Ankhwa. Well built, thick-limbed, the granite statue's thyroid face is capped by a heavy wig. He has a boat-builder's adze slung on his shoulder in the same denominative manner in which the relief sculptors drew a scribal palette on the chest of Hesi-re. Like others of the group, the half-life-sized figure has been pounded from a hefty block of speckled Aswan granite, and Ankhwa's name is lightly cut into his linen kilt.

Here too is another doughty statue of a courtier, wrapped in the leopard skin of priestly office and wearing a necklace shaped like a circle with a horizontal line attached to it, in the form of the so-called *shen* hieroglyph. In the times of Djer and Djet and Den, the same sign had been drawn on some of the picture plaques underneath a notched and curving palm rib, signifying the years of pharaoh's rule. Later, the same round sign would also serve as the determining image for the phrase signifying the endless circuit of the sun; later still, it would be stretched into the so-called 'cartouche' that holds the names of kings.

The shen sign

And there are princesses in this stony court, round-kneed, full-breasted, high-shining sculptures, one of them described as a 'true daughter of the king'. Pounded out of jet-black blocks of stone, their steady staring faces enlivened by thin chisel lines drawn with considerable artifice around their eyes and mouths, they also bear resemblance to the statues of their king.

To the modern eye, this small community holds the beginnings of a formal definition of human individuality that you can also see in Hesi-re's reliefs. Queens and scribes, boat builders and priests, all staring confidently ahead, the bright-faced members of a brand-new social order that, even as their tombs were made, was overseeing the construction of the first Egyptian pyramid.

PART FOUR

Step Pyramid
(2675–2650 BC)

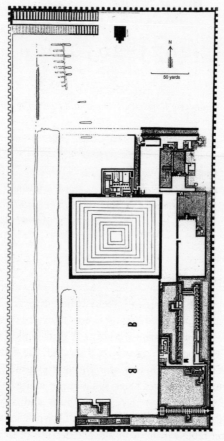

The excavators' plan of the Step Pyramid enclosure, circa 1928

22

Djoser's Kingdom

When conducting a visit to Sakkara don't miss the following sites:

   The Step Pyramid of King Zoser, and its surrounding complex:

   The Pyramid of King Titi:

   The tomb of Mereruka and the tomb of Kagimni:

   The Mastaba tomb of Ti, and the tomb of Ptah-Hotep:

                                             Ask-Aladdin.com

Of the ten million tourists that visit Egypt every year, a fair number take a charabanc to the desert cemeteries of Saqqara, an hour from Cairo along bumpy roads, past onion fields and pyramids half buried in the sand, through groves of palms, until they are disgorged with a pneumatic swish, onto a windy plateau. A slow walk through yellow sand, down a narrow passageway and through the flicking shadows of an oddly fluted colonnade, and Djoser's pyramid, that strange familiar monument, is revealed across a bright white court.

Excavated and explored during the 1920s and 1930s by James Quibell and Cecil Firth and other officers of Egypt's Service des Antiquités, and later rebuilt from the millennial detritus of stone plunderers and lime burning by the architect Jean-Philippe Lauer, the pyramid and its remarkable enclosure places visitors in a four-thousand-year-old environment and at the same time sets their imaginations running through a maze of ancient festivals and spirit palaces, and hoary tales of King Djoser and a famous vizier.

And through all of this, plain, uninscribed and largely unexplained, the ancient buildings stand silently around. And you might never guess that this grand enclosure, with its enormous pyramid and a faint air of the Champ de Mars, had been the place where many ancient Egyptians had thought their history had begun.

At the beginning, Djoser's builders had not meant to make a pyramid at all, having started the construction of the royal tomb with a scheme to make a different architectural novelty; a 200-foot-square slope-sided mastaba entirely built from blocks of well-cut stone. Only after two decades of change and alteration did the 'Step Pyramid', as the construction is now known, emerge; an oblong architectural pile rising in six slanting steps to a height of around 200 feet to form the first Egyptian pyramid; a work that in the making, had consumed 600,000 tons of limestone blocks, 120 tons of granite, and some 70 tons of copper chisels.

The pyramid, however, was but half the work that Djoser's builders undertook at Saqqara. By the time of his death, it was standing at the centre of a near-forty-acre enclosure, a rectangle of beautifully made stone walls niched in the serekh pattern of the early mastabas. And inside this mile-long perimeter were row upon row of dummy buildings, entirely made of blocks of fine white stone. To the west of the pyramid, there were long, low, stone buildings with the appearance of extended mastabas, whose labyrinthine underground galleries have yet to be fully explored and which appear to have held huge quantities of wheat. To the north, there is a colossal three-tiered altar and other long, low buildings that are also as yet largely uninvestigated. To the east, there was a beautiful series of open courts, each one lined with groups of finely finished buildings whose elegant façades gave the appearance of simple buildings thinly made from wood and rush, but in reality were entirely solid structures sheathed in fine white limestone and filled with rough-cut blocks. To the south, set against the perimeter wall, there is a mysterious mastaba of stone with a splendid frieze of spitting cobras. It has a royal burial chamber set beneath it that is the equal of the one beneath the pyramid, and it is similarly constructed from a dozen massive granite blocks set in a deep, wide shaft. And the volume of stone required to make this unique environment, these architectural masterpieces that are the world's oldest stone-block buildings, was equal to the volume of stone required to build the pyramid itself.

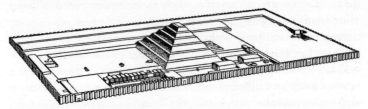

A reconstruction of the ancient appearance of the Step Pyramid enclosure. The so-called 'Heb-sed Court' lies in the narrow area to the left of the pyramid and has rows of little buildings set along its sides

DJOSER AND HISTORY

It is sometimes said that the first indisputable proof that the earth is round was the photographs taken by the first astronauts. In similar vein, the erection of Djoser's pyramid provided pharaoh's subjects with visible evidence of the power of the transport and supply systems that they had built over the previous half-millennium and which were the very essence of the state.

Nor was the unique role of Djoser and his monuments in the making of the pharaonic state forgotten during the later dynasties. Graffiti written by pharaonic scribes on the half-tumbled stones of his great enclosure in the following millennium say that it was as if 'heaven were within it'; as if it were 'a place from which the sun might rise', while in later lists of kings, court scribes would write Djoser's name in red ink rather than their usual black. And in texts and temples from Aswan to Alexandria, both the king and his fabled courtier Imhotep were offered prayers and admiration as the originators of everything from stone building to the arts of medicine.

Before King Djoser, so some later texts describe, the kingdom had been ruled by a succession of near-mythic monarchs. Only after Djoser, so the pharaonic lists and classical sources agree, had Egypt been ruled by mortal men, and it is their stories that make up the best part of the heroes in the noisy narratives of Greek histories. In the twentieth century of the present era, the great philologist-egyptologist Sir Alan Gardiner would still describe the vast unlettered ages before the times of Djoser and the pyramids as a time 'where a solid foothold of evidence is so lamentably absent'.

Yet the information available for Djoser's reign, as for all the monarchs of the Third Dynasty – which Djoser is considered to have founded – is as thin as that for earlier dynasties, and there are hardly any footholds for traditional historians; 'Data currently available are sufficient neither for determining the length of reigns for each king nor the length of the dynasty as a whole,' as a leading chronologist recently observed. So traditional history books fall back on later legends and the oldest surviving record of the period, a fragmented papyrus known as the 'Turin Canon', which was written at least fourteen centuries later and which gives Djoser nineteen years of rule, while Manetho's account in the *Aigyptiaka*, written a thousand years after that, awards him twenty-nine. Djoser, then, is still a semi-legendary monarch, his very name, indeed, a word meaning 'hallowed' or 'holy', being a later literary invention used by people like the scribes who wrote the name in the graffiti they left within his pyramid enclosure. Contemporary inscriptions, on the other hand, name its builder as King Netjerikhet.

It is the buildings, the buildings by themselves, the impressive remnants of his monuments, that provide the name of Djoser/Netjerikhet with an air of substance. His pyramid stands as a marker for the train leaving the tunnel of the Second Dynasty, where surviving monuments are thin on the ground and those that yet remain have none of the resonance of Djoser's unique pyramid enclosure, with its courts and their solid full-sized model buildings. Here, history is architectural, and it is to be found in both the buildings' forms and also in the materials from which they are made – in the extraordinary switch, especially, from mud brick to the stone block, which immediately became the supreme medium of the courts of all the later pharaohs.

The fundamental skills required for such a change, of course, were already available. Stone-working skills had long been held in great abundance in the royal workshops, whilst the support systems of transport and supply required for the realization of such an ambitious project had been built up over the previous half-millennium; they were, indeed, the sanctified quintessence of the state itself. What, then, was required of Djoser's courtiers and craftsmen was the imagination to conceive of making royal funerary architecture out of the traditional materials used by the stone-vase workshops: that, and the energy and administrative abilities to ensure that the court system of supply and control would work as it never had before.

THE SWITCH TO STONE

By Djoser's day, as the fragments of tens of thousands of splendid vases found at Abydos testify, the production of hard-stone vessels had been a major court activity for several centuries. Such wares were clearly prized. That other examples of this same courtly industry have been recovered from relatively modest tombs throughout the lower Nile suggests that they may also have been used as a kind of courtly commerce in fine things, as royal favours; a function that would appear to have been graphically acknowledged during the Second Dynasty with the invention of a hieroglyph of a stone pot with legs, a composite sign used to denominate the phrase 'that which is brought'. Long before stone was taken up for building pyramids, therefore, worked stone of itself had held a special status at court. Nor were those special qualities denied when the prime use of that material was switched from vase to block.

Dull-grey mud brick, on the other hand, had been used by all and sundry for a millennium and more, and for a variety of mundane purposes as well as for the royal tombs and the architecture of their accompanying enclosures. Made from water and Nile silt, and often with the judicious addition of chopped straw or sand, the ingredients of mud bricks were readily available throughout the region of the lower Nile and were manufactured simply by laying out their wet, new-made forms in the sun. Such huge structures as the nobles' mastabas and the royal tombs and funerary enclosures of the early dynasties were swiftly built and easily set up. And they have proved so durable in the Nile-side deserts that, though weather-beaten and eroded, many of them yet survive.

Stone, on the other hand, is intractable and slow to work, and requires metal tools to both extract and shape it. Much of the Step Pyramid enclosure, too, is made of varieties of stone that had been previously favoured by the court stone-vase manufacturers, and could only be obtained from relatively distant sources. Right from the outset, therefore, the making of King Djoser's stone-block funerary architecture was building on a very different scale from anything that had been done before.

Of the three types of stone used in Djoser's monuments, two were shipped along the Nile. Only the coarse limestones used for much of the filling and foundations of his buildings seem to have originated at Saqqara, mined directly from the plateau just outside the great enclosure so that part of its white walls would have appeared to stand above a great dry moat. The monuments' facing stone, however, a fine-grained limestone, was probably quarried from the desert cliffs and hills that lie behind the modern town of Tura, a few miles to the north of Helwan on the east bank of the river, the masons' appreciation of that pure unblemished rock having begun long since, in the heyday of the stone-vase makers. Barged in blocks of up to thirty tons or so and pulled from canal-side quays up through the desert onto the cliff-top plateau, Tura limestone was used for both the body and the casing of the Step Pyramid, for its grand enclosure walls and also for the facing of all the other buildings in the enclosure, which are themselves as finely finished as an archaic vase.

Djoser's burial chamber, though, is a rough affair made up of ten blocks of granite, each weighing twelve and a half tons, the numbers that are marked on their surfaces suggesting that they had been designed and trimmed to fit in their allotted places before they were erected at the bottom of the burial pits. Along with a second set of blocks that make up a second burial chamber which lies beneath the southern mastaba, all these granite blocks were quarried at Aswan and shipped downstream to Memphis.

So the Step Pyramid and all the buildings in its grand enclosure are manifestly products of the state's supply lines, as indeed were the huge cargoes of tools and provisions required to support King Djoser's various labour forces. So the wooden river boats that first appeared within the painted tomb at Hierakonpolis, which had provisioned the Naqadan communities of Memphis and supplied the delta estates with implements and labourers, and whose cargoes had filled the royal tombs at Abydos, were reorganized in Djoser's time to sustain the work of the three-thousand-odd core craftsmen who, it may be estimated, were required to build the royal monuments. And special barges of unprecedented size must have been constructed to accommodate the huge blocks of stone which were also being shipped.

The skill and confidence that the masonry of Djoser's compounds displays from the very outset of the work show that the craftsmen who formed the hard core of this enormous enterprise were already seasoned stonemasons. They were thus drawn from the court vase-making workshops, the only workforce of any size that would have had the necessary experience and ability. Nor did this radical change of product, from vase to block, necessarily represent a challenge in the amount of work these craftsmen masons had undertaken. A statistical analysis of the energy required to manufacture the extraordinary quantities of vessels that were deposited in the archaic cemeteries shows that the court workshops' previous levels of production of hard stone represents a greater expenditure of labour than that required for cutting the relatively soft limestone building blocks employed in Djoser's monuments.

Underlining the direct connection between vase and block and the remarkably rapid shift of focus undertaken by this traditional court workforce, archaeologists excavating Djoser's complex found the distinctive marks of vase makers' flint drills on dozens of stones. The craftsmen, it appears, were still employing some of their old methods. The fundamental change, however, from vase to block signalled the ending of that grand archaic industry. After Djoser, as more and larger pyramids were built, though the physical dimensions of stone vases tended to increase, the level of their production went into a severe decline and the ancient craft never regained its previous position as the major consumer of the court's resources. That role had been taken over by the entirely novel profession of stonemasonry, which in a single generation would come to hold an unsung though defining role in the culture of the later pharaonic court.

The decision to use rectangular stone building blocks on such an unprecedented scale not only demanded the immediate attention of the court's vase workshops, but also unprecedented numbers of copper chisels and of the little hand saws which can cut soft limestone with a surprising ease. That the Abydos burial chamber of Djoser's father, Khasekhemui, had been lined with blocks of limestone smoothed and marked with small copper chisels – a novel architectural finish, and a previously unrecorded usage of a traditional tool – suggests that the pharaonic prospecting gangs were already surveying the mountains of the Eastern Desert and the Sinai peninsula for mining sites. They were now producing relatively plentiful amounts of the soft red metal that, until the introduction of iron tools into Egypt in the first millennium BC, would be the primary material of pharaonic tools and weapons.

Given that copper chisels quickly wear away, even when working a material as chalky as fresh-cut limestone, building on the scale of Djoser monuments required considerable amounts of that malleable metal. In fact, the million and more tons of cut stone blocks which comprise King Djoser's pyramid enclosure would have probably required some seventy tons of copper for their fashioning, an unprecedented quantity of such material in the ancient world. Cast in little desert furnaces set up close to the mines, the ingots would presumably have been transported to Memphis and Saqqara for recasting, for the most part, into small stone-working chisels, a few of which the archaeologists found in the Step Pyramid Enclosure.

This, then, was a logistic undertaking on a previously unknown scale: the years of quarrying, mining, barging and building that such grand monuments as pyramids require for their completion necessitating the establishment of settlements of labourers, quarrymen, sailors, shipwrights and miners all over pharaoh's kingdom. And of course, in common with the courtiers and the king, all these professionals would have required provisioning.

In common with most of the activities of ancient life, evidence of these extraordinary labours has almost disappeared, and is only tokened now by the buildings in the Step Pyramid enclosure, by the reliefs of Djoser on the rocks of Sinai, and by a variety of mud seals stamped with the royal name that have been found in excavations in settlements and cemeteries all through the valley, from the delta to the cataract at Aswan.

Now, though, the sturdy little statue of the boat-builder Ankhwa, with a wood-worker's adze hooked on his shoulder and the scribal pens and inks that are similarly worn by Hesi-re on some of his reliefs, speaks of the growing importance of those two professions at King Djoser's court. Just as the pyramid marks the beginning of the new-made profession of the stonemason, so those courtly images speak of the rise of a new kind of bureaucracy, a core element of Djoser's changing kingdom, and another augury of the later order of the state.

Just as the pharaonic scribes of later ages who graffitied the Step Pyramid's enclosure had understood, Djoser's reign marked the beginning of a brand-new era. As his buildings had risen on the Saqqara plateau, the very process of their making came to define the size, the structure and the outreach of the later state. At a single stroke, the change from mud to stone became the catalyst that would facilitate the transformation of a precocious prehistoric culture into an elegant and millennially successful kingdom.

TO MAKE A PYRAMID

The decision to break with the traditional construction techniques of mud brick, and in effect turn Khasekhemui's limestone block burial chamber inside out, involved considerable amounts of trial and error and large amounts of time and court resources, as the complex *mélange* of block sizes and bonding visible in the lower portions of King Djoser's pyramid still clearly testify. That these elaborate experiments in construction were being undertaken at the same time as additions were being built onto the original square stone mastaba shows that, at exactly that same time, a new and distinctive architectural vision was arising. This was a vision that, if present estimates of the length of Djoser's reign are accurate, grew for the best part of a quarter-century.

Various antecedents have been claimed for the architectural form of Djoser's pyramid at Saqqara, modest mud-brick structures, mostly, that had been built over some of the great mud-brick burial chambers of the First Dynasty and which by Djoser's day had been buried for a century and more. And, of course, the indelible outline of King Djoser's pyramid is self-evidently something other than the happenstance of copying the bonding of mud brick. At the same time, though, the pyramid's fundamental qualities derive from a venerable design tradition. Its crisp silhouette and fine, pure form, the concentration on a superb finish which, though now largely missing from the pyramid, is still evident amongst the other buildings in the Step Pyramid's enclosure hark back to the design tradition of Naqadan craftsmen and the finest products of the court vase-making workshops.

Strictly speaking, stone-block building had not been an innovation of King Djoser's time. Slabs and shafts of granite and fine limestone had long been used as paving stones and doorjambs and portcullises in the corridors of the great mastabas of the First Dynasty, whilst stone slabs had also been employed as wall linings in some smaller near-contemporary tombs at Helwan, as well as that of Khasekhemui at Abydos. In similar fashion, the stacks of dry, rough stone which compose the foundations and the fillings of some of the buildings within Djoser's great enclosure bear resemblance to the fieldstone walls of the enormous stone enclosure, as yet largely unexcavated, that was erected in the time of Khasekhemui, in the desert behind Djoser's enclosure.

By Djoser's day, however, there were pressing practical reasons for the tomb makers to abandon mud-brick architecture, for the superstructures of some of the contemporary mastabas were reaching sizes close to the limits of mud brick as a building medium. The great contemporary mastabas at Beit Khallaf, for example – the largest of which is 280 feet long and almost 40 feet high – would have disintegrated under their own weight had their builders stacked more bricks on top of them without providing additional support in wood or stone. Stone alone, in fact, could stand as high as Djoser's pyramid, and stone alone could be set in such crisp, straight and enduring lines.

The pyramid, however, was not the form that Djoser's builders had originally intended. As we have seen, they had first made a square, slope-sided mastaba whose simple forms were probably derived from the modest superstructures of the earlier royal tombs on the Umm el-Qa'ab at Abydos, and whose dimensions were considerable smaller than some of the contemporary mud-brick mastabas. From the beginning, though, the unique ambition of King Djoser's builders had been to make a monument of stone. This was the mastaba that may still be seen today – for it is part-visible in the body of the later pyramid – and it was laid out in straight and perfectly levelled lines on the surface of the desert, its sides and corners set to rise with the symmetry and precision of a fine stone vase.

These novel architectural qualities, it appears, had immediately impressed. So, with the mastaba finished, yet with the national supply systems still sending provisions to the workforce at Saqqara, with the miners smelting ingots of desert copper and gangs of quarrymen producing considerable quantities of fine stone blocks, the craftsmen masons first set a series of larger mastabas against and over the finished original before piling a succession of more slope-sided mastabas one atop the other in a series of steps – a feat utterly unrealizable in mud brick – so that finally they created a unique, unmoving, solid structure almost 200 feet high, whose crisp, clean lines were entirely clad with Tura limestone as finely finished as a limestone vase.

To keep such an enormous structure straight without the aid of modern surveying equipment presents a special range of problems that modern builders never have to consider. Clearly, the earlier experience of building enormous mud-brick structures greatly aided the work in its first phases. The influence of brick building shows as well in the battered walls of the first stone mastabas, which are typical mud-brick forms, an angle that is repeated at the rise of the pyramid's six steps. Now, though, as they built ever higher, the masons were able to employ the unyielding qualities of stone to stop their building crumbling under pressure, and also to keep a constant check on the building's shape and level; for, as always with such large and solid structures, there was a constant danger of it shifting out of true as it rose higher and its weight increased. And so, by using blocks of stone and water as a level, and stretched lines of cord, and plumb bobs, and the touch of fingertips across two adjacent stones to check for the slightest movement, and by constant observation and alignments with the night stars, which are the oldest known of all fixed points, they made a perfect pyramid that could be seen from Memphis far below them on the plain and from across the river at Helwan, and ten miles and more, north and south, all up and down the river.

ANTIQUARIAN

A mere Antiquarian is a rugged being.

Samuel Johnson

At the same time that Djoser's builders were busily creating a brand-new architecture with blocks of stone, the craftsmen working on the other buildings inside the pyramid's enclosure were carefully recreating in blocks of stone the forms of some of the traditional indigenous architecture of the settlements of the lower Nile. As Djoser's pyramid makers were building the foundations of future pharaonic culture, therefore, the other half of his workforce was working in an atmosphere that was self-consciously antiquarian.

Though a few of the galleries and tunnels beneath the Step Pyramid may have lain open since ancient times, the best part of them were blocked off by Djoser's builders, by drifting sand and rock falls, so it was only in the 1920s, when the archaeologists of the Service des Antiquités undertook their full clearance, that some forty thousand fine stone vessels were discovered lying in the long dark corridors. Collected up by Djoser's work gangs, they had been stacked and stored in sacks: vases, cups and dishes by the ton, many of them cracked and broken and looking for all the world like dusty clutches of dinosaur eggs, a grand accumulation of the products of the royal stone-working workshops since their beginnings. And the oldest of them bore King Narmer's name.

Engraved or scratched into their surfaces, or sometimes simply inked in red and black by practised scribal hands, dozens of these vessels bore laconic and often enigmatic inscriptions – this, after all, was not a literary age – that between them named most of the kings who had reigned before Djoser, and recorded specific events. Some of them recorded the names of two or three successive kings, while others announced or commemorated various courtly events. Others still, named regions and settlements in the Nile Valley, most frequently the great quarry in Middle Egypt, anciently called Hatnub, that had supplied the alabaster from which a great part of the subterranean store of vases had been made. In sum, the vases held a partial history of their times, a court circular in stone.

That Djoser's agents had gathered such a vast collection and stored it carefully beneath the royal pyramid suggests a kind of retrospection in the court, especially as many of the inscriptions bear a direct resemblance to others found in the far earlier royal tombs at Abydos. That the Second Dynasty kings are equally well represented in these texts suggests that those vases, too, may also have been collected from their tombs, for certainly the substructures of at least two of them lie just outside the Step Pyramid's eastern enclosure wall. Perhaps King Djoser's builders had dismantled some of those missing royal tombs; or, and more intriguingly, perhaps the superstructures of those missing tombs are buried within some of the dummy buildings in King Djoser's own enclosure, whose varied architecture, like the cache of vases, is itself a grand collection of much older forms.

At all events, there was, clearly, a whole lot of thinking going on inside King Djoser's funerary enclosure: nothing less than a reprise, an architectural restatement, of the royal presence in the regions of the lower Nile. Its very form, indeed, those long white walls with the niched patterns of the serekh and the palace façade, was derived from the great brick constructions of the earlier dynasties. Yet more remarkably, the lengths of those same walls were made precisely ten times larger than those of the mud-brick mastaba of Naqada built three centuries earlier and 300 miles to the south, in the Naqadan heartlands. In similar fashion, the forms and proportions of the dummy buildings within the great enclosure were derived from building types that had been erected in the lower valley of the Nile since mid-Naqadan times. Those modest constructions, whose images appear upon a range of archaic engravings and whose architectural traces Michael Hoffman and his colleagues had excavated at Hierakonpolis, were made of wood and reed, and mud and basketry. In Djoser's day, those particular structures would have been some eight centuries old. Nonetheless, along with other early building types, the forms and the proportions of at least one of those building types were faithfully and resplendently reproduced in stone within the six open courtyards that lie along the east side of Djoser's enclosure.

As well as making a geometric synthesis of some of the traditional forms of Nilotic architecture, the royal stonemasons also made clever reproductions of those buildings' original materials. Columns that reproduced the forms of reed and rush, of wooden masts, of building frames and wicket fences, of plastered mud-brick walls and wooden doors left open or ajar, were all smoothly and symmetrically rendered in an elegant petrifaction that has direct precedent in the earlier productions of the stone-vase workshops which had transposed the forms of woven rush and leaves and baskets into dishes made from desert stone. Nor were these merely rococo demonstrations of the craftsmen builders' skills nor, certainly, as is sometimes claimed, examples of their naive simplicity. These were painstaking reproductions of aspects of the traditional Nilotic world made with abstract blocks of fine white limestone.

What, then, were these dummy buildings for? That many of them take the form of archaic shrines suggests they may be related to the rites of royal audience, of slaughtering, offering and tithing: the usual subject matter of many of the scenes in which the images of those shrines appear. It would be reasonable, therefore, to suppose that the courts in which these dummy buildings stand are representations of the environments in which the ancient originals had stood. Thus they are stony imitations of the ambience of the living rites of audience that, along with the shrines and the other buildings associated with the royal court, had been established in some of the settlements along the lower Nile for many centuries.

Unfortunately, the archaeologists found very little in most of these open courts to support or contradict such theories. In two of them, however, they discovered that King Djoser's masons had carefully reproduced a throne dais in polished blocks of Tura stone, such as appear in early scenes of royal audience. And one of these stood at the southern end of a narrow court about a hundred yards in length, whose sides had once been lined by rows of dummy buildings with the appearance of archaic shrines.

As its excavators realized, the complicated shape of the throne dais in the narrow court was somewhat similar to those drawn in the hieroglyphic image of a double throne and canopy set up on a podium. This was a hieroglyph which appears from the time of the First Dynasty and was later used as the determining sign to designate the term '*heb sed*', the name of a millennially celebrated series of court rituals now known as Sed festivals. Here, then, Djoser himself may well have sat, in spirit or in flesh, in regal ceremonial.

The hieroglyph of a double throne with steps – the so-called 'heb sed' throne base; from Petrie's drawing of fragments of a white stone vase recovered from a royal tomb upon the Umm el-Qa'ab

Distinctive statues that were found scattered throughout Djoser's great enclosure give further credibility to the impression that some of these open courts were reproductions of the courts of royal audience and, especially, of slaughtering and tithing. The statues bear a strong resemblance in their technique to the high-shining sculptures of Djoser's nobles and are of equal if not superior quality, yet have entirely different subject matter. Though complete works in themselves, these sculptures are simply busts or heads, or rows of heads, thrust forward in the age-old pose of prisoners waiting, with the same dignified resignation that you sometimes see on modern news reports, for the *coup de grâce*.

An earlier example of this same tragic genre had been found at Hierakonpolis, in the mud-brick enclosure of Djoser's predecessor, Khasekhemui, where it had served as a door post, the socket grinding into the back of the out-thrust neck. At Hierakonpolis as well, in the archaic temple, Quibell and Green had excavated some near-life-sized sculptures of bound and kneeling prisoners with their heads set in the same distinctive attitude. Nearby, in the great cache, they also found many objects of both ivory and clay with drawings of prisoners in that same vulnerable pose which, of course, is a part of that considerable repertoire of images of slaughter and confinement that frequently appear on courtly objects of the First Dynasty. And after Djoser, too, similarly posed figures, near-life-sized sculptures, were set up in the courtyards of several of the royal pyramids, where they appear to mark out areas where offerings are made, demarcating a zone that, in the manner of the archaic courts, is at the very edges of the living world. These sculptures, then, bespeak royal appearance and ceremonial.

Another aspect of these same occasions is represented by a small group of unusual statues of bearded, standing males that were also made in Djoser's era but which, being smaller and more portable, have been gathered up by dealers and taken out of Egypt, and thus have no known provenance. Though a different statue type from the so-called 'prisoner' statues, they are of the same tradition and may have been made in the same skilled workshops. These statues, though, are far rarer than those of prisoners, and all of them are smashed. Even the best example, which must have stood about a foot high, is broken at the knees. At first glance, perhaps, it does not impress. Then you notice that, like the reliefs of Hesi-re, it has an unusual vivacity of line and an exquisite finish, that it is cut from mottled desert gneiss, that it wears a penis sheath as prehistoric images of men had done, and that, rather than clutching a stick, as would usually be the case in Djoser's day, its right hand grips a flint-bladed slaughtering knife such as the Naqadans had used. This group of little statues, therefore, which may well have come from the excavation of King Djoser's great enclosure, inhabits the same zone between death and life as the prisoner statues; that zone which, in reality, was once held in the archaic royal courts.

Human sacrifice had long since ceased by Djoser's day, nor is there

An image of a bound prisoner carved three centuries before the Step Pyramid complex was built; a five inch ivory found in the great cache of Hierakonpolis and drawn by Annie Quibell

evidence of its return in later periods. What makes these powerful images especially fascinating, therefore, is that even as the pharaonic court was engaged in building the first pyramid, making the world's first state, the long Naqadan heritage of tithe and offering and its particular environment, that zone of life and death held in the earlier settlements, was being carefully examined, and parts of it were being set into the centre of the state.

23

Heb Sediana

Visions of the Pyramid

History has been committed here today.
Unknown Super Bowl commentator, 2008

At the same time that the excavation of Djoser's pyramid enclosure was uncovering a mass of practical information, it was also creating a stage for the enactment of an entirely different kind of history. And a springboard of the better part of that is the so-called 'Heb Sed Court', a narrow yard lined with dummy shrine-like buildings with a dais set up at its southern end where Djoser may have sat enthroned.

It is not difficult to picture such proceedings. King Narmer's mace head has already shown the king in audience, installed on a similar if somewhat simpler podium, whilst comparable installations are represented on a number of ivory picture plaques and may even have been recovered, in bricks and mortar, by archaeologists working in the oval court at Hierakonpolis. And certainly, *heb sed* imagery is present in some of those archaic images, just as it is also represented on a number of the stone vases stacked in the corridors beneath King Djoser's pyramid. During the following millennia, as well, until the coming of the Greeks, many of the same archaic images would be periodically remade and reassembled at the pharaonic court, and celebrated in texts and images that describe a variety of Sed festivals. These appear to have consisted of a number of formal appearances in which the king performed a variety of rites dressed in archaic costumes. All this, then, might suggest a connection between these later Sed festivals and the podium by Djoser's pyramid. And that, in turn, led to the identification of Sed festivals, after the Old Testament's prescriptions, as a pharaonic jubilee, as a festival of jubilation, restoration and renewal, for many texts describe the later Sed festivals as being undertaken at specific intervals in a pharaoh's rule. And that, naturally, led to the proposal that the dummy buildings and the courts inside the Step Pyramid's enclosure had been built so that Djoser's spirit could celebrate the elaborate rites of just such jubilees.

Unfortunately, though a great deal has been written about these Sed festivals, they remain essentially mysterious. Despite the biblical resonances, and beyond the fact that some of the organizing officials of later times record that they carefully collected a raft of archaic customs and costumes for their re-enactment and display, there is precious little information as to their point and purposes. Even the origins of the term *heb sed* remain unknown. So naming of one or more of the courts inside King Djoser's pyramid enclosure as a 'Heb Sed Court' offers no genuine explanation of its function. With its air of biblical jubilee, it also provides those silent courts with false scenarios based on Western ideologies of divinity and kings.

Thou shalt halowe the fyftith year . . . he is forsothe the jubilee (Leviticus 25.10)

Given that the methods of early egyptological research were largely drawn from those of nineteenth-century biblical scholarship, the identification of Sed festivals with biblical jubilee was probably unavoidable. In similar fashion it was also conflated with the theories propounded in Sir James Frazer's *The Golden Bough*, a twelve-volume, twenty-five-year *magnum opus* and monument of late Victorian erudition, fine writing and judicious publishing, that came to a triumphant climax in a single-volume abridgment published in 1922, just four years before the excavation of the Step Pyramid complex had begun.

An underlying, if unstated, argument of *The Golden Bough*, and one that, at the time, was of considerable novelty, was that the key Christian themes of a dying and resurrecting god were also present in savage superstitions, in ancient history and in pagan faiths around the world – an idea that held such broad contemporary appeal, that, along with Stravinsky, T. S. Eliot and Freud, numerous egyptologists read and absorbed the various volumes as they emerged from Frazer's study. So Sed festivals were frequently viewed, as Frazer had previously outlined in great and gory detail in several chapters of volume 3 on 'The Killing of the Divine King', as having their roots in a world of prehistoric savagery. This was a world in which elderly or impotent rulers were physically tested and, if found weak or insufficient, were murdered by their successors; a fate that the semi-civilized pharaohs, it was opined, had managed to avoid by the cunning invention of a ceremonial involving a ritual renewal; an Egyptian jubilee!

Even as the archaeologists were cleaning the sand from the enormous puzzle of King Djoser's tumbled architecture, Frazer's theories were animating their interpretations. So his dying and resurrecting god sat easily upon the podium in Djoser's Heb Sed Court where, by an entirely circular logic, the king's spirit performed Frazerian rites to prove his fitness for eternal rule. This was a convenient scenario, one that corresponded nicely with the then current belief that pharaohs were considered to have been divine – another daydream, born of an imperial age in which many colonial administrators had imagined that, when tribal peoples, those simple souls, bowed the knee before them, they were regarding their foreign masters in exactly that same light.

THE EGYPTIAN LEONARDO

Fantasies of a somewhat similar vintage to that of the Frazerian Sed festival have also grown up around the making of the Step Pyramid itself, providing an unspoken answer to the essentially modern question as to the name of its designer. Most of these fancies are centred on the courtier Imhotep, a man 'who, because of his medical skill,' as Manetho told in his *Aigyptiaka*, 'has the reputation of Asklepios amongst the Egyptians and who was the inventor of the art of building with hewn stone . . .'. Such was Imhotep's fame in later millennia, indeed, that scribes would sprinkle a few drops of water in deference to him before they began to mix their inks, and in the classical manner, several of the chapels that were erected in his honour became sanatoria and Imhotep himself a god of healing.

Despite this autumn fame, however, the pharaonic Egyptians never credited Imhotep with designing the Step Pyramid nor indeed with the invention of stone architecture. All of that is a mix of Hellenizing myth and traditional translations of a single inscription from the time of Djoser, which was recovered during the excavation of the Step Pyramid's enclosure: 'The chancellor of the king of Lower Egypt, the first after the king of Upper Egypt, administrator of the great palace, hereditary lord, Greatest of Seers, Imhotep, the builder, the sculptor, the maker of stone vases.' Beautifully inscribed upon a royal statue base in fine archaic hieroglyphs, this ancient and somewhat oblique text has been widely interpreted as stating that Imhotep had been the first minister of the kingdom, a royal chamberlain and high priest, and that he had made sculpture and stone vases and designed the first Egyptian pyramid; that he was, in fact, as one commentator recently described him, 'an Egyptian Leonardo'.

Yet the contemporary meaning of such translations is as elusive as are the modern terms 'King of Jazz' or 'Lord Privy Seal'. What little evidence that has survived suggests that, rather than serving as literal descriptions of an individual personality or a list of job descriptions, they are, in common with the titles of most other cultures, coded representations of a person's standing in a community, such as a royal court or the world of jazz or even in a cemetery, or any other setting in which the text was destined to be placed.

A further objection to the casting of Imhotep in the role of Leonardo da Vinci is that it is based on the belief that history is dependent on individual psychologies, characters like Hegel's 'Men of Destiny', whose names alone give the illusion of providing answers to such loaded questions as 'who designed the Step Pyramid?' – to which, of course, the only possible answer is the name of an individual with the qualities of a nineteenth-century 'Renaissance Genius'. Yet, just as christening a part of Djoser's enclosure as a 'Heb Sed Court' tells little of its ancient purposes, so too the provision of a single ancient name offers no convincing explanation of the creation of his pyramid.

FORMS AND FUNCTIONS

Back on the ground and in reality, the various contemporary activities that find genuine architectural expression in Djoser's limestone architecture, and those on which his builders expended the better part of their energies, were connected with the physical well-being of the dead king: the hefty burial chamber set beneath the prodigious pyramid, the enormous magazines of wheat, and a maze-like building set over the sloping passageway that leads down to the royal burial chamber at the bottom of the pyramid's north face and which is now known as a pyramid temple. This building had great alabaster basins set into its floors to collect the blood of cattle that, in the age-old manner of Naqadan cemetery feasts, could be slaughtered at the graveside.

The other parts of Djoser's funeral enclosure, however, the courts of dummy buildings that appear to have been formal replicas of the key environments of the living state, seem to have been concerned in some way with the king's incorporeal needs. It is these, of course, that are now haunted by the ghosts of Frazer's resurrecting gods and by the modern studies of a variety of Sed festivals.

Six good clues, two groups of three limestone reliefs, point to the contemporary purposes of those dummy buildings with rather more precision. Vigorous and celebrated works of limestone carving, with qualities similar to those of Hesi-re's reliefs, they were engraved upon the walls of some of the subterranean chambers that lie underneath the pyramid and the southern mastaba. Set close to the two great granite burial vaults, the six reliefs were set in niches framed with splendid faience tiles whose forms give the impression of a building whose walls have been hung with matting made from fresh rushes.

Each of these six panels holds two columns of hieroglyphs and an image of King Djoser engaged in various activities that are differentiated by two different poses. Three of the panels show the king with legs akimbo, either running or striding. The other three place him in the standard ancient Egyptian pose of a figure with one leg in front of the other – a pose that, though it gives a Western eye the immediate impression of walking, actually shows him, as an examination of the musculature and the accompanying texts will indicate, as a stationary, standing figure.

In his standing pose, Djoser wears either the traditional Red or White Crown and holds a mace and a stick, the tools of royal slaughter. The accompanying cryptic hieroglyphs appear to indicate that he is visiting buildings whose hieroglyphic images resembled some of the

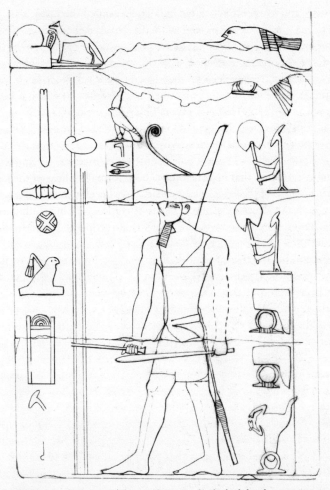

The king stands before a shrine: the central relief of the three images set beneath the Southern Mastaba. Djoser's figure is about half life size

dummy buildings in the pyramid enclosure. One of these buildings is identified as the shrine of the hawk that stood beneath the town of modern Edfu in Upper Egypt, another, as a shrine that stood on the site of the present town of Ausim to the north of Cairo, whilst the third appears to be the 'Great House' – the palace – of the king himself.

The king runs: the northernmost of the three reliefs that were set beneath the Southern Mastaba. Djoser's figure is about half life size

The three panels that hold the running figure show Djoser stripped for exercise. It is an ancient pose. An image of King Den, for example, performs the same action on an ivory label, and the figures of both Den and Djoser are accompanied by two groups of semicircular images which, as later hieroglyphs, served to denominate a term for the two banks of the Nile. Here, though, in these early images, the schematic drawings representing tongues of river silt may refer to some kind of boundary, for they are drawn on both sides of pharaoh's striding legs, as if they were delineating a span of cultivable land, such as would have been remeasured every year after the inundation of the river. Remarkably enough, two groups of those same signs were also reproduced in two solid constructions some thirty-five feet long and made of blocks of stone, which were set up along the centre line of one of the open courts in Djoser's pyramid enclosure. Lined up with a throne dais, which was situated against the southern baseline of the pyramid, these two distinctive structures appear like turning points upon a running track.

These monumental hieroglyphs in the open court beside King Djoser's pyramid certainly suggest the accommodation of some kind of ceremonial, and this, in turn, has led to its being interpreted as an element of Sed festival architecture, for, though none of the inscriptions on Djoser's six reliefs specifically refer to *heb sed*, the running pose appears in later images of those festivals. And so this open court with its throne base and two boundary posts was represented as a place where Djoser or his spirit ran in festivals of jubilee that,

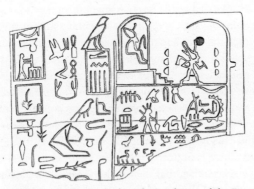

The king runs: Petrie's drawing of an ebony plaque of the First Dynasty showing a king running (?) between six images of banks of river silt set in an archaic court, beside a throne upon a plinth

according to the followers of Frazer, had replaced the savage earlier custom in which archaic pharaohs had been running for their lives!

Halfway to Hollywood or a scientific reconstruction of the ancient past? Even with the second throne dais in the so-called Heb Sed Court, the presence of an arena next to Djoser's pyramid is hardly sufficient evidence to conclude that the grand settlement of dummy buildings beside the Step Pyramid were set up for the enactment of eternal Sed festivals. And certainly our present knowledge of the early dynasties hardly supports the notion that, in spirit or in flesh, the first pharaohs had been Frazerian savages decked out on occasion in a collected mishmash of scholarly Heb Sediana.

What Djoser's six reliefs do carefully and clearly show, however, are images of the king visiting a palace and two shrines and engaging in another activity involving two structures that apparently denoted tracts of land. Now replicas of similar buildings, as we have seen, stood in the open courts in Djoser's great enclosure, as did two monumental structures representing tracts of land. Taken as a whole, therefore, this would imply that Djoser's enclosures, with their sculptures and their throne bases, their open courts, their dummy shrines and palaces, were an elaboration of the architecture of various offices of the living kingdom: the kingdom that under royal aegis had provisioned the living court of Memphis for centuries.

Such an explanation would naturally accommodate the notion of the celebration of Sed festivals in whatever form they may have taken in King Djoser's day, for, as reproductions of the formal environments through which the king had moved in life, they would encompass the courts in which such rites and festivals were celebrated. At the same time, it also supplies a resolution to the puzzle of the two great tombs that lie just 700 feet apart inside Djoser's funerary enclosure; for now they may be seen as examples of the two courtly tomb types of Saqqara and Abydos.

As to the enclosure's purposes, it is significant, though seldom noticed, that there is no trace of a master plan in its surviving buildings; no evidence, either, that their makers were following a symbolic programme in the manner of the makers of mosques or churches. Quite the reverse, in fact. Many parts of Djoser's funerary architecture were altered many times and in a variety of ways, and some, such as the so-called Heb Sed Court, were never finished. Like Djoser's pyramid, therefore, they are the residue of constantly changing ideas and processes. And of course, and at the same time, those courtyards and dummy buildings also represent the offices of state. Whatever else they may have represented, both the forms and the materials of Djoser's architecture show a continuing urge to elaborate and reappraise the offices of that state. So today, when you are visiting Saqqara and walking through those beautiful stone quadrangles that are still haunted by the overwhelming presence of the king, you are witnessing part of that slow translation in which the domains and networks of the archaic kings became the kingdom of the pharaohs.

24

Deus Absconditus

The Hidden God

The single most impressive image of King Djoser to have survived is a life-sized cloaked and seated statue that was found by the archaeologists of the Service des Antiquités during the excavation of his funerary enclosure. One of a number of similar works that have been reduced to fragments, it was found still standing in its original position, set up inside a small stone chamber on the pyramid's northern baseline next to the pyramid's offering temple. Djoser's 'serdab' (which, following Mariette's borrowing of an Arabic word for cellar, has become the common term for such enclosed compartments) had a pair of two-inch holes drilled through its north wall at the height of the statue's eyes, a device which would have enabled it to 'see' through the blocks of fine white limestone and also have enabled an officiant to waft incense into the serdab and around the statue, for a serdab has no door.

Robbers had long since chiselled out the figure's eyes, which appear to have been inlaid. If later examples of such work may stand as guides, they might have been made of polished crystal and set in strips of gold. Otherwise, the little serdab had preserved its statue well, even down to its numerous coats of paint and gesso; yellow for skin, black for the wig and beard and white for the enfolding cloak, which appears to have been repainted on numerous occasions and which, therefore, suggests that, like Hesi-re's reliefs, it may have originally stood in a more open place.

Despite its disfigurement – even perhaps, in part, because of it – this is one of the greatest of Egyptian sculptures. It is also one of the most original, for, though the cache at Hierakonpolis had preserved two small, similarly posed statues of Djoser's predecessor, when set beside this masterwork, a focal point of Djoser's funeral estate, they appear tentative and inconclusive.

This statue, then, is an epitome of earlier representations: like the buildings in the pyramid enclosure, a majestic summation of centuries of courtly development, its mass and detail most beautifully balanced and designed. Yet it is not those formal qualities that make it stand out from the rest – many later works are its equal in all of those respects – but rather that the figure of itself, the tension and control in its every line that, despite its blinded eyes, gives it superhuman presence.

THE DEMESNE OF THE SHRINE

That such a splendid image had been so cleverly employed in Djoser's funerary complex made it easy to imagine that the numerous empty niches in the rows of dummy buildings which line the courts by Djoser's pyramid had sheltered a great wealth of statues, and that some of them may have represented the deities whose shrines the royal stonemasons had so carefully reproduced. If that were true, if some of the dummy buildings inside Djoser's pyramid enclosure that are stony versions of settlement shrines rebuilt on the Saqqara plateau had housed a pantheon of traditional deities, an enormous light would then be cast on the beginnings of ancient Egyptian religion. Just as Frazer and his contemporaries had sought the origins of ritual and great gods in primitive settings, so, too, it would now appear, the later courtly gods of ancient Egypt had sprung from the worship of local prehistoric deities.

Of the several early shrines that have been excavated, one of the most remarkable was that found by Petrie in the winter of 1893/4 whilst digging on the east bank of the river opposite Abydos, at the ancient settlement of Coptos. Excavating inside the massive mudbrick walls of an enclosure that had housed some later temples of an ithyphallic deity known today as Min, he came across the scanty remnants of a circular, hut-like building sprinkled with sherds of late Naqadan pottery and nearby, in an open area, the remains of three colossal siltstone statues.

Dating, apparently, from around the time of Narmer and standing, before their destruction, at a height of around thirteen feet, the great grey sculptures had been made in a manner typical for male Naqadan statues, their forms outlined by a series of grooves and lines cut and abraded into three long thin slips of stone. At least two of these statues had once grasped their erect, though now largely shattered, penises in their right hands, a pose which in later ages would become typical of images of Min, and all three had elaborate engravings on their thighs – careful drawings of Red Sea shells, antelope heads, catfish, cows – and an archaic sign that is sometimes identified as an image of a lightning bolt and which would later serve as an emblem of Min.

May we not, therefore, assume that the hut-like building which had stood by the statues had been an archaic shrine? And that the statues are early manifestations of the god Min, for whom the later pharaohs built the nearby temples? Was this not proof, therefore, that the origins of the deities of the pharaonic state were to be found in the shrines of local prehistoric deities?

Unfortunately, however, not one of ancient Egypt's celebrated gods, from Amun to Thoth, makes an unambiguous appearance in the surviving relics of ancient Egypt until decades after the death of Djoser. In this respect, if the statues that Petrie found at Coptos had been much older images of the god Min, whose later temples stood close by, they would be a unique exception. Of all the distinctive signs that are shown beside the images of shrines on archaic engravings – the stork, the lightning bolt, the hawk and all the rest that had been employed in a variety of contexts since Naqadan times – only a handful would become the attributes of later deities of state. Nor is there evidence that those ancient motifs were regarded as the original manifestations of later deities. What, then, or who, could have inhabited the niches in the archaic shrines of Djoser's revolutionary stone architecture?

Since Petrie's time, excavations at many sites both in the delta and the Nile Valley have uncovered a variety of archaic shrines which have all contained a remarkable similarity of furnishings: a diversity of modest figurines of animals and humans made in a variety of materials, some palettes, some pottery and mace heads, and some slaughtering knives and incense burners. A very well-preserved collection of just such objects has recently been recovered in excavations at the delta site of Tell el-Farkha. The objects had been deposited on a number of different occasions in a succession of shrines set one above the other, a find that, apart from the usual pottery and knives, comprised a lively collection of tiny ivory models. These included baboons and little boats and people, some miniature hedgehogs, scorpions, birds and fish, shells, geese, cobras and, most remarkable of all, two gold-plated, stiff-standing male statues around one and two feet tall that bear no specific resemblance to any later deity and whose sculptural style is similar to that of the Coptos Colossi.

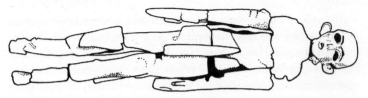

The smaller of the two rotted figures which had been covered in sheets of gold, shown as it was found, lying in the soil of Tell el-Farkha in the eastern Delta

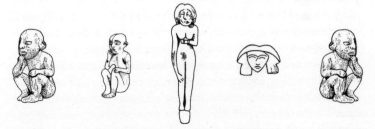

Some of the little ivories from Tell el-Farkha

Such myriad images are typical of the surviving contents of these early shrines. None of them, however, holds images that identify them as those of the later gods of the pharaonic temples. Nor is there coherent evidence of an organized religion with a fixed repertoire of deities in the times of the first dynasties of kings. The very hieroglyph, indeed, that is commonly translated as 'god' is a rendering of the ancient Egyptian *neter* sign, which though in later dynasties the sign may, indeed, be part-equated with classical and early Christian conceptions of a god, may well have held somewhat different connotations in the period of the early dynasties.

A neter *sign*

And still, in Djoser's time, as in earlier periods, there is no evidence of a developed state religion beyond that of royal ceremonial. Outside the panoply of the royal court, indeed, with its slaughtering and tith-ing, all the surviving signs of piety and of a confrontation with the supernatural are focused in the cemeteries. And here, at least, there may be a genuine continuity, for the *neter* hieroglyph, a kind of flying flag or banner on a stick, may originally have signalled the positions of individual graves or, more simply, places that of themselves held special power – a common strand of piety that runs through a great many systems of belief.

It is unlikely, therefore, that the prehistoric shrines that Djoser's architecture imitates in blocks of stone would have housed images of greater sanctity than, say, the flags of modern nation-states that make their appearance beside modern heads of state. These could be seen in something of the same manner as the images of storks and hawks and the rest of the prehistoric signs that appear beside the early images of shrines. Such shrines, therefore, need not have housed images of spe-cific gods at all, but have been holy places of themselves. And if that were true, their reproduction inside Djoser's enclosure would repre-sent a gathering of their special power from all over Djoser's kingdom.

As for the three great torsos that Petrie found at Coptos, though they certainly grasp at least one of the god Min's leading attributes, even the most ardent adherents to the belief that they are primitive images of that later god could hardly claim that these are images of the deity that texts will describe as a god of perfume and of deserts, as the husband of a half-dozen foreigners and the consort of the goddess Hathor, who in her aspect as a cow, complements another of Min's roles as the bull, Khamutef, in which aspect he is united with the Theban state god Amun which, however, is separate from his identification as an aspect of the god Horus, in which guise – Horus-Min – he occasionally appears as the husband of the goddess Isis. That, after all, is but another Heb Sed-style speculative compilation, taken from the pages of two centuries of egyptology.

However, Barry Kemp's recent re-examination of Petrie's Coptos excavation has shown that both the statues and their accompanying shrine had indeed been set up in an environment not unlike that of a Naqadan burial ground, where ashy offerings were made. This in turn suggests that the spirit of the place had been closer to that of a contemporary cemetery than that of the state temples of later ages. Better then, to think of this 'Min' – a name that is itself a Greek version of an ancient Egyptian original – as a kaleidoscopic personification. Aspects of Min were variously employed over the millennia to describe a variety of conditions and relationships, and later manifestations often used archaic signage, as did the Sed festivals, to denote that their subjects held unfathomably ancient powers.

It is hardly likely, therefore, that the numerous niches in the shrine-like buildings beside King Djoser's pyramid had held statues of the later gods, of which not a single trace has been found within the great enclosure. It is more probable that they had accommodated statues of the king himself, of which a large number of fragmentary sculptures have been recovered from the Step Pyramid's enclosure. These show Djoser enthroned, Djoser seated with a woman and children; Djoser posed like a caryatid dressed in the same distinctive kilt that Narmer wears upon his siltstone palette and Djoser's feet – a beautiful broken relic of a life-sized seated statue, resting on three images of the *rekhyt* – and many other well-made and intricately decorated scraps that are so fractured and dispersed that even their poses have been entirely lost.

At this same time, too, stony images of pharaoh were also being set up under royal auspices in some of the old settlements. Random limestone fragments from early twentieth-century Italian excavations at Gebelein in the Naqadan heartlands and Heliopolis north of

Memphis hold images of Djoser and, perhaps, of his predecessor Khasekhemui, most beautifully engraved on blocks of stone. Though lacking the expansiveness and confidence of the subterranean reliefs at Saqqara, the hieroglyphs, the hairstyles and the accoutrements of the royal court are represented in jewel-like detail. They show a king moving vigorously across a wall, and the legs of a huge enthroned image of Djoser being grasped by tiny images of women, queens and daughters, some of whom will be buried close to his pyramid at Saqqara. It is as if, in Djoser's time, the royal presence held in the stones of his pyramid enclosure was moving out into the land, and the aura of the archaic kings had started to suffuse the pieties of local shrines.

Enlarged and petrified, the offices of kingship and of the state itself had been vividly and concretely realized at Saqqara; in later times, the royal court, its sculptors and its masons would move throughout the land of the lower Nile, building pyramids, tombs and temples, with palaces and offering places. And sometimes, too, they marked their projects with images of prisoners' heads, those wretched figures from the deep archaic past that would always serve to mark the zone between life and death through which the pharaoh moved: the Deus Absconditus.

25

In Consequence

The Pyramid's Effect

> *Egypt is the classic case of ethnogenesis by means of building.*
> Jan Assmann, 2002

That in the time of Djoser the majority of court craftsmen had changed from stone-vase making to stone-block building had a profound effect on many different aspects of pharaonic culture.

Previously, each and every craftsman had produced a series of individual pieces, just as they had done since prehistoric times, each vase maker displaying a particular sensitivity to the translucence and iridescence, the veins and flecks, of each separate piece of stone they worked. Now, though, in the reign of Djoser, most of the court craftsmen had changed their way of working to accommodate the production of regularly sized quarry blocks that, when set together, made a single enormous form. Now, too, the craftsmen were working with stones that were physically so large that their quarrying, transportation and manipulation required the co-operation of a large number of people from a variety of professions. This, then, was a profound change in the manufacturing of courtly objects, a change of scale and procedure, that produced in turn a change of mentality and sensibility right across the court community, from the craftsmen to the courtiers who organized such enormous enterprises.

There was, of course, an immediate and visible transformation in the quality of court architecture; from buildings that were largely, though not exclusively, made of organic materials, with handmade and often lively finishes, to something with the abstract perfection of a fine vase. They have something of those same qualities, indeed, that to the modern eye can provide the erroneous impression that this ancient architecture was as smoothly practical as the buildings of the modern world.

At the same time, the repetitious nature of the labour required to produce tens of thousands of separate blocks of stone of near-equal size, many of which were extracted from seamless quarries of white and perfect cliffs, was an entirely different process from working relatively small boulders of desert rock, each one of which had been individually selected. Previously, the vase makers had usually begun their work by using hand-operated drills with flint tips that cut right into the centre of the stone. Now, though, work proceeded by shaping the blocks' exterior surfaces with the use of mallets and small copper chisels, a process requiring a precise knowledge of the qualities of limestone so that the stone could be worked efficiently and accurately in straight, flat lines without the tools bending or wearing at too fast a rate.

Consequently, the work of the stonemasons and the other craftsmen of the royal workshops obtained an expansiveness, a confidence, in the reign of Djoser that it had never had before. Responding directly to the mass production of large rectangular blocks of quarried stone, the notion of the block itself, as an abstract unit of design, was taken up by all branches of the court craftsmen and quickly found reflection in the designs of sculpture, furniture and architecture. As witnessed in the grand sculpture of Djoser from his serdab, the work of the court sculptors, especially, found a new sense of scale and form after adopting what would later become a standard ancient Egyptian method of making statues; a process by which the appropriate plans and elevations of the intended sculpture were drawn as silhouettes onto the various faces of a single abstract block of stone, each one of which was then cut down to leave a single sculpted form which could be smoothed, polished and embellished.

That process in its turn, that novel and precise drafting of the human form, led to the draughtsmen who were working in relief undertaking a rigorous re-examination of their traditional ways of drawing. Images of the human figure, which had previously enjoyed a considerable plasticity within a set of none-too-strictly applied conventions, were submitted to severe procedures. It was a kind of formal mapping in which, for example, silhouettes of the heads of Hesi-re or Djoser would be set in profile, just as they would appear on one of the sides of a sculptor's block, while the eye and the shoulders of that same figure would be drawn 'full-face', that is, as they would appear on the front of a sculptor's block. Building pyramids, therefore, not only served to change the scale of pharaoh's court and government, but affected the way in which the human figure was itself perceived: the very body image of the pharaoh and his courtiers.

The reliefs of Djoser – both those in the subterranean corridors at Saqqara and the fragments from the shrine at Heliopolis – are also the first known examples to have been sculpted on walls composed of many different blocks of stone. Previously, the craftsmen had conceived and placed such images upon a single slab of wood or stone or ivory, and often the placing of those images had reflected the specific qualities of the particular piece of material on which they worked. Now, though, the linear arts were freed from such traditional restraints, and their images had been enlarged to the extent that they could be drawn across whole walls. Djoser's reliefs, in fact, show these processes in transition, for, though the figures and their accompanying hieroglyphs have already been enlarged to cover large areas of a stone-block wall, some of them are yet possessed of that minuteness of detail found in the smaller earlier reliefs and even in the siltstone palettes, when the craftsmen were working on a single, unique piece of stone.

This opening up of size and scale, the freeing of the traditional images developed in the archaic workshops, is another aspect of the new way of working at the court: not as individuals, but as a group. Now, master drawings on portable materials such as limestone chips – and, probably, though they are now lost, sheets of papyrus – could serve as exemplars for statue making or relief engravings such as those set on the rocks of Sinai, which, though clumsy in their execution, show a sophisticated knowledge of royal regalia and a careful eye for composition. Such large-scale work, of course, could also be undertaken by groups of people working side by side and simultaneously, a process that led to the creation of communities of court craftsmen who would work together in extraordinary harmony on everything from pyramids to temples and colossal statues.

It is no exaggeration, therefore, to say that the fundamentals of later ancient Egyptian courtly culture were crystallized during the construction of Djoser's pyramid complex. Neither is it an exaggeration to say that, at this same time, and equally remarkably, the making of those same buildings served as well to further define the nature of the pharaonic state, not only in the span of the materials used in their construction, which were brought from various locations throughout the realm, from Sinai to Aswan, but also in the conception of the state itself.

Though the state had long since named and marked out its specific zones of interest in the architecture of great tombs and brick enclosures and in farms, estates and quarries, it had never before specified anything as abstract as the territory of a state. Now, though, the architecture of the Step Pyramid complex set up the boundaries of pharaoh's realm in a variety of ways. Nor was this an incidental or unthinking process, but a conscious preoccupation of the times, one indeed that is reflected in contemporary inscriptions, for the first known hieroglyphic inscriptions to contain the structure of a sentence demarcate the properties of one of Djoser's courtiers.

At least three different sets of boundary markers have been recovered in excavations by the Step Pyramid's enclosure, and they appear to have delineated and defined three tracts of land on the desert plateau. Two of these sets were made of rough blocks of limestone set up as cairns of stones, some of which bore Djoser's name. None of these blocks, however, have been found in their original locations, and it appears they had been dismantled and reused during later phases of the building work – this, perhaps, as the plans for the contents and extent of the enclosure had changed in the course of Djoser's reign.

The third demarcation, on the other hand, comprises the two hieroglyphic markers that were set up in the great open court on the pyramid's south face, around which, in flesh or spirit, Djoser may have run or strolled or danced, just as he is shown in three of the subterranean reliefs. Now these elegant 'turn-rounds', as later images of similar boundary markers are sometimes described, are set, as are the lands of the lower Nile, upon a north–south axis. That they will become the denominating hieroglyph from the term for 'bank' or 'shore' points to their further use as a geographic designation, for, in later inscriptions, the kingdom of itself will be described as the 'two banks' or indeed the 'banks of the north and south'. That these two turn-rounds lie between the king's two tombs, that of the northern mastaba and the pyramid with its southern, Abydos-style tomb beneath, adds to the sense that this is an abbreviated geography of pharaoh's realm, drawn out in stone within a single court.

In somewhat similar fashion, two other hieroglyphic signs that accompany all of the six figures of King Djoser on his subterranean reliefs, represent two halves of the 'sky' hieroglyph, which will later be called the 'point of turning back'. Along with the silt-bank markers which are drawn beneath them, they are the boundaries of the pharaonic state; of its earth and of its sky. And, suitably enough, the two half-sky signs are supported by two *shen* signs that will signify the circuit of the sun. This, then, represents an entirely different aspect of pharaoh's kingdom; one partly articulated in the images of the ivory comb from the reign of Djet; a kingdom, not of farms and estates, quarries, mines and traffic networks, but one with a broad conceptual extent, from the silt to the sky.

No wonder, then, that there are no buried boats in Djoser's funerary enclosure. They were not necessary. All of pharaonic Egypt had been gathered up inside that great stone rectangle. Shaped like the sign of pharaoh's residence, it was the state defined.

PART FIVE

Building Ancient Egypt
(2650–2550 BC)

26

A Diadem of Pyramids

2650–2625 BC

After Djoser, the royal masons moved a few hundred yards to the south and west of the Step Pyramid's enclosure and began to build a slightly larger pyramid at the centre of a somewhat narrower enclosure. And they rationalized the work, using larger and more regularly sized building blocks and employing smaller quantities of imported stone. But the new pharaoh, one Sekhemkhet, seems to have died after only a few years of rule, for building at the enclosure was stopped whilst the best part of it had yet to be completed.

Although the pyramid itself had barely reached the top of its first step, the quarrying of rows of subterranean magazines and the corridors and staircases leading to the royal burial crypt had been well advanced. And in the 1950s, on their way down to the burial chamber which lies beneath the centre of the pyramid, archaeologists found stone vases, the remains of wooden furniture and some gold jewellery which, along with a well-made wall that blocked their further progress, led them to believe that a royal burial lay undisturbed beneath the pyramid. This conviction was further encouraged when the sealed wall was breached to reveal another, and then another, until finally they entered a low, square room, roughly cut into the desert limestone. A fine sarcophagus lay at its centre, made from a single shining block of fine-veined Hatnub alabaster with what seemed to be an ancient wreath draped extravagantly across its top. In the heady days of 1954, just two years after the Egyptian Revolution, major excavations at Saqqara were being controlled and led for the first time by an Egyptian, Zakaria Goneim, the pyramid's discoverer, and suddenly the world's press was camping at the doorway of the old government inspectorate where he was living. 'From a Pharaoh's Tomb Comes a

Gleam of Gold,' the headlines yelled, for there was no evidence of robbery within the tomb, and the sarcophagus was plastered shut. So for a month and more, journalists in their hundreds trailed through the loose sand and down into that hot, dark cavern, a pilgrimage that ceased abruptly when the sarcophagus was opened and found to be entirely and mysteriously empty. Now, the press reported, it was a 'Pharaoh Fiasco'.

Nonetheless, Sekhemkhet's unfinished pyramid holds many treasures, for the drifts of sand and chip that cover a great part of the enclosure had hidden the relics of ancient pyramid building in progress; the masons' yards and the stone-hauling ramps that had ceased operation in mid-flow when the work was stopped. Sand drifts also covered parts of the pyramid's enclosure walls, which are skilful duplications of those that the craftsmen masons had made earlier for Djoser. And here, the pristine surface of a new-made wall had invited dozens of graffiti and builders' marks, some scribbled pictures and a few short texts, one of which names Imhotep as if he were still alive. Inked by practised hands, the swift and abbreviate hieroglyphics of some of these graffiti underline the loss of a wealth of contemporary documentation that had presumably been written out on papyrus or other fragile media and stored away from the preserving deserts, in settlements beside the valley farmlands, where the bulk of the population lived.

Following Sekhemkhet, another pyramid was started to house the burial of another shadowy monarch named, so it would appear, King Kha'ba. Whilst showing little ambition to build larger or higher than the earlier pyramids, once again the new project rationalized their previous work, and this was the beginning of a process of development and change that the pyramid builders would continue throughout the next half-century. Yet this pyramid, too, was never finished and as for the next king in the line, his burial place remains unknown; his very name, Sanakht, is only recorded in some scattered seal impressions and a few rare inscriptions. Beyond the two unfinished pyramids, a handful of inscriptions and some rock reliefs around the copper mines at Sinai, hardly any history has been preserved from the decades that followed Djoser and his mass of monuments. Even the reign of Sekhemkhet had passed unrecognized until Goneim found evidence of the king's name on some jar sealings and some other fragments left in the corridors of his unfinished pyramid.

Then, at the ending of these hazy reigns, a sprinkling of little pyramids was cast down along the valley of the lower Nile. Built in the distinctive manner of the earlier pyramids, each one rose in three or four sloping steps and, with one exception, each was around sixty feet square at its base. None of them, however, shows any trace of burial arrangements and most of them, it appears, were made in the reign of a single monarch, the last pharaoh of the Third Dynasty, a king called Huni. In common with his predecessors, little is known of Huni, nor has his tomb been found, though it is likely that it lay to the south of Saqqara, on the wide desert plain behind the village of Minshat Dahshur, from where a few rare monuments of his age – two grand alabaster sarcophagi and a splendid relief panel of the king himself – appear to have originated.

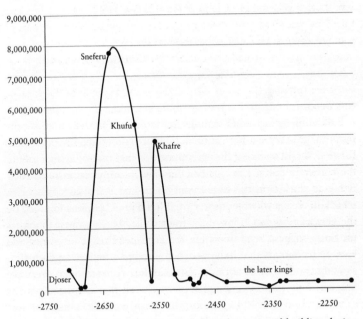

Chart showing the quantities of stone employed in pyramid building during the centuries after Djoser

Standard – though far later – ancient sources record that the last king of the Third Dynasty, who was, presumably, the man we now call Huni, reigned for some twenty years. Whilst conveniently corresponding with the present mathematics of Egyptian chronology, such information would be of little import were it not for the fact that this now largely empty period of time must have been one of considerable enrichment and enlargement for the kingdom on the lower Nile. For the reign which followed Huni's, that of the first king of Manetho's Fourth Dynasty, was that of Sneferu, in which some twenty million tons of cut stone blocks were quarried, transported and set up on three great royal pyramids; a dizzying progress in monumental engineering that culminated in the reign of Sneferu's successor, Khufu, and the construction of the largest and most perfect pyramid of all, the Great Pyramid of Giza.

IN THE PROVINCES

Egypt was probably always a village society.
                                              Christopher Eyre, 1999

Just as a great part of the history of the beginning of pharaonic Egypt is held in the pottery and sealings found on the late Naqadan supply routes, so too a great part of the kingdom's continuing history is held in the well-laid stones of the early pyramids that rise today, like mountains from the desert. It is a history, therefore, of ambition and efficiency. A history based on the state's continuing and increasing prosperity, which, in an age when monetary wealth did not exist, was founded on the increasing populations of the lower Nile, which so best estimates presently suggest, rose steeply in the centuries between Narmer and Sneferu from under a million people to around a million and a half.

What is remarkable in this is that such fast-rising populations were able not only to grow enough food to sustain themselves, but at the same time produce sufficient surpluses to maintain a huge labour force that was not working on the land at all, but building a succession of gigantic pyramids.

Such enormous surpluses could hardly have been derived from tithing subsistence farmers and were, in fact, a product of several different factors. Fundamentally, there was the phenomenal and constant fertility of the valley of the lower Nile, and a radical change in the court's system of collection and distribution of the kingdom's resources. Founded in the First Dynasty, a system that appears to have depended on the presence of the king in audience at the various settlements had by the time of the Fourth Dynasty been replaced by a class of yeomen land managers operating at a local level as part of a nationwide system of court provision and supply.

In common with most of the activities of ancient life along the lower Nile, most of the evidence of this development has disappeared. Two elements, however, survive: the standing pyramids, which hold mountains of statistics concerning the materials and energies required for their creation; and the agricultural lands that ultimately fuelled their construction and which still hold information about the pyramid makers' resources that is as fundamental as that which is contained within the pyramids themselves. For though different tools and seed stocks were introduced into the Nile Valley in classical times and little specific is known about farming methods in early dynastic Egypt, the fundamental parameters of food production in the mono-environment of the lower Nile hardly changed until a century and a half ago, when the great river dams started to be constructed and engine-driven water pumps came into use.

Remarkably, the millennial processes of agriculture on the lower Nile were mapped in the last years of the eighteenth century, as part of a Napoleonic 'Domesday Book' compiled during the course of the French invasion of Egypt. As you would expect, the French surveyors' plans show a narrow limestone valley cut deep into the desert, with the great river at its centre and a natural flood plain lying on either side of it, deep in river silt. In the Naqadan heartlands, this band of black and cultivatable land was but a mile or so across, a pattern that remained until the introduction of land reclamation and desert farming in the last half-century. In its day, however, that narrow natural flood plain had been a practical width for farmers working with hand tools, for, with the aid of skilfully sited embankments set at angles to the river's bank, they had trapped the receding floodwaters of the annual inundation and thus prolonged the land's fertility. In direct consequence of this same system, millennially applied, the French maps show a continuous ribbon of cultivated land running right down the centre of the desert valley, dotted with settlements and farmed, as were the fields of Europe before the arrival of the tractor, in narrow strips in which crops were planted side by side, as if in a garden. This, then, was the broad pattern of the cultivated lands in Sneferu's kingdom, though at that time the regions of cultivation would have been interspersed between considerable areas of uncultivated land. A large part of the subsequent economic history of the pharaonic state, indeed, is the history of the colonization of those scrub lands and wild water-meadows and the creation of that unbroken stable landscape that Napoleon's geographers would so diligently map.

Samples of the remaining seed from Djoser's enormous underground granaries have been found to contain more than thirty plant species; a similar mix of grain and field weeds, darnel, canary grass and vetches and the rest, that was to be found in Egyptian wheat fields until a century or so ago. Watered by basin irrigation, this single annual crop took so little from the fruitful silt that it could be planted each and every year without further effort or ado. This was the fundamental unit of pharaonic agriculture. In contrast, most of the remaining crops were cultivated, as they had been until quite recently, either in more protected areas that held the water of the inundation longer and were the last to dry out in the summer's heat, or on plantations set close to canals or the natural branches of the river that ran parallel to the main stream in many sections of its valley, which were then watered throughout every season so that, in the natural hothouse of the Nile Valley, vegetables would grow around the year.

Only the delta, where an estimated fifth of the population of King Sneferu's kingdom lived, would have presented a different agricultural environment. Sown in part brackish salty wetlands, and part fen and water-meadow, the seeds that have been gathered from the remains of farming settlements of those times show a growing emphasis on the cultivation of animal fodder, which was not the case, as similarly detailed studies have shown, in Upper Egypt.

Such specialization appears to have been a growing trend from

Djoser's time, if not earlier, in which some delta farms had developed a regime of rearing beef cattle in stalls, so that the animals grew to a considerable size and would develop long, curved hoofs due to lack of exercise – a quality that reflects the description of such animals in later pharaonic tax registers as 'fattened' cattle. Seeds from such farming units show that their principal fodder was probably the same kind of dense, dark clover that is still widely used throughout provincial Egypt, where it is called *berseem* and is harvested continuously, as required. Interestingly, the seeds of wild mustard and dock that have been found mixed in with those of delta clover appear to have been imported from Upper Egypt, along with the clover seed itself.

Some of the delta estates, therefore, seem to have been specialized agricultural centres that, apart from producing the usual field crops such as wheat and flax, were developing an export industry in which large numbers of the cattle that were especially favoured as beasts of ritual offering were shipped all over Egypt. Some of these animals, indeed, may have been slaughtered in Djoser's pyramid temple, where the drains and basins are large enough to hold the great beasts' blood after their throats had been cut.

At the same time, in those undocumented decades between the reigns of Djoser and Sneferu, the ongoing spread of cemeteries shows that sections of the central river valley known now as Middle Egypt, where the flood plain could not be easily adapted to the small-scale methods of basin irrigation used by the earlier farmers, were being increasingly colonized. At this same time, too, some of the most ancient centres of Naqadan society, which had previously been depopulated, were enlarging once again. Though mostly unexcavated, the remains of substantial settlements at Abydos, Hierakonpolis and Naqada show that those traditional centres were flourishing, whilst a string of excavations in the huge desert cemeteries that lie downstream from Abydos, at sites like el-Raqaqna and Nag' el-Deir, have recorded thousands of burials of this same period. These, presumably, were of people who had been supported by the produce of local farms. Underlining their direct and continuing relationship with the court at Memphis, one of the enormous contemporary mud-brick mastabas at Beit Khallaf, another of the sites near Abydos, contained mud jar sealings bearing the impression of the name of Djoser, while another mastaba contained a seal impression of one of Huni's predecessors, King Sanakht.

At first it would appear that Sanakht's broken seal impression by itself is hardly proof of the growing power and reach of a centralizing state. It is, however, typical of the evidence available from those lost decades of a vast and enlarging national network, whose existence could only otherwise be inferred from the statistics of provision and supply that are built into the pyramids' own stones. For though Sanakht himself has hardly left a mark on history and his very tomb is lost, wherever his name is found, it is always connected to the networks of state supply. It is found, for example, on a seal impression excavated in Djoser's pyramid temple at Saqqara that testifies to the continuance of offerings at Djoser's funerary compound long after that king's demise. It is in the tomb at Beit Khallaf, and, at the Sinai copper mines, two reliefs of that elusive king are set close to those of Djoser, Sekhemkhet and Sneferu. And it is also found at the Aswan cataract where, in the course of the German Archaeological Institute's excavations, Sanakht's name was found impressed into a tiny blob of fine Nile mud that, as the indentations on its reverse revealed, had once sealed a long-perished roll of papyrus.

Recovered from the debris of the office that had been established in the Second Dynasty on a small island next to the great brick fortress of the First Dynasty, the seal that held Sanakht's name had belonged to an administrator and was one of twenty similar sealings which the ruined building had inadvertently preserved. In the manner of the times, the sealings held the names and titles of several individuals, some descriptions of various quantities of now-vanished goods and the years of rule of some of the kings – unfortunately unnamed – in which those goods were sealed. Underlining the connection of these islands with the state systems of distribution and supply, several other seal impressions bearing the names of Third Dynasty kings have also been found in the Aswan excavations, and these, too, had come from mud-sealed storage jars.

Though less informative and far less plentiful, similar seal impressions have also been found at a scattering of other sites. At el-Kab, for example, which lies on the opposing bank of the river to Hierakonpolis, a Belgian expedition recovered another seal impression of an 'inspector of the granary', and some fine pieces made in the court workshops including a hard-stone vessel bearing the name of Sneferu, were excavated from the largest tombs within the local cemetery. Together with similar goods that have been found in cemeteries both in the valley and the delta, these are the earliest evidence of royal patronage and, apparently, of provincial officials who were in contact with the royal court.

Aswan, however, offers further insight into the transformations that were taking place during those lost decades, and evidence of a strengthening network of authority and obligation throughout the kingdom. Close by the office on its little granite island in the middle of the river's stream, there stands one of the small stepped pyramids that were placed along the valley of the lower Nile at the end of the Third Dynasty. Sixty feet square and built of limestone blocks in a manner typical of its times, the little pyramid, which was set at the island's highest point, once rose in three angled steps to a height of around thirty-five feet. And a brief inscription on a single cone-shaped block of granite informs us that its name was 'The Diadem of King Huni'.

Six similar pyramids are known at present and others may well lie undetected. All are small and stepped and, before their part-demolition by nineteenth-century treasure seekers, they had been completely solid. One stands near Edfu, some of the others near Hierakonpolis, Naqada and Abydos, and all of them were, apparently, anonymous. Then, in the late 1980s, excavations at the northernmost of these distinctive pyramids, which is set close to the modern village of Seila in the hills between Lake Faiyum and the valley of the Nile, uncovered an alabaster offering altar, some fragments of a royal statue and a stela bearing the name of Huni's immediate successor, Sneferu.

In conjunction with the discovery of the office set close to the pyramid at Aswan, the discoveries at the Seila pyramid solved one of the minor mysteries of egyptology. For now it appeared that, although they had no burial chambers of their own, these small stepped pyramids had been built as miniature versions of the grand royal pyramids – particularly the finished pyramid of Djoser, with its statues and offering temple – and that they had performed similar roles, by proxy, to that of Djoser's pyramid temple, marking offering and tithing

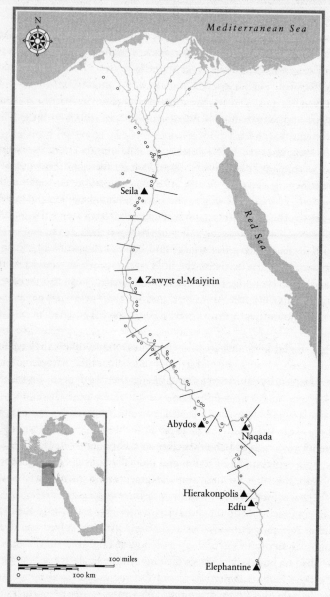

Map showing the locations of the little step pyramids that were built up and down the Nile in the late Third Dynasty; some of the later nome divisions are shown as ruled lines

places of the royal cult, and serving as markers for the reception and dispatch of goods gathered and dispensed in the royal name, just as the sealings found at Aswan had implied.

As Stephan Seidlmayer, the excavator of the Aswan office first observed, the positions of these little pyramids up and down the valley of the Nile is reminiscent of some of the later divisions of the Nile Valley into the twenty-odd provinces which, along with an equal number of others in the Nile Delta, are now known under the Greek term of 'nomes'. Though the origins of this system of provinces are unknown, some of these nomes are already named in the short texts inscribed on the vases that were stored underneath King Djoser's pyramid; amongst others, the so-called Oryx Nome – the province in which the alabaster quarries of Hatnub were situated. By Sneferu's time, however, a far wider range of these province names appears on a variety of inscriptions. That some of these record the names of provincial officials and others describe landholdings by the names of the nomes in which they were situated suggests that the nome system was part of a parcelling out of Egypt, part of the kingdom's developing systems of provision and supply and a further stage, as well, in the continuing process of internal colonization along the valley of the lower Nile.

With its inscription of King Sneferu, the Seila pyramid is somewhat different from the others, the rest of this group of little pyramids are so similar in their sizes and methods of construction that is it likely that they were all built at the same time – and probably, therefore, during Huni's reign. And if that is true, then the diadem of little pyramids that had been sprinkled out along the Nile in the age before the building of Egypt's greatest pyramids, would appear as an elaborate architectural expression of the rites of audience and offering that, from the very beginning, had been the quintessence of the state.

27

Court and Country

Metjen and the Early Reign of Sneferu,
2625–2600 BC

Walk north past the walls of the Step Pyramid's enclosure and up the dusty track that led to the old Government Inspectorate and Merka's mastaba, and you will pass by a number of undistinguished stacks of mud brick that are slowly dissolving into the sand. In all probability, though in the absence of any inscriptions it is no longer possible to be entirely sure, one of these fast-fading structures, the ruined remnants of a considerable cemetery, belonged to a certain Metjen, an official of King Sneferu's court, whose mastaba once held a remarkable series of stone reliefs that in the nineteenth century were shipped to Europe for exhibition in Berlin.

> Cairo. July 10th [1845]
>
> . . . the rest of my companions have left me here alone. They departed hence yesterday. How gladly should I have accompanied them, as to-day the third anniversary of my departure from Berlin has already borne round; but the taking down of the pyramid tombs yet keeps me back. The four workmen, who were sent me from Berlin as assistants, have arrived; they are strong young men, and I took them immediately with me to the Pyramids. We ensconced ourselves in a conveniently situated grave; a field-smithy and a scaffolding for the crane was erected, and the work was quickly commenced.
>
> Richard Lepsius

Unlike the tomb of Hesi-re, with its row of wooden panels, each one in a separate niche spaced out along a corridor, the reliefs that Lepsius took from Metjen's tomb chapel had been arranged so that their images were set all altogether, focused in a single corridor-like nine-foot niche built of stone blocks that ran into the body of the mud-brick

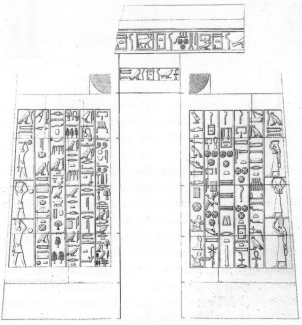

Lepsius' record of the doorway to Metjen's tomb chapel. The texts to the right of the entrance, which is some seven feet high, would appear to describe part of Metjen's role in government, and are usually described as 'titles': those on the other side concern the establishment of estates in the western delta; where 'wine in great quantities' was made. The flanking figures on either side of the texts are shown in the act of delivering produce to the altar in the chapel, which lies beyond the doorway

mastaba. At the ending of this passageway there had stood an offering altar set below a copy of a house door made in stone – a so-called 'false door' – in which there was an engraved image of Metjen, standing in the manner of Hesi-re and Djoser. Together with a serdab that had been set nearby into the body of the mastaba and which had contained a lovely little granite statue of Metjen, this innovative ensemble, the most elaborate of a dozen other examples that have survived from this same time, had comprised one of the oldest decorated so-called 'tomb chapels' ever to have been found in Egypt.

Durchschnitt nach c d.　　　Grundriss.　　　Durchschnitt nach a b.

Lepsius' plan of Metjen's tomb chapel – a narrow corridor made of limestone blocks whose stone roof imitates the palm log ceilings of domestic dwellings. The size of the mud brick mastaba in which this chapel was embedded was not recorded

Made, in all likelihood, some two generations after the nearby tomb of Hesi-re, this novel rearrangement provided more space for texts and images and, by combining the various elements of sculpture, inscriptions and tomb reliefs – image and text – in a single architectural composition, allowed for a greater coherence, an eloquence even, in the dialogue of the tomb. It is precisely this same new-made expansiveness that makes the texts within the tomb of Metjen of such outstanding interest, for they are far more expansive than any earlier examples; and more informative, as well, than any other surviving texts of Metjen's time. Here, then, for the first time in Egyptian history, are writings concerning an individual's role within the court, his ownership of various estates and texts, and even passages that describe some of the landholdings of his mother and his father. Taken all together, they show something of the mundane realities of courtly life during an extraordinary period of history.

Metjen, so these inscriptions tell, had travelled to Sneferu's court from a family home in the broad farmlands of Middle Egypt and, as the reliefs from his tomb chapel seem to show, he lived to a ripe old age. And that may indeed be the reason why the old man's tomb was on the Saqqara plateau by King Djoser's pyramid, in the burying grounds of previous generations, rather than with most of the courtly tombs of Sneferu's day, which are located in the deserts to the south of Saqqara, beside the royal pyramids.

What first holds the eye in Metjen's tomb chapel is a lively series of reliefs, exquisitely delineating the essential actors of a courtly expedition to the desert. Lines of servants carrying supplies and bedding – for a midday siesta? – and lively images of the chase drawn with a hunter's eye; hares and desert rats and a small flock of Dorcas gazelle, some of which the hounds have caught by the leg. Metjen, whose very name when it is translated from hieroglyphic conjures visions of a desert sheikh, appears to have been an administrator of the deserts and a controller of the royal hunt. Walk further into the narrow chapel and other elegant reliefs show produce being brought from Metjen's various estates for offering at his tomb: pictures of some of the provisions that earlier generations had piled up in reality within the storerooms of the mastabas, images that from this time on will form a main part of the decorations of the nobles' tomb chapels.

It is the lengthy lines and columns of hieroglyphs, however, that hold especial interest in Metjen's tomb chapel, for they contain some of the oldest known sentences in the Egyptian language. Nor is this merely an early surviving example of the appearance of a subject and predicate within a line of hieroglyphs. Though they lack the precision of later inscriptions, there is a vivacity in some of these texts that to the modern ear appears to echo elements of speech.

Clearly, such novel textual constructions were the products of earlier developments in which writing as a medium of lists, which had recorded little more than objects and quantities, names and sounds and whose understanding was dependent on its setting within the state-wide accounting system, had been transformed into writing that could stand alone as an independent medium, in which lines of signs held grammar in them and something, even, of a speaking voice. Beyond some simple phrases – wishes for long life, for many years of rule and the like – which were composed in the times of the first kings, there is hardly any surviving evidence of the introduction of grammatic structure into hieroglyphic, most of which must have taken place in the few decades between King Djoser and King Sneferu. That Metjen's inscriptions tell us directly that they were copied from 'writing in a royal document', suggests that those advances had been made in texts written on fragile media that have since perished and serves again to underline the loss of a great mass of early writing that was set down on less permanent materials than Tura limestone.

Stonily preserved, parts of Metjen's texts give details of his inheritance and properties, some describe his status at the court, whilst others address that perennial concern of earlier communities of the lower Nile, the provision of offerings to the dead. And with all of that, they show aspects of state administration in the reign of Sneferu that are otherwise virtually undocumented: a glimpse of the organization that had embarked upon the largest programme of stone-block building the world would ever see.

Metjen was not a member of the royal family; his texts record that he had inherited his father's property with royal assent, however, and that it had come down to him 'without wheat and barley ... but with dependants, and herds of pigs and donkeys'. Ownership of such a fine-made and well-sited tomb, therefore, had probably resulted from personal contact with the king. In his capacity of master of the hunt, indeed, Metjen may well have spent much time with the inner circle of the royal family, for hunting had long been a popular royal pastime; favoured hounds of the early kings had been buried close to their masters in their own graves, and some of their names – 'Nub' and 'Sed' – had been individually recorded on stone stelae.

As well as a royal hunt master, Metjen's tomb texts also describe him as a court official charged with the production of the royal linen, with managing some of the royal estates and with overseeing the 'offices of provisioning'. These were posts which, if their words are literally true, would have provided him with a broad overview of the kingdom and enabled him, with the aid of royal patronage, to accumulate a spread of property which, so his tomb chapel records, consisted of several considerable estates including landholdings of 150 acres in the old Naqadan heartlands. So much land did Metjen accumulate, in fact, that his tomb texts tell us he had ceded some fifty acres for the upkeep of his mother's household.

The holdings of which Metjen was most proud, however, or at least those that his inscriptions describe in lively detail, are his properties in the western delta, in various new settlements near the northern settlements of Buto and Damanhur and others in nomes closer to Memphis. There, too, as well as controlling various crown estates and developing a series of landholdings in his own name, Metjen also appears to have undertaken civic duties, serving as an arbitrator of disputes. And so successful were these enterprises that he was able to entail the produce of one estate so that it would be sent as offerings to his tomb, where, presumably, it served to support a family of cemetery officials who undertook regular offerings in his tomb chapel.

Above all else, however, and 'very much!', as a translation of one of the phrases in his inscriptions frequently proclaims, Metjen founded a series of smallholdings such as you may still see in the Egyptian countryside. These were large walled gardens with date palms, fig trees and vines, and where, on occasion, salad and other vegetable crops were cultivated, grapes were pressed and, as Metjen describes, a 'very large quantity of wine was made'. These, indeed, were the same shaded gardens that, in later ages, pharaonic artists would describe in pictures painted in the nobles' tomb chapels, for both the produce and the luscious perfumed environments of these little paradises were greatly prized.

One of Metjen's gardens, so his inscriptions tell, was a generous square of silt of some two and three-quarter acres. Such establishments required a good deal of experience and skill both to establish and to run. Unlike the usual open irrigation systems, which were dependent on the annual inundation, these walled plots required the excavation of an artificial lake or pond from which the gardeners could water their crops around the year. Such work, therefore, required a permanent staff and continuous supplies of water which, so later pictures show, was supplied by digging through the silt to tap the Nile's water table. Such systems also required a careful grading of the soil, even perhaps the addition of manure and extra silt, so that the constant watering that would produce three or four crops of vegetables each year would drain down swiftly through the rows of trees and plants, and not lie in stagnant pools which, with evaporation, would cause white crusts of salt to form and kill the tender shoots.

The opening of such intensive agricultural developments alongside the building of embankments to contain the inundation, and the cleaning and clearing of the wild wetlands – the continuing colonization of the lower Nile – was fundamental to the early pharaonic state. And in Metjen's day, his texts imply, the king and his courtiers were directly involved in the establishment of just such fresh sources of food production, while at the same time establishing a class of yeomen farmers – Metjen's land managers – who had direct allegiance, through Metjen, to the court and to the king.

THE MEANINGS OF WORDS

Well, pull in your reel, Mr Fielding, you're barking up the wrong fish.

I. A. L. Diamond, 1959

It is remarkable that the texts in Metjen's tomb chapel, some of the oldest documents to have survived from ancient Egypt, appear to celebrate the ownership of land and proudly record Metjen's status at a royal court: it is almost as if he were an eighteenth-century country gentlemen sitting for a Gainsborough portrait. Great care, however, must be taken with the interpretation of such texts. Though ancient Egyptian writing has a powerful and developing grammatical consistency, and two centuries of Western scholarship has enabled its translation with some precision, there yet remain far greater difficulties in its accurate comprehension than is the case with the translation of a living language.

Some outstanding questions concerning Metjen's landholdings, for example, would be solved if there were any indication of the identity of the authors – of the 'voice' or 'voices' – of the various texts that describe them. Are those inscriptions simply copies of commercial dealings that were originally recorded in a similar manner to that of modern land registries? Or, if the voice of those texts is not that of a state bureaucracy but Metjen's own, are his texts to be understood as a 'biography', as a list of lands and courtly titles granted by King Sneferu as favours to his hunting master?

Choose one of those two different voices over another and you choose a different vision of the order within Sneferu's kingdom. If the first alternative were true, then some obscure details perhaps describing Metjen purchasing land from 'royal colonists' would serve to underline his role as a magnate acquiring lands that had previously been awarded to some settlers by royal warrant: as a man, that is, operating in a laissez-faire economy, with an equivalent to money and with the state acting, in the modern manner, as guarantor of personal property. If the second alternative is correct, however, and those texts are a record of his personal achievements at the court, then they would depict Sneferu's economy as one controlled entirely by the crown; a kingdom in which, in the words of a later autocrat, 'l'État, c'est moi'. Traditional translations of Metjen's texts tended to the latter; modern versions sometimes supply caveats to their interpretations.

Another obstacle in the accurate comprehension of Metjen's tomb texts, along with others of his time, is that they were written in a period when the hieroglyphic writing system was just beginning to reflect an oral language. Of itself, this slow move into written texts would have been a profound transition for court society and administration, though it is one that is difficult to readily appreciate today since writing, as Roland Barthes once famously observed, has long been the fundamental medium through which our society constructs its institutions, its entertainments and religions. It is precisely our long-cultivated tradition of literary precision, indeed, that prompts specific questions as to the 'voice' of Metjen's texts, and the ownership and usufruct of his estates. In Metjen's day, such exactitude may not yet have formed a part of everyday experience.

A further difficulty in understanding such early texts is that their translation can only be accomplished by reference to other, later texts. And here a paradox arises, for to assume that Metjen's inscriptions are merely 'primitive' versions of later similar examples, and that gaps in their understanding may be resolved by reference to the fuller texts of later times serves to deny internal change within a society that, in Sneferu's day, was clearly undergoing a series of colossal transformations. It is the very nature of most grammars and dictionaries, moreover, to provide compacted, generalizing visions of the language of the culture in which they deal and this, as far as the traditional vision of 'ancient Egypt' is concerned, has created a jargon-filled vocabulary with its own internal mythologies, so that, however rigorous or erudite the act of translation may have been, it often serves to bewitch the genuine relics of the past and reinforce a vision of an 'ancient Egypt' held by earlier generations of lexicographers and philologists. That, of course, is how Metjen can appear to be like an English squire, and Imhotep, an Egyptian Leonardo.

How, then, to proceed, when the very language that we use to describe Metjen's world – words like 'king', 'courtier', 'Egypt', 'estate' and all the rest – threatens to turn that lost society into a little England? Or, indeed, given that the fundamental hieroglyphic dictionaries in daily use were founded in nineteenth-century Berlin – a warmer Prussia? A simple litmus test, it seems to me, is whether or not our understanding of the ancient texts is reliant on explications of such things as 'ancient symbols' or 'primitive mentalities'. Though such dismal metaphysics were second nature to Western colonial societies, there is little evidence of their presence in ancient times. Better to assume, as John Baines puts it, that 'the developers of writing . . . were surely more intelligent than the generality of their modern interpreters', and to approach the scraps of early writing that survive with humility and the assumption that their present understanding is extremely limited, and that, when they are cast into translation, all ancient words are as quicksilver on the shards of an ancient mirror in which we must inevitably, glimpse phantoms of ourselves.

Some of the vertical inscriptions above the offering altar in Metjen's tomb chapel listing more of Metjen's titles and detailing a grant of a 35-acre farm to his mother

28

High Society

Sneferu at Maidum, 2625–2600 BC

A royal palace or, at least, some of the offices of Sneferu's government, once stood upon the desert at Maidum, some thirty miles south of Memphis and on the west bank of the river. For in the first years of his prodigious reign, that great wide plain had been chosen as the location for the royal tomb and, though the area itself has never been systematically surveyed, the archaeology of other sites and later texts both show that the pyramid-building kings built settlements beside such works: a palace, the offices and households of the courtiers, and the workshops and habitations of the craftsmen pyramid builders.

The presence of government offices on the Maidum plain is further suggested by the nearby pyramid of Seila, one of the little pyramids that had been sprinkled down the valley of the lower Nile in the reigns of Sneferu and his predecessor, Huni. Set on a ridge of desert hills that overlooks both Lake Faiyum and the valley of the Nile, the little pyramid with its offering table and its stela bearing Sneferu's name is a solid, well-made structure set on a plinth of fine white limestone blocks. When it had stood to its full height, it would have looked down across the wide plain of Maidum and thus would have been clearly visible from Sneferu's pyramid below: two near-contemporary monuments six miles apart, with the royal residence nearby.

None of these monuments, however, would have appeared as they do today. A great part of the Maidum plain is now deep in sand, Seila's pyramid has been part-dismantled by treasure seekers, and the Maidum pyramid itself, though sufficiently colossal to discourage such desultory invasions, is so broken and distorted that in the 1870s it was described by an English tourist, somewhat unkindly if not entirely inaccurately, as looking 'like a slice of double Gloucester'.

The locations of the pyramids of Djoser, Sneferu and Khufu

Once, though, that steep-sided block, with the appearance more of a fortress than a tomb, had been a high, white pyramid of seven steps that, before their various catastrophic collapses, had risen just a little higher than Djoser's great original.

From its beginning, the building work at Maidum had been different from that at all earlier pyramid sites. Having planned at least three royal pyramid enclosures during the previous half-century, the court builders had already streamlined their building methods. Now, though, the changes were more drastic; the royal burial chamber was reduced to a small room set at the centre of the pyramid, and the best part of the earlier pyramids' external architecture, including the grand enclosure walls, was entirely discarded, so that, apart from a low surrounding field-stone wall and a tiny offering temple, the king's pyramid was to stand alone.

Though the new pyramid was designed to be a little higher than previous ones, given that the project to complete the royal tomb complex required less than half the stone it had before, one would expect it to have been completed quickly. At all events, when the pyramid's cladding of smooth limestone was completed, work nonetheless continued, just as it had done at Djoser's tomb, and the pyramid was enlarged with the addition of another fine stone cladding and an additional step.

COUNTRY LIFE

All work on Sneferu's stepped pyramid seems to have stopped by the fourteenth year of his reign; that, at least, is suggested by the graffiti scribbled on many of its building blocks. And at exactly that same time, so a later text describes, two doorways were erected for King Sneferu as part of a palace that, in all probability, stood on the plain at Dahshur, some twenty-five miles to the north of Maidum and close by Saqqara, where Sneferu's workforce had started work upon a brand-new pyramid.

It is likely, therefore, that the several cemeteries of Sneferu's time which lie in the plain around the Maidum pyramid were established during the first fourteen years of his rule, along with the splendid line of mastabas that lay along a ridge half a mile to its north. Though standing in a similar relationship to the Maidum pyramid as did the tombs of Metjen and other nobles of the time to Djoser's pyramid at Saqqara, these mastabas were far larger and had simpler chapels set into their eastern sides.

Two of these tombs are of considerable importance for the later history of pharaonic culture. Not only did they hold works of extraordinary quality and originality and some of the finest draughtsmanship to have survived from ancient Egypt, but they are the first known examples of a canon of tomb decoration that would be followed throughout the succeeding millennia by craftsmen working in cemeteries in every part of the ancient kingdom.

The vast, unfinished mastaba that stands beside the Maidum pyramid, and which is still dwarfed by that colossal ruin, was probably one of the first of these great tombs to have been built. Made of enormous blocks of limestone, its superb burial crypt holds one of the oldest known granite sarcophagi in Egypt; its chapel, however, is undecorated, the tomb anonymous. By contrast, the largest of these mastabas, and the first in the line that lies to the pyramid's north, was

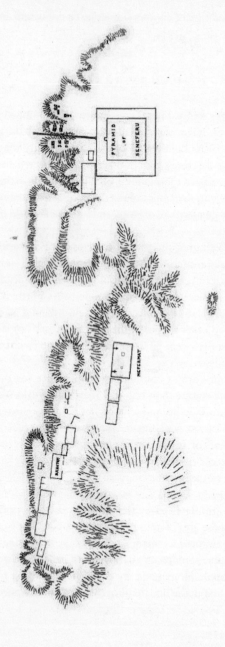

Petrie's map of the monuments at Maidum. Drawn in the late 1890s, it shows the two stone-lined chapels that were set into the eastern side of the mastaba of Nefermaat and Itet, which is 206 feet long.

20. The stela of King Djet, found by Amélineau beside the king's tomb at Abydos and now in the Louvre Museum. Made of two slabs of fine limestone, it is one of the finest pieces to have survived the millennial plunder of the Umm el-Qa'ab, and hints at the precocious elegance of the royal workshops of the first kings. It is 4 feet 8 inches tall.

21. One of the five beautiful panels found by Auguste Mariette in 1860 in a mud-brick mastaba at Saqqara and taken to Cairo for exhibition in the Middle East's first national museum. Originally one of eleven similar pieces, it depicts and names King Djoser's courtier Hesi-re, who is shown holding the inks and palette of a scribe. Each of the panels stood around 3 feet 9 inches high, and had been cut from a single slab of acacia wood.

22. The life-sized statue of King Djoser found in the 1920s during the excavations of Firth and Quibell, still standing in its original position close to the base of the Step Pyramid at Saqqara. The statue's eyes, which were probably inlaid with highly polished stones and set in precious metal, had been hacked out.

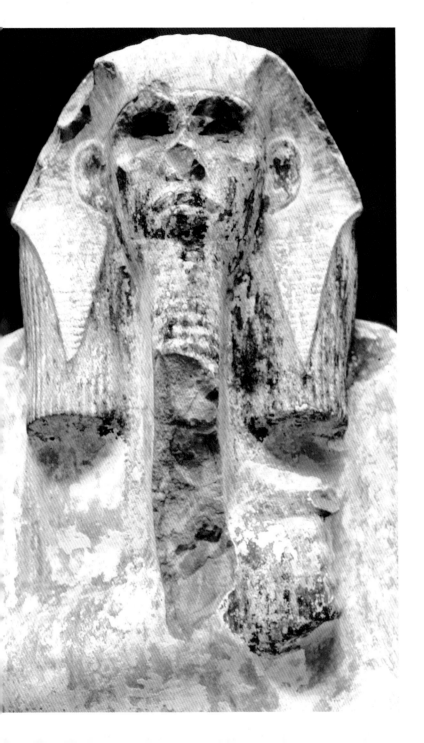

23. The Step Pyramid and the gateway to Djoser's great enclosure under reconstruction in the 1970s. The re-built doorway, which had originally provided the only access to the royal enclosure, shows the original height of its mile-long enclosure wall. The structure that forms the boundary of the stonemasons' yard in the foreground is a mastaba tomb of later date.

24. Two of Petrie's tracings, drawn in 1890, of the scenes on part of the stone walls that formed the entrance to the chapel of Nefermaat in the mastaba of the courtiers Nefermaat and Itet at Maidum. The panel to the left, part of the chapel's northern doorjamb, bore the images and names of Nefermaat and Itet and their family. The right hand panel, which was some four feet wide, was the northern part of the chapel's façade. Its inscriptions tell that two of the offering bearers in the upper registers are bringing wine and figs into the tomb and names the fowlers beneath them as two of the sons of Nefermaat and Itet just as, in all probability, is the anonymous little boy in the register below them, who is playing with some of the family's pet animals.

25. Twenty years after Petrie made these drawings he was asked to dismantle the decorated tomb chapels of Maidum, and their stone blocks were dispatched to a wide number of museums. This modern photograph of a detail of the bottom block of the same scene shows the unique cloisonné technique employed by the ancient craftsmen to great effect. It is now in Copenhagen.

26. The southern section of the enormous mastaba of Nefermaat and Itet today, which had once stood to a height of some thirty feet and more. The large hole at the centre of the photograph is the product of the erosion that followed the removal of the limestone blocks of Nefermaat's great decorated chapel.

27 and 28. A singular preoccupation with perfection.

The vase is cut from Egyptian basalt. The precision of its form, its surface texture and the marks of its manufacture make it likely that it was made in an anonymous Badarian encampment. Just 11 inches high and of unknown provenance, it is now in the British Museum.

Made some fifteen centuries later, the Great Pyramid of Giza was built in the reign of Khufu of the Fourth Dynasty of Egyptian Kings. Though stripped now, of its smooth outer casing stone of fine limestone, each of its four baselines were once set to near perfection; each one measuring 755½ feet and holding between them all, a discrepancy of less than 7 inches. This is the pyramid's eastern face, which overlooks the valley of the Nile.

29 and 30. The upper photograph shows Hetep-heres's rock-cut tomb chamber as discovered by Reisner's archaeologists in March 1925. The queen's alabaster sarcophagus is on the left, and the golden shells of the wooden poles of her funeral canopy lie on top of it. On the floor beside it are the decayed fragments of her other tomb furnishings – the bed and chairs, the palanquin, the boxes, the jewellery and hundreds of other smaller pieces. The lower photograph shows Hetep-heres's bed and one of her chairs after their restoration, set up again inside her canopy, at the Cairo Museum.

made, so its inscriptions tell, for a man and a woman: Nefermaat and Itet, who were each provided with individual burial chambers in two deep shafts within the body of the mastaba, and with their own separate tomb chapels as well, which were set at the opposing ends of the mastaba's eastern face.

The inscriptions in these chapels tell that Nefermaat and Itet had children, and that Nefermaat had been a royal prince and Sneferu's eldest son. It is convenient then, to call the couple man and wife, though there is no known ceremony from any period of pharaonic history that equates to a modern wedding, and only in later periods do property settlements appear that, in detailing the disposal of the household goods of 'divorcing' couples, imply that some formal state of espousal had been considered to exist between them. In similar fashion, Nefermaat's often-translated title of 'king's son' does not necessarily imply that he was the physical offspring of the monarch, for some other courtiers of the time are described as having been a 'son' of successive kings or, even, as 'eldest son of the king's own body'. Better, perhaps, to think of such richly provided individuals as people who, unlike Metjen, held but few provincial titles and were members of the inner circle of the royal court.

Whatever their DNA – and surely not even the most ardent royalist would hold that such tests would invariably equate with the official versions of regal ancestry – Nefermaat and Itet had shared a magnificent tomb. A solid rectangle 420 feet long and some 30 feet high, it had walls of mud brick strengthened with lavish amounts of chopped straw, and had been entirely filled with huge quantities of liquid mud capped with several feet of gravel. Plastered with fine-ground desert gesso that was so highly polished as to appear as straight and sharp as stone, the huge tomb would have shone as brightly in the yellow desert as the limestone of the nearby pyramid. In similarly extravagant fashion, the mastaba's two chapels were built from beautifully fitted blocks of fine white limestone weighing ten, twenty, thirty tons apiece. Even in its ruin, it remains triumphantly impressive, the ground plans of its now-vanished chapels marked by a few blocks of limestone lying at the bottom of two high gorges of eroded mud and dust that have been brought down from the broken mastaba that looms above.

Once, though, the high-paired walls of the two missing chapels had stood like sloping pylon doorways, their façades and inner surfaces covered in beautifully drawn registers filled with images of Nefermaat and Itet going about their lives, accompanied by the members of their family and a menagerie of exotic animals: the great man carried in a palanquin to view the various work on the estates, ploughing, slaughtering, butchering and boatbuilding; the family hunting in the desert with their dogs, or fishing, fowling and trapping waterbirds in the marshes by the riverside. All those activities, in fact, that had since Naqadan times been recorded in a diversity of media in graves along the lower Nile, were given new life in these two chapels in a grand procession of lively images, laid out, row on row, on the high white walls. And at the same time, too, it is as if the narrative structures of later texts were being rehearsed within these measured pastorals; each one with its subject and its object, and with many of the images employed being identical to those of hieroglyphics.

Just as in Metjen's chapel at Saqqara, the tomb owners are shown receiving trains of people carrying offerings to their tomb chapels; bringing geese and stall-kept animals from their farms, wine and figs from the kitchen gardens and the produce of the open fields, all borne on the heads of men and women from estates whose names are written out beside the bearers. Here as well are two of the couple's sons, 'the courtiers Seref-kha and Wehem-kha' who are trapping ducks, whilst little children – other sons, perhaps – play with their pets, one of which, a grey baboon with the air of a naughty child, tweaks the feathers of a handsome crane, a cameo splendidly balanced on the opposing face of the other chapel by a line of desert foxes, the fine brown bushy tail of one of which is firmly grasped by the jaws of one of Nefermaat's dappled hounds.

Though these scenes are often described as reliefs, they are, in fact, a kind of *cloisonné* work; an outlandish technique in which each image, or even differently coloured parts of a single image, are first drawn in silhouette on the flat surface of the stone, which is then excavated to a depth of an inch or so before being infilled with hefty slabs of pure pigment. Today, with much of the pigment gone, the empty *cloisons* hold an inadvertent and confusing internal pattern of keyed chisel marks. What still makes these scenes remarkable, however, is that the *cloisons*' outline drawings are so fresh, so original and so filled with amused observation that, as well as fulfilling the requirements of a mortuary chapel, they hold genuine and fond observations of courtly country life. That the same scenes still hold a rare archaic grandeur, that new-found scale which had emerged within the figurative

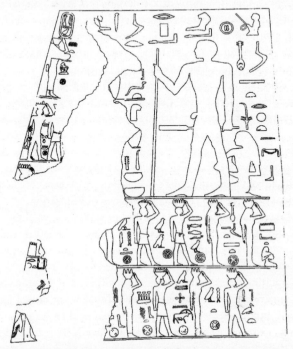

Nefermaat with Nofret kneeling by his side, are shown looking eastwards across the living Nile Valley while underneath, rows of bearers are bringing offerings into the chapel from his estates. Drawing by Flinders Petrie of the cloisons cut into one of the inner doorjambs of Nefermaat's tomb chapel. The principle figures are close to life size; the cartouche of Sneferu, one of the earliest appearances of the royal name in that distinctive form, appears at the top left

arts in the time of Djoser and of Hesi-re, transforms their seemingly simple subject matter into a remarkable remembrance of things past.

The idiosyncratic technique of setting slabs of pigment into the surface of a stone wall appears to have been unique to this tomb and may have been intended to serve a practical purpose. For the high pylons of the mastaba's two stone chapels had once stood open and exposed upon a desert plain, a place where a thin layer of pigment painted in the usual way upon the wall would not have survived for very long, so that, like most of the designs that were painted on the exteriors of earlier mastabas, they would have been quickly lost. Indeed, a brief text written beside one of the figures of Nefermaat describes the inlaid images as being made in a way 'which does not disappear', seems to address exactly that concern.

The writer need not have worried. Just as Sneferu's first step pyramid had been covered with a second coat of stone, so many of the Maidum mastabas were similarly treated, their exteriors enlarged and beautifully plastered, once again, in fine white gesso. The new skin, though, would have buried the entrances to the two stone chapels under twelve feet of mud brick, and so a narrow corridor was made to connect them to the mastaba's new façade. And those two new narrow corridors were also covered in registers of decoration.

That there had long been very skilful draughtsmen working at the royal court is testified by the quality of Hesi-re's reliefs. Freed now from the usual constraints of working with sculptors and engravers, the master draughtsmen came into their own in these two narrow corridors; painting directly onto the smooth-surfaced, light-grey walls in watery and fine-ground pigments, they show an easy skill, a balance of design and a clarity of vision that would seldom be matched in later ages. Here, once again, were images of Itet, Nefermaat and members of their family, inspecting work on their estates and watching the lines of offerings arriving at the tomb. Amongst these scenes was one of the minor surviving masterpieces of Egyptian art, the famous fragments known as the 'Geese of Maidum', which, to a modern eye, are drawn with such bucolic brio that Metjen's phrase of 'very much!' still seems an apt description.

LIFE AND DEATH AT MAIDUM

In later years, the second enlargement of the mastaba of Nefermaat and Itet was followed by a third, which, again, was precisely finished

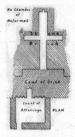

Petrie's plan of Nefermaat's cruciform tomb chapel and its subsequent enlargements. At a little under thirty feet, the chapel was similar if a little larger, to that of Itet's. Both were made of limestone blocks, and both were blocked off by the mastaba's second coating of mud brick, as shown upon this plan.

with a glass-like coat of desert gesso. Several of the other smaller tombs were similarly enlarged, once, twice, three times over, so that in 1871 the unveiling of these second skins, which had so long protected and obscured parts of the tomb chapels' interiors, provided one of egyptology's periodic popular sensations.

It would appear that in the autumn of that year, a certain Monsieur Vigne of Alexandria had set a dozen labourers to digging in the drifted sand around the rows of Maidum's buried mastabas, searching, so he later said, for 'ancient animal bones'. What Vigne actually uncovered, however, was a 'high pillar of stone' – part of the portal of a tomb chapel – at which point the sheikh of the nearby village of Maidum had stopped his explorations and reported the discovery to the authorities in Cairo. Even as the sheikh had sent his letter, however, the celebrations for the opening of the Suez Canal were concluding in Cairo, and the head of the government's Service des Antiquités, Auguste Mariette, was working at the Opera House, engaged in the final rehearsals for the Christmas Eve premiere of Verdi's *Aida*, an event for which he had written the preliminary libretto and designed the sets and costumes.

Unable to attend in person, Mariette dispatched his assistant, Daninos Pasha, to Maidum, where he was met at the local railway station, so he later recalled, by a thousand workmen, Mariette's habitual workforce, raised in corvée on the orders of the Khedive Ismail himself. In just two days, this enormous body of men had cleared the sand from the outlines of several of the northern mastabas, one of which, so the inscriptions on an outer wall of one of its two tomb chapels announced, had been made for another of Sneferu's sons, the Prince Rahotep and Nofret, his wife. Then came the discovery. As they continued digging, one of the workmen broke a small hole in a brick wall that had been built across the corridor of the prince's inner chapel. To everyone's amazement, Daninos Pasha and his reis found themselves gazing through the darkness at two brightly painted statues of Rahotep and his wife, as large as life and sitting side by side, their crystal eyes flashing in the Egyptian sunlight, after an utter quietude of four and a half millennia.

That the scenes on the walls of the chapels of Rahotep and Nofret were more tightly organized and better balanced than those of Nefermaat and Itet suggested that their chapels had been made at a slightly later date, by which time the artists had abandoned the *cloisonné* technique and were cutting their images in raised relief, a technique that would remain the standard form of tomb chapel decoration for the following five centuries.

It is the statues, though, set at the centre of the chapel, that most impressed the visitors. Not simply because of their uncanny eyes but also because, in their near-perfect state of preservation, they hold a genuinely lifelike presence. Unlike earlier statues, such as those of Djoser and his courtiers, those of Rahotep and Nofret have the same freshness as the domestic scenes on their chapel walls and they appear as vulnerable human beings, so that, though their right arms are set across their chests in a traditional hieratic pose, that commanding action is transformed, so that it appears as a brave and touching human gesture, as these two people stare ahead, alive, together and alone.

A great deal of traditional art-historical study has been devoted to the school of sculptors that made these two exquisite works. Clearly, they are highly complex sculptures that, like others of their time, hold the aesthetics of the Naqadan craft tradition, the lively silhouette, the synthetic rendering of natural form, inside the newly emerged space frame of stone-block sculpture. What is immediately engaging about these two stone sculptures, however, is their reality; their clothes, their jewellery, her wig, his moustache, how the splayed toes of their feet have never been trapped inside a shoe, how the vigour of Rahotep's fist upon his chest is answered by the gentleness of the same pose in Nofret's statue, where her fingers press against her costume to bring out the curve of her breast.

The celebrated statues of Rahotep and Nofret, as drawn by the architect Geslin for the initial publication of Mariette's notes concerning their discovery

Not surprisingly, the pair created a sensation when they were transported to Cairo for exhibition in Egypt's national museum, the first such in the Middle East. A photograph of a celebrated diva dressed in the costume of Aida was displayed next to Nofret and it was remarked how very much alike they looked; this, the beginning of a long line of similar connections that are made down to this day, for Rahotep and his wife tend to provoke strong feelings of affinity.

Along with the two statues, Mariette also ordered the removal of some fragile fragments of the tomb chapels' decorations, including the six fine geese from Itet's tomb chapel, which were dispatched, so a contemporary tourist remarked, to graze in Mariette's museum. And naturally the exhibition of those remarkable new finds provoked a steady stream of visitors to the desert of Maidum, and over the following years other sections of the paintings and reliefs were carved up and detached and many of the cakes of colour in the chapels of Nefermaat and Itet were prised out of the walls.

In December 1890, Flinders Petrie came to Maidum to survey and excavate the broken pyramid, and whilst he was engaged in one of his periodic battles with the Service des Antiquités for permission to dig, he set about making facsimiles of the tomb chapels' remaining decorations. Along with the hand copies of the hieroglyphs that Mariette had made when the chapels had been opened, these drawings are the only record of the original positions of the fragments that survive.

Here I am, [Petrie happily confided in a letter to a friend] once more in peace in this land . . . In a narrow tomb, with the figure of Nefermaat standing on each side of me – as he has stood through all that we know as human history. I have just room for my bed, and a row of good reading in which I can take my pleasure when I retire to the blankets after dinner. Behind me is that Great Peace, the Desert. It is an entity – a power – just as much as the sea is.

Twenty years later, with the Maidum paintings and reliefs still suffering depredation, the authorities of the Service des Antiquités invited

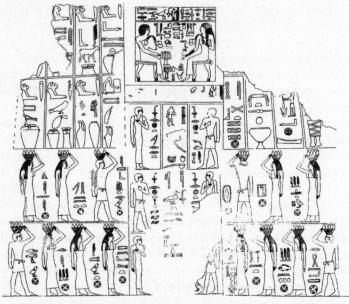

The climax of the decorations of Nofret's tomb chapel in which she is shown seated together with Rahotep within a square panel set above the offering altar. Six of their children are shown standing underneath in attendance, and on the narrow walls on either side are lists of various offerings and images of more offering bearers bringing fresh produce from their estates

Petrie to return to Maidum and dismantle the tomb chapels, whose great stones would then be divided up; half to the Cairo Museum, and half to Petrie's patrons.

> Meydum is not yet finished, [Petrie wrote to Hilda, his wife, in March 1910] as the removal and packing of the sculptured tombs is a long work. Rahotep is now in the Cairo Museum. Nefermaat is being packed. Atet[-Itet] is nearly packed and is coming altogether to England, beside the remaining portion of Nefert[-Nofret] ... As there is altogether about 30 feet length of it, 10 feet high, there will be enough for several museums.

So the beauteous chapels of Rahotep and Nofret, Nefermaat and Itet are no more, their fragments, apart from those that were part-reassembled in Cairo, scattered in museums throughout the West; in Oxford and Cambridge, in New York and Boston, in Munich and London, Liverpool and Bristol, in Brussels and Chicago, Philadelphia and Copenhagen.

THE STATE IN LIFE AND DEATH

The traditional explanation of such scenes as were laid out in the tomb chapels of Nefermaat and Itet and Rahotep and Nofret is that the ancient Egyptians believed them to be magical; that the lines of offering-bearers were carrying substitutes for the real provisions that were traditionally offered to the spirits of the people in the tomb, and that the scenes of 'daily life' were constructed so that their spirits could visit and enjoy the world again.

Such explanations, of course, would be offensive were they employed to explain the impulses that lead modern governments to maintain war cemeteries, or the sentiments involved in setting toys or flowers on a family grave: activities which are not dissimilar to some of those performed in the chapels of the Maidum mastabas, both through their paintings and by the staffs of professionals who lived close by and were supported, as was the case at Metjen's tomb, by the produce of an estate that had been entailed for those particular purposes by the tombs' owners during their own lifetimes.

Another explanation that goes some way to explain the intensity and the huge amounts of time and labour expended on these decorated tombs is that their owners wished to celebrate their lives in images and inscriptions while they were still alive; that they represent, therefore, the beginnings of the construction of personal identity in the people of the pharaonic court. And indeed, to modern eyes, the reliefs of Hesi-re or the statues of Nofret and Rahotep have an air of individuality about them that encourages us to speculate about their lives and personal biographies.

Yet for the most part, the scenes in these tombs will be repeated over and over again, down through the ages, so that they quickly became generic and repetitive, while the texts that will accompany them will usually hold little more than the names of the tombs' intended occupants, and those of some of their family members, and lists of offerings and courtly designations.

It would appear, therefore, that with their leisured descriptions of the richness and continuity of courtly life, and the unblinking equanimity with which both their texts and images confront life and death, the tomb chapels' decorations are something more than magic images or brief attempts at describing the qualities of individuals. What these tomb chapels actually provide are confident descriptions of an ordered and secure society; an order to contain the courtiers in life and death. An order, too, that in real life, in Sneferu's day, was held within the endless lines of stone haulers working at the royal pyramid and also in the tomb chapels of his nobles, in images of lines of offerers and offerings.

Such chapels are, therefore, essentially an extension of the Naqadan practices of burial, a part of a dialogue of care between the living and the dead that maintained their joint community, and also a kind of afterlife. Offering at the tomb, of course, a tithing of the living by the dead, had been undertaken since Badarian times. By Sneferu's day, however, the notion had taken the essential form of an image of a well-dressed courtier, sitting on a fine-made chair, beside a table stacked with loaves of bread, with both those images precisely set within a well-proportioned panel whose empty spaces were entirely filled with lists of offerings of food and linen. That such panels were often placed at the centre of the tomb chapel, above an offering slab and in full view of the entrance doorway, shows how the arrangements for the noble dead echoed the order of the living kingdom; how the vigorous systems of supply, whose energy and prosperity were enabling the construction of great pyramids, also sustained the households of the courtiers in life and death.

That, too, is the underlying meaning of the hieroglyphic formula, the so-called '*hetep di nesut*' that, since the time of Metjen, had accompanied such lists of offerings, and which is traditionally translated as 'a boon that the king gives'. Not that this need imply that the kings sent real food to physically feed the spirits of the noble dead, but that the existence of the tombs themselves, their imported stone, their situation in the royal cemeteries, the employment of the finest craftsmen of the royal court to work on their offering chapels, and the royal guarantee underlying the entailment of land to support continued offerings at the tomb, were all products of the good order of the living state. And that, quite literally, was a boon provided by the kings, for that office was the embodiment, the personification, of the state itself.

So these first decorated tomb chapels were filled with images and sentiments of the everyday, rendered as aspects of the living state; that state which through the office of the king, the arbiter of life and death, the conduit between the living and the dead, extended to the realms of death.

OFFERING AT THE PYRAMID

After copying the scenes in the courtiers' tomb chapels and securing a licence to excavate at Maidum, Petrie put his workforce to digging into the mounds of chip and dust that roll around the oddly devastated pyramid – a product of stone robbers and collapse – with the aim of discovering the identity of its owner, which was not then known. After several weeks of hard and largely fruitless labour, he then bit the bullet and dug directly into the huge mound at the centre of the pyramid's east face where, experience had told him, a royal temple might have stood. And there it was that, after further weeks of dust storms and rock falls, at the bottom of a loose and dangerous cutting which by this time 'would have held two or three good-sized London houses', he came down upon the roof of a small, slope-sided building. Unfortunately, the little temple, though as sturdy as a pillbox, was entirely uninscribed. Even the pair of splendid fourteen-feet-high stelae that still stood beside it, and which resembled some of those put up in the Abydos cemeteries, were completely blank. This disappointment was part-redeemed, however, by the graffiti of some pharaonic tourists who had visited the temple twelve centuries after the pyramid's construction and had affably recorded in inky hieroglyphs how very pleased they had been to visit the 'very great pyramid of King Sneferu'.

Built of blocks of limestone weighing twenty to thirty tons, the little temple's gigantic roofing blocks had protected its interior during the pyramid's disastrous collapses, most of which had occurred in the generations after the ancient scribes had written their graffiti. A simple chicane like those that had been built in front of some of the shrines of Djoser's great enclosure had led those visitors up to a small door that had opened into a tiny courtyard, whose back wall was the dizzily sloping surface of the rising pyramid. And there, between the feet of the two high-standing stelae, lay the focus of this tough little monument: a great stone offering altar, shaped like the *hetep* hieroglyph – a formal image of a loaf of bread set on a papyrus mat.

Petrie's modest sketch of the temple he uncovered at the Maidum pyramid. Taken from the east side of the pyramid, it shows the two great limestone stelae with the alabaster offering table set between them

Kings, of course, had always received offerings at their tombs. Unlike the offering chapels in the nearby courtiers' tombs, however, and indeed unlike all the earlier royal monuments, this royal offering temple had been connected to a great long causeway lined with blocks of stone that had run down from the pyramid to the edge of the cultivated land. Here, presumably, there had been a dockside, with a canal linked to the Nile and, thus, to all of living Egypt. When Sneferu was alive, his workforce had shipped building blocks from distant quarries along the river and up canals and, finally, slid them up great building ramps onto his rising pyramid. So too, this causeway made architectural provision for lines of offerers to follow exactly that same progress, to bring produce from the royal estates up and down the lower Nile to the offering slab within the little temple at the pyramid. The pyramid, the causeway and the tiny temple: a stone synopsis of the state's essential systems.

ANNALS

By modern standards, the monuments of Djoser and Sneferu hold silent histories of their own. Their construction was so large, so all-consuming for the state that made them, that their manufacture had been far and away the major happening of their times. And yet, beyond the presence of their monuments, there is scarcely any contemporary record of the lives of the kings whose names they bear.

Three centuries later, however, in the Sixth Dynasty, some scribes compiled an elaborate record of that period. The oldest known account of the reigns of the early kings, it was essentially a kind of diary, an annual court circular that in gnomic phrases listed some of the activities of the court.

Small parts of that record survive in the form of some broken and fragmentary inscribed stones known as the Annals, the most celebrated piece of which is the so-called Palermo Stone, a portentous slab of engraved basalt, shipped, so it appears, from Memphis in the eighteenth century and marooned today in a Sicilian museum. Along with a number of similar though smaller pieces housed in museums in London and Cairo, these fragments seem to have come from a single six-foot slab that might once have formed part of a sarcophagus. Lightly tapped in tiny rows of hieroglyphs on both sides of the slabs' two shining faces, the Annals were set within the lines of an accounting grid that, in a deliberately archaizing manner, gives them the appearance of rows of First Dynasty ivory picture plaques, with the individual boxes measuring out the years of each king's reign. Though most of the great stone slab is lost, the grid had been accurately divided, so it may be reasonably estimated that it had once held the names of at least a hundred prehistoric rulers and that it had also provided a calendar of the reigns of the first five dynasties of kings.

Starting with a list of odd-sounding names of otherwise unrecorded rulers, the texts first took their readers back to the beginning and then to the times of Manetho's First Dynasty, where, though the kings' names are lost, it yet records the years when the gods were born and worshipped, when statues were first made, and when palaces and temples were measured out upon the earth. At the same time, it also tells of royal rounds of offering and tithing, the years when cattle, gold and people were counted and recorded, records similar in many ways to those in the descriptions copied from the *Aigyptiaka*. And always and inevitably, these little records are literally underpinned by rows of hieroglyphic numbers giving the exact height of the annual inundation of the Nile, the foundation of state wealth.

Just as they had done with ancient texts from Herodotus to the Old Testament, traditional historians generally divided the surviving texts of the Annals into those that appear probable and those that seem improbable, plucking the 'real' from the 'mythical', like plums from a pudding. Taken all together, however, as the ancient scribes had done, the broken fragments carefully record that a stone temple had been erected long before King Djoser's time when Min himself – or perhaps a statue of that god? – had been born. The texts then go on to tell us, though here there is a considerable gap in the surviving record, that,

The events of Sneferu's reign as described on the Palermo Stone. The three columns of text are laid out in a manner similar to the First Dynasty picture plaques, and are of similar size

in the two-year period between the twelfth and fourteenth years of Sneferu's reign, the king had brought thousands of people and great herds of cattle from the south; that a royal palace was erected, and that the shipyards were building dozens of boats and barges, some of which were 100 cubits – over 170 feet – in length. This is information that, as far as the reign of Sneferu is concerned, describes valid if not essential components of the projects in which, so modern archaeology informs us, King Sneferu's court was then engaged, yet which the Annals never mention: the construction of the king's new pyramids.

Here, then, is early evidence of the opening of the gulf between the modern view of history and that held in the majority of the surviving records of pharaonic culture. For there are no contemporary records that in any way describe the creation of the early pyramids, nor does the memory of their manufacture, or even a notice of their enduring presence in the Memphis landscape, impinge on the records of their time, nor, indeed, of any later ages.

It is as if the ancient culture had lived entirely in the present: that the lists of kings compiled in the First Dynasty had not been made for historical purposes at all, but to define the continuing office of kingship of itself. In similar fashion, the Annals only record events outside the usual rhythms of the court's routine: the exact height of the annual flood, the birth of gods and year of a temple's founding; events that were unique. In such a world, pyramids and pyramid making would not have been regarded as a part of history, not as monuments to memorialize the lives of individual kings; for the work of their construction was part of the daily and yearly processes of the living state.

Building, setting stone on stone and making pyramids, is hardly a symbolic enterprise. In similar fashion, the people of the lower Nile had long since understood that their communities were sustained by economy and practicality, and the Naqadans, whose craftsmen had carefully observed and classified their bountiful environment, had ordered their settlements in the belief that the survival of the community of both the living and the dead was dependent on those same processes.

After three centuries of kingship and the royal court, after three centuries of such continuous change that Djet's little comb with its engraving of a model universe seems more like a proposition than a settled statement of ideology, the royal court had gathered and defined the vital elements of their culture at the royal pyramids in precisely the same way as their Naqadan predecessors had done: by extending the processes of burial. Now, though, the scale of these processes of definition had entirely changed so that, in the generations after Djoser, as an ever-enlarging state machine quarried and laid blocks of stone at ever greater rates, there was a delirium of building.

29

A Building Passion

Sneferu at Dahshur, 2600–2575 BC

The real adventure of Sneferu's reign began in its fourteenth year when, as the Palermo Stone helpfully records, the gates of a royal residence were erected and, as the graffiti and statistics of Sneferu's building works both show, Sneferu's pyramid makers had started the construction of the first of the pyramids that would be built on the plain at Dahshur. It would appear, therefore, that those two new gates, one facing north towards the delta and the other towards the south and the Nile Valley, were the entrances of a royal palace, and that the court had moved from Maidum back to Dahshur close by Saqqara, where Sneferu's predecessor, Huni, may also have been buried.

The work of building Sneferu's two pyramids at Dahshur was, and yet remains, an unparalleled human labour, and the amounts of stone and ambition that were required, gargantuan. Whereas the stepped pyramid at Maidum had been similar in size in both its phases to the earlier stepped pyramids, the two monuments built by Sneferu at Dahshur, one following the other, were three and five times larger than their predecessors so that, for their completion whilst the king yet lived, the labour force must on occasion have been tripled in its size. And when the work was at its height, those building programmes would have engaged some 25,000 workers, more than ten per cent of the adult male workforce in the kingdom and a depletion that, in an agrarian society in less fertile climates and in less ordered states, would have had a similar effect to that of a medieval plague.

Nor were those two pyramids the ending of the work. Upon completing that architectural extravaganza, the royal workforce returned to Maidum, where it again enlarged the baselines of Sneferu's stepped pyramid and smoothed out its sides, transforming it into the first classically proportioned pyramid.

A HISTORY IN STONE

Like all the other early pharaohs, Sneferu, the man himself, has virtually disappeared; only spare and eroded images of him have survived, and certainly, we have no idea of his role in the making of his pyramids, nothing beyond the graffiti on some of the blocks which record the time they were either quarried or set up on a pyramid. One thing, though, is sure; just like the earlier monuments of Djoser, Sneferu's three great pyramids are products of a lengthy reign. And Sneferu certainly reigned for a very long time – present estimates ranging between twenty-three and forty-six years.

A great part of the problem of calculating the length of Sneferu's reign more precisely is that the numbers of the stone workers' graffiti may not record the years of Sneferu's rule at all, but those of a biennial cattle count. Recent evidence, however, has shown that in later reigns the cattle count occurred more frequently, though it is not yet clear whether this was also true in Sneferu's time. The colossal work of pyramid construction, however, would tend to indicate that it was not, for even with a biennial cattle count, which would allow Sneferu a full forty-six years, this would have made the building of his second pyramid at Dahshur a ten-year sprint which, in the first years of construction, for example, would have required the setting of 150 two-and-a-half-ton limestone blocks up onto the pyramid in each hour of every working day!

If a cattle count had taken place in every year of Sneferu's reign, therefore, the pyramid's 3.8 million tons of stone would have had to have been laid in half the time, a work that, even if conditions at the site could have provided the physical space for such a large labour force, would have required the labours of a quarter of the adult male population which, given the resources of the kingdom, would have been economically unsustainable. Thus, I have based my estimates of the length of Sneferu's building works on a reign of forty-six years; a timeframe that sets the beginning of his second Dahshur pyramid around the thirtieth year of his rule.

At some 720 feet along its baselines and almost 345 feet high, Sneferu's second pyramid at Dahshur would have been far larger than anything ever built before. The decision to build it at such an extraordinary rate, therefore, represents a change of gear in the mechanisms of the pharaonic state, another fundamental change following the introduction of stone-block building in the reign of Djoser that saw the state's available resources enlarge fivefold in fifty years.

In great part, this extraordinary change of scale in state resources was based on practical considerations, for the first pyramid that Sneferu's work gangs began to build at Dahshur had become so unstable during its construction that it was abandoned. Unfortunately, the conservative methods of the court builders had led them to start work at Dahshur in the same way that, some fifty years before, King Djoser's craftsmen had started building pyramids, by laying out the baselines directly on the desert, in a line of cut stone blocks bedded in a little sand. At Saqqara, the weight of Djoser's pyramid, a structure a quarter of the size of Sneferu's new pyramid, had been supported by the desert's underling rock; at Maidum as well, a prehistoric riverbed of cemented clay and gravel still holds that pyramid in an equally firm fashion. At Dahshur, however, the underlying geology of the part of the plain they chose for the new pyramid was erratic and unreliable, so that, as it had begun to rise and more than a million tons of rock – the largest gathering of cut stone that the world had ever seen – was set onto its shallow baselines, it began to sink unevenly, and twist.

Adding further to its woes, the failing pyramid had been planned differently from all the others. It was, for example, to have been the first smooth-sided pyramid, a form derived, perhaps, from the building methods employed at the Maidum pyramid, which, judging by the appearance of its ruin, had been erected by adding a series of stepped enlargements onto a smooth-sided central core. At the same time, the failing pyramid had also been set to rise at a far steeper angle than any other pyramid, so that, had it been completed, it would have stood at an unprecedented height of 400 feet. Even had the ground beneath been stable, the pressure on its baselines would have been tremendous.

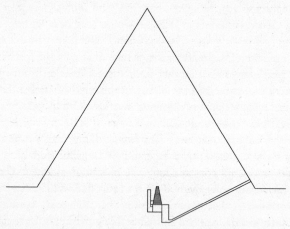

A reconstruction of the original design of Sneferu's first-planned pyramid at Dahshur. Had it been finished, it would have stood some 405 feet high, just 75 feet short of the Great Pyramid of Giza. The section shown is from south to north

Unremittingly, as the building blocks were piled up, day on day, ton by ton, they began to crack and shift until the entire structure was so unstable that the burial chamber and other rooms set at the centre of the pyramid had to be part-filled with stacks of stone and wooden buttresses, some of which are still in place today. Nothing, though, could stabilize the structure, and, after fifteen years of labour, Sneferu's builders stopped piling further blocks of stone onto the failing pyramid.

When the work was at its height, the pyramid makers had been quarrying and transporting, cutting, hauling and setting well over 1,000 two-and-a-half-ton blocks of limestone every working day on this pyramid. What a disaster, then, with stone blocks arriving at Dahshur at such a rate, that the pyramid on which they were being emplaced was sinking and twisting ever further under their accumulating weight!

A practical solution – but only in the modern meaning of that term – would have been to return the king to Maidum for burial within his first-built pyramid. Yet the pyramid makers, or at least the officers of Sneferu's court who controlled that masterpiece of Bronze Age organization, did not stop the state building machine, but simply moved the location of its stone deliveries a mile to the north and started the construction of another and yet larger pyramid.

Before the age of pyramids, the principal function of the court and king had been the provisioning of the living court at Memphis and the production of stone vases. Pyramid building, however, the expanded networks of the state, its colonies and quarries, its shipyards and storage enclosures, its mines and estates, had become the main factor of the enlarging prosperity of the living state. So, just as the labour of pyramid making had been transferred from Maidum to Dahshur with the court, the work of Sneferu's pyramid makers had not stopped when the pyramid on which they were working could not sustain more stone.

The work of pyramid making only stopped, indeed, when a pharaoh died – not a single unfinished pyramid is known to have been started by one pharaoh and finished by another – a new one was begun with the beginning of each new reign, a procedure that literally regathered the resources and organization of the state together around the offices of the new king.

So, in the thirtieth year of Sneferu's rule, after abandoning the failing and half-finished pyramid, the royal workforce had started on another. With generations of experience, their supply lines already up and running, the masons building the largest stone-block buildings in the world with the simplest of equipment, this was a state machine the like of which the world – let alone the lower valley of the Nile – had never seen before. Employing, in all probability, gangs of between ten and twenty men – a practical number of people for working on the pyramid's standard two-and-a-half-ton limestone blocks – thousands of quarrymen were engaged in extracting and shaping blocks of stone and hauling them down ramps onto the docksides so that they could be transported in a fleet of boats to Dahshur, where thousands more men were employed in hauling the blocks up other ramps and finally onto the new pyramid, where, under the eyes of master craftsmen and with an extraordinary care, they were set into position. Thousands upon thousands of huts, compounds and settlements must have been scattered in the fields and deserts all around the Dahshur plain so that, together with the royal residence, they would have made a sort of city.

BUILDING THE MACHINE

Though its four sides had been bravely and ambitiously set at the unprecedented length of over 700 feet, the new pyramid at Dahshur had been designed to rise at a far lower slope than its failed neighbour, so the mass and the pressure on its baselines were considerably reduced. The sheer size of the new pyramid's footprint, however, meant that the tonnage of quarried stone required for its completion was more than one and a half times that of the earlier one. At previous work rates, therefore, the new-planned pyramid would have taken some thirty years to finish, and this at a time when Sneferu had already spent a similar length of time upon the throne and was, by ancient standards, an old man. Yet, as its graffiti show, the vast new pyramid – known now as the 'Red Pyramid' – appears to have been built in less than eleven years, which means that the size of the royal workforce was approximately tripled.

Given their geometric regularity, the mathematics are inevitable. Though appearing today as if the work of their building had just

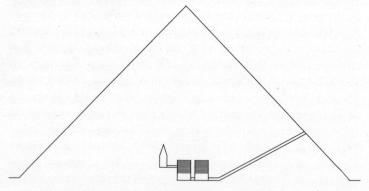

Sneferu's second-built pyramid at Dahshur, known as the 'Red Pyramid'. The base is 719 feet long; the section shown is from south to north

begun, several unfinished pyramids actually hold half the stone of a completed one. For the low-angled Red Pyramid to have been finished in less than eleven years, half of its stone would have had to have been laid by the second year of its construction. And in those early years, of course, when the pyramid was at its widest, many gangs could have worked side by side, but their numbers would, perforce, have tapered with the pyramid itself, as the work continued.

Sneferu's workforce, therefore, had varied greatly in its size throughout his reign. Seven times more people would have been required during the first years of the building of his three main pyramid projects than at their ending. In this economy, therefore, where large labour forces were erratically employed, the presence of a permanent core community of craftsmen would have been essential, for pyramid making requires extraordinary skills – a nucleus, it may be estimated, of around five thousand people, a community with generational experience in such tasks. Employed from the beginning to the ending of the work, this core group would have provided each new king with the expertise to lay out a new pyramid's baselines with extraordinary precision, to select and organize suitable quarries from which to bring the stone, to construct the building ramps, to plan and to construct the pyramid's internal corridors and chambers, and to ensure that the building rose up straight and true until the capstone was put into position.

It is probably no accident that this estimate of five thousand pyramid makers is similar to the number of craftsmen, so it has been calculated, that were working in the court's stone-vase industry before the reign of Djoser. It is likely, therefore, that the core workforce of pyramid makers were the descendants of the same community of craftsmen that, half a century before, in Djoser's time, had made the switch from stone vases to stone-block buildings, and whose labours and aesthetics had guided stone architecture from its beginnings. This core of craftsmen, directly subsidized by the state systems of supply, was in effect part of the royal court, and down through the following millennia would cultivate and maintain its unique cultural identity.

RUNNING THE MACHINE

In the last decade of Sneferu's lengthy reign, as work on the Red Pyramid was nearing its completion, the state machine continued quarrying and transporting stone at such a rate that, in those last few years, almost a quarter of all the building blocks that were used in Sneferu's reign, a further two million tons of them, were quarried, transported and emplaced.

Throughout pharaonic history, such unusually lengthy reigns as those of Sneferu and Djoser were often periods of architectural innovation; periods, that is, when the standard monuments of royalty had been built, yet the royal workforce was still cutting and transporting stone.

Thus, at a time late in Sneferu's reign, both the failed pyramid at Dahshur and Sneferu's pyramid at Maidum were provided with small temples on their eastern sides. Both these temples were approached through chicanes and both had two large offering stones set between a pair of enormous stelae. In all likelihood, therefore, these two pyramids had been integrated, along with the pyramid of Seila and the diadem of other little pyramids strung out along the valley of the Nile, into the cult that had been created around the offices of the king and the court's systems of collection and supply.

At Dahshur, at this same time, an expert eye was also cast over the failed pyramid. Trained now by a further furious decade of experience in pyramid making, a decade in which the techniques of every part of pyramid making, from lime burning to stone setting, had entirely changed, the masons first built a girdle of large and fine-cut blocks of the densest limestone around the bottom of the failed pyramid and then, extravagantly, they capped the unfinished pyramid with another, pitched at a lower angle. Even as they laid new blocks upon the failed pyramid, it had begun to twist and move again, and huge fresh cracks appeared. Now, though, the pyramid makers dealt with every wrench and subsidence as it occurred, setting new building lines and refitting blocks of stone. And in so doing, they built a series of controlled tensions into the rising monument, so that the 'Bent Pyramid', as it is now known, is the strongest and best preserved of all the pyramids of Egypt.

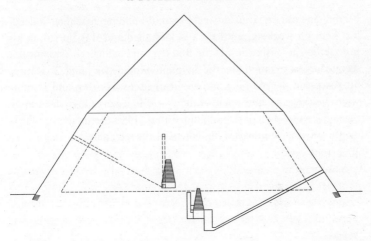

The final form of Sneferu's first-built pyramid at Dahshur, known as the 'Bent Pyramid'. The base is 621½ feet long; the section shown is from south to north

In those same years, the pyramid makers went back to Maidum. And there as well, they built a girdling wall around the base of the old pyramid, smoothed out its stepped sides and raised its apex to a new

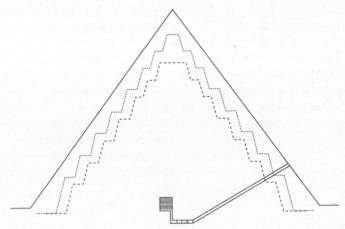

The final form of Sneferu's Maidum pyramid, which encased the two earlier stepped pyramids. It was 473½ feet long at its base lines; the section shown is from south to north

height. Sneferu's extraordinary pyramid-building machine, indeed, just kept on working, until the old king died and was buried, in all probability, at Dashur inside the Red Pyramid, which yet remains the second largest pyramid that the Egyptians would ever build. To Khufu, his successor, the old king had bequeathed a workforce and a state-wide building machine such as the world had never known. And at the same time, the court had gained that cultural confidence which would become an indelible ingredient of the later state.

30

Making the Gods

Deity at Dahshur, 2600–2575 BC

In the winter of 1951, Ahmed Fakhry, a professor at the University of Cairo, undertook the clearance of a causeway at Dahshur which, in the manner of the causeway of the Maidum pyramid, had run down from the Bent Pyramid towards the cultivation. And at its end, almost half a mile from the pyramid itself, he found the ruins of a fine stone building that had been erected as a place of offering, as a focus of a cult of King Sneferu which had continued for a millennium and more. The detritus of generations of the cult's officials, statues, stelae, offering tables, family memorials, seals and document boxes, lay all around it in the sand.

Before it had been stripped to its foundations and the better part of its stonework rendered into quicklime in a nearby kiln, the cult temple had been a handsome structure, almost 160 feet long, made in the simple form of a large, plain-sided mastaba with gently sloping walls. Passing from the causeway through a pair of wooden doors, a single entrance at the centre of its eastern side had given access to a central corridor, a passageway set between four storerooms, which had opened into a large bright courtyard. Here, in the shadows at the far end, behind two rows of foursquare pillars, had stood six sleek statues of King Sneferu, each one standing high in its own niche.

As the surviving fragments showed, the temple's interior had been covered in reliefs – the oldest known decorated temple to have survived from ancient Egypt – which had been cut in the same strong and lively manner as those within the near-contemporary tomb chapels of Metjen at Saqqara and Rahotep and Nofret at Maidum. The same fragments also showed that some of the subject matter of these reliefs had been similar to that of the nobles' tomb chapels: the king

Sneferu's so-called 'Valley temple' at Dahshur. It measured 160 feet from the entrance to the interior shrines

overseeing the rearing of exotic and domesticated animals, holding audience and receiving offerings; and there were some of the same scenes, as well, as those set down in earlier centuries on picture plaques and mace heads.

The only intact reliefs that Fakhry found in their original positions were some rows of offering bearers carved in nicely measured registers along the half-broken walls of the corridor which had given access to the courtyard and the shrines. Listed, identified and quantified, they held dozens of images of women who, on one wall, had been carrying provisions from Sneferu's estates in the Nile Valley and, on the other, from his estates in the delta.

The destination of these offerings, which was indicated by the direction of the offerers' procession, had been the life-sized statues of King Sneferu in the shadowed niches at the end of the open court. Though their surfaces had been damaged by the eruption of the limestone's natural salts, and some of their eyes had been plucked out, two of these six figures had yet survived relatively intact, along with fragments of the others; over-life-sized, idealized images of a calm young king that had impassively overseen generations of offerings by the resident ritualists, whose relics Fakhry had found scattered round the temple.

The temple's continuing endowment, so these relics told, had been

Women bearing offerings from Sneferu's farm estates; a fragment of relief from the east wall of the entrance corridor of Sneferu's temple. Personifications of some of the king's delta estates, each one carries a little offering table with loaves of bread and a hes vase in one hand, and an ankh sign in the other. The figures were some 3 feet high

sustained by the produce of some of Sneferu's estates, an arrangement that a later pharaoh had reaffirmed in a decree which had been carved in stone and set up beside the temple. In such documents, the administrators of the cult are usually described as 'the servants of the god' or, as it is frequently translated, as 'temple priests'. In hieroglyphic writing, however, the term typically employs the *neter* sign, an enigmatic image of a flag flying from a decorated stick, which, as we have already seen, is usually taken to signify a 'god' yet which first appeared as part of the name of an early king, and which in the times before King Sneferu may equally well have signified an ancestor or grave or indeed a plot of land or shrine that held a special power. What precise significance the sign may have held for Sneferu's contemporaries, therefore, is not known. It is highly unlikely, however, that it had simply signified those well-known 'gods' that, in the popular imagination, indiscriminately inhabit all periods of ancient Egypt. For in this modest temple, amongst the innumerable fragments of relief, Fakhry found some of the oldest known images of the pharaonic gods in the form of human figures – or, in the case of several of them, in that typical ancient Egyptian combination of later times – of a human body with the head of a lion, a jackal or another animal.

IN THE IMAGE OF THE KING

Seen now, in drawings made from reconstructions of the gathered fragments of relief, some of the most celebrated of the pharaonic gods, some of which are named and others whose images are but preserved in tiny fragments, make their first appearance in this temple, one at a time. Several of them were shown embracing Sneferu in the manner of thousands of later royal reliefs. Others were in yet closer contact with the king, nose to nose and face to face with pharaoh, and the encounter holds remarkable intensity, as if the single images of Hesi-re or Djoser that are so filled with pulse and sentience had suddenly been placed in intimate contact with another similar being.

Earlier examples of images of these gods in human or semi-human form are very rare. In a unique relief that came onto the antiquities market in the 1960s, Sneferu's predecessor, Huni, is shown being embraced by a god who is drawn as a man with the head of a hawk and is identified as Horus. A single limestone slab, less than two feet high, this remarkable relief was carved in a gentler style than those of the time of Sneferu; it is more similar, indeed, to Djoser's six reliefs, and, like those earlier works, may have been set close to the royal burial.

Older still, the only other unambiguous early image of a god in human form that is known to have survived was sculpted on a broken door jamb, from a mud-brick building which had been set up at Hierakonpolis for Khasekhemui, Djoser's predecessor. Decorated with a variety of odd and complex scenes that appear to hold several images of the king posed in the usual manner, in one of them, though they are all very damaged, he appears to be accompanied by a woman engaged in marking out a plot of land and who carries the hieroglyphic attributes of the goddess Seshat. In later ages, Seshat is similarly pictured helping the king found temples by marking out plots of land. Appropriately, given the insistent harmonies of pharaonic architecture, Seshat will also be associated with counting and with mathematics, qualities that are present in the subtle symmetries of Sneferu's limestone temple, where she had also once appeared.

On the assumption that the ancient Egyptian gods hailed from a savage prehistoric past, their ancestry, as we have seen, used to be traced back to the earliest occurrences of some of the attributes with which they became associated – those signs that originated deep in Naqadan times. Similarly, the graphic conventions of drawing human figures with the heads of animals was sometimes said to have been derived from masks such as had been worn in settlements along the lower Nile since early prehistoric times. And, as it is difficult for many Westerners to imagine gods without written explanations and accompanying stories, so the 'lost histories' of these faux-archaic deities were unthinkingly ascribed to a lost 'oral tradition'. There is no evidence, however, that the human-figured gods in Sneferu's temple were the products of such Frazerian imaginings. Quite the reverse, in fact. Rather than being personifications of 'primitive powers' or chthonic deities, these gods are newly made.

As the rows of offerers in the tombs of Djoser's courtiers most elegantly demonstrate, the graphic device of personification used to create these novel deities had been employed to identify other aspects of the state for at least the previous half-century. In Sneferu's Dahshur temple, the brief written texts which accompany these standard offering figures are now a major source of information about the order of King Sneferu's state, for they record the names of the estates and the types of goods that they produced. These estates are identified by the nomes in which they were situated, many of which, though not all of them, make their first known appearance beside the rows of offering figures in Sneferu's temple. The figures and the texts together, therefore, hold a large part of the early history of the royal estates and also of temple endowments.

Gathered thus, from mud sealings, a few tomb chapels and the fragmented reliefs of Sneferu's temple, the emerging bureaucratic structures of King Sneferu's state are still little understood. Nonetheless, it is clear that, in that strange elusive age, in the dramatic half-century between the death of Djoser and the reign of Sneferu, the kingdom was divided and subdivided and came into its own. Its farmlands and estates were identified, listed and personified along with other equally vital yet less easily defined aspects of the kingdom such as the voluptuous plenty of the inundation, of wild rush, marsh and water, whose small, anonymous personifications make their appearance in the broken reliefs of Sneferu's temple as a row of fat, blue-painted male figures. Early egyptologists had identified these little chaps, a common feature of temple decoration throughout pharaonic history, as Nile gods, a term that fell out of fashion when it was recognized that these gynaecomastic figures were personifications of abundance and fertility, rather than of the Nile itself.

The first age of pyramid building – the half-century from Djoser to Sneferu – had seen an intellectual revolution conducted in architecture and stone images. And part of that took place within this limestone temple, with the dust of pyramid making rising from the desert plain behind them, as some of Sneferu's courtiers and craftsmen created images personifying the various aspects of the kingdom, from the rhythms of the river and the order of the state to the gods themselves; and all of them identified, drawn and situated as elements of the economic engine, natural and man-made, that would fuel the pharaonic state till its ending.

What, if anything, the individual gods gathered in this temple may specifically have personified, however, is not clear. Certainly, these images of Seshat, Min and Ptah, and many others, did not embody the descriptions of the gods listed in dictionaries of ancient Egypt, those elderly Victorian deities who were described as the gods of Memphis or of mathematics, of beer or craftsmen, of foreigners and childbirth, and all the other things that at one time or another their images may have accompanied or embodied. These have been diligently collected from the accumulated faith of ages in a manner that has been described as showing the 'impatient objectivity of the lepidopterist, who aesthetically but terminally arranges his creatures . . . in those famous glass boxes which might look instructive but convey little about the splendor of the living being'. These figures, however, are entirely different; these scraps from Sneferu's temple are the first known appearances of those mysterious deities that generations of pharaonic scribes will name in their writings throughout the following millennia.

Sneferu's gods, however, were created in a pre-literary environment, one in which the manipulation of stone, wood and pigment was a prime mover in the processes of human thought. They could not, therefore, have started life as illustrations to a written literature, so it is hardly likely that they were born of theological endeavour.

It is precisely because these images were not designed to symbolize abstract ideas and were made in absolute conformity to the craftsmen's rules of image making, that any intellectual processes that may have been involved in their creation have been effectively disguised. What is left, however, is something of the environment in which they were created; their time and place, that dramatic point in time when work on Sneferu's pyramids was coming to its conclusion, an age that had seen an unprecedented mass of humanity linked in a single purpose, building for the king who was the centre of the state, the sustainer of its order and the prosperity of the court. Here, then, the relief artists drew out the vital qualities of the state machine in human form and, in so doing, they created some of the oldest known images of the pharaonic gods.

A clue to the origins of these gods and to their roles in Sneferu's state is held in some of the images that were set on the rows of columns that shadowed the statues of the royal cult: images of Sneferu carrying a mace and stick, those archetypal tools of slaughter that, as the fundamental tools of offering and kingship, had long served as the keys to another world.

These images of the king had marked the place in Sneferu's temple where, behind the columns, in the shadows, offerings were made; ten close-set pillars demarcating the edges of the offering place, a zone at the edge of this world and the next, where the image of the king, cast in his roles as the receiver of offerings and the conduit between life and death, would be particularly appropriate. All the architecture of the temple, the dark corridor beyond the entrance, the open court, the shaded columns, the royal statues and the altars, lead to a powerful place set between this world and the next: a zone that is precisely described as 'sacred' and thus holds more than words within it.

Here, within the temple, above the rows of offering-bearers and the blue fertility figures, were also carved and painted images of the gods. Given human or quasi-human form, they appear, as did the figures of estates and abundance, as personifications. Unlike those other figures, however, the gods are personifications based on the images of the king. They stood in close physical proximity to Sneferu and they were drawn in some of the same poses, with the same build and at exactly the same height. And they embrace the figure of the king as he enters into the temple, into that zone between this world and the next, as if they were inducting him through the looking glass of the offering altar into a world beyond.

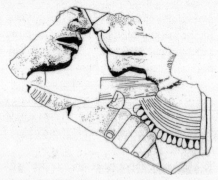

King Sneferu and a lion goddess? – an identification of a relief fragment from Sneferu's temple suggested by later examples of similar images. The royal figures in the temple were around life size

THE PLACE OF KINGS

In the half-century since Djoser's day, the vision of the court had shifted. Rather than reproducing the buildings of the living kingdom in stone, as Djoser's craftsmen had once done, Sneferu's temple, with its king and gods and plentiful estates, held images of the entirety of the pharaonic state.

And the centre of that ordered imagery was the figure of the pharaoh. In sheer economic terms, in pyramids and palaces, in estates and offering temples, the king took up far more of the state's resources than the newly envisaged deities who embraced him in the shadows of his temple. Throughout pharaonic history, indeed, images of gods will usually be shown in the company of kings. That is their place. As many later temple texts describe, the royal state was a precondition of their presence, for it is the king who builds the houses of the gods, so that they may dwell within his kingdom.

And at the same time that the gods appear, the image of the king within the order of the state visibly changes. For the images of the gods have given a new and powerful physical dimension to the sacred. Rather than the indistinct sanctity of the earlier shrines, the human figures of the gods have brought air and life and space with them: another world. And simultaneously, as he is set into their company in the chapels and in temples in which offerings are made, the office of the king, the arbiter of life and death on earth, has also changed.

At this same time, the royal name is isolated from all others, its hieroglyphs circumscribed inside an oval ring – the so-called cartouche – which is at one and the same time an elongated *shen* sign, used to describe the eternal circuit of the sun and also a ring of the multi-stranded rope employed by the pyramid's stone-hauling gangs. Though it had made its first appearance in earlier reigns, from the time of Sneferu the cartouche is regularly used to frame the names of kings, and its distinctive form will serve to highlight the royal dona-tion that is announced in the offering chapels of the nobles' tombs.

Nor need this continuing definition of the office of the pharaoh have been the cunning plan of a propagandizing dictator, as tradition once explained. Nor indeed need it have been the product of someone who believed himself to be divine or even possessed of the divine rights of a baroque king. The true story is one of continuing inventive-ness and change, and once again it is to be found within the surviving architecture. From one project to the next, the early pyramids show an utter lack of standardization. Each one was constructed in a differ-ent way. And just as they were not built by labourers employing primitive versions of modern equipment, so neither were they built by rule and rote, or driven by principles of practicality or modern eco-nomics. Even the ramps up which the stones were hauled onto the early pyramids, several of which still survive, show different methods of construction and design. The shapes and sizes of the pyramids' buildings blocks were often changed, sometimes during the course of building a single pyramid, and, in similar manner, the finishing of the various pyramids' exteriors shows the use of a wide range of implements and diverse techniques. With the success and failure of their half-dozen projects, however, Sneferu's stone workers learned that better finished stones were more stable than rough blocks, learned, too, how carefully fired plaster was more suited for the tasks that it had to perform than the raw material, learned also how to triple a workforce and yet maintain the necessary provisions and supplies; learned, in short how to make a better pyramid.

Just as there is little evidence that the system of nomes and estates that provisioned those extraordinary enterprises was part of a sternly centralizing organization, so, too, beyond the near-perfection of their silhouettes, the early pyramids were hardly the products of a massive mono-enterprise controlled in a modern way, but rather the products of a system which had allowed the practical free-flow of intelligence, and retained that accumulated knowledge down through generations.

As for Sneferu's role in all this, as the linchpin of the living state, both his office and his state gained clarity and definition with the building of his pyramids, with the invention of the gods, and the personification of almost every aspect of the kingdom. After Sneferu, the 'boon that the king gives' is that the monarch and the officers of the court will continue to control all the aspects of the state that they so vigorously defined and refined, so that it caters both for the living and for the dead; a contract measured out on the horizon of the living land in Sneferu's pyramids.

This, then, tells something of the impulses which kept Sneferu's masons bending at their work for half a century yet left the scribes of later ages straining to explain it in dense religious texts. Pyramid building, of itself, had become a ritual activity, not in the sense that it required priests, or incense, or incantations, but as a national enterprise of offering in which all the different spaces of the pharaonic state, in life and death, had been defined and unified.

31

The Perfect Pyramid

Khufu and Giza, 2575–2550 BC

> *the state ... is not a partnership in things subservient only to*
> *the gross animal existence of a temporary and perishable*
> *nature ... It is a partnership in all science; a partnership in all*
> *art; a partnership in every virtue and in all perfection ... a*
> *partnership not only between those who are living, but*
> *between those who are living, those who are dead, and those*
> *who are to be born.*
>
> Edmund Burke, 1790

Sneferu's successor to the throne, and probably one of the old man's sons, was a certain Khufu, whose tomb is known today as the Great Pyramid of Giza.

As with King Sneferu, the best part of the known history of Khufu's life and times is held within his building works, within his great unlettered pyramid, whose vast dimensions, extreme precisions and subtle architectural harmonies were never to be repeated in all pharaonic history – nor indeed, in any other culture.

In practical terms, the labour of the Great Pyramid's construction was nothing that Sneferu's pyramid makers had not already undertaken during the previous half-century. Such an outrageous building project, indeed, could only have been realized at that specific moment in pharaonic history, when the dynamic of Sneferu's state machine was running fast and a second and third generation of core craftsmen still held the ability and experience to undertake such work: to build a pyramid, that is, whose completed bulk would be more than half as large again than any earlier pyramid, yet could be built within the lifetime of a king who, given Sneferu's long reign, was probably already past the first flush of youth.

The pyramid was built upon the past. Virtually every technical aspect of King Sneferu's pyramid-building projects was re-assessed and rationalized and put to work at the Great Pyramid. In exactly similar fashion, the architecture of King Khufu's pyramid is the perfection of all earlier pyramids; the epitome of a powerful aesthetic that had driven the craftsmen of the lower Nile since the time of the Badarian potters: to make a perfect abstract form within a chosen medium. Unlike the earlier pyramids, however, which show continuous processes of development and change in almost every aspect of their manufacture, the Great Pyramid immediately became the vademecum of royal tombs for the best part of a millennium.

The reign of Khufu, therefore, represents both an ending and a beginning.

IMAGINING THE PYRAMID

Given the ambitions of Khufu's pyramid makers, it is hardly surprising that practical considerations underpinned the planning of his pyramid, not the least of which was the selection of its location. All three of Sneferu's pyramids had been set on compacted beds of clay and gravel. There is precious little local building stone at either Maidum or Dahshur, and what stone there is in the nearby deserts is of such poor quality that its use may well have contributed to the Bent Pyramid's dramatic failure.

So the substance of those three enormous pyramids had been shipped to their building sites, and some of it from considerable distances. The Red Pyramid, for example, derives its modern name from the unusual tint of its limestone blocks, and the only known quarries for such stone are in the Mokkatam Hills, close by Cairo some twenty miles away and on the east bank of the river. The enterprise of its acquisition – shipping, hauling, barge, canal and harbour building – must have been a major element in that pyramid's construction, absorbing considerable amounts of the state's resources.

Unlike the valley plains of Maidum and Dahshur, the limestone plateau of Giza, one of the last ridges of valley limestone before the delta plains, held enormous reservoirs of good, strong limestone. Nearby, as well, there was a sheltered desert valley in the cliffs, ideal for the siting of a harbour through which the pyramid's fine Tura limestones and Aswan granite could be conveniently shipped, along with provisions for the pyramid builders, a community that at its height would have consisted of at least fifty thousand people.

Above all else, however, the Great Pyramid's creation seems to have been dominated by the bitter experience of the Bent Pyramid's dramatic failure. For the same rock formation of which the Giza Plateau is composed not only held large quantities of good-quality building rock just a ramp's length from the pyramid's projected baselines, but also promised a firm footing for the pyramid itself, which at its conclusion would consist of some 5.5 million tons of rock piled on a thirteen-acre base. So, even though the pyramid was planned to stand upon a cliff top some 300 feet above the river's plain and would be situated far further north of Memphis than any earlier royal tomb, it was in fact a perfect place to build a great, grand pyramid.

Nonetheless, the anxiety of its builders to continuously check and control the pyramid's stability during all phases of its construction suffuses every element of the Great Pyramid's architecture. In previous generations, at Sneferu's Bent Pyramid, as the building blocks were delivered and emplaced, and as the baselines and the internal corridors and chambers had twisted out of true, the masons had attempted to correct the distorting architecture, for it was essential to the accurate progress of the pyramid to maintain straight building lines as the pyramid rose up into the sky. Given the tools available, however, the pyramid makers had no means of measuring the mass of movements that were taking place within the rising pyramid nor, indeed, those under way within the ground on which the pyramid stood.

King Khufu's masons solved this problem by laying out their pyramid at the beginning of the work with an extraordinary accuracy and then rechecking its continuing integrity with almost every stone they laid, so that every tiny subsidence within that enormous and accumulating stack of stone was corrected as it occurred. At the same time, too, whilst conforming to the architectural specifications for a pharaoh's burial that had been developed in the time of Sneferu, the plan of the Great Pyramid's internal architecture was elaborated so that it contained a further set of architectural checks and balances, simple geometries by which the rising pyramid could be calibrated and controlled at almost every level of its stonework. So as the pyramid rose ever higher, a cat's cradle of verticals and diagonals was set down in the pyramid's internal architecture with an extraordinary precision that would continue to show the slightest movement in the stonework, such as occurred during the later stages of its construction, when some of the fifty-ton granite blocks from which the burial chamber had been constructed, subsided, and then snapped and twisted out of true.

From its beginning, therefore, the Great Pyramid was specifically designed to serve as its own theodolite, an instrument with which every stone was checked against another as it was laid, and the whole was checked against the point of north, as established in an alignment of the stars. And the system was adhered to with such extraordinary tenacity that it was only with the arrival of Napoleon's surveyors at the ending of the eighteenth century that any deviation from absolute geometrical perfection was measured at the pyramid. Before that time, most scientists had thought the Great Pyramid to be a perfect abstract measure; Isaac

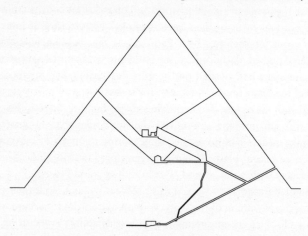

Khufu's pyramid at Giza; the 'Great Pyramid'. When complete, it stood 480 feet high and its baselines were, on an average, 718 feet 8 inches long, the maximum error between them being just 7 inches. The section shown is from south to north

Newton, for example, had considered that, along with Solomon's temple, King Khufu's pyramid had held the measure of the universe within it.

THE STATE MACHINE

The Great Pyramid's baselines would have been established at the beginning of King Khufu's reign; that is, around the first quarter of the twenty-fifth century BC. Earlier, on the death of Sneferu, the master builders must have surveyed and selected the site of the Giza Plateau and thus made the novel decision to set their pyramid upon a cliff. Then, we may imagine, the craftsmen masons and their families, a courtly community several thousand strong, had set out from their settlements at Maidum and Dahshur and travelled north to Giza to establish the support networks that such grand-scale pyramid building required: to plan and oversee the excavation of canals to run from the river to the new harbour that would be situated in the valley by the Giza cliff. At this same time, too they had to oversee the construction of accommodations, dockyards and warehouses, and to open local quarries and secure the supply lines for the delivery of fine limestone from the Tura quarries that was to be employed at certain key locations from the beginning of the work. Now, too, they had to re-establish the granite quarries at Aswan, for, though it had not been greatly used for building since King Djoser's day, blocks of Aswan granite would be used to build King Khufu's burial chamber and also for the various gigantic plugs and portcullises which, in the traditional manner, were to block parts of the pyramid's internal corridors after the royal burial had taken place. Such was the amount of Aswan granite that would be required – some 2,300 tons of the dull-red stone, and some of it quite early in construction – that its quarrying must have begun at the same time as work started on the pyramid itself.

When the quarries and the supply lines were established, when the site had been surveyed and measured, and a small but perfectly aligned corridor had been cut into the rock to serve as the pyramid's first fixed point; when four fifty-ton blocks of Tura limestone had been set down to mark out the pyramid's cornerstones; then the avalanche would have begun. Some forty thousand workers were gathered to quarry and to ship and haul the blocks of stone onto the rising pyramid. If Khufu's pyramid makers had engaged the same-sized workforce and built at the same rates as their predecessors had done at Sneferu's Red Pyramid, it would have taken less than fourteen years to finish: a labour that at its height would have required 4,000 tons of limestone blocks to have been hauled up along the slick mud of the stone-hauling ramps on each and every working day and set with great precision on the rising pyramid. For the first few years, therefore, when half of the pyramid's bulk would have been put in place, there would have been a considerable community of pyramid makers and their families living around the Giza Plateau, and indeed the sparse remains of huts and fires from just this period have been excavated in the surrounding areas.

No trace, however, has been found of Khufu's residence, which must have surely stood at Giza. There, too, would have been the households of the royal court, many of the people who would be buried in the neatly laid-out rows of stone-block mastabas and little pyramids that flank the royal pyramid. The eastern cemeteries of this unique assembly contain the tombs of queens and members of the royal family group; those to the west of the Great Pyramid, members of the state administration, amongst them one Hemiunu, who appears to have been the eldest son of Nefermaat and Itet and thus part of the inner circle of the royal family.

Judging by the position of his tomb, however, Hemiunu may also have taken an active part in the royal administration and indeed his court titles, as they are written on a remarkable statue from his tomb, describe him as a king's son and a considerable priest, with a variety of benefices, as a courtier, a royal scribe and seal bearer, and as director of the music of the north and south. That another of Hemiunu's titles also describes him as 'overseer of all the royal construction projects' has led some to claim him to have been Khufu's very own Imhotep and the Great Pyramid's designer. Yet there is little chance that an ancient noblemen could have performed such a modern function, in the construction of a structure that is as much an exercise in craftsmanship and state logistics as in architectural design. Given the exceptionally fine workmanship of his tomb, however, and the remarkable graffiti that keep a tally of its building, it would not appear unlikely that Hemiunu was involved in the organization of the royal building projects. His tomb, indeed, is surrounded by the tombs of other courtiers, whose titularies imply that they too may have been concerned with the organization of the royal labour force. In the manner of the times, however, the elegant fragments of relief that have survived the sad destruction of Hemiunu's tomb chapel depict a bucolic idyll, similar to that drawn in his parents' tomb at Maidum, rather than the dusty day-to-day realities of a pyramid-building court that was part of a unique urban community, living beside an ancient building site quite isolated from the rhythms of rural life.

Rather than their decorations, it is the mastabas themselves that show something of the air of Khufu's court. Conservative and severe, these massive tombs, built entirely of rough stone blocks, are finished with a light and skilful touch, a pervading elegance, an austere perfection. Like the pyramid in whose shadow they all stand, their design is highly regulated, all of them in line, most of them the same size as their neighbours, and all of them faced with colossal yet precisely rusticated blocks of stone. And at their south-eastern corners, many of these mastabas once displayed a special single slab of stone, a small rectangle of fine Tura limestone, most beautifully carved and painted, which named the person who was to be buried in the tomb. The same person whose image is also shown on the slab, seated most elegantly at a table loaded with loaves of bread and surrounded by lists of offerings: the continuing transaction of the state in life and death that, under Khufu, had become a highly regulated reduction of the expansive arrangements of the earlier tomb chapels. Rarely, as in the case of Hemiunu's tomb, is there a niche or serdab in these lines of mastabas to accommodate statues. Down in their burial chambers, at the bottom of a considerable shaft, a plain, rectangular wooden coffin held a linen-wrapped corpse, and set beside it were utensils, a few ceramic pots, some vessels of copper and of stone and, on occasion, a beautiful life-sized head, an ideal portrait made of fine white limestone. Every one of these is individually memorable, and all of them bear the curious rough scars of a line of chisel marks cut into their perfect finish, as if the sculpture had been scalped.

As for Khufu's pyramid, though the very sizes of its blocks of stone, its orientation to the stars and even the exact angle of its rise were all derived from Sneferu's pyramids, everything had been elaborated and made more precise. In 1881, when the young Flinders Petrie undertook the definitive survey of its architecture, he could find no error whatsoever in the angle of the first of its internal corridors, and errors of less than a few inches – and many, indeed, far less than that – between the craggy reality of the pyramid's exterior, which has been largely stripped of its fine outer casing, and the perfections of an ideal pyramid of the same size. The four final baselines, for example, hold a combined error in them, a deviation from geometrical perfection, of less than 7 inches in 755 feet 9 inches.

Such extreme precisions would be very difficult for modern builders to maintain. The ancient builders worked to tolerances far smaller than those of modern building codes, and their errors, as far as they exist at all, would be undetectable with the use of a metal surveyor's tape, which in the sun's heat would expand by yet larger amounts. Khufu's pyramid makers did not use modern plans and numbers but the pyramid's own geometry, and they worked at full size. Apart from those rare instances where some subsidence has occurred, the only places in this extraordinary monument in which modern surveying equipment can detect substantial inaccuracies are those where the pyramid makers could not control their architecture with the tools available to them: a finger's touch along a row of stones, the comparison of a horizontal line with a line of water, or a vertical line with a plummet and a cord.

The builder's reliance upon geometry, upon stretched cords and the stars, meant that they used very few fixed measurements during the pyramid's construction. Apart from the baselines, which were fixed at 440 cubits, the best part of its specifications were derived from two related grids whose squares were one-sixth of the baseline's length, and between them these controlled both the geometric web of corridors inside the pyramid and the angle of its sides. Such grids had been used in pyramid construction from the beginning. Drawings from both Djoser's and Sneferu's times show ancient builders using grid co-ordinates to set up similar angles in their architecture, whilst the horizontal lines of the stepped pyramids, of course, had provided the pioneer stone-block builders with a system of co-ordinates that was built into the stone of their exteriors.

Such simple methods – a line divided and then subdivided several times and angles set on grids – had controlled the weaving of the Faiyum farmers, where the weft and warp of looms had held the geometric complexities that underpin all weaving work. Similar geometries were built into the Faiyum farmers' grain baskets; later, they would control some of the designs of the Naqadan pottery painters. By itself, of course, such pattern making did not employ the mathematics that we now often use to explain how such ancient processes were undertaken, but they were, quite simply, the lifeblood of the ancient crafts and it was natural for the pyramid makers to employ them.

In similar fashion, the Great Pyramid's architectural design was also based upon those of its predecessors, the angle of its rise precisely imitating the smoothed surfaces of the final phase of Sneferu's pyramid at Maidum. Neither Sneferu's nor Khufu's designers, however, used the modern expression of 51° 50' to measure the angle of that rise, employing instead a simple system of grid co-ordinates. In similar fashion, the eccentricities of the Great Pyramid's interior architecture are but elaborations of traditional designs. The ceiling of the corridor that leads to the burial chamber, for example, the celebrated Grand Gallery, with its soaring corbel vault built on enormous blocks of stone, resembles the modest prehistoric constructions made in mud brick that were first reproduced in rough stone in Sneferu's Maidum pyramid. Inside the Great Pyramid the ancient forms of its predecessors were enlarged and then distorted by the application of its particular design grid. In similar fashion, Khufu's burial chamber, a vast prefabricated granite box, is but an enlargement and adaption of Djoser's funerary vault; likewise, the mechanisms of the granite plugs and portcullises, that series of colossal mobile geometries designed to block parts of the pyramid's internal architecture after Khufu's burial, were all derived from those used in earlier tombs. As with everything in this perfect pyramid, the difference is one of scale and of the perfection of its workmanship: the culture of most ancient Egypt taken to another level.

AFTER THE PYRAMID

When the pyramid had been finished, when its four great cliffs of Tura limestone were polished to a shine, when the great stone-hauling ramps that had stood upon its southern face had been taken down and the volume of its stone and rubble had refilled the quarry which had supplied the bulk of the pyramid's building stone; after all of that, the builders kept on working.

The nobles' cemeteries were extended. Chapels were built onto many of the mastabas and sometimes their original designs were enlarged and altered. The graffiti in Hemiunu's tomb, for example, suggest that he was still alive when the Great Pyramid was finished, but that he had died by the nineteenth year of Khufu's rule, when his mastaba was in a third stage of enlargement.

Now, too, when the pyramid was finished, buildings could be constructed in areas that were previously inaccessible due to the construction work. Three minor pyramids were built close to the pyramid's eastern side to house some royal queens, and another miniature pyramid, such as had stood by some of Sneferu's pyramids, was set close to them, this last addition perhaps an echo of the secondary sepulchral complex that had been built in Djoser's pyramid enclosure.

At the same time, too, a splendid offering temple of basalt, granite and limestone with an open courtyard and a shadowed columned hall with statues of the king, was set at the centre of the pyramid's east face. An enormous causeway was constructed that, with the support of a high stone ramp, ran from this temple, over the cliff top and down to the edge of the cultivation in the plain below, where, it would appear, another temple had once stood. On the walls of these now largely vanished buildings the royal craftsmen cut fine reliefs, of which the merest fragments have survived; images of offering-bearers carrying the goods of Khufu's estates up to the temple by the pyramid; fragments of scenes of woodcutting, cattle wrangling and other activities on the royal estates, and of boat-building and Sed festivals; all beautifully made, but pitifully broken.

Khufu died after ruling for at least twenty-six years, and his funeral rites, as some graffiti by his pyramid record, were conducted under the aegis of Djedefre, who appears to have been his son and successor to the throne. After his sarcophagus was closed, the portcullises had thudded into place, and the great granite plugs had filled parts of the pyramid's internal architecture, after the entrance to the pyramid had been closed with blocks of Tura limestone, the work of Khufu's court was finished. Only the continuing ceremonies of the royal cult in the pyramid's dark temple witnessed to state activity continuing in Khufu's name. As for the pyramid makers, they had moved northwards to another hill, where they would build a pyramid for Djedefre.

Nothing of Khufu the man is known. As in the days of Sneferu, the usual inscriptions were set into the red rocks of the Sinai copper mines; Khufu's quarrymen made another, too, in the alabaster quarries at Hatnub, whilst a few brief graffiti cut into the boulders at Aswan record the presence of some of the members of his court at the settlement which provided granite both for his pyramid and for his plain and uninscribed sarcophagus. In 1900, at Abydos, in an ancient temple built over the remnants of an archaic shrine, Petrie found a unique tiny ivory figure of an enthroned king bearing Khufu's name. Its chubby face bears some resemblance to a few royal heads of granite and limestone which, though uninscribed, are from the same period and are often claimed to represent King Khufu. In the year 2000, deep in the Sahara, some 300 miles west of Memphis, a desert explorer found the names of Khufu and Djedefre scratched into the surface of an enormous cone of rock. It seems that both those kings had sent expeditions into the Western Desert to recover a substance that the text describes as *mefat*, which appears to have been a red ochre of especial brilliance. The rock on which the ancient expedition leaders, Beby and Iymery, left their graffiti had been a way station for desert voyagers since Naqadan times. Expeditions such as the pharaohs had mounted required hundreds of men and donkeys, both to sustain mining and to travel on such distant tracks, which stretch far further and, mysteriously, deep into the Sahara, south and west towards Chad and the Sudan. That the rock graffito naming Khufu announces that it was made at the time of his thirteenth cattle count provides the unique information that the king had probably enjoyed a twenty-six year reign at least; ample time, therefore, to build the Great Pyramid of Giza.

Like many kings before him, Khufu was provided with a means of river transport after death. Five wooden boats were buried in deep pits beside his pyramid, two of which were obscured by later building works and thus, remarkably, survived. One of them still lies, disassembled, underground. The other was excavated in the 1950s and restored with an extraordinary skill by Hag Ahmed Youssef and a team of restorers from the Service des Antiquités. The beautiful result, after many years of work, was the reappearance of one of Khufu's river craft, its planks still shining from the wear of the ancient ropes that its crew had coiled up and buried with the boat. It is a swing-hulled vessel with the same profile that the Naqadan artists had drawn upon the wall of the painted tomb at Hierakonpolis almost a thousand years before, a design that, even in those far-off days, had echoed the shapes of yet more ancient craft that groups of hunter-gatherer fishermen had made from bundles of papyrus stalks pulled up into a graceful curve, to ply the prehistoric Nile.

THE TOMB OF KHUFU'S MOTHER

Thursday, February 19, 1925
A curious patch of cement [= plaster // GAR] from 5 – 7 cm thick and about 320 cm from north to south and 90 from east to west has been found a little way west of G 7101 P. This has been mapped and as the rock has been cut as for a door or pit-mouth at the south it will be explored carefully.

Scribbled in the excavation diaries of the Harvard–Boston Giza expedition, and annotated by its stern director, Dr George Andrew Reisner (= GAR), this terse note signalled the beginnings of one of the most remarkable archaeological enterprises ever undertaken, and much of it performed close to the Great Pyramid, in an ancient rock-cut vault no larger than a suburban drawing room and set some eighty feet beneath the surface of the plateau.

Most of the cemeteries of King Khufu's nobles, those bleak rows of repeating mastabas as regular as plots in a modern cemetery, were excavated during the first half of the last century by two great archaeologists – Herman Junker, a German Jesuit professor at the University of Vienna, who after some fifteen seasons left the windy plateau to investigate the prehistoric settlement of Merimda, and George Reisner, a Harvard professor, who had started work at Giza in 1902 and died there, forty years later, in his expedition house.

Both men had studied at Berlin, the great centre of egyptology during the early twentieth century, and both of them had imbibed its curious vision of ancient Egypt as a culture at once primitive and savage and yet as intellectually consistent as Henry Ford's production line. Like all great archaeologists, Reisner had supreme self-confidence. He also had great affection for Egypt and especially for the villagers with whom he worked throughout his life. He trained them to excavate, photograph and document in his demanding way, and thus built one of the finest excavating teams ever to have worked in Egypt, a team, so it transpired, suitable not only for doggedly working through the lines of tombs of Khufu's nobles, but also for the excavation of the decayed contents of a single tiny chamber with unremitting care, and thus preserve one of those rare points of immediacy, those vivid flashes of reality, that stand out from the usual run of ancient history.

Mohammedani Ibrahimi, one of Reisner's photographers, had first spotted a tongue of plaster in the freshly excavated bedrock of an open area behind the line of the three small pyramids that stand to the east of Khufu's pyramid. The following week, the plaster slab was cut away to reveal several rows of chunky Tura limestone blocks, a building method regularly employed by the funerary masons of King Khufu's day to seal the shafts that lead into the burial chambers of the Giza mastabas. That these blocks were undisturbed signalled to the archaeologists that they had uncovered the mouth of a shaft which had been sealed since the day of its ancient closure. At the same time too, the shaft's position in the middle of the open area that Reisner had dubbed 'Queens Street' rather than at the centre of a mastaba informed its excavators that it may have been part of a tomb which had been cleared away when the three nearby pyramids were built – a reorganization of the cemetery that had hidden the shaft from the plunderers who had visited most of the other tombs within the Giza cemeteries.

After removing some thirty feet of filling from the shaft, a mix of limestone blocks, dust, stones and plaster, the archaeologists came across a small side chamber which held an ox head and some beer jars; an offering, it appeared, that had been made at the time the tomb was sealed. And then, at almost ninety feet and at the bottom of the pit, they came across another wall of limestone blocks which closed its southern side.

On taking down the wall, the archaeologists found themselves in a short open corridor whose ending was blocked by yet another stone-block wall. At first, a single stone was taken out. 'It was then late in the afternoon and the sunlight had gone,' Reisner reported. 'By the light of a candle he [an expedition archaeologist, Alan Rowe] saw only dimly a chamber, a sarcophagus, and a glimmer of gold.' Without further opening up the chamber, which was brimful of antiquity, a mass of gold, silver, pottery and faience lying in a gossamer of decay beside a stone sarcophagus, it took three days of gazing through a pair of field glasses to make out the cartouche of Sneferu emblazoned on a thick gold sheet.

Rowe had opened an intact tomb of a member of the royal family, a tomb some fifteen centuries older than Tutankhamun's, whose discovery just three years earlier had already attuned the world's media to thrilling tales of pharaoh's hidden gold. This tomb, however, did not contain the treasure of an unknown boy king, but quite possibly that of Khufu, the builder of the Great Pyramid or that of his father, Sneferu. At all events, the discovery promised a fresh pharaonical sensation.

Reisner was teaching in America as his team were clearing the burial shaft at Giza, and when he heard their news he ordered the shaft to be reblocked, the surrounding area fenced off, and a guard to be mounted at the end of Queens Street to await his arrival. Ten months later, when press excitement had abated and after a deal of careful planning, he travelled to Egypt, 'leisurely back through London and Paris', and then, and only then, was the ancient shaft reopened and the last wall taken down so that the work could begin.

In the four and a half millennia that the treasure had rested in its tiny limestone vault, the wood of which the best part of its contents had been made had desiccated, shrunk and twisted and, following a leak of water into the chamber, it had further suffered the effects of a slow-growing fungus. In consequence, the joints of the furniture and the numerous storage boxes which had been stacked around the alabaster sarcophagus had been forced apart and had then decayed so that, over the centuries, much of their golden coverings and inlays had shucked like lizard skins, dropping down in the silent darkness to lie amongst an accumulating mass of dust and decay. So Reisner and his assistants had to deal with a royal treasure that time had rendered into a tumbled mass which lay across the chamber floor like cigar ash mixed with golden foil, with broken basketry, leather and linens and a mass of precious inlay scattered all about, as well as a considerable store of pottery that had originally been piled up against the furniture within the chamber but which, as the woodwork had disintegrated, had dropped down and rolled through the accumulating debris on the floor.

That this most fragile of all ancient treasures was not blown away in a blast of publicity and hasty archaeology is entirely due to Reisner; to a stubbornness that month on month insisted on a forensic deposition of everything within the tomb, with artists, photographers and restorers in continual attendance, and with Reisner lying on a mattress, inching week by week ever further into the little room, accompanied by a series of assistants, one of whom, he noted approvingly, possessed 'especially long arms'.

They were a full two months into the work before they knew whose tomb it was that they were emptying. Then, one day, as he was lifting lines of some beautiful golden hieroglyphs that had been part buried in the dust, Reisner reassembled them and translated them as the titles of the 'mother of the King of Upper and Lower Egypt', 'guide of the ruler', 'favourite lady whose every word is done for her' and finally, the name of Hetep-heres, an entirely unknown person who, so her titles seem to tell, had been a daughter of King Huni, a wife of King Sneferu, and the mother of King Khufu, whose funerary workshops, so some of the impressions on the mud sealings found on jars within the chamber now showed, had prepared her tomb for burial.

On they went, measuring, drawing, photographing, and note-taking in the tomb chamber of Queen Hetep-heres; clearing fragments of her furniture and jewellery, of her baskets, her storage boxes and her caskets, some of which had been so heavily inlaid with semi-precious stones and faience that they looked for all the world like the inlaid decorations in the chapels of the queen's relatives at Maidum. Here, then, were piles of sticks, and a royal bed complete with a wooden half-moon headrest. Here, too, were the disassembled elements of a great golden canopy, whose poles, along with its accompanying golden boxes made to hold the linen curtains, had been laid on top of the sarcophagus. And in the deep, grey dust they found the decayed remnants of the queen's jewellery box still holding twenty silver bracelets, each one inlaid with fragments of lapis lazuli, turquoise and carnelian, set in the form of butterflies. Given the manner of her times, Hetep-heres might well have worn these bracelets all at once. Though such parures had long since been pictured in the tomb reliefs, this set is the only one that is known to have survived.

There were, however, but a few fine, hard-stone jars within the tomb, the rest being cut from soft alabaster and for the most part rather badly finished, an indication that the venerable industry had all but disappeared. Here, though, were heaps of domestic pottery, all newly made and smashed and never used; lamps and basins, storage pots, cooking bowls and jars for yoghurt making, and a most elegant pair of cups with a small serving jug all made of bright yellow gold. And there, too, was a boxed set of toiletries, little pots for oils and unguents, some copper razors and flints, and a copper washing basin with a jug.

These then, are the personal possessions of a grand old lady, the relics of a courtly life transformed into a deathly trousseau, packed into an underground chamber measuring seventeen feet by nine.

And at the ending of the work, when all the fragments had been mapped, measured and photographed and placed on a series of wooden trays and lifted to the surface, a small gathering of the great and the good came down into the tomb to welcome the ancient queen back into the realm of the living. Then, finally, the lid of the sarcophagus was opened and, like that of King Sekhemkhet, it proved to be, as Reisner dolefully described, as empty as the day it had been made.

Even with Reisner's detailed records of their clearance, it took twenty years to restore Hetep-heres's belongings to something like their original condition; among those involved in the work being a young man, Ahmed Youssef, who would later be responsible for the near-thirty-year programme of conservation and restoration of one of Khufu's cedar boats.

Two magnificently proportioned short-legged chairs were reconstructed from among the mass of furnishings. One of them had been heavily inlaid with semi-precious stones and faience in the same dense, carpet-like patterns of some of the boxes in the tomb, a manner that resembled the chequered designs which had been painted on the exterior walls of some of the archaic mastabas. The second chair, however, was a light and clever design of abstract panels, and set into its sides were two elegant versions of the hieroglyph for 'delta': a bunch of curved papyrus stems tied heraldically together in a motif that would be constantly repeated in furniture and architecture throughout pharaonic history.

The golden inscription bearing the names and titularies of King Sneferu that Rowe had spotted at the tomb's first opening proved to have fallen from the side pillars of the great golden canopy, an ingenious copper-jointed structure made of wood, entirely covered in gold sheet soldered with pure silver. Restored and re-erected, gold and linen in the sunlight, it formed a rectangular frame some ten and a half feet long and seven feet high with four round poles shaped like some of the slimly swelling columns of King Djoser's architecture set along three of its sides. This grand open tent could have served as a canopy for the royal bed inside the royal palace, or for a sunshade in the desert, just as it could also have served as the queen's embalming tent and, later, as a catafalque to cover the sarcophagus in a full-sized burial chamber. Nearby, inside the Great Pyramid, within its colossal burial chamber, Khufu's sarcophagus would probably have been surrounded with a similarly refined range of objects.

Yet there was no body in the little chamber. All the archaeologists recovered of the queen herself were four small packets of her entrails, some of them still steeping in a solution of natron which had been poured into the various partitions of a splendid alabaster chest that had been placed in a carefully sealed recess in the chamber wall. In explanation of Hetep-heres's absence, the normally taciturn Reisner proposed an Ali Baba-ry of tales. More recent and less elaborate hypotheses have proposed that she may originally have been buried with her grave goods in a full-sized burial chamber underneath a modest pyramid which, late in Khufu's reign, and after the Great Pyramid had been finished, had been taken down as part of the new plan for the cemetery of the royal family. At which point, her body may have been taken for reburial, possibly beneath one of the three now-ruined pyramids that stand close by, whilst her original burial goods had been reburied in the jumbled heap that Reisner would so painstakingly retrieve.

What is so typical of ancient Egypt, and so touching in all this, is the extraordinary change of scale: the tantalizing contrast between the queen's cups and razors and the blank enormity of the Great Pyramid. Yet both Hetep-heres's golden cups and the stones of Khufu's pyramid hold a similar integrity of skill and workmanship within them. Only the scale of the enterprise had changed. And they are all the products of a vision of profound simplicity, a vision that in earlier millennia had perceived a unity and symmetry in the luscious environment of the valley of the lower Nile and had created a society in harmony with those unique surroundings. And in the reign of Khufu of the Fourth Dynasty, they built a pyramid whose harmonious perfection was the perfection of the prehistoric state.

Judging by the size of Hetep-heres's restored palanquin, a box-like chair with two long carrying poles, she must have been a tiny woman. Looking at its hard, flat, plain seat, one wishes her cushions for the ride, such as are shown in images of carrying chairs in later tomb chapels, where nobles are pictured visiting their farms and tombs: a little lady with a stick, dressed in linen, with silver bracelets on her arms.

From the golden caps of its two carrying poles to the plain box of its wooden chair, which is edged in stripes of glittering gold patterned in the manner of a reed mat, the palanquin, like all the queen's possessions, is exquisitely proportioned. Similarly, the golden hieroglyphs from which Reisner had recovered Hetep-heres's name – jewellers' masterpieces that, though but a fraction of their size, are the equal of the painted hieroglyphs from the Maidum mastabas – had been set in three thin columns and mounted on strips of ebony fixed to the outside of the palanquin's back rest. Though small, this flashing chair would have identified the little queen as she was carried out from the palace to visit her estates and, perhaps, to view the progress of her tomb beside her son's great pyramid, high on the desert cliff.

And yet our real knowledge of these ancient people hardly extends beyond their pyramids, their tomb chapels and names and titularies. We know nothing, for example, of those who carried Hetep-heres in her palanquin, and though we possess her very intestines, we know nothing of the woman or the queen at all. As we have seen, it is convention, rather than hard proof, that describes her as the daughter of King Huni, the wife of Sneferu and the mother of King Khufu. And it is precisely this mix of intimacy, anonymity and grandeur, at once alien and familiar, which is so very fascinating. But then again, the greater part of what survives from early Egypt is exactly what those ancient people took pains to store and thus preserve within the dryness of the desert; an ancient presentation.

King Khufu's cartouche, from an inscription set up in a Nubian hard-stone quarry

Chronology

All dates BC

Faiyum farmers	5000–4000
Merimda settlements	4800–4300
Badarian culture	4400–4000
early Maadi–Buto culture	4000–3300
early Naqadan culture	4000–3500
middle Naqadan culture	3500–3200
later Buto culture	3200–3000
later Naqadan culture	3200–3000

DYNASTY ONE: 3000–2825 (175 YEARS)

kings: attested years of rule:

Narmer	30?
Aha	?
Djer	47?
Djet	7 to 13
Den	42 to 47
Anedjib	6 to 7
Semerkhet	7 to 8
Qa'a	23 to 25

DYNASTY TWO: 2825–2675 (150 YEARS)

kings: attested years of rule:

Hetepsekhemui	28?
Raneb	15?
Nynetjer	40 to 43
Peribsen	10 to 28
Sekhemib	11?
Sened	?
Khasekhemui	17 to 28

DYNASTY THREE: 2675–2625 (50 YEARS)

kings: attested years of rule:

Djoser	19 to 26
Sekhemkhet	6 to 8
Kha'ba	3 to 6
Sanakht	?
Huni	24?

DYNASTY FOUR: 2625–2500 (125 YEARS)

kings: attested years of rule:

Sneferu	24 to 46
Khufu	23 to 27
Djedefre	8 to 11
Khafre	24 to 26
Menkaure	5 to 28
Shepseskaf	5

NOTES

Details of the short titles and abbreviations cited below can found in the Bibliography.

The fundamental problem of ancient Egyptian chronology is that the ancients did not employ an absolute dating system such as we use today, but only recorded the years that each king ruled. Thus, the absolute dates of reigns and dynasties can only be calculated by the addition of the attested years of individual reigns. Errors, therefore, are both cumulative and frequent, and are especially large in the earliest periods of history where the surviving records are also fragmented and sparse.

An anchor of sorts, though only for those kings in this chronology who reigned after Khasekhemui, has recently been provided by Christopher Bronk Ramsey *et al.*, 'Radiocarbon-based Chronology for Dynastic Egypt', *Science*, 328 (June 2010), which employs a Bayesian analysis of a new set of carefully controlled radiocarbon dates and two recent traditionally compiled egyptological chronologies; Shaw (ed.), *The Oxford History of Ancient Egypt*, pp. 479–83, and *AEC*, pp. 490–95. Both these traditionally compiled chronologies had employed a well-established range of archaeological and literary information, and both were in general agreement about the order and the years of rule of individual kings. Yet in the early phases of Egyptian history they differ in their absolute dates by a century and more.

Bronk Ramsey's groundbreaking analysis, which I have followed in this chronology, served to underline some fundamental facts about the present state of modern chronologies of ancient Egypt. First, it showed that modern Carbon 14 dating confirms the general time-frames and order of the ancient kings established by traditional scholarship. At the same time, however, it also showed that there was considerable uncertainty about the absolute dates of the kings throughout the early dynastic period, which at present can only be dated to within three-quarters of a century. So, while they may well give the impression of a well-ordered and established history, chronological tables that list the dates of Djoser, for example, as 'Djoser 2592–2544 ± 25' are providing their readers with a largely spurious reassurance of accuracy.

I have therefore resisted the temptation to provide another list of monarchs with illusory columns of the dates they may have ruled, preferring instead to give the numbers of years for which their rule is presently – though often ambiguously – attested: figures that are largely derived from *AEC*. Given these present uncertainties, I have used multiples of twenty-five years when approximating the lengths of the first four dynasties, and also in my estimations of the reigns of such long-lived kings as Sneferu and Djoser.

Overall, the greatest period of uncertainty in this loose web of dates is the Second Dynasty. The order of succession is far from clear. Some of the kings I have listed may have reigned simultaneously; some of those names, alternatively, might be those of a single individual, while other kings may yet remain unknown (see further, Kahl, 'Inscriptional Evidence', in *AEC* pp. 102ff.). So though the order of the First Dynasty kings seems clear enough, the date of its beginning, which, ultimately, is dependent on the length of the Second Dynasty, is yet uncertain. I have set it, nominally, at 3000 BC.

For the Predynastic periods, the divisions of my chronology follow contemporary academic consensus, which is largely founded on the basis of changing pottery styles. The dates I have given for these divisions are based on those of Hendrickx, 'Predynastic-Early Dynastic Chronology', and pp. 487–8, in *AEC*, with minor modifications as suggested by Midant-Reynes, *The Prehistory of Egypt*, p. 108; Wengrow, *The Archaeology of Early Egypt*, table 2, p. 273; and Wenke, *The Ancient Egyptian State*, p. 177.

The radiocarbon dates for the Predynastic periods are founded on a wide variety of different samples, and contain discrepancies of several centuries. My chronology for those periods, therefore, inevitably contains inherent contradictions, especially in the uneasy conjunction between prehistory and the early dynasties, and also in the detail of the relative chronologies of the Uruk and Naqadan cultures. My figures, however, are an up-to-date reflection of present knowledge and consensus; they are inherently conservative and probably represent the minimum time spans they describe.

There are especially large differences of opinion concerning the dating of Merimda and the three phases of its occupation; compare for example, Midant-Reynes, *The Prehistory of Egypt*, pp. 108–18 and chart 3, p. 264, with Wengrow, *The Archaeology of Early Egypt*, and Wenke, *The Ancient Egyptian State*, p. 177. I have opted for a middle course.

NAMES AND NOMENCLATURES

My 'Faiyum farmers' are technically described as the 'Faiyum A culture'; 'early Maadi–Buto culture' denotes the similar cultures of the Maadi and Buto periods during the phases that are presently designated 'I' and 'II'; 'later Buto culture' denotes the period from Maadi–Buto Phase III until the beginning of the First Dynasty. Like Naqadan pottery, the northern wares continued to be made during the period of the early dynasties. See further Hendrickx, 'Predynastic-Early Dynastic Chronology', in *AEC*.

The three phases of the Naqadan culture that I have named 'early', 'middle' and 'later' are more precisely identified as follows: 'early' = Naqada I – IIB: 'middle' = Naqada IIC – IID2: 'late' = Naqada IIIA1 – IIIC1. Though in my text I stop using this terminology at the beginning of Dynasty One, it should be noted that Naqada III period pottery continued through various later phases and several further centuries – Naqada IIID3 is presently the latest sub-division – until some of the forms were adopted by the studios of the so-called 'Early Old Kingdom' potters; see further, Hendrickx, 'Predynastic-Early Dynastic Chronology', and pp. 487–8 in *AEC*.

Note that one of the casualties of Bronk Ramsey's analyses was the ingenious method for dating pyramids proposed in Kate Spence, 'Egyptian Chronology and the Astronomical Orientation of Pyramids', *Nature*, 408 (2000), which has also been criticized by archaeo-astronomers. So, though I employed dates derived from that method in my previous book, Romer, *The Great Pyramid*, I now prefer the chronology set out above.

Bibliography

This is not a complete bibliography of the subject matter of this book. Were one to be compiled, it would be larger than the book itself.

In way of compromise, I have provided a short general reading list of works that have been fundamental to the compilation of my text. Along with Ludwig Wittgenstein's *Notes upon Frazer's Golden Bough* ed. Rush Rees (Oxford, 1979), which I employed as a specific antidote to the nonsense that continues to be written about ancient and tribal peoples, these books were usually beside me as I wrote.

I have also provided bibliographic notes to every chapter citing the sources of its subject matter – mostly excavation reports – and some other works – usually recent publications – that are especially relevant to the chapter's arguments. I have kept these secondary citations limited in number and preferred English texts whenever they were available. Most of these works contain plentiful references to older texts which though they may not be named in this bibliography, are often the intellectual bedrock of the subject in hand. Their omission here is simply one of practicality.

Many of these works appeared as articles in specialist publications, some of whose titles are given in the form of the abbreviations listed below. After their first citation, all references are given in a shortened form.

ABBREVIATIONS

AEC   Erik Hornung, Rolf Krauss and David A. Warburton (eds.), *Ancient Egyptian Chronology* (Leiden, 2006)

AEE   Jeffrey Spencer (ed.), *Aspects of Early Egypt* (London, 1996)

AEMT   Paul T. Nicholson and Ian Shaw (eds.), *Ancient Egyptian Materials and Technology* (Cambridge, 2000)

BMS   *British Museum Studies in Ancient Egypt and Sudan* (on-line journal)

CAJ   *Cambridge Archaeological Journal*

EAAP   *Egyptian Art in the Age of the Pyramids*, Metropolitan Museum Exhibition Catalogue (New York, 1999)

EL   Edwin C. M. van den Brink and Thomas E. Levy (eds.), *Egypt and the Levant: interrelations from the 4th through the early 3rd millennium* BCE (London, 2002)

EOI   S. Hendrickx, R. F. Friedman, K. M. Ciałowicz and M. Chłodnicki (eds.), *Egypt at its Origins [1]: studies in memory of Barbara Adams* (Liège, 2004)

JARCE *Journal of the American Research Centre in Egypt*

JEA   *Journal of Egyptian Archaeology*

JNES   *Journal of Near Eastern Studies*

MDAIK *Mitteilungen des Deutschen Archäologischen Instituts Abteilung Kairo*

ZÄS   *Zeitschrift für Ägyptische Sprache und Altertumskunde*

GENERAL WORKS

The *Atlas of Ancient Egypt* by John Baines and Jaromir Málek (Oxford, 2002), is a basic guide to the physical and historical geography of the lands of the lower Nile.

Karl W. Butzer's pioneering work, *Early Hydraulic Civilisation in Egypt* (Chicago, 1976) remains fundamental to an overall understanding of the ancient Egyptian environment; Wilma Wetterstrom's essay 'Foraging and Farming in Egypt: the transition from hunting and gathering to horticulture in the Nile Valley', in Thurstan Shaw, Paul Sinclair, Bassey Andah and Alex Okpoko (eds.), *The Archaeology of Africa: food, metals and towns* (London, 1993), provides an excellent overview of early food production.

A. M. T. Moore, G. C. Hillman, A. J. Legge *et al.*, *Village on the Euphrates: from foraging to farming at Abu Hureyra* (New York,

2000) describes that primary transition in remarkable and illuminating detail. Jacques Cauvin's *The Birth of the Gods and the Origins of Agriculture* (Cambridge, 2000), trans. Trevor Watkins from *Naissance des divinités, naissance de l'agriculture* (Paris, 1994), is an eloquent account of the intellectual processes that appear to have motivated the people of that period.

The gulf between French- and English–speaking approaches to this vital period of early history is underlined in Alexander Joffe's short review of Cauvin's *Birth of the Gods* in *JNES* 62.3 (2003) and also in the lengthy review articles of that same book in *CAJ* 11.1 (2001). The debate, it seems to me, is rooted in a fundamental disagreement about the nature of humanity itself, and for ancient Egyptian history as for all other histories, the implications are profound.

Béatrix Midant-Reynes, *The Prehistory of Egypt: from the first Egyptians to the first pharaohs* (Oxford, 2000), trans. Ian Shaw from *Préhistoire de L'Égypte* (Paris, 1992), provides a lucid account of the archaeology of those periods. David Wengrow, *The Archaeology of Early Egypt: social transformations in north-east Africa, 10,000 to 2650 BC* (Cambridge, 2006), is an up-to-date anthropologically based interpretation of the development of the ancient Egyptian state; Barry Kemp's *Ancient Egypt: anatomy of a civilisation* (London, 2nd edn., 2006), offers a unique archaeologically based commentary upon the same subject.

While conservative in its approach, Toby Wilkinson's *Early Dynastic Egypt* (London, 1999) contains an extensive catalogue of the relevant subject matter, which is further illuminated and extended by a wealth of essays in *EL*.

For the later sections of the book, my own *The Great Pyramid: ancient Egypt revisited* (Cambridge, 2007), provides a detailed and relatively up-to-date overview of pyramid-building.

PREFACE

Epigraph: from *Flaubert in Egypt: a sensibility on tour*, trans. and ed. Francis Steegmuller (London, 1973), p. 75.

Roland Barthes (p. xv) is quoted from *The Semiotic Challenge* (New York, 1988), trans. Richard Howard from *l'Aventure sémiologique*

(Paris, 1985), p. 136; 'evolutionary trajectories . . .' (p. xix) from Norman Yoffee, *Myths of the Archaic State: evolution of the earliest cities, states, and civilisations* (Cambridge, 2005), p. 197.

The analysis of years per page in modern histories of ancient Egypt (p. xx) has been culled from Ian Shaw (ed.), *The Oxford History of Ancient Egypt* (Oxford, 2000); such figures would, perforce, be typical of other less honourable and level-headed histories.

The description of the new archaeology as 'vulgar materialism' (p. xx) is Alexander Joffe's, from his review of Cauvin, *Birth of the Gods* in *JNES* 62.3 (2003).

CHAPTER I. BESIDE THE PALE LAKE

Gertrude Caton-Thompson and Eleanor Gardner's *The Desert Fayum* (London, 1934), is fundamental to any account of the first Faiyum farmers; Caton-Thompson's autobiography, *Mixed Memoirs* (Gateshead, 1983), contains fascinating information on that remarkable woman and her work in the Faiyum.

In 'Egypt's Earliest Granaries: evidence from the Fayum', *Egyptian Archaeology*, 27 (2005), Willeke Wendrich and René Cappers outline their present excavations and discoveries at one of Caton-Thompson's most important Faiyum sites; in *AEMT*, 'Basketry', Wendrich further discusses and describes the Faiyum farmers' baskets.

Midant-Reynes, *Prehistory of Egypt*, pp. 100–108, and Robert J. Wenke, *The Ancient Egyptian State: the origins of Egyptian culture (c. 8000–2000 BC)* (Cambridge, 2009), pp. 159–80, summarize archaeological activity in the Faiyum since Caton-Thompson's discoveries, to which the field reports of Pawlikowski, Ginter and Kozłowski *et al.*, in *MDAIK* 36 (1980), 38 (1982), 40 (1984) and 42 (1986) add considerable detail. Maciej Pawlikowski 'Reasons for the Predynastic–Early Dynastic Transition in Egypt: geological and climatic evidence', in *EO1*, provides an interesting footnote linking archaeological and climatic evidence.

Midant-Reynes' *Prehistory of Egypt*, and Stan Hendrickx and Pierre Vermeersch in chapter 2 of Ian Shaw (ed.), *The Oxford History of Ancient Egypt* (Oxford, 2000), contain broad-based descriptions of the Faiyum farmers' hunter-gatherer antecedents.

Moore *et al.*, *Village on the Euphrates* documents and analyses primary data on the origins and practices of the Middle Eastern agricultural revolution; Cauvin, *Birth of the Gods*, offers an intelligent commentary upon the impact of that chosen way of life within communities of early Middle Eastern farmers.

While Butzer, *Early Hydraulic Civilisation* provides a framework for an understanding of the pharaonic environment and farming year, Stephan Kröpelin and Rudolf Kuper, 'Climate-controlled Holocene Occupation in the Sahara: motor of Africa's evolution' in *Science*, 313 (2006) and Kröpelin *et al.*, 'Climate-driven Ecosystem Succession in the Sahara: the past 6000 years' *Science*, 320 (2008), give up-to-date commentaries upon climate and climate change during the beginning of that period.

Wetterstrom, *Foraging and Farming*, provides a lively account of the contemporary flora and fauna; Gillian Vogelsang-Eastwood describes ancient Egyptian linen manufacture in *AEMT*. My remarks on looms follow the observations of Grace Crowfoot and Henry Ling Roth *Hand Spinning and Woolcombing*, Bankfield Museum Notes, series 2 no. 12 (Halifax, 1931).

The biblical quotation on p. 4 is from Genesis 41: 48–9; the brief quotation at the chapter's ending, from Cauvin's *Birth of the Gods*, pp. 125–6.

CHAPTER 2. SICKLE SHEEN

Epigraph: from Georges Charbonnier, *Conversations with Claude Lévi-Strauss* (London, 1969), trans. J. and D. Weightman from *Entretiens avec Claude Lévi-Strauss* (Paris, 1961), pp. 27–8.

As in the previous chapter, Moore *et al. Village on the Euphrates*, and Cauvin, *Birth of the Gods*, supply data and commentary on the origins of the agricultural revolution in the Middle East, while part three of Midant-Reynes, *Prehistory of Egypt*, sets the Faiyum farmers in the wider contemporary archaeological context of hunter-gathering communities, and Wengrow, *The Archaeology of Early Egypt*, provides a thoughtful commentary upon recent theories concerning the diffusion of Middle Eastern agriculture.

David Phillipson discusses the diet of the Sudanese herders in 'The

Antiquity of Cultivation and Herding in Ethiopia', in Shaw *et al.*, *Archaeology of Africa*. In that same volume, Juliet Clutton Brock's and R. M. Blench's essays, 'The Spread of Domestic Animals in Africa' and 'Ethnographic and Linguistic Evidence for the Prehistory of African Ruminant Livestock, Horses and Ponies' respectively, list and discuss the animals of the time.

The adaptations to the usual Middle Eastern neolithic farming round that were required for successful Nile-side farming are described in Karl W. Butzer's 'Geoarchaeological Implications of Recent Research in the Nile Delta', in *EL*.

CHAPTER 3. MERIMDA AND EL-OMARI

Epigraph: from Wittgenstein, *Remarks on Frazer's Golden Bough*, p. 3e.

Josef Eiwanger's *Merimde-Benisalame*, 3 vols. (Mainz 1984–92), is fundamental to any treatment of that site. Bruce William's review of Eiwanger's vol. 2, *Die Funde der mittleren Merimdekultur* in *JARCE* 27 (1990), discusses the cache of objects that Eiwanger found within a pot, while accounts of Merimda, both in William Hayes, *Most Ancient Egypt* (Chicago, 1965), and Wengrow, *The Archaeology of Early Egypt*, emphasize details that are easily missed in Eiwanger's voluminous reports.

Pierre M. Vermeersch *et al.* describe the excavations at the so-called Sodmein Cave in 'Neolithic Occupation of the Sodmein Area, Red Sea Mountains, Egypt', in *Aspects of African Archaeology: papers from the 10th Congress of the Pan African Association for Prehistory and Related Studies* (Harare, 1996).

In *El Omari: a neolithic settlement and other sites in the vicinity of Wadi Hof, Helwan* (Mainz, 1990), Fernand Debono and Bodil Mortensen document the excavation of the cemeteries at those sites; the volume's appendices, by Douglas Derry, Hala Barakat and Vivi Täckholm, describe the skeletal and faunal remains.

To the general discussion of ancient Near Eastern Neolithic imagery in Cauvin, *Birth of the Gods*, Alexandra Fletcher, Jessica Pearson and Janet Ambers add pertinent and precise observations concerning the sculpted images of heads in 'The Manipulation of Social and Physical Identity in the Pre-pottery Neolithic: radiographic evidence for cranial modification at Jericho and its implications for the plastering of skulls', *CAJ* 18.3 (2008).

In Moore *et al.*, *Village on the Euphrates*, T. I. Molleson details the effects of the activity of wheat grinding on female skeletons at Abu Hureyra. The same phenomena are reported in central American sites in Kent V. Flannery and Joyce Marcus, *Zapotec Civilisation: how urban society evolved in Mexico's Oaxaca Valley* (London, 1996), who also discuss the sociological implications of the architecture associated with such activities.

Claude Lévi–Strauss's observations upon axes and neo-evolutionism (p. 26) are taken from the Introduction of his *Structural Anthropology*, trans. Claire Jacobson and Brook Grundfest Schoepf (New York, 1963). The 'prehistorian' quoted on p. 29 is Michael A. Hoffman, and is taken from *Egypt before the Pharaohs: the prehistoric foundations of Egyptian civilization* (London, 1991), p. 176.

The intellectual climate in which Gordon Childe coined his phrase the 'Neolithic Revolution' is outlined in Bruce Trigger, *Gordon Childe: revolutions in archaeology* (London, 1980). Along with many other works, V. Gordon Childe, *What Happened in History* (London, 1942; new edn., rev. Grahame Clark, London, 1964), provides a flavour of the man himself.

Lewis Binford has been quoted (p. 33) from Cauvin, *Birth of the Gods*, p. 7, whose thoughts inspired this chapter's final paragraphs.

CHAPTER 4. THE BADARIANS

Guy Brunton and Gertrude Caton-Thompson's *The Badarian Civilisation and Predynastic Remains near Badari* (London, 1928), remains the fundamental volume on its subject and is the source of the greater part of the quotations in this chapter. Published in the previous year, Brunton's *Qau and Badari* (London, 1927) contains invaluable information about that pioneering expedition and the region of Badari.

A fascinating report upon the partial re-excavation of one of Caton-Thompson's key sites is Diane L. Holmes, 'Recent Investigations in the Badarian Region (Middle Egypt)', in Lech Krzyżaniak, Karla Kroeper and Michał Kobusiewicz (eds.), *Interregional Contacts in the Later Prehistory of Northeastern Africa* (Poznán, 1996). For more recently excavated Badarian sites, see also Midant-Reynes, *Prehistory of Egypt*, pp. 152 ff., and Deborah Darnell's various preliminary accounts of her 'Rayayna Culture' on the splendid website of the Oriental Institute, University of Chicago.

The first publication and explication of the Sequence Dating System is W. M. Flinders Petrie, *Diospolis Parva: the cemeteries of Abadiyeh and Hu* (London, 1901). Stan Hendrickx, 'The Relative Chronology of the Naqada Culture: problems and possibilities' in *AEE*, provides a commentary upon the system's subsequent refinement and also a description of Werner Kaiser's re-evaluation of Petrie's sequence dating system, which he initiated in the 1950s – see, for example, Kaiser, 'Zur Inneren Chronologie der Naqadakulture', *Archaeologica Geographica*, 61 (1957).

Mahgar Dendera is described in Stan Hendrickx and Béatrix Midant-Reynes, 'Preliminary Report on the Predynastic Living Site Maghara 2 (Upper Egypt)', *Orientalia Lovaniensia Periodica*, 19 (1988), and also in the same authors' full report with Wim Van Neer, in *Mahgar Dendera 2 (Haute Égypte): un site d'occupation Badarien* (Liège, 2001).

Some stimulating observations on domestic pottery production are made by Kostalena Michelaki in 'Making Pots and Potters in the Bronze Age Maros Villages of Kiszombor-Új-Élet and Klárafalva-Hajdova', *CAJ* 18.3 (2008). For a remote Tasian-type desert grave, see Renée Friedman and Joseph J. Hobbs, 'A "Tasian" Tomb in Egypt's Eastern Desert', in Renée Friedman (ed.), *Egypt and Nubia: gifts of the desert* (London, 2002).

Wengrow, *The Archaeology of Early Egypt*, offers several discussions of the conception and implications of graves as presentations, or, as he prefers, as 'theatres'; Winifred Needler *et al.*, in *Predynastic and Archaic Egypt in The Brooklyn Museum* (New York, 1984), provides illuminating insights into many aspects of the material cultures of the prehistoric lower Nile.

The technical report on Badarian woven linens is by Thomas Midgley, and has been taken from Brunton and Caton-Thompson, *The Badarian Civilisation*, p. 66; the epigraph to the section 'The Burial of the Dead' (p. 54) is from p. 41 of that same volume.

CHAPTER 5. BLACK-TOPPED, WHITE-LINED

The remark (p. 57) that naming archaeological evidence of ancient cultures after the sites at which they were first found is 'cumbrous and inexact' is from Petrie, *Diospolis Parva*.

Apart from the numerous publications of Petrie and his contemporaries, Jean Capart, *Primitive Art in Egypt* (London, 1905), still provides a handy visual overview of Naqadan graphics.

Dorothea Arnold and Janine Bourriau (eds.), *An Introduction to Ancient Egyptian Pottery* (Mainz, 1993), contains a fine description of the production of the various types of ancient Egyptian ceramics; Janine Bourriau's *Umm el-Ga'ab: pottery from the Nile Valley before the Arab Conquest* (Cambridge, 1981) a perceptive overview of its changing styles, and Anna Maria Donadoni Roveri and Francesco Tiradritti (eds.), *Kemet: al sorgente del tempo* (Milan, 1998), a splendid photographic portfolio of Badarian and Naqadan ceramics and hard stone ware.

The figures for Badarian and Naqadan communities along the lower Nile have been extracted from data presented in Stan Hendrickx and Edwin C. M. van den Brink, 'Inventory of Predynastic and Early Dynastic Cemetery and Settlement Sites in the Egyptian Nile Valley, Egypt', in *EL* (note that I have added together their figures for Naqada and Ballas and treated them as a single centre of settlement).

For local differentiations between various Naqadan settlements, see Diane L. Holmes, 'Lithic Assemblages from Hierakonpolis and Interregional Relations in Predynastic Egypt', in Lech Krzyżaniak, Karla Kroeper and Michał Kobusiewicz (eds.), *Interregional Contacts in the Later Prehistory of Northeastern Africa* (Poznán, 1996). See too, Holmes, 'The Evidence and Nature of Contacts between Upper and Lower Egypt during the Predynastic: a view from Upper Egypt', in Edwin C. M. van den Brink (ed.), *The Nile Delta in Transition 4th–3rd Millennium B.C.* (Tel Aviv, 1992).

The pioneering works on local pottery styles are: Elizabeth Finkenstaedt, 'Regional Painting Style in Prehistoric Egypt', *ZÄS* 107 (1980), and her 'The Location of Styles in Painting: white cross-lined ware at Naqada', *JARCE* 18 (1981). See also, and more recently; Barbara

Adams, 'Decorated Sherds from Renewed Excavations at Locality 6, Hierakonpolis', *Cahiers caribéens d'égyptologie*, 3/4 (Feb./March 2002), and Renée Friedman, 'Variations on a Theme: regional diversity in the predynastic pottery of Upper Egyptian settlements', in Carol A. Redmount and Cathleen A. Keller (eds.), *Egyptian Pottery: proceedings of the 1990 symposium at the University of California, Berkeley* (Berkeley, 2003).

The published material on the excavations at Hierakonpolis is as wide-ranging and diffuse as the various excavations at the site. Barbara Adams, *Ancient Nekhen: Garstang in the City of Hierakonpolis* (New Maldon, 1990), gives an overview of previous work, whilst Hierakonpolis Online – especially the articles in *Nekhen News* – has vivid accounts of the ongoing researches of the American expedition.

For the potteries, see Michael A. Hoffman, 'A Rectangular Amratian House from Hierakonpolis and its Significance for Predynastic Research', *JNES* 39 (1980), and Stan Hendrickx *et al.*, 'Experimental Archaeology concerning Black-topped Pottery from Ancient Egypt and the Sudan', *Cahiers de la céramique égyptienne*, 6 (2000).

For the breweries, see Jeremy R. Geller 'From Prehistory to History: beer in Egypt', in Renée Friedman and Barbara Adams (eds.), *The Followers of Horus: studies dedicated to Michael Allen Hoffman* (Oxford, 1992); and Delwen Samuel, 'Brewing and Baking', in *AEMT*.

For the elephants, see Renée F. Friedman 'Elephants at Hierakonpolis', in *EO1*.

CHAPTER 6. A CLOUD ACROSS THE MOON

Epigraph: from Gananath Obeyesekere *The Apotheosis of Captain Cook* (Princeton, 1992), p. 10.

The quotation at the heading of the section 'Great Tombs' (p. 77) is from Wittgenstein *Remarks on Frazer's Golden Bough*, p. 10e.

The first excavations at the oval court of Hierakonpolis are described by Renée Friedman in 'The Ceremonial Centre at Hierakonpolis, Locality HK29A', in *AEE*, this interpretation of the site having since been updated by further excavations which are variously described by Friedman and others on the Hierakonpolis Online website.

The fundamental study of flint slaughtering knives is Béatrix

Midant-Reynes, 'Contribution à l'étude de la société prédynastique: le cas du couteau "ripple-flake"', *Studien zur Altägyptischen Kultur*, 14 (1987).

A small and early Naqadan slaughtering centre is described in David A. Anderson, 'Power and Competition in Upper Egyptian Predynastic: a view from the predynastic settlement at el-Mahasna, Egypt', Ph.D. thesis, Pittsburgh, 2006 (published online).

For the great tombs at Hierakonpolis, see Barbara Adams, 'Elite Tombs at Hierakonpolis', in *AEE*, and the same author's *Excavations in the Locality 6 Cemetery at Hierakonpolis 1979–1985* (Oxford, 2000). See also Diane L. Holmes, 'Chipped Stone-working Craftsmen: Hierakonpolis and the rise of civilization in Egypt', in Friedman and Adams (eds.), *The Followers of Horus*. The animal burials of the time are discussed by Diane Victoria Flores, 'Funerary Sacrifice of Animals in the Egyptian Predynastic Period', in *EO1*.

The remarkable masks found at the great graves are pictured at Hierakonpolis Online; see also, Barbara Adams, 'Unprecedented Discoveries at Hierakonpolis', in *Egyptian Archaeology*, 15 (1999).

The modest tombs within the Hierakonpolis cemetery KH43 are widely reported at Hierakonpolis Online, especially in *Nekhen News* 8–19. See also, Ahmed Gamal-El-Din Fahmy, 'Plant Remains in Gut Contents of Ancient Egyptian Predynastic Mummies (3750–3300 BC)', *OnLine Journal of Biological Sciences*, 1 (8) (2001).

The quotation on p. 80, 'dominated by the political advantage etc.', is taken from Wengrow, *The Archaeology of Early Egypt*, p. 75, quoting M. J. Rowlands and S. Frankenstein in K. Kristiansen and M. Rowlands, *Social Transformations in Archaeology: global and local perspectives* (London, 1998). For 'powerfacts' etc., see Alain Anselin, 'Le Harpon et la Barque: des powerfacts aux hiéroglyphes', which is published online as part of an occasional series, Aegyptio-Graphica.

For a modern rationale of power and force as the main mover of late Naqadan history see Wilkinson, *Early Dynastic Egypt*, pp. 31ff. 'The Iconography and Ideology of Rule'; Yoffee, *Myths of the Archaic State*, provides a general overview of such ways of thinking; Barry Kemp's observations in his *Ancient Egypt*, pp. 395–6, n. 31, point up its limitations and its underlying dangers.

The notion of 'potter kings' comes from a recollection of a conversation with the late Michael Hoffman.

CHAPTER 7. BOATS AND DONKEYS

Epigraph: from the opening paragraphs of Thomas De Quincey, *Autobiographic Sketches* (London, 1845).

James Quibell, *Hierakonpolis I. Plates of discoveries in 1898* (London, 1900), and *Hierakonpolis II* by James Quibell and Frederick Green (London, 1902) are yet fundamental to this area of research at Hierakonpolis. The Naqadan painted tomb, however, has been revisited with great effect by Joan Crowfoot Payne and Humphrey Case, 'Tomb 100: the decorated tomb at Hierakonpolis', *JEA* 48 (1962), and by Joan Crowfoot Payne, 'Tomb 100: the decorated tomb at Hierakonpolis confirmed', and Barry Kemp, 'Photographs of the Decorated Tomb at Hierakonpolis', both in *JEA* 59 (1973).

Careful descriptions of the various ceramic fabrics of the lower Nile are provided by Janine Bourriau and Hans-Åke Nordström, in Arnold and Bourriau (eds.), *An Introduction to Ancient Egyptian Pottery*.

A recent commentary upon the decorated red buff ware named 'D' or Decorated Ware in Petrie's classification system is John Baines and David Wengrow, 'Images, Human Bodies and the Ritual Construction of Memory in Late Predynastic Egypt', in *EO 1*; Needler *et al.*, *Predynastic and Archaic Egypt*, pp. 202 ff., discusses the origins of 'D' Wares' various forms.

For descriptions of some of the environments in which similarly scaled pottery manufactories have thrived, see Bryant G. Wood, *The Sociology of Pottery in Ancient Palestine: the ceramic industry and the diffusion of ceramic style in the Bronze and Iron Ages* (Sheffield, 1990), and Barbara K. Larson, 'The Structure and Function of Village Markets in Contemporary Egypt', *JARCE* 19 (1982). Though not necessarily appropriate to Naqadan realities, they provide practical alternatives to many common ill-founded assumptions.

David Jeffreys, 'Hierakonpolis and Memphis in Predynastic Tradition', in *EO 1*, discusses the relative geographies of those two sites, and, in that same volume, Diana Craig Patch, 'Settlement Patterns and

Cultural Change in the Predynastic Period', treats the changing settlement patterns at Hierakonpolis.

For importations of both produce and farming methods into Egypt during the so-called 'second wave' of innovation, see Wengrow, *The Archaeology of Early Egypt*, pp. 135 ff; Pierre de Miroschedji, 'The Socio-political Dynamics of Egyptian-Canaanite Interaction in the Early Bronze Age', in *EL*; Justin Jennings *et al.*, '"Drinking Beer in a Blissful Mood": alcohol production, operation chains, and festing in the ancient world', *Current Anthropology*, 46.2 (2005), and Jaimie L. Lovell, 'Horticulture, Status and Long-range Trade in Chalcolithic Southern Levant: early connections with Egypt', in Béatrix Midant-Reynes, Yann Tristant, J. Rowland and Stan Hendrickx (eds.), *Egypt at its Origins [2]: proceedings of the international conference 'Origin of the State: predynastic and early Dynastic Egypt'* (Liège, 2008).

Cheryl A. Ward, *Sacred and Secular: ancient Egyptian ships and boats* (Philadelphia, 2000), and the same author's 'Boat Building and its Social Context in Early Egypt: interpretations from the First Dynasty boat-grave cemetery at Abydos', *Antiquity*, 80 (2006), provide splendid commentaries upon the rise of large wooden boat construction on the lower Nile.

Ibrahim Rizkana and Jürgen Seeher, *Maadi*, 4 vols. (Mainz, 1987–90), hold the fundamental treatment of this settlement; further excavation at the site, which is endangered by housing development, is reported in Ulrich Hartung *et al.*, 'Vorbericht über neue Untersuchungen in der prädynastischen Siedlung von Maadi-West', *MDAIK* 59 (2003).

A recent discussion of Egyptian stone jars and Levantine basalt vessels at Maadi can be found in Andrew Bevan, *Stone Vessels and Values in the Bronze Age Mediterranean* (Cambridge, 2007).

Miriam Tadmor, 'The Kfar Monash Hoard Again: a view from Egypt and Nubia', in *EL*, provides a useful overview of copper tool and weapon making during this period. For fine pictures of ancient mines at Timna, see Benno Rothenberg, 'Archaeo-metallurgical Survey Methodology', in Feisal A. Esmael (ed.), *Proc. 1st Int. Conference on Ancient Egyptian Mining* (Cairo, 1995); for technical descriptions of the processes of copper smelting, see Benno Rothenberg *et al.*, *The Ancient Metallurgy of Copper: archaeology-experiment-theory, researches in the Arabah, 1959–84*, vol. 2 (London, 1990).

Buto has been excavated by German archaeologists since 1983. For an overview of work at that site before that time see Dina Faltings, 'Ergebnisse der neuen Ausgrabungen in Buto: Chronologie und Fernbeziehungen der Buto-Maadi Kultur neu überdacht', in Heike Guksche and Daniel Polz (eds.), *Stationen. Beiträge zur Kulturgeschichte Ägyptens Rainer Stadelmann gewidmet* (Mainz, 1998); see also the later reports of Dina Faltings *et al.* in *MDAIK* 52–9 (1996–2003). Note that Faltings essay in *EL*, 'The Chronological Frame and Social Structure of Buto in the Fourth Millennium BCE', makes important modifications to the earlier findings, and lists other important analyses of material from the site.

Guy Brunton's identification of the Naqadan painted tomb as a 'foreign shrine' is to be found in his essay, 'The Predynastic Town-site at Hierakonpolis', in Stephen Glanville (ed.), *Studies presented to F. Ll. Griffith* (London, 1932).

The observation upon the similarities between the modern fellah and the ancient Maadians is from Sandor Bokonyi, 'The Animal Remains of Maadi, Egypt: a preliminary report', in Mario Liverani, Alba Palmieri and Renato Peroni (eds.), *Studi di paletonologia in onore di Salvatore M. Puglisi* (Rome, 1985).

CHAPTER 8. ROLLING ALONG

The seals and seal impressions are treated in an invaluable and wide-ranging survey of importations into late predynastic Naqadan society by Ulrich Hartung *et al.*, *Umm el-Qaab II: Importkeramik aus dem Friedhof U in Abydos (Umm el-Qaab) und die Beziehungen Ägyptens zu Vorderasien im 4. Jahrtausend v. Chr.* (Mainz, 2001).

The nature and pattern of Uruk expansion is discussed in Guillermo Algaze, *The Uruk World System: the dynamics of expansion of early Mesopotamian civilisation* (Chicago, 1993), while the chronology of these movements is re-examined and updated in Alexander H. Joffe, 'Egypt and Syro-Mesopotamia in the 4th Millennium: implications of the new chronology(1)', in *Current Anthropology*, 41 (2000), which also contains an overview of the perceived relationships between those two cultural centres, a subject that prompted a substantial and impressive literature in the course of the last century.

Wengrow, *The Archaeology of Early Egypt*, chapter 9, pp. 176 ff. contains a broad overview of the considerable mass of late Naqadan graphics: once again, the splendid plates in Donadoni Roveri and Tiradritti (eds.), *Kemet*, provide glimpses of the tactile qualities of these rare and unusual objects.

CHAPTER 9. SCORPION AND HAWK

A full account of the circumstances and contents of this Naqadan desert graffito can be found in John Coleman Darnell *et al.*, *Theban Desert Road Survey in the Egyptian Western Desert*, vol. 1: *Gebel Tjauty Rock Inscriptions and Wadi el Hol Rock Inscriptions* (Chicago, 2002), pp. 5 ff. and Catalogue 'Inscription 1'. The Nubian 'scorpion' graffito is carefully examined in William J. Murnane, 'The Gebel Sheik Suleiman Monument: epigraphic remarks', *JNES* 46 (1987).

The fundamental record of the architecture and contents of the tomb U-j at Abydos is Günter Dreyer, *Umm el-Qaab I: Das prädynastische Königsgrab U-j und seine frühen Schriftzeugnisse* (Mainz, 1998); Ulrich Hartung *et al.*, *Umm el-Qaab II*, places the finds within a broad contemporary context.

For 'Dynasty Zero' see Wilkinson, *Early Dynastic Egypt*, pp. 52 ff. The term itself appears to have been invented by Petrie; see the ending of the letter of 13 December 1919 in John A. Larson (ed.), *Letters from James Henry Breasted to his Family: August 1919–July 1920* (Chicago, 2010).

The quotes from Norman Yoffee (p. 125 ff.) have been variously extracted from his *Myths of the Archaic State*.

CHAPTER 10. THE COMING OF THE KING

Epigraph: from Shakespeare, *The Merchant of Venice* V. iv. 90.

The main sources of information on the early digs at Hierakonpolis are Quibell and Green, *Hierakonpolis II*, and Adams, *Ancient Nekhen*; see also Günter Dreyer, *Elephantine VIII: der Tempel der Satet, die Funde der Frühzeit und des Alten Reiches* (Mainz, 1986), chapter 2, where Green's working notes are edited and published. In *A Wayfarer in*

Egypt (London, 1925), Annie A. Quibell provides a graphic description of the work at Hierakonpolis and also the observation (p. 128) that the uncovered ivories 'resembled potted salmon'. The ongoing work of the ivories' conservation is described by Helen Whitehouse, 'A Decorated Knife Handle from the "Main Deposit" at Hierakonpolis', *MDAIK* 58 (2002).

Dreyer, *Umm el-Qaab I* contains a full catalogue of the signs recovered from tomb U-j; John Baines, 'The Earliest Egyptian Writing: development, context, purpose', in Stephen D. Houston (ed.), *The First Writing* (Cambridge, 2004), provides a thoughtful discussion of them. See also, Baines's further observations on this subject in chapter 5 of his *Visual and Written Culture in Ancient Egypt* (Oxford, 2007).

A lively cross-section of commentary and interpretation of the Narmer Palette can be found in chapter 1 of Orly Goldwasser, *From Icon to Metaphor: studies in the semiotics of the hieroglyphs* (Fribourg and Göttingen, 2002); another, somewhat more down to earth, is David O'Connor, 'Context Function and Program: understanding ceremonial slate palettes', *JARCE* 39 (2002).

Hans Goedicke, '"Narmer"', *Wiener Zeitschrift für die Kunde des Morgenlandes*, 85 (1995), provides a list of Narmer's various modern names. In his essay, 'Language and Script in Ancient Egypt', in Asma Afsaruddin and A. H. Mathias Zahniser (eds.), *Humanism, Culture, and Language in the Near East: essays in honor of Georg Krotkoff* (Winona Lake, Ind., 1997), pp. 427–8, the same author makes some apposite comments upon the relationship of language and hieroglyphics.

For the serekh sign, see Sir Alan Gardiner, *Egyptian Grammar* (Oxford, 3rd edn., 1957), pp. 72 and 75, and, latterly, Wilkinson, *Early Dynastic Egypt*, pp. 224 ff. See also Klaus Peter Kuhlmann, 'Serif-style Architecture and the Design of the Archaic Egyptian Palace (Königszelt)', in Manfred Bietak (ed.), *Haus und Palast im Alten Ägypten* (Vienna, 1996).

The quotation on p. 135, 'a complex history of loss, etc.', is from James P. Allen, 'The Egyptian Language', in Richard H. Wilkinson (ed.), *Egyptology Today* (Cambridge, 2008), p. 194. Colin Renfrew's 'the symbol in its real, actual substance etc.' (p. 131) is from his *Prehistory: the making of the human mind* (London, 2007), p. 135.

It is Wittgenstein, *Remarks on Frazer's Golden Bough*, p. 12e, who observes that not everyone acts upon the opinions they hold (p. 130), whilst the 'pure products of old Egypt' (p. 135) as William Carlos Williams might have said, has been bowdlerized, with grateful acknowledgements, from a chapter heading in James Clifford, *The Predicament of Culture: twentieth-century ethnography, literature, and art* (Cambridge, Mass., 1988).

CHAPTER 11. NARMER'S PALETTE

Epigraph: extracted from Wittgenstein's notebook entry of 29 September 1914, as translated in Anthony Kenny, *Wittgenstein* (Oxford, 2006), pp. 42–3.

My account of the making of the Narmer Palette has benefited from Mark Warden's online essay in *Nekhen News*, 12 (2000), 'Recarving the Narmer Palette'; the enlarged plate in Donadoni Roveri and Tiradritti (eds.), *Kemet*, p. 286, shows the marks of a palette maker at work. For Narmer's siltstone quarry, see Barbara A. Aston *et al.*, in *AEMT* pp. 57–8.

Basic documentation of the White and Red Crowns is provided by Wilkinson, *Early Dynastic Egypt*, pp. 192–5. Gardiner, *Egypt of the Pharaohs* (Oxford, 1961), pp. 400 ff., offers some traditional readings of the sign groups on the Narmer Palette. Alternatively, E. Christiana Köhler, 'History or Ideology? new reflections on the Narmer Palette and the nature of foreign relations in pre- and early Dynastic Egypt', in *EL*, shows how some egyptological interpretations have shifted since Gardiner's day, and provides an overview of the intervening scholarship.

A detailed account of another shrine of similar age to the one found by Quibell and Green at Hierakonpolis is Dreyer, *Elephantine VIII*; for more examples, see further, chapter 24 below.

CHAPTER 12. THE HAWK UPON THE WALL

Epigraph: from the last paragraph of Christopher J. Eyre, 'The Village Economy in Pharaonic Egypt', in Alan K. Bowman and Eugene Rogan (eds.), *Agriculture in Egypt from Pharaonic to Modern Times* (Oxford, 1999).

A clear chronological discussion of the ancient names of Egypt is Ogden Goelet, 'Kemet and Other Egyptian Terms for their Land', in Robert Chazan, William W. Hallo and Lawrence H. Schiffman (eds.), *Ki Barich Hu: ancient Near Eastern, biblical, and Judaic studies in honor of Baruch A. Levine* (Winona Lake, Ind., 1999). Some pertinent comments on the nature of ancient states are to be found in part 1 of David A. Warburton, *State and Economy in Ancient Egypt* (Fribourg and Göttingen, 1997).

The epigraph to the section 'Migrations' (p. 149) is from a dedicatory poem in William Lithgow's *The Totall Discourse Of the Rare Aduentures, and painefull Peregrinations of long nineteene Yeares Travayles from Scotland, to the Most Famous Kingdomes in Europe, Asia and Affrica* (London, 1632).

The relatively impoverished burials in some of the southern cemeteries of this period are described in Joan Crowfoot Payne, 'Chronology at Naqada', in Renée Friedman and Barbara Adams (eds.), *The Followers of Horus: studies dedicated to Michael Allen Hoffman* (Oxford, 1992). The Naqadans' contemporary northward movements are clearly reflected in the lists of dated cemeteries and settlements given in Stan Hendrickx and Edwin C. M. van den Brink, 'Inventory of Predynastic and Early Dynastic Cemetery and Settlement Sites in the Egyptian Nile Valley', in *EL*.

Though stressed somewhat differently to the argument of my text, two articles by E. Christiana Köhler are of fundamental importance to discussions of this period; see 'The State of Research on Late Predynastic Egypt: new evidence', *Göttinger Miszellen*, 147 (1995), and 'Evidence for Interregional Contacts between Late Prehistoric Lower and Upper Egypt: a view from Buto', in Lech Krzyżaniak, Karla Kroeper and Michał Kobusiewicz (eds.), *Interregional Contacts in the Later Prehistory of Northeastern Africa* (Poznán, 1996).

Herodotus (p. 151) is quoted from Book 2, chapter 99; trans. George Rawlinson, with J. Gardner Wilkinson and Henry Rawlinson, *The Histories of Herodotus*, 4 vols. (London, 1858).

The extent of Horus shrines along the lower Nile is outlined in Hans Goedicke, 'Cult-temple and "State" during the Old Kingdom in Egypt', in Edward Lipinski (ed.), *State and Temple Economy in the Ancient Near East* (Liège, 1979), whilst the ancient description of the establishment of the shrine of the hawk at Edfu is discussed in fascinating detail in E. A. E. Reymond, *The Mythical Origin of the Egyptian Temple* (Manchester, 1969).

CHAPTER 13. TAKING WING

Epigraph: from Ludwig Wittgenstein, *Lectures and Conversations on Aesthetics, Psychology and Religious Belief*, ed. Cyril Barrett (Oxford, 1966), p. 3.

For a broad background to my statements on Delta settlement see Köhler's 'Evidence for Interregional Contacts', Faltings, 'The Chronological Frame', and, more recently, the opening pages of Penelope Wilson, 'Prehistoric Settlement in the Western Delta: a regional and local view from Sais (Sa El-Hagar)', *JEA* 92 (2006).

For a list of possible ancient Levantine names employed for locations in the Nile Delta, see Donald Redford, 'Some Observations on the Northern and North-eastern Delta in the Late Predynastic Period', in Betsy Bryan and David Lorton (eds.), *Essays in Egyptology in Honor of Hans Goedicke* (San Antonio, Tex., 1994).

A recent description of the prehistoric geography of the Nile Delta is Karl W. Butzer, 'Geoarchaeological Implications of Recent Research'; once again, the statistical basis of my description of Delta settlement is based upon Hendrickx and van den Brink, 'Inventory', in *EL*.

The delta's ancient delights and thus its extraordinary potential for future pharaonic histories have been thoroughly revealed in the work of Manfred Bietak; see, for example, his *Avaris, the Capital of the Hyksos* (London, 1996), and, more recently, Ursula Thanheiser, 'Venice on the Nile?: on the maritime character of Tell Dab'a/Avaris', in Ernst Czerny *et al.* (eds.), *Timelines: studies in honour of Manfred Bietak*, 3 vols. (Liège, 2006).

A selection of recently uncovered Naqadan settlements in the delta can be found in the reports of ongoing excavations at various sites in Zahi Hawass, with Lyla Pinch Brock (eds.), *Proceedings of the Eighth International Congress of Egyptology*, 3 vols. (Cairo, 2002).

Detailed recent accounts of Naqadan settlement in the southern Levant are reported and discussed in *EL*, from where the bulk of information in the section 'Into the Levant' has been derived. The source of my remarks upon Nahal Tillah/Tell Halif is Eric Kansa and Thomas E. Levy, 'Ceramics, Identity and the Role of the State: the view from Nahal Tillah', in that same volume.

Wengrow, *The Archaeology of Early Egypt*, pp. 33ff. and 166ff. provides an up-to-date account of A Group culture. For recent discussions of the porous mix of Naqadan and Nubian cultures in southern Upper Egypt and Nubia, see Dietrich Raue, 'Who Was Who in Elephantine of the Third Millennium BC?', in *BMS* 9 (2008), and Maria Carmelo Gatto, 'Egypt and Nubia in the 5th–4th millennia BCE: a view from the First Cataract and its surroundings', in *BMS* 13 (2009). See also Izumi H. Takamiya, 'Egyptian Pottery Distribution in A-Group Cemeteries, Lower Nubia: towards an understanding of exchange systems between the Naqada Culture and the A-Group Culture', *JEA* 90 (2004).

CHAPTER 14. TAKING STOCK

A brief modern overview of the site that Petrie dug in the years before the First World War – W. M. Flinders Petrie *et al.*, *Tarkhan I and II* (London, 1913–14) – is given in Lisa Mawdsley, 'The Corpus of Potmarks from Tarkhan', *BMS* 13 (2009).

Naqadan delta farms are presently being excavated at a number of locations. For a fine example, see Martin Ziermann *et al.*, 'Tell el-Fara'in – Buto: Bericht über die Arbeiten am Gebäudekomplex der Schicht V und die Vorarbeiten auf dem Nordhügel (Site A)', *MDAIK* 58 (2002), and Ulrich Hartung *et al.*, 'Tell el-Fara'in – Buto 8: Vorbericht', *MDAIK* 59 (2003).

For an important early study of delta seed and crops, see Ursula Thanheiser, 'Local Crop Production versus Import of Cereals in the Predynastic Period in the Nile Delta', in Lech Krzyżaniak, Karla Kroeper and Michał Kobusiewicz (eds.), *Interregional Contacts in the Later Prehistory of Northeastern Africa* (Poznán, 1996).

The low Nile floods of the period have been noticed by Maciej Pawlikowski, 'Reasons for the Predynastic–Early Dynastic Transition in Egypt: geological and climatic evidence', in *EOI*; Butzer, *Early Hydraulic Civilisation*, draws comparison between the Nile flood plain and that of other African rivers.

The death rates of populations in Upper Egypt contemporaneous to those of the Naqadan delta farms are part-taken from appendix V by Andreas Nerlich and Albert Zink, in Günter Dreyer *et al.* 'Umm el-Qaab, Nachuntersuchungen im frühzeitlichen Königsfriedhof 13./14./15: Vorbericht', *MDAIK* 59 (2003).

Renée Friedman's phrase, 'striking and complete loss . . .' (p. 167), is from her unpublished doctoral dissertation 'Predynastic Settlement Ceramics of Upper Egypt', Ann Arbor, 1994 (University Microfilms); see also, Takamiya, 'Egyptian Pottery Distribution'.

For a representative list of these early serekhs, see Edwin C. M. van den Brink, 'The Incised Serekh-signs of Dynasties 0–1 Part I: complete vessels', in *EL*; for a convenient listing of contemporary desert serekhs, and an interpretation of their significance which is different from mine, see Toby Wilkinson, 'Political Unification: towards a reconstruction', *MDAIK* 56 (2000).

The fundamental elements of early Mesopotamian writing are outlined in Denise Schmandt-Besserat, *Before Writing* (Austin, Tex., 1992); for the constituents of ancient Egyptian, Antonio Loprieno, *Ancient Egyptian: a linguistic introduction* (Cambridge, 1995).

John Wilson's much-quoted phrase 'civilization without cities' (p. 171) is taken from his essay 'Egypt through the New Kingdom: civilization without cities', in Carl H. Kraeling and Robert McC. Adams (eds.), *City Invincible* (Chicago, 1960).

The fundamental source of information on the brick tombs that were set along the Memphis skyline is Walter B. Emery *et al.*, *Great Tombs of the First Dynasty*, 3 vols. (Cairo, 1949; London, 1954 and 1958).

CHAPTER 15. THE SHADOWS OF BIRDS

Adam Kuper, *The Invention of Primitive Society: transformations of an illusion* (London, 1988), charts the history of this ugly modern myth, which yet lives on in egyptology. A subtle remedy, though its curious English title lacks the poetry of the French original, is the classic volume of Claude Lévi-Strauss, *The Savage Mind* (London, 1966), trans. of 'La Pensée sauvage' (Paris, 1962).

Fundamental statistics of the surviving picture plaques are provided in the study of Kathryn E. Piquette, 'Representing the Human

Body on Late Predynastic and Early Dynastic Labels', in *EO1*. A list of the known knife handles of the period is given in Whitehouse, 'A Decorated Knife Handle', while Emma Swan Hall, *The Pharaoh Smites his Enemies* (Munich, 1986), offers a handy, if somewhat dated, checklist of such scenes.

The evidence for human sacrifice in Naqadan times is dissected and discussed in a varied collection of essays on the subject; Jean-Pierre Albert and Béatrix Midant-Reynes (eds.), *Le Sacrifice humain en Égypte ancienne et ailleurs* (Paris, 2006).

The epigraph to the section 'Tithe and Ceremonial' (pp. 179–80) is from Wittgenstein, *Remarks on Frazer's Golden Bough*, p. 16e.

Following its discovery by Michael Hoffman in the 1980s, the excavation of the oval court was reported by Renée Friedman, 'The Ceremonial Centre at Hierakonpolis, Locality HK29A', in *AEE*. Its further excavation has been variously recorded at Hierakonpolis Online, where it is designated as the 'Temple' at site HK29A. See, especially, the four weekly excavation reports, November–December 2002.

Hermes Trisgemistus, Libellus XVI paragraph 1, describes Greek philosophy as 'a noise of talk' and quite unable to contain the holy force of things Egyptian (p. 184); translation from Walter Scott, *Hermetica* (Oxford, 1924).

CHAPTER 16. THE SEREKH TOMB

Petrie's work at Naqada was published in the year it was completed; see W. M. Flinders Petrie, *Naqada and Ballas* (London, 1896). Note that the uncertainties of Petrie and his team as to what they had found evaporated in the next few years, along with the mythical 'New Race' that he proposes in the text of this same volume.

The publications that documented the excavation and re-excavation of the Naqada mastaba were but a small part of a remarkable series of excavations undertaken in Upper Egypt at the turn of the twentieth century. As with Petrie, all these reports were published in the same year that the excavations they record had been concluded. They are: Jacques de Morgan, *Recherches sur les origines de l'Égypte*, vol. 2:

Ethnographie préhistorique et tombeau royal de Négadah (Paris, 1897); Ludwig Borchardt, 'Das Grab des Menes', *ZÄS* 36 (1899); John Garstang, 'The Tablet of Mena', *ZÄS* 42 (1905). See also, James Quibell, *Catalogue général des antiquité Égyptiennes du Musée du Caire: archaic objects*, 2 vols. (Cairo, 1904–1905).

For a flavour of the intense rivalries of those days, see W. M Flinders Petrie, *Seventy Years in Archaeology* (London, 1933), and, latterly, Élisabeth David, *Gaston Maspero 1846–1916: le gentleman égyptologue* (Paris, 1994).

The epigraph to the section 'Uruk in Egypt' (p. 191) is from Adam T. Smith, 'The Politics of Loss: comments on a powerful death', in Nicola Laneri (ed.), *Performing Death: social analysis of funerary traditions in the ancient Near East and Mediterranean* (Chicago, 2007), p. 165.

For Habuba Kabira, see, for example, Eva Strommenger, 'Fünfter vorläufiger Bericht über die von der Deutschen Orient-Gesellschaft mit Mitteln der Stiftung Volkswagenwerk in Habuba Kabira unternommenen archäologischen Untersuchungen', *Mitteilungen der Deutschen Orient Gesellschaft*, 108 (1976); Algaze, *The Uruk World System*, is a convenient general source for much similar material, as is Joffe, 'Egypt and Syro-Mesopotamia'.

CHAPTER 17. A LINE OF KINGS

Epigraph: from the first paragraph of the first volume of W. M. Flinders Petrie, *The Royal Tombs of the First Dynasty*, 2 vols. (London, 1900–1901), which are an indispensable record of the excavation of the Umm el-Qa'ab.

A recent guide to the huge site of Abydos by one of its most eminent excavators is David O'Connor, *Abydos: Egypt's first pharaohs and the cult of Osiris* (London, 2009). The demon that once haunted that ancient site is described by John Ray in his essay 'Ancient Egypt', in Michael Loewe and Carmen Blacker (eds.), *Divinations and Oracles* (London, 1981), pp. 175–6.

Margaret S. Drower, *Flinders Petrie: a life in archaeology* (London, 1985), pp. 256ff., recounts his work at Abydos; an echo of the scale and tenor of that enterprise is provided in Stan Hendrickx *et al.*,

'Excavating in the Museum: the stone vessel fragments from the royal tombs at Umm el-Qaab in the Egyptian collection of the Royal Museums for Art and History at Brussels', *MDAIK* 57 (2001). In similar fashion, Luc Watrin, 'Tributes and the Rise of a Predatory Power: unraveling the intrigue of EBI Palestinian jars found by E. Amélineau at Abydos', in *EL*, provides a brief overview of Amélineau's excavations.

A scientific analysis of the organic contents of some of the jars that Petrie recovered on the Umm el-Qa'ab is Margaret Serpico and Raymond White, 'A Report on the Analysis of the Contents of a Cache of Jars from the Tomb of Djer', in *AEE*.

Reports on the German Archaeological Institute's on-going work upon the Umm el-Qa'ab – in which Petrie's plans and observations of the site are being enlarged and refined – have appeared regularly in *MDAIK* since 1979; the re-excavation of the tombs of Narmer and Aha, for example, are described by Günter Dreyer *et al.* in *MDAIK* 35 (1979) and 38 (1982).

Alongside a discussion of various archaeo-anthropological theories, Ellen F. Morris 'Sacrifice for the State: First Dynasty royal funerals and the rites of Macramallah's rectangle', in Nicola Laneri (ed.), *Performing Death*, provides an up-to-date overview of funerary practices upon the Umm el-Qa'ab, while Laurel D. Bestock, 'Finding the First Dynasty Royal Family', in Zahi Hawass and Janet Richards (eds.), *The Archaeology and Art of Ancient Egypt: essays in honor of David B. O'Connor* (Cairo, 2007), places the Abydos enclosures in a contemporary setting. See also, David O'Connor, *Abydos*, chapter 10.

Later records concerning 'storehouses' at Abydos are discussed by Jaroslav Černý in his article 'Storehouses of This', in *Studi in memoria di Ippolito Rosellini nel primo centenario della morte II* (Pisa, 1955), pp. 29 ff.

A recent discussion of the king lists on the Abydos seals can be found in Josep Cervelló-Autuori, 'Narmer, Menes and the Seals from Abydos', in Zahi Hawass, with Lyla Pinch Brock (eds.), *Proceedings of the Eighth International Congress of Egyptology*, 3 vols. (Cairo, 2002).

The epigraph to the section '*Aigyptiaka*' (p. 212) is from John Van

Seters, *In Search of History: historiography in the ancient world and the origins of biblical history* (Princeton, 1983), p. 193.

The standard translation of the remaining fragments of Manetho's *Aigyptiaka* is that of W. G. Waddell, *Manetho* (London, 1940). For more recent attitudes to those texts, see, for example, Stanley M. Burstein, 'Images of Egypt in Greek Historiography', in Antonio Loprieno (ed.), *Ancient Egyptian Literature: history and forms* (Leiden, 1996), and John Dillery, 'The First Egyptian Narrative History: Manetho and Greek historiography', *Zeitschrift für Papyrologie und Epigraphik*, 127 (1999).

CHAPTER 18. THE LOST DYNASTY

Petrie's descriptions of the tombs of Khasekhemui and Peribsen are to be found in Petrie, *Royal Tombs*; the German Archaeological Institute's ongoing re-investigation of those structures, in Dreyer *et al.*, *MDAIK* 35 (1979), 54 (1998), 56 (2000) and 59 (2003).

Joris Van Wetering 'The Royal Cemetery of the Early Dynastic period at Saqqara and the Second Dynasty Royal Tombs', in *EO1*, provides a recent discussion of the present knowledge of these monuments.

Sir Alan Gardiner is quoted (p. 218) from the preface of his *Egypt of the Pharaohs*, p. v. For a recent account of the use of hieroglyphs at the Abydos royal tombs, see Elise V. MacArthur, 'In Search of the sḏm=f: the conception and development of hieroglyphic writing through the reign of Aha', a paper delivered at 'Egypt at its Origins [3]', and published online; MacArthur discusses Petrie's 'sweetheart' under the heading 'Kahl Quelle Nr. 286'.

The tales of Peribsen and Khasekhemui are recounted in chapter 3, 'Historical Outline', in Wilkinson, *Early Dynastic Egypt*, pp. 89–94.

The German Archaeological Institute's excavations on the Isle of Elephantine at Aswan have been extensively documented in *MDAIK* since vol. 26 (1970). An overview of this ongoing work, with extensive maps, is given in *MDAIK* 55 (1999).

Stephan J. Seidlmayer, 'Town and State in the Early Old Kingdom: a view from Elephantine', in *AEE*, provides a thoughtful synthesis of the history of the island settlement in its early phases; Martin

Ziermann, *Elephantine* XXVIII: *Die Baustrukturen der älteren Stadt (Frühzeit und Altes Reich)* (Mainz, 2003), documents and reconstructs the buildings of the earliest settlements.

CHAPTER 19. THE WHEELING HAWK

Pierre de Miroschedji, 'The Socio-political Dynamics of Egyptian–Canaanite Interaction in the Early Bronze Age', in *EL* describes the dynamics of settlement of this period within the south Levant – the differences between the beginning and ending of Dynasty One are graphically underlined in a comparison of his figures 2.4 and 2.5.

Ezra Marcus, 'Early Seafaring and Maritime Activity in the Southern Levant from Prehistory through the Third Millennium BCE', in *EL* brings together much disparate information concerning ancient seafaring in the southern Mediterranean, and is the source of much of my detail on this subject. In that same compendious volume, Stan Hendrickx and Laurent Bavay, 'Chronological Position of Egyptian Predynastic and Early Dynastic Tombs with Objects Imported from the Near East and the Nature of Interregional Contacts', list and quantify the foreign objects found in proto and early dynastic tombs. Modern discussions of these materials, with extensive bibliographies, can be found in *AEMT*. See also Dietrich D. Klemm, with Rosemarie Klemm and Andreas Murr, 'Ancient Gold Mining in the Eastern Desert of Egypt and the Nubian Desert of Sudan', in Renée Friedman (ed.), *Egypt and Nubia: gifts of the desert* (London, 2002); and also, Hartung *et al.*, *Umm el-Qaab II*.

That histories of this period can still be based on concepts of political power and social coercion – and even, that, as a chapter epigraph informs us, 'War is the father of all things' – is demonstrated in Wenke, *The Ancient Egyptian State* pp. 189ff., which contains a potted version of the history of this period similar in tone to that outlined in my section 'Trading clichés'. A more carefully argued version of the same historical genre is Yoffee, *Myths of the Archaic State*, where it is exemplified by the title of chapter 2, 'Dimensions of Power in the Earliest States'.

Some of the evidence that the culture of the early court was closing in upon itself is presented – though from a different perspective – by Toby Wilkinson, 'Reality versus Ideology: the evidence for "Asiatics" in predynastic and early dynastic Egypt', in *EL*.

CHAPTER 20. THE REALMS OF PHARAOH

The quotation from Tertullian (p. 242) is from chapter 50 of his *Apologeticus*. O'Connor, *Abydos*, provides an outline of the later history of the Umm el-Qa'ab and Abydos.

W. M. Flinders Petrie *et al.*, *Tombs of the Courtiers and Oxyrhynkhos* (London, 1925) contains his account of his return to Abydos; plate XII has his drawing of the comb that bears the serekh of King Djet. Petrie's notebooks for that season's work – and for many others – have been published on CD ROM by the Petrie Museum of Archaeology, University College London, and have supplied some further detail for my text.

For differing interpretations of the signs upon the ivory comb, compare Hans Goedicke, 'Unity and Diversity in the Oldest Religion of Ancient Egypt', in G. Ernest Wright (ed.), *The Bible and the Ancient Near East: essays in honor of William Foxwell Albright* (New York, 1961), and Stephen Quirke, *Ancient Egyptian Religion* (London 1992).

Human sacrifice in the early royal tombs was described as 'suttee' in George Andrew Reisner, *The Development of the Egyptian Tomb down to the Succession of Cheops* (Oxford, 1936); Wilkinson, *Early Dynastic Egypt*, p. 266, suggests that the practice may have belonged to 'an ancient African substratum' of Egyptian culture.

The Sinai smiting inscriptions are published in Alan Gardiner, Jaroslav Černý *et al.*, *The Inscriptions of Sinai*, 2 vols. (London, 1952 and 1955).

The *Opferplatz* by the tomb U-j is described in Dreyer, *Umm el-Qaab I*, section 4.2; some of the other offering grounds upon the Umm el-Qaab are variously recorded in the reports of the German Expedition's work, in Dreyer *et al.*, in *MDAIK*.

The precipitate decrease in human sacrifice throughout the First Dynasty is shown in chart 2.2, 'Numbers of Subsidiary Burials at Abydos', in Morris, 'Sacrifice for the State'.

CHAPTER 21. TWO GENTLEMEN OF SAQQARA

Epigraph: from the opening paragraphs of James Quibell, *Archaic Mastabas (1912–1914)* (Cairo, 1923).

The best description of the Memphite region during this period is David Jeffreys and Anna Tavares, 'The Historic Landscape of Early Dynastic Memphis', *MDAIK* 50 (1994). See also Katy Lutley and Judith Bunbury, 'The Nile on the Move', *Egyptian Archaeology*, 32 (2008) and the succeeding article in that same journal by David Jeffreys, 'Archaeological Implications of the Moving Nile'.

Merka's tomb is numbered 3505 in Emery, *Great Tombs II*, which records its clearance and provides elaborate, if schematic, plans.

Merka's stela is placed in historical context in John Baines, 'Forerunners of Narrative Biographies', in Anthony Leahy and John Tait (eds.), *Studies on Ancient Egypt in Honour of H. S. Smith* (London, 1999); the same author's 'Origins of Egyptian Kingship', in David O'Connor and David P. Silverman (eds.), *Ancient Egyptian Kingship* (Leiden, 1995), pp. 133ff., discusses the terms *sem*, *iry-pet* and *rekhyt*. See also Bruce Williams, 'The Wearer of the Leopard Skin in the Naqada Period', in Jacke Phillips (ed.), *Ancient Egypt, the Aegean and the Near East: studies in honor of Martha Rhoades Bell* (San Antonio, Tex., 1997).

Élisabeth David, *Mariette Pacha 1821–1881* (Paris, 1994), provides a portrait of this elusive pioneer. To my knowledge, Auguste Mariette, *Les Mastabas de l'ancien Empire* (extracted *post mortem* from his papers, by Gaston Maspero) (Paris, 1885) contains the only notice of the discovery of Hesi-re's tomb; James Quibell, *Excavations at Saqqara (1911–12): the tomb of Hesy* (Cairo, 1913), provides a full account of that tomb and its subsequent re-excavation. Catalogue entry 4 in Edward L. B. Terrace and H. G. Fischer, *Treasures of the Cairo Museum* (London, 1970), offers a succinct appreciation of one of Hesi-re's reliefs; see also Henry G. Fischer, 'Some Emblematic Uses of Hieroglyphs with Particular Reference to an Archaic Ritual Vessel', *Metropolitan Museum Journal*, 5 (1972), and Baines, 'Forerunners', pp. 28–9.

The epigraph to the section 'Order and the Court' (p. 264) is from Spenser, *The Faerie Queene*, book 2, canto 7; that to the section

'Constancy and Change', from Shakespeare, *Titus Andronicus*, I. i. 228.

For some early pharaonic sculptures whose makers appear to have paid particular attention to the physical appearance of their subjects, see Romer, *The Great Pyramid*, chapter 9.

Seidlmayer, 'Town and State', provides a geographic overview of some of the officials who were emerging at this time. A gallery of black-and-white photographs of the sculptures of the same period is given in plates 2–4 of W. Stevenson Smith, *A History of Egyptian Sculpture and Painting in the Old Kingdom* (Oxford, 2nd edn., 1949). See also *EAAP*, catalogue numbers 11–16, and Marianne Eaton-Krauss, 'Two Masterpieces of Early Egyptian Statuary', *Oudheidkundige mededeelingen uit het Rijksmuseum van Oudheden te Leiden*, 77 (1997).

CHAPTER 22. DJOSER'S KINGDOM

The excavation of the Step Pyramid complex is documented in Cecil Firth and James Quibell, *The Step Pyramid*, 2 vols. (Cairo, 1935). Some of the changes in the design and construction of the complex are outlined in Jean-Philippe Lauer, *Histoire monumentale des pyramides d'Égypte* (Cairo, 1962), which contains elaborate plans of the compound and reconstructions of its original appearance. Note, however, that it is now widely accepted that the processes of building King Djoser's monuments were more complex than Lauer describes; see, for example, Rainer Stadelmann, 'Origins and Development of the Funerary Complex of Djoser', in Peter Der Manuelian (ed.), *Studies in Honor of William Kelly Simpson*, 2 vols. (Boston, 1996).

The graffiti that later scribes left at the Step Pyramid are numbered 90, 193, 195 and 196 in Kenneth Kitchen, *Ramesside Inscriptions* (Oxford, 1988–). Gardiner is quoted from his *Egypt of the Pharaohs*, p. 427, whilst the 'contemporary chronologist' is Stephan J. Seidlmayer, 'The Relative Chronology of Dynasty 3', in *AEC* p. 122.

Much of the architectural data in this chapter has been drawn from Romer, *The Great Pyramid*, especially from chapters 25–6. See also, Bevan, *Stone Vessels*, pp. 62–72.

John Garstang, *Mahâsna and Bêt Khallâf* (London, 1903), records his excavations at Beit Khallaf (p. 267) and provides plans of its huge brick mastabas.

The epigraph to the 'Antiquarian' section (p. 286) is taken from Boswell's *Life of Samuel Johnson, LL.d.* (London, 1791), vol. 3, p. 61.

The fundamental publications of the inscriptions upon the Step Pyramid's stores of vases, which have come to support a considerable further literature, are Pierre Lacau and Jean-Philippe Lauer, *La Pyramide à degrés*, vols. 4 (two parts) and 5 (Cairo, 1959–61 and 1965). See also, Sydney H. Aufrère, 'L'Origine de l'albâtre à la 1re dynastie d'après les inscriptions des vases provenant des galeries de la pyramide à degrés', *Bulletin de l'institut français d'archéologie orientale*, 103 (2003).

The stonemasons' syntheses of natural forms in the architecture of the Step Pyramid complex is described by I. E. S. Edwards, *The Pyramids of Egypt* (London, 1999), chapter 2. A useful introduction to the possible purposes of the stone throne dais within the Step Pyramid complex, is Alexei A. Krol, 'The Representation of the "Sed-Platform" in the Early Dynastic Monuments', *Göttinger Miszellen*, 184 (2001).

For a splendid picture gallery – though to my mind a somewhat overwrought discussion – of the so-called 'prisoner' statues, see Bernard Bothmer, 'On Realism in Egyptian Funerary Sculpture of the Old Kingdom', *Expedition Magazine* (Penn Museum), 24 (1982). The image of the bound and kneeling captive is ubiquitous in early Dynastic art; see, for example, Quibell, *Hierakonpolis I, passim*. For the small statue of a man carrying a flint knife, see *EAAP*, catalogue number 10.

CHAPTER 23. HEB SEDIANA

An orthodox overview of the Sed festival may be found in Wilkinson, *Early Dynastic Egypt*, pp. 212ff.; note that he observes that 'there is surprisingly little explicit evidence for [its] details'.

Leviticus (p. 293) is quoted from the translation of John Wycliffe (1384).

The history and contemporary impact of Frazer's *Golden Bough* is described in Robert J. Ackerman, *J. G. Fraser: his life and work* (Cambridge, 1987).

For Imhotep, see Dietrich Wildung, *Imhotep und Amenhotep:*

Gottwerdung im alten Ägypten (Munich, 1977). The translation of Imhotep's titles on the statue base (p. 295) is taken from John Ray, *Reflections on Osiris: lives from ancient Egypt* (Oxford, 2002), p. 13, as is the quotation from Manetho; see also, Waddell, *Manetho*, fr. 11, p. 41.

For alternative conceptions of the significance of the six reliefs of Djoser that were set beneath his pyramid complex, see Florence Dunn Friedman, 'Notions of Cosmos in the Step Pyramid Complex', in Peter der Manuelian (ed.), *Studies in Honor of William Kelley Simpson*, 2 vols. (Boston, 1996); and Hans Goedicke, 'Zoser's Funerary Monument 2: The "Heb-sed" court', *Bulletin of the Egyptological Seminar*, 8 (1997). See also A. J. Spencer, 'Two Enigmatic Hieroglyphs and their Relation to the Sed-festival', *JEA* 64 (1978).

CHAPTER 24. DEUS ABSCONDITUS

Djoser's celebrated statue is placed in its contemporary context in Hourig Sourouzian 'L'Iconographie du roi dans la statuaire des trois premières dynasties', in *Kunst des Alten Reiches* (Mainz, 1995).

Petrie's report of the early shrine he found at Coptos is carefully re-examined, along with its statuary, in Barry Kemp, 'The Colossi from the Early Shrine at Coptos in Egypt', *CAJ* 10.2 (2000), and subsequently, in Kemp, *Ancient Egypt*, pp. 129–31; pp. 112–35 of the same volume contain an illuminating treatment of early shrines. For an account of the extraordinary cache found in an early shrine at Tell el-Farkha, see Marek Chłodnicki and Krzysztof Ciałowicz, 'Tell el-Farkha (Ghazala) 2006, Preliminary Report on the Activities of the Polish Archaeological Mission', *Annales du service des antiquités de l'Égypte*, 83 (2009); and Marek Chłodnicki and Krzysztof Ciałowicz, 'Golden Figures from Tell el-Farkha', *Studies in Ancient Arts and Civilisation*, 10 (2007); and Krzysztof M. Ciałowicz, 'The Early Dynastic Administrative-cultic Centre and Tell el Farkha', *BMS* 13 (2009).

The history of professorial investigations into the meaning of *neter* are outlined in Erik Hornung, *Conceptions of God in Ancient Egypt: the one and the many* (London, 1982), trans. John Baines from *Der Eine und die Vielen* (Darmstadt, 1971), pp. 105ff. See also the apposite remarks in Hans Goedicke, 'God', *Journal of the Society of the Study of Egyptian Antiquities*, 16 (1986).

Some of the largest of the many fragments of early relief that were excavated at Gebelein and Heliopolis in the first years of the twentieth century are described and pictured in Donadoni Roveri and Tiradritti (eds.), *Kemet*, catalogue numbers 235, 239–41.

CHAPTER 25. IN CONSEQUENCE

Epigraph: from Jan Assmann, *The Mind of Egypt: history and meaning in the time of the pharaohs* (New York, 2002), trans. by Andrew Jenkins from *Ägypten: Eine Sinngeschichte* (Munich, 1996), p. 53.

The method of drawing a series of appropriate profiles on each face of a stone block and then cutting them down to make a sculpture was still employed in Egypt millennia later, and the surviving examples from those later times elaborate the ancient procedure: see, for example, Nadja Samir Tomoum, *The Sculptors' Models of the Late and Ptolemaic Periods* (Cairo, 2005), pp. 35–41. For examples of the same process being undertaken in the time of the early kings, see the unfinished statues in *EAAP*, catalogue member 73; for hard evidence of its use in Djoser's day, see Sourouzian, 'L'Iconographie du roi', plate 54 (a).

For the demarcation of Djoser's various estates, see Spencer, 'Two Enigmatic Hieroglyphs'; also, A. D. Espinel, 'The Boundary Stelae of Djoser's Funerary Complex at Saqqara: an interpretation through artistic and textual evidence', in Zahi Hawass, with Lyla Pinch Brock (eds.), *Proceedings of the Eighth International Congress of Egyptology*, 3 vols. (Cairo, 2002).

CHAPTER 26. A DIADEM OF PYRAMIDS.

The full record of the excavation of the pyramid of Sekhemkhet is M. Zakaria Goneim, *Excavations at Saqqara: Horus Sekhem-khet* (Cairo, 1957). The same author's popular book *The Lost Pyramid* (New York, 1956) gives his account of the media debacle at the time the tomb was discovered.

Mark Lehner, *The Complete Pyramids* (London, 1997), provides a modern compendium of all the royal pyramids of Egypt.

The panel of an otherwise unknown king, 'Qahedjet', presently in the Louvre (see also *EAAP*, catalogue number 9), has been identified as belonging to the king known now as Huni who, in the manner of later monarchs, appears to have had more than one name; see, for example, Seidlmayer, 'The Relative Chronology', and Rainer Stadelmann, 'King Huni: his monuments and his place in the history of the Old Kingdom', in Zahi Hawass, and Janet Richards (eds.), *The Archaeology and Art of Ancient Egypt: essays in honor of David B. O'Connor*, 2 vols. (Cairo, 2007).

The epigraph to the section 'In the Provinces' (p. 320) is from Eyre, 'The Village Economy', p. 35; the same essay provides a fundamental discussion of the ancient countryside and its pharaonic inhabitants. See, too, the same author's 'The Water Regime for Orchards and Plantations in Pharaonic Egypt', *JEA* 80 (1994).

The results of an analysis of seed taken from Djoser's granaries is presented in J.-P. Lauer, V. Laurent-Täckholm and E. Åberg, 'Les Plantes découvertes dans les souterrains de l'enceinte du roi Zoser à Saqqarah (IIIe dynastie)', *Bulletin de l'Institut Égyptien*, 32 (1932). For the produce of contemporary farms in the Delta region, see Marie-Francine Moens and Wilma Wetterstrom, 'The Agricultural Economy of an Old Kingdom Town in Egypt's West Delta: insight from the plant remains', *JNES* 47.3 (1988). Parts of the region around Abydos at this time are described by Edward Brovarski in the entries for 'Naga (Nag')-ed Der' and 'Thinis', in Wolfgang Helk, Eberhard Otto and Wolfhart Westendorf (eds.), *Lexikon der Ägyptologie*, 7 vols. (Wiesbaden, 1975–92).

For the occurrence of Sanakht's name in Upper Egypt, see Seidlmayer, 'The Relative Chronology'. Note that the southern tip of the modern island of Elephantine is composed of two anciently adjacent islands that were joined together by silt brought down in the annual inundation at a time after the building of the fortress and the pyramid upon the eastern island.

An elegant catalogue of the little Third Dynasty pyramids is presented by Günter Dreyer and Werner Kaiser, 'Zu den kleinen Stufenpyramiden Ober- und Mittelägyptens', *MDAIK* 36 (1980). In November 2009, a lecture by Kerry Muhlestein of Brigham Young University with an accompanying press release announced the discovery of a relief bearing Sneferu's name on a stela at the Seila pyramid; see for example, heritage-key.com.

Seidlmayer, 'Town and State', describes his theory of the connection between the little pyramids and the confines of pharaonic provinces.

CHAPTER 27. COURT AND COUNTRY

Lepsius (p. 328) is quoted from letter 36 of Richard Lepsius, *Discoveries in Egypt, Ethiopia and the Peninsula of Sinai in the years 1842–1845*, trans. Kenneth R. H. Mackenzie (London, 1852).

The reliefs from Metjen's tomb were first published in Lepsius' *magnum opus*: *Denkmäler aus Aegypten und Aethiopien*, 12 vols. (Berlin and Leipzig, 1849–1913), volume 2, plates 3–7; and latterly, in photograph, by Hans Goedicke 'Die Laufbahn des *Mtn*', *MDAIK* 21 (1966).

Baines, 'Forerunners', contains interesting observations upon the interrelationship of the architecture and decoration of Metjen's tomb. My brief quotations from translations of the tomb texts generally follow those of Baines within that essay; my comments on Metjen's small holdings, their description in Eyre, 'The Water Regime for Orchards and Plantations'.

'writing in a royal document' (p. 331): the use of papyrus at the early court is discussed in John Baines, *Visual and Written Culture in Ancient Egypt* (Oxford, 2007), pp. 128ff.

There is a considerable academic literature concerning the names of dogs in ancient Egypt; for a recent overview of the subject, see Michael Rice, *Swifter than the Arrow: the golden hunting hounds of ancient Egypt* (London, 2006).

The epigraph to the section 'The Meanings of Words' (p. 334) is taken from lines spoken by 'Jerry/Geraldine' in Billy Wilder's film *Some Like It Hot* (1959).

Broadly speaking, the two differing 'voices' of the Metjen inscriptions are those detected, on the one hand, by Goedicke, 'Die Laufbahn des *mtn*', by Baines, 'Forerunners', and by Eyre, 'The Water Regime', who consider that they were intended to describe aspects of an individual and, on the other hand, by those who see Metjen's texts primarily as a record of his titles and legal documents; see, for example, Karin Barbara Gödecken, *Eine Betrachtung der Inschriften des Meten im Rahmen der sozialen und rechtlichen Stellung von Privatleuten im ägyptischen Alten Reich* (Wiesbaden, 1976), and Nigel Strudwick, *Texts from the Pyramid Age* (Leiden, 2005).

Roland Barthes's well-known discussion of the effects of literature is to be found in Barthes, *The Semiotic Challenge*, pp. 164ff.

The quotation on p. 336 is from Baines, 'The Earliest Egyptian Writing', p. 183.

CHAPTER 28. HIGH SOCIETY

The locations of royal residences of this period are discussed by Rainer Stadelmann, 'La Ville de pyramides à l'Ancien Empire', *Revue d'Égyptologie*, 33 (1981).

'like a slice of double Gloucester' (p. 337): extracted from W. J. Loftie's delicious *A Ride in Egypt from Sioot to Luxor* (London, 1879), p. 204.

Maidum and its pyramid are described in Romer, *The Great Pyramid*, pp. 263ff, as are the problems of the history of Sneferu's time; see also Rainer Stadelmann, 'Beiträge zur Geschichte des Alten Reiches: die Länge der Regierung des Snofru', *MDAIK* 43 (1987), and Miroslav Verner, 'Contemporary Evidence for the Relative Chronology of Dyns. 4 and 5', in *AEC*.

The site of Maidum is relatively little documented, the fundamental record still that of Flinders Petrie; W. M. Flinders Petrie *et al.*, *Medum* (London, 1892), and W. M. Flinders Petrie, Ernest Mackay and Gerald Wainwright, *Meydum and Memphis (III)* (London, 1910). The latter volume contains Petrie's astute observations upon the mastabas' construction; a brief modern commentary on the two decorated tomb chapels is to be found in *EAAP*, catalogue numbers 24A–C to 26A–C.

A fundamental work upon the tomb chapels of this period is Yvonne Harpur, *Decoration in Egyptian Tombs of the Old Kingdom* (London, 1987); see also, the same author's 'The Identity and Positions of Relief Fragments in Museums and Private Collections: the reliefs of R'-ḥtp and Nfrt from Meydum', *JEA* 72 (1986), and 'Further Reliefs from the Chapel of R'-ḥtp at Meydum', *JEA* 73 (1987).

For recent observations upon marriage and divorce in ancient

Egypt (p. 341), see Christopher J. Eyre, 'The Evil Stepmother and the Rights of a Second Wife', *JEA* 93 (2007).

My account of the circumstances of Daninos Pasha's opening of the Maidum Mastabas is taken both from David, *Mariette Pacha*, and Gaston Maspero, 'Deux documents relatifs aux fouilles de Mariette', *Recueil de travaux relatifs à la philologie et à l'archéologie égyptiennes et assyriennes*, 12 (1892).

The first-quoted letter (p. 348ff.) written by Petrie from Maidum is from his autobiography: W. M. Flinders Petrie, *Seventy Years in Archaeology* (London, 1933), p. 125; the second, from Flinders and Hilda Petrie, *Letters from the Desert*, ed. Margaret Drower (Oxford, 2004), p. 192.

Detlef Franke, 'The Middle Kingdom Offering Formulas – a Challenge', *JEA* 89 (2003), provides a recent overview of the problems connected with the ubiquitous phrase now known as the *hetep di nesut*; Romer, *The Great Pyramid*, chapter 10, provides a near-contemporary context for its use during the early dynasties.

The quotation on p. 351 is from W. M. Flinders Petrie, *Ten Years Digging in Egypt* (London, 1893), p. 139.

A full account of the Palermo Stone by one of its recent investigators is Toby Wilkinson, *Royal Annals of Ancient Egypt: the Palermo Stone and its associated fragments* (London, 2000). See also Jochem Kahl, 'Inscriptional Evidence for the Relative Chronology of Dyn. 0–2', in *AEC* pp. 125ff.

CHAPTER 29. A BUILDING PASSION

The statistics and mechanics of pyramid building of Sneferu's time are detailed in Romer, *The Great Pyramid*, chapters 6 and 28–31, this information having been extrapolated, in part, from fundamental information supplied in Rolf Krauss, 'The Length of Sneferu's Reign and How Long it Took to Build the "Red Pyramid"', *JEA* 82 (1996) [work rates]; K. S. Sandford and W. J. Arkell, *Paleolithic Man and the Nile-Faiyum Divide* (Chicago, 1929) [geology]; Josef Dorner, 'Form und Ausmaße der Knickpyramide: neue Beobachtungen und Messungen', *MDAIK* 42 (1986), and the same author's 'Neue Messungen an der Roten Pyramide', in Heike Guksche and Daniel Polz (eds.),

Stationen. Beiträge zur Kulturgeschichte Ägyptens Rainer Stadelmann gewidmet (Mainz, 1998) [architecture]. See, too, more generally, Edwards, *The Pyramids of Egypt*; Rainer Stadelmann, *Die Ägyptischen Pyramiden: vom Ziegelbau zum Weltwunder* (Mainz, 1997), and Lehner, *The Complete Pyramids*.

The scant surviving images of Sneferu are discussed in Rainer Stadelmann, 'Der Strenge Stil der frühen Vierten Dynastie', in *Kunst des Alten Reiches* (Mainz, 1995).

For a fresh view of the issue of the so-called 'cattle counts', see J. S. Nolan, 'The Original Lunar Calendar and Cattle Counts in Old Kingdom Egypt', in Susanne Bickel and Antonio Loprieno (eds.), *Basle Egyptology Prize I* (Basle, 2003).

CHAPTER 30. MAKING THE GODS

The fundamental source of information for this chapter is Ahmed Fakhry, *The Monuments of Sneferu at Dahshur*, volume 2: *The Valley Temple*, 2 vols. (Cairo, 1961); Dorothea Arnold, 'Royal reliefs', and catalogue entry 22A–B in *EAAP*, containing some useful updates and some additional visual material. See, too, Elmar Edel, 'Studien zu den Relieffragmenten aus dem Taltempel des Königs Snofru', in Peter Der Manuelian (ed.), *Studies in Honor of William Kelly Simpson*, 2 vols. (Boston, 1996).

The door-jamb of Khasekhemui is pictured in Quibell, *Hierakonpolis I*, plate II. Further reliefs on that same block of stone were first noticed in the 1930s at the Cairo Museum; see Rex Engelbach, 'A Foundation Scene of the Second Dynasty', *JEA* 20 (1934). For the relief of Huni/Qahedjet, see the bibliographic note to chapter 26 above.

For some traditional views upon the gods of Egypt, see Hornung, *Conceptions of God*, and Wilkinson, *Early Dynastic Egypt*, chapter 8. The quotation concerning lepidopterists is taken from Goedicke, 'God'.

The rows of offering figures in Sneferu's temple are placed in their contemporary context in Helen K. Jacquet-Gordon, *Les Noms des domaines funéraires sous l'ancien empire égyptien* (Cairo, 1962).

The *shen* sign and the cartouche are numbered as V9 and 10 respectively in Gardiner's sign list; see Gardiner, *Egyptian Grammar*.

Presently, the oldest known example of a royal cartouche is from the reign of Huni's predecessor Sanakht and was recovered from one of the mastabas at Beit Khallaf; see Seidlmayer, 'The Relative Chronology'.

CHAPTER 31. THE PERFECT PYRAMID

Epigraph: from Edmund Burke, *Reflections on the Revolution in France* (London, 1790).

The statistics and mechanics of the Great Pyramid's construction is taken from Romer, *The Great Pyramid*, these having been derived, in part, from fundamental information supplied in Krauss, 'The Length of Sneferu's Reign' [work rates], by Mark Lehner, 'Development of the Giza Necropolis: the Khufu Project', *MDAIK* 41 (1985) [geography], and by W. M. Flinders Petrie, *The Pyramids and Temples of Gizeh* (London, 1st edn., 1883) [architecture]. See, too, Edwards, *The Pyramids of Egypt*; Stadelmann, *Die Ägyptischen Pyramiden*, and Lehner, *The Complete Pyramids*.

For a recent account of Hemiunu, see *EAAP*, catalogue numbers 44–5; the translation of his titles is taken from that of James P. Allen in that publication. For Hemiunu's tomb, see also Peter Jánosi, *Giza in der 4. Dynastie: die Baugeschichte und Belegung einer Nekropole des alten Reiches,* vol. 1: *die Mastabas der Kernfriedhöfe und die Felsgräber* (Vienna, 2004), *passim*. That same work provides a careful analysis of the building chronology of the cemeteries surrounding the Great Pyramid.

Catherine H. Roehrig, 'Reserve Heads: an enigma of Old Kingdom sculpture', in *EAAP*, is an overview of those remarkable works; see also, catalogue entries 46–9 in that same volume.

Dieter Arnold, 'Royal Cult Complexes of the Old and Middle Kingdoms', in Byron E. Shafer (ed.), *Temples of Ancient Egypt* (New York, 1997), offers an overview of the developing royal pyramid temple. Though I share Stadelmann's reservations about parts of Arnold's general theory, I have nonetheless followed him in the belief that Khufu's Pyramid temple held statues of the king at its rear, rather than the false door proposed by Stadelmann in, for example, 'The Development of the Pyramid Temple in the Fourth Dynasty', in Stephen

Quirke (ed.), *The Temple in Ancient Egypt: new discoveries and recent research* (London, 1997).

Many of the surviving sculpted blocks from Khufu's causeway are described in Hans Goedicke, *Re-used Blocks from the Pyramid of Amenemhet I at Lisht* (New York, 1971); *EAAP*, catalogue numbers 23, 38–43 and 66 supply a recent commentary upon some of those same pieces.

The recently discovered rock in the Western Desert that, amongst many other inscriptions, was found to bear King Khufu's name is published by Klaus Peter Kuhlmann, 'Der Wasserberg des Djedefre (Chufu 0111): ein Lagerplatz mit Expeditionsinschriften der 4. Dynastie im Raum der Oase Dachla', *MDAIK* 61 (2005). For the ancient context and the surrounding deserts, see Rudolf Kuper, 'Between the Oases and the Nile-Djara: Rohlfs' cave in the Western Desert', *Cahiers de Recherches de l'Institut de Papyrologie et d'Égyptologie de Lille*, 26 (2006–2007).

John Ross's photographs in Nancy Jenkins, *The Boat beneath the Pyramids* (London, 1980), hold the elegance of Khufu's restored boat. For a fascinating record of the work of its restoration, see Mohammed Zaki Iskander, Ahmad Youssaf Moustafa *et al.*, *The Cheops Boats* (Cairo, 1960).

The extract on p. 388 is taken from the pages of the expedition's notebooks, which are published on the splendid website of the Giza Archives of the Museum of Fine Arts, Boston at www.gizapyramids.org.

For an appreciation of Reisner and Junker at Giza, see John A. Wilson, *Signs and Wonders upon Pharaoh: a history of American egyptology* (Chicago, 1964).

I have employed the translations of the inscriptions found in Hetepheres' tomb that are given in Reisner's publications. In similar fashion, my description of the contents and the clearance of that tomb is largely based on his publications: 'The Tomb of Queen Hetep-heres', in a *Supplement* to *Bulletin of the Museum of Fine Arts Boston* (May 1927); 'The Empty Sarcophagus of the Mother of Cheops', *Bulletin of the Museum of Fine Arts Boston* (26 Oct. 1928); *A History of the Giza Necropolis*, vol. 2: *The Tomb of Hetep-heres, Mother of Cheops*, completed and revised by William Stevenson Smith (Cambridge, Mass., 1955).

Note, however, that, following Mark Lehner's careful reinvestigation of Reisner's theories in *The Pyramid Tomb of Hetep-heres and the Satellite Pyramid of Khufu* (Mainz, 1985), Reisner's account of the ancient history of that tomb is no longer accepted. Note also, that Lehner's proposal in that volume, that the pyramid whose foundation trenches lie above the Hetep-heres cache was a secondary pyramid of Khufu's can no longer be sustained either, since another smaller pyramid lying closer to the Great Pyramid was discovered in the 1990s, and is reported by Zahi Hawass as 'The Discovery of the Satellite Pyramid of Khufu (GI-d)', in Peter der Manuelian (ed.), *Studies in Honor of William Kelley Simpson*, 2 vols. (Boston, 1996).

List of Maps and Figures

Whenever practicable, the excavator's original plans and drawings have been reproduced. Many of these figures, therefore, are historical documents in their own right.

The maps are based upon modern physical geography, the ancient geography of the area during the periods discussed in the book being insufficiently established to allow accurate reconstructions. Recent researches, however, have shown that the river moved erratically within its valley down throughout millennia, and generally towards the east. Similarly, in the times of most ancient Egypt, the Delta appears to have been smaller and to have been less well-defined along its coast-line. See, for example, Karl W. Butzer's 'Geoarchaeological Implications of Recent Research in the Nile Delta', in *EL*; and Katy Lutley and Judith Bunbury, 'The Nile on the Move', in *Egyptian Archaeology* 32 (2008).

After their first citation, all references are given in a shortened form. A key to the abbreviations employed may be found at the head of the Bibliography.

in sheets of gold, shown as it was found, lying in the soil of Tell el-Farkha in the eastern Delta. Drawing by Elizabeth Romer from material presented in the excavation report of Marek Chłodnicki and Krzysztof Ciałowicz, 'Tell el-Farkha (Ghazala) 2006, Preliminary Report on the Activities of the Polish Archaeological Mission', in *Annales du service des antiquités de l'Égypte* 83 (2009).

List of Plates

Though ancient Egyptian things usually look very well in the modern media, no photographs can catch the reality of them, which is seen to their best advantage under the Egyptian sun.

These plates have been specifically chosen to illustrate the qualities of some of the objects discussed in the text.

Unless otherwise indicated, all plates are by John Romer.

1. Neolithic grain silo. A plate from Gertrude Caton-Thompson and Eleanor Gardner, *The Desert Fayum* (London, 1934).

2. Neolithic cup from Lake Faiyum. Petrie Museum UC 2500. Electa, Milan.

3. The Nile Valley north of Aswan.

4. Badarian ripple ware bowl from grave 5128 at Badari. Petrie Museum UC 9240. Electa, Milan.

5. An early Naqadan pot. British Museum EA 49022.

6. An early Naqadan pot. British Museum EA 27754.

7. The predynastic cemeteries of Naqada, photographed in 1976.

8. A mid-Naqadan burial, numbered H 23, from a plate in the memoir of Edward R. Ayrton and W. L. S. Loat, *Pre-Dynastic Cemetery at el-Mahasna* (London, 1911).

9. A mid-Naqadan burial, numbered H 112, from a plate in the memoir of Edward R. Ayrton and W. L. S. Loat, *Pre-Dynastic Cemetery at el-Mahasna* (London, 1911).

10. Two mid-Naqadan decorated buff ware pots. British Museum EA 26636 (left) & EA 47996 (right).

11. Part of the Ballas desert potteries, photographed in December 1980.

12. Ballas water pots stacked by their kilns and awaiting transportation, photographed in December 1980.

13. Ballas water pots stacked on a felucca in the traditional manner, photographed at Luxor, on the West Bank, in February 1981.

14. The Painted Tomb of Hierakonpolis under excavation. See Barry J. Kemp, 'Photographs of the Decorated Tomb at Hierakonpolis', *Journal of Egyptian Archaeology* 59 (1973).

15. The southern end of the Naqadan tomb painting found at Hierakonpolis; one of a series of plates illustrating that tomb in J. E. Quibell and F. W. Green, *Hierakonpolis*, vol. 2 (London, 1902).

16. A detail of the so-called 'Battlefield Palette'. British Museum EA 20791.

17. Objects from the great cache at Hierakonpolis; a plate from J. E. Quibell and F. W. Green, *Hierakonpolis*, vol. 2 (London, 1902).

18. The tomb of King Djer at Abydos. German Archaeological Institute, Cairo.

19. Four golden bracelets recovered from the tomb of King Djer at Abydos. Plate from W. M. Flinders Petrie, *The Royal Tombs of the First Dynasty*, vol. 2 (London, 1901).

20. The stela of King Djet. Louvre Museum E 11007.

21. Wooden panel from the mastaba of Hesi-re at Saqqara. Cairo Museum.

22. A statue of King Djoser. Cairo Museum.

23. The Step Pyramid at Saqqara.

24. The northern doorjamb and façade of the chapel of Itet in the mastaba of Nefermaat and Itet at Maidum. A plate from W. M. Flinders Petrie *et al.*, *Medum* (London, 1892).

25. A monkey torments a crane. Detail of a block from the chapel of Itet. Ny Carlsberg Glyptotek, Copenhagen AEIN 1133 A.

Index

ALLEN LANE
an imprint of
PENGUIN BOOKS

Recently Published

Evgeny Morozov, *To Save Everything, Click Here: Technology, Solutionism, and the Urge to Fix Problems that Don't Exist*

David Cannadine, *The Undivided Past: History Beyond Our Differences*

Michael Axworthy, *Revolutionary Iran: A History of the Islamic Republic*

Jaron Lanier, *Who Owns the Future?*

John Gray, *The Silence of Animals: On Progress and Other Modern Myths*

Paul Kildea, *Benjamin Britten: A Life in the Twentieth Century*

Jared Diamond, *The World Until Yesterday: What Can We Learn from Traditional Societies?*

Nassim Nicholas Taleb, *Antifragile: How to Live in a World We Don't Understand*

Alan Ryan, *On Politics: A History of Political Thought from Herodotus to the Present*

Roberto Calasso, *La Folie Baudelaire*

Carolyn Abbate and Roger Parker, *A History of Opera: The Last Four Hundred Years*

Yang Jisheng, *Tombstone: The Untold Story of Mao's Great Famine*

Caleb Scharf, *Gravity's Engines: The Other Side of Black Holes*

Jancis Robinson, Julia Harding and José Vouillamoz, *Wine Grapes: A Complete Guide to 1,368 Vine Varieties, including their Origins and Flavours*

David Bownes, Oliver Green and Sam Mullins, *Underground: How the Tube Shaped London*

Niall Ferguson, *The Great Degeneration: How Institutions Decay and Economies Die*

Chrystia Freeland, *Plutocrats: The Rise of the New Global Super-Rich*

David Thomson, *The Big Screen: The Story of the Movies and What They Did to Us*

Halik Kochanski, *The Eagle Unbowed: Poland and the Poles in the Second World War*

Kofi Annan with Nader Mousavizadeh, *Interventions: A Life in War and Peace*

Mark Mazower, *Governing the World: The History of an Idea*

Anne Applebaum, *Iron Curtain: The Crushing of Eastern Europe 1944-56*

Steven Johnson, *Future Perfect: The Case for Progress in a Networked Age*

Christopher Clark, *The Sleepwalkers: How Europe Went to War in 1914*

Neil MacGregor, *Shakespeare's Restless World*

Nate Silver, *The Signal and the Noise: The Art and Science of Prediction*

Chinua Achebe, *There Was a Country: A Personal History of Biafra*

John Darwin, *Unfinished Empire: The Global Expansion of Britain*

Jerry Brotton, *A History of the World in Twelve Maps*

Patrick Hennessey, *KANDAK: Fighting with Afghans*

Katherine Angel, *Unmastered: A Book on Desire, Most Difficult to Tell*

David Priestland, *Merchant, Soldier, Sage: A New History of Power*

Stephen Alford, *The Watchers: A Secret History of the Reign of Elizabeth I*

Tom Feiling, *Short Walks from Bogotá: Journeys in the New Colombia*

Pankaj Mishra, *From the Ruins of Empire: The Revolt Against the West and the Remaking of Asia*

Geza Vermes, *Christian Beginnings: From Nazareth to Nicaea, AD 30-325*

Steve Coll, *Private Empire: ExxonMobil and American Power*

Joseph Stiglitz, *The Price of Inequality*

Dambisa Moyo, *Winner Take All: China's Race for Resources and What it Means for Us*

Robert Skidelsky and Edward Skidelsky, *How Much is Enough? The Love of Money, and the Case for the Good Life*

Frances Ashcroft, *The Spark of Life: Electricity in the Human Body*

Sebastian Seung, *Connectome: How the Brain's Wiring Makes Us Who We Are*

Callum Roberts, *Ocean of Life*

Orlando Figes, *Just Send Me Word: A True Story of Love and Survival in the Gulag*

Leonard Mlodinow, *Subliminal: The Revolution of the New Unconscious and What it Teaches Us about Ourselves*

John Romer, *A History of Ancient Egypt: From the First Farmers to the Great Pyramid*

Ruchir Sharma, *Breakout Nations: In Pursuit of the Next Economic Miracle*

Michael J. Sandel, *What Money Can't Buy: The Moral Limits of Markets*

Dominic Sandbrook, *Seasons in the Sun: The Battle for Britain, 1974-1979*

Tariq Ramadan, *The Arab Awakening: Islam and the New Middle East*

Jonathan Haidt, *The Righteous Mind: Why Good People are Divided by Politics and Religion*

Ahmed Rashid, *Pakistan on the Brink: The Future of Pakistan, Afghanistan and the West*

Tim Weiner, *Enemies: A History of the FBI*

Mark Pagel, *Wired for Culture: The Natural History of Human Cooperation*

George Dyson, *Turing's Cathedral: The Origins of the Digital Universe*

Cullen Murphy, *God's Jury: The Inquisition and the Making of the Modern World*

Richard Sennett, *Together: The Rituals, Pleasures and Politics of Co-operation*

Faramerz Dabhoiwala, *The Origins of Sex: A History of the First Sexual Revolution*

Roy F. Baumeister and John Tierney, *Willpower: Rediscovering Our Greatest Strength*

Jesse J. Prinz, *Beyond Human Nature: How Culture and Experience Shape Our Lives*

Robert Holland, *Blue-Water Empire: The British in the Mediterranean since 1800*

Jodi Kantor, *The Obamas: A Mission, A Marriage*

Philip Coggan, *Paper Promises: Money, Debt and the New World Order*

Charles Nicholl, *Traces Remain: Essays and Explorations*

Daniel Kahneman, *Thinking, Fast and Slow*

Hunter S. Thompson, *Fear and Loathing at Rolling Stone: The Essential Writing of Hunter S. Thompson*

Duncan Campbell-Smith, *Masters of the Post: The Authorized History of the Royal Mail*

Colin McEvedy, *Cities of the Classical World: An Atlas and Gazetteer of 120 Centres of Ancient Civilization*

Heike B. Görtemaker, *Eva Braun: Life with Hitler*

Brian Cox and Jeff Forshaw, *The Quantum Universe: Everything that Can Happen Does Happen*

Nathan D. Wolfe, *The Viral Storm: The Dawn of a New Pandemic Age*

Norman Davies, *Vanished Kingdoms: The History of Half-Forgotten Europe*

Michael Lewis, *Boomerang: The Meltdown Tour*

Steven Pinker, *The Better Angels of Our Nature: The Decline of Violence in History and Its Causes*

Robert Trivers, *Deceit and Self-Deception: Fooling Yourself the Better to Fool Others*

Thomas Penn, *Winter King: The Dawn of Tudor England*

Daniel Yergin, *The Quest: Energy, Security and the Remaking of the Modern World*

Michael Moore, *Here Comes Trouble: Stories from My Life*

Ali Soufan, *The Black Banners: Inside the Hunt for Al Qaeda*

Jason Burke, *The 9/11 Wars*

Timothy D. Wilson, *Redirect: The Surprising New Science of Psychological Change*

Ian Kershaw, *The End: Hitler's Germany, 1944-45*

T M Devine, *To the Ends of the Earth: Scotland's Global Diaspora, 1750-2010*

Catherine Hakim, *Honey Money: The Power of Erotic Capital*

Douglas Edwards, *I'm Feeling Lucky: The Confessions of Google Employee Number 59*

John Bradshaw, *In Defence of Dogs*

Chris Stringer, *The Origin of Our Species*

Lila Azam Zanganeh, *The Enchanter: Nabokov and Happiness*

David Stevenson, *With Our Backs to the Wall: Victory and Defeat in 1918*

Evelyn Juers, *House of Exile: War, Love and Literature, from Berlin to Los Angeles*

Henry Kissinger, *On China*

Michio Kaku, *Physics of the Future: How Science Will Shape Human Destiny and Our Daily Lives by the Year 2100*